Agenda Formation

Agenda Formation

William H. Riker, Editor

Ann Arbor
THE UNIVERSITY OF MICHIGAN PRESS

Copyright © by the University of Michigan 1993
All rights reserved
Published in the United States of America by
The University of Michigan Press
Manufactured in the United States of America

1996   1995   1994   1993   4   3   2   1

Library of Congress Cataloging-in-Publication Data

Agenda formation / William H. Riker, editor.
        p.   cm.
    Includes bibliographical references.
    ISBN 0-472-10381-4 (alk. paper)
    1. Political planning.   2. Policy sciences.   I. Riker, William H.
  H97.A36   1993
  320′.6—dc20   93-16150
                                                              CIP

A CIP catalogue record for this book is available from the British Library.

Preface

During the 1990–91 school year, the authors of the essays in this volume presented their work to an audience of faculty and graduate students in the Department of Political Science at the University of Rochester. Subsequently, the authors discussed their papers with each other at a conference in Rochester, June 21–22, 1991. We thank the departmental audience at the presentations and conference for their patience, criticism, and hospitality.

The sponsor of these papers is the Central Intelligence Agency. Since it collects political information, analyzes it, and forecasts on the basis of it, the agency has a common interest with social scientists in the development of political theory, which is necessary both to gather and to interpret information. We thank the agency for joining with us in this effort to understand the complexities of the succession of issues and the construction of agendas.

Contents

Introduction

William H. Riker

Agendas foreshadow outcomes: the shape of an agenda influences the choices made from it. Today we are intensely aware of this fact, but our knowledge about it is relatively new. Eighteenth-century writers did not, as far as I can discover, discuss it at all. Only near the end of the nineteenth century, with the swift increase in the amount of legislative business in European and American countries, did it strike observers as important. In the twentieth century, however, as governments have grown in size and complexity, the agenda function of setting alternatives and priorities for decision has become wholly apparent, so much so that making agendas seems just about as significant as actually passing legislation.

In the last half-century, political theory has revealed just how significant agendas are. In 1948, Duncan Black published his rediscovery of the paradox of voting (Black 1948; also see Black 1958). This is the fact that, under pairwise voting, alternatives may cycle; that is, alternative a may beat b, b beat c, and c beat a, so that there is no clear winner in the sense that one alternative beats both of the others. Black established a sufficient condition for the existence of a clear winner: the median voter theorem. If voters' ideal points can be arranged on a continuum so that, for each voter, the further an alternative is from his or her ideal point, the less desired it is, then the winning alternative is that alternative at the ideal point of the median voter. That is, the median's ideal can beat all other alternatives in pairwise contests. Thus, the median's ideal is a social equilibrium in the sense that the group must, by reason of members' tastes, choose and retain the median's ideal. This sufficient condition, of course, defines and reveals the circumstances under which a clear winner does not exist and, by extension, when cycles exist. Using this theorem, a prospective loser can, of course, bring a cycle into existence in order to avoid a loss or even to bring about a triumph.

Soon after Black published his theorem, Arrow (1963) proved that some inconsistency like the paradox might occur under any minimally fair system of amalgamating individual preferences. This means that the difficulty resides

not in the method of amalgamation, but in the profile of voters' tastes or values. Hence, there is no mechanical way to escape social inconsistencies. If the profile does not produce a transitive social order of alternatives, regardless of the method of voting, then the inconsistency must exist or some unfair method of amalgamation must be used. The significance of this fact is, as Arrow remarked, that transitivity ensures "the independence of the final choice from the path to it."

The path to the final choice is, of course, determined by the agenda; indeed, the path is the agenda. Thus, whenever something like the paradox occurs, the path or agenda partially determines the outcome. Furthermore, as McKelvey (1976 and 1979), Schofield (1978), and McKelvey and Schofield (1986) have shown, when there is more than one dimension of judgment, intransitivity is almost certain. In any complicated situation, the agenda as well as the individual tastes are necessarily involved in the final choice. Characteristically, social groups escape from intransitivity by some device that restricts the alternatives to be considered or restricts the individual preference orders allowed or counted.

The sum of these restrictions is embodied in an agenda. At the most general level there are the things people talk about as possible subjects for group decision. Call this the feasible set. From this misty swamp, politicians—by constitutional restrictions and directives and by rhetorical and heresthetical maneuvers—form the set of considered issues. The act of defining this set necessarily involves admitting some issues from the feasible set and excluding others. This is the first step in restricting tastes. As the considered set is (temporarily) fixed, politicians also maneuver to form the alternative set, which is the set of admissible alternatives when some issue in the considered set is discussed. This is the second step in restricting tastes. Finally, politicians form a set of procedures (e.g., parliamentary rules and customs) for choosing one alternative from the alternative set. This is the third and final step in agenda formation.

Since cycles almost certainly exist at the first and second steps and often exist at the third, it follows that the path of sequential narrowing partly determines the final choice. Hence, the process of forming agendas has as much social consequence as individual tastes. As political scientists, we ought, therefore, to study agenda formation just as much as we study public opinion, political socialization, and the like.

This is what we attempt in this volume. It includes essays on:

  (a) the specification of political issues (Budge; Poole and Rosenthal; and Riker),
  (b) the origin of issues (Bueno de Mesquita and Lalman; Carmines and Simpson; Laver and Shepsle; and Smith), and

(*c*) the manipulation of issues (Johnston, Blais, Brady and Crête; Graham; Iyengar; and Smith).

Some of the essays (those in group *a*) relate to the first stage of agenda formation; those in group *b* and most in group *c* relate to the second stage, while the essays by Laver and Shepsle and, to a lesser degree, Smith relate to the third stage.

The Specification of Issues

Just what is a political issue is itself a political issue. Often, political disputants say with fervor: "That's not an issue." What they usually mean is, "That's not an issue on which I have a winning position." The only escape from such futile disputes about the specification of issues is to treat as issues whatever some people think are issues. This is the procedure followed by all the authors in this volume.

But no matter what method is used, the specification of issues is a tedious enterprise. Budge's work is based on the analysis of a collection of every party manifesto (or platform) issued from 1945 through 1981 in 23 democracies, mostly European, though including Australia, Canada, India, Israel, New Zealand, Sri Lanka, and the United States. Budge and his co-workers summarized the themes of the manifestos into about 60 categories and then used the categories to interpret party interaction and to locate parties on spatial dimensions. Poole and Rosenthal, utilizing all legislators' votes on all roll calls in the U.S. House of Representatives, 1789–1985, in a multidimensional scaling process, located both voters and possible roll call outcomes in a multidimensional space. The calculation of the dimensions of the space and the location of roll call outcomes for a particular session is a massive arithmetical problem, but it does yield a revealing spatial map of legislators and issues. Finally, Riker based his work on a summary of a large sample of all written materials in the national campaign for the ratification of the Constitution, 1787–88. He categorized the material into themes, weighting each theme by its quantity of words and the frequency of their printing.

Each of these methods has advantages and disadvantages. Both Budge's method and Poole's and Rosenthal's method provide insight into the temporal sequence of issues over a long period of time and permit a spatial characterization of issues at a single point in time. Riker's method does not permit spatial characterization, but does facilitate observation of partisan interaction over short periods of time.

While the underlying data are quite different for the three papers, several conclusions are remarkably similar. Since these authors worked individually,

the similarity of their results increases the credibility of their generalizations about political debate.

Both Budge and Riker emphasize that partisan themes are orthogonal to each other. Budge distinguishes between a party's efforts to persuade voters that some party issue is salient to voters' decisions and a party's confrontation on issues with another party. He finds that they devote more effort to demonstrating salience than to confronting others. It follows, then, that parties do not debate positions on a single issue, but try instead to make end runs around each other on different issues.

In a similar vein, Riker offers two principles: the Dominance Principle and the Dispersion Principle. The Dominance Principle is that, when one party has a clear-cut advantage on an issue, it regularly emphasizes that issue, while the other party abandons it. The Dispersion Principle is that, when neither side has a clear advantage on an issue, both abandon it. As in Budge's analysis, this implies that campaigns are mostly about salience, not confrontation, although Riker points out that there is a steady, though small, amount of ad hominem castigation of others.

In contrast to the similar conclusions by Budge and Riker, Smith finds that, in the debate on the legislative enactment he studies, there is a substantial amount of direct confrontation. I think this difference is a function of context, of legislative rather than electoral dispute. A bill (like an indictment in a court) defines an issue and forces confrontation, tending to reduce the dispute to a single dimension on which the two sides take different positions, while elections can be fought on many dimensions at once.

This leads to a second point of agreement in these essays, namely that issue spaces tend to be one dimensional over time. Using factor analysis on quite different data, both Budge and Poole and Rosenthal discover that one factor carries most of the weight. For Budge this means a left-right dimension (socialism, welfare statism, and social service expansion at the left and capitalism and social conservatism on the right) characterizes party disputes over the long run, with parties tending to converge toward the median over the period from 1946 to 1980—except when new politics issues ("greens") upset the balance. For Poole and Rosenthal, the main dimension is economic, though both parties may move dramatically in the same direction, as in the leftward movement of the 1930s. Still, they find two periods, the early 1850s and the late 1950s to early 1960s, when a second dimension, race, crosscut the economic dimension.

Altogether, then, there are two very important observations supported by these three very different ways of identifying issues.

1. In the short run of campaigns, debate is orthogonal. Parties talk past each other in several dimensions.

2. In legislative decisions and, electorally, in the long run, these dimensions usually collapse into one dimension, though from time to time politics may become two dimensional.

While the orthogonality of debate has previously been observed (e.g., "parties own issues"), the connection between the orthogonality of debate and the long-run undimensionality of the issue space has not previously been emphasized. Thus, these conclusions constitute important new ideas.

The Origin of Issues

While there is less comparability of themes in the essays in Part 2 than in Part 1, one general theme does run through Carmines and Stimson's essay and Bueno de Mesquita and Lalman's essay and, less centrally, through Budge's essay. Political issues, they agree, reflect the objective problems of society. Carmines and Stimson define realigning issues, certainly the most important ones in politics, as salient in the long term and crosscutting to the existing alignment, as in the examples of the New Deal and racial issues. (Note that Poole and Rosenthal agree that race was crosscutting, but economic issues of the New Deal were not. Both authors agree, however, on salience.) Bueno de Mesquita and Lalman show that foreign policy decisions derive not simply from the international context, but also from domestic issues strong enough to override international concerns. All these authors are thus in accord with Budge's observation that the issues that dominate in his manifestos and factor analyses are main public concerns.

Since, otherwise, there is less comparability in this set of essays, I summarize their main discoveries individually.

Smith describes, in precise terms, one very important, but possibly infrequent, source of new issues, namely the special concerns of interest groups. If a group can present its desired position to legislators in such a way that they will vote as the group wishes, then, clearly, the group can generate issues (and perhaps even outcomes) entirely on its own. This essay is all the more important because it flatly reverses the conventional wisdom in political science that pressure groups have little effect on legislators' actions. Smith shows, on the contrary, just how and when a pressure group can successfully influence legislators and he describes in detail one such event, the enactment of the statute creating the Department of Education, as forced by the National Education Association.

Smith assumes that group lobbyists can influence a legislator's decisions by presenting him or her with interpretations of issues favorable to the group's goals, by endorsing and financially supporting him or her in elections, and by making it difficult for him or her to offer their members an acceptable explana-

tion when he or she does not vote as the lobbyists wish. Smith then hypothe-
sizes that a legislator can defect from the group's desired position only if there
are weak spots in the lobbyists' relationship with the legislator, weak spots
that Smith calls defection conditions: (1) the constituency condition that the
group has relatively few members in the legislator's district, (2) the communication condition that the group's members do not do grass roots lobbying, and
(3) the contribution condition that the group and its members contributed
relatively little money to the legislator's campaign. Finally, by a careful
historical analysis of the issue of creating a Department of Education, Smith
shows that, in fact, legislators defected from pressure group positions only
when at least one of these conditions was present and that they were more
likely to defect when more than one condition was present.

In contrast to Smith's single-group-generated issue, Carmines and
Stimson deal with the whole range of issues in political life. They are concerned with the fact that, while there are myriad possibilities for new issues,
only some come into being and even fewer flourish. Using evolutionary biology as a metaphor, they explain the development of issues in terms of conscious political forces and unconscious environmental ones. The political
forces are the interests of politicians: previous winners, of course, seek to
maintain the status quo of issues on which they have won, while previous
losers seek to bring up new issues on which they can win. But beyond the
conscious manipulation of politicians, there are environmental forces (such as
unexpected wars, depressions, and so forth) as well as internal contradictions
in old issues that force new issues into political life. Carmines and Stimson
then offer several possible models of evolutionary adaption by which these
developing issues might flourish. One is the notion of "cataclysmic adaption"
that they equate with the theory of critical elections. In rejecting this model,
they offer a powerful and definitive critique of the idea. In its place, they offer
instead the accepted Darwinian notion of gradualism. Issues succeed each
other after gradual and successful refinement of the winners. One especially
important feature of this model is the emphasis on chance and the absence of
teleological direction for development. Just as successful species are a product of the fit between internal drive and external circumstance, so successful
issues are the product of their value to politicians and their fit with the whole
political environment.

Bueno de Mesquita and Lalman deal with issues of foreign policy, resolving theoretically and, to some degree, empirically, the epistemological
issue between "realists" and "liberals." This is probably the fundamental
philosophical issue in the field of international politics and the resolution of it
is a major scientific advance.

After pointing out that these two irreconcilable traditions dominate in the
very description of foreign policy, they define the realist position, which is
currently more popular in U.S. academia, as the proposition that the makers

of foreign policy select their objectives entirely in terms of the constraints and opportunities of the international world. The liberal position, on the other hand, is the proposition that makers of foreign policy respond to the domestic considerations of pressure group interests, electoral objectives, and so forth. (Thus, the liberal position could accommodate Smith's analysis, while the realist position could not.)

In order to choose between those competing assumptions, Bueno de Mesquita and Lalman construct a sequential game with two variants of actions taken in accord with foreign policies. The realist and liberal variants have quite different solutions. When they compare these solutions with data about international disputes from 1815 to recently, they find that the liberal solution is consonant with observed reality, while the realist solution is not. Hence, they can definitively reject the realist position. This is a remarkable breakthrough in the settlement of an ancient and heretofore unresolvable question about the origin of issues in foreign affairs.

Laver and Shepsle deal, at the most abstract level, with the origin of issues in parliamentary governments with coalitions of more than one party. In contrast to the currently conventional view that the possibilities for different policies are limited to the number of possible feasible coalitions, Laver and Shepsle set up a model in which the number of possible policies is defined in the following way. Each potential governing coalition consists of a cabinet with ministers having more-or-less complete authority over the area of policy within their portfolios. The range of possible policies for each coalition is the number of ways that parties in the coalition can fill the ministries. Thus, if there are two feasible coalitions, say, between parties A and B and parties A and C, if there are two portfolios in the cabinet, and if each party can offer one leader for the main portfolio and two alternative subordinate leaders for the second portfolio, then there are twelve possible policies. Not all these policy points are likely to be in equilibrium, however. Two kinds of equilibria are possible. One is an empty winset equilibrium wherein, for a given assignment of portfolios in a feasible coalition, all the alternative assignments in this and other feasible coalitions are unable to beat the given assignment; that is, the winset is empty. Alternatively, there is a veto-generated equilibrium wherein some alternatives to a given assignment are in its winset, but some party to the coalition has an incentive to veto all the alternatives in the winset. This model is extraordinarily rich and offers the promise of inferring a number of nonobvious restrictions on governing coalitions, not just in theory but also in the real world.

The Manipulation of Issues

One of the received propositions in the contemporary study of political campaigns is that campaign advertising is not efficacious. This follows directly

from the behaviorist theory of politics in which voters' choices are determined by party identification and not much else and is in direct conflict with the rational choice theory of politics in which voters' choices are determined by their calculation of advantage given the supply of information. In this latter theory, campaign information should, at least sometimes, generate voters' choices contrary to those determined by party identification. Since the rational choice model utilizes the common meaning of persuasion and allows for the assumption that persuasion is sometimes efficacious, the behaviorist propositions are suspect from the rational choice point of view, even though political scientists and psychologists have accumulated, since the 1950s, a substantial amount of evidence to support the behaviorist theory. The three essays on the manipulation of issues (by Iyengar; Johnston, Blais, Brady and Crête; and Graham) provide powerful evidence that persuasion does occur and that the behaviorist model is essentially incorrect.

Iyengar summarizes and interprets the discoveries from some of his remarkable experiments with agenda setting in television news. Since public opinion on issues is shifting and complex, the role of the media lies in making issues accessible in the sense that the news renders the subject matter easily retrievable from popular memory. Furthermore, the form of retrieval significantly affects the public's judgment. Iyengar shows that those subjects made accessible by television news are more *salient* than others, salient in the sense that they are more influential on opinion and on the choice of candidates. Furthermore, the way the media present stories frames them by constraining the kind of public response that the news generates. Especially interesting in this respect is the distinction in consequences between "episodic" news (i.e., dramatic stories about the effect of policies on particular persons) and "thematic" news (i.e., stories about news placed in abstract or theoretical contexts). While episodic news may be more dramatic, thematic news has, counterintuitively perhaps, far more impact on public opinion. Iyengar's evidence and discussion seem definitively to reject received behaviorist opinion and to emphasize the need for the detailed study of media effects within a rational choice context.

One obvious elaboration of Iyengar's work is to examine the effect of framing, or, more broadly, heresthetical manipulation, when political opponents are struggling to dominate the process. Johnston, Blais, Brady, and Crête provide a valuable case study of just such a situation in both the long run and the short run. In the long period, 1890–1970, Canadian Conservatives favored protection while Liberals favored free trade, which, however, they were never able to enact, despite their usual dominance in this period, because Conservatives beat them on this issue. In a complicated shift of stances involving not only trade considerations but also issues of price supports for agricultural and forestry products, the parties reversed positions. Conserva-

tives favored free trade and Liberals favored protection. The test of this Conservative-initiated heresthetical maneuver came in the election of 1988, fought almost entirely over the free trade, which survey research showed to be losing support. Midway in the campaign (day 25 out of 50 days), free trade was less popular than the protectionist status quo by a margin of 39 percent to 42 percent. Primarily because of the Liberals' success in identifying free trade with the controversial Conservative prime minister and by heresthetically suggesting that free trade would endanger Canadian social programs (i.e., especially the health service), free-trade support fell abruptly by day 29 to 31 percent. By the campaign's end (day 50), however, Conservatives won. Opinion on free trade was divided about as at the beginning: 40 percent in favor and 44 percent opposed. Again, successful Conservative persuasion accounted for the revival, first, by refutation of the argument—sophistic on its face—that free trade threatened social programs and, second, by impressing Canadians with the danger of dropping out of the North American market. This remarkable flip-flop, the result of successful heresthetical and rhetorical manipulation by the two sides successively, is convincing evidence that campaign persuasion does occur and is, probably, determinative of outcomes.

Finally, Graham's essay is inspired by the failure of political scientists (or anyone else) to predict or even to anticipate in more than casual speculation the remarkable transformations during 1989–90 in the former Soviet Union and other East European countries. Consequently, Graham constructs a model within which regime changes can occur and offers suggestions about the use of the model for empirical investigation. He defines the features that determine the maintenance or transformation of regimes as (1) the degree of perceived well-being of citizens, (2) the perceived ability of the regime to coerce citizens, and (3) the degree of popular risk aversion. Windows of opportunity for regime change occur as perceptions of well-being become dismal, as the expectation of coercion declines, and, as a consequence of these changes, popular risk aversion decreases. His problem is to identify those windows. Graham argues that these perceptions of well-being and coercive capacity can, perhaps, be inferred from easily available statistical series (if they are reliable), but the impact of these perceptions on the citizenry depends on rhetorical emphases on the events these series reflect. As a method of estimating the impact, Graham offers the Vanderbilt archive of national television news programs. The attention given to well-being and coercion in these programs can serve as a leading indicator of popular perceptions and, hence, of windows of opportunity. While Graham concedes that U.S. news programs are not closely geared to political concerns of other nations, he argues, nevertheless, that this television filter does reveal the truly significant events, so that a careful tracking via the archive is one possible method of successfully predicting regime change. Obviously, however, a similar archive

for other nations would be helpful for tracking their rhetorical interpretation of events.

BIBLIOGRAPHY

Arrow, Kenneth. 1963. *Social Choice and Individual Values*. 2d. ed. New Haven: Yale University Press.
Black, Duncan. 1948. "On the Rationale of Group Decision Making." *Journal of Political Economy* 56:23–34.
Black, Duncan. 1958. *The Theory of Committees and Elections*. Cambridge: Cambridge University Press.
McKelvey, Richard D. 1976. "Intransitivities in Multidimensional Voting Models and Some Implications for Agenda Control." *Journal of Economic Theory* 12:472–82.
McKelvey, Richard D. 1979. "General Conditions for Global Intransitivities in Formal Voting Models." *Econometrica* 47:1085–1112.
McKelvey, Richard D., and Norman Schofield. 1986. "Structural Instability of the Core." *Journal of Mathematical Economics* 15:179–98.
Schofield, Norman. 1978. "Instability of Simple Dynamic Games." *Review of Economic Studies* 45:575–94.

Part 1
The Specification of Issues

Spatial Realignment and the Mapping of Issues in U.S. History: The Evidence from Roll Call Voting

Keith T. Poole and Howard Rosenthal

Fifty years ago E. E. Schattschneider, in his classic *Party Government*, wrote that the "political parties created democracy" and that "modern democracy is unthinkable save in terms of the parties" (1940, 1). Schattschneider argued that freedom of association and the guarantee of regular elections with plurality winners made the development of two mass-based political parties inevitable in the United States. U.S. political history can be written almost entirely as a conflict *between* and *within* political parties. The political parties have mirrored the great social and economic conflicts that have divided Americans. When they have failed to do so, they have been torn apart and replaced by new parties better representing mass opinion.

The realignment literature in political science is concerned with changes in mass support for the political parties and how leaders of the parties responded to them. The prevailing view in this literature is that there have been three major realignments: one in the 1850s over the extension of slavery to the territories; one in the 1890s over the creation of inflation either by abandoning the gold standard or by monetizing silver; and one in the 1930s because of the collapse of the economy during the Great Depression.[1]

The most complete statement of this thesis is by Sundquist (1983). He argues that a realignment is a durable change in patterns of political behavior (1983, 4). In his basic model of realignment, a new issue emerges that cuts across the existing cleavage and reorganizes the political parties around it.

We thank Douglas Skiba and Albert Robertson for their assistance and a member of the *Advocate* for perfecting amendments. Final work on this manuscript, including superb editing by Kathleen Much, was completed while Rosenthal was a Fellow at the Center for Advanced Study in the Behavioral Sciences. He is grateful for a grant of financial support provided by the National Science Foundation, #BNS-8700864, during his stay at CASBS.

1. All authors agree on these three (see Burnham 1970; Ginsberg 1972 and 1976; Sinclair 1977 and 1981; Brady 1982; Sundquist 1983). Ginsberg (1976) finds evidence for substantial differences between the two political parties during the 1880s.

"[T]he party system has a new rationale, an old conflict has been displaced by a new one for a segment of the electorate, and that segment of the electorate has formed . . . new party attachments on the basis of that rationale. If the segment is large enough . . . a new party system supplants the old one" (1983, 37).

Sundquist, relying mainly on changes in party registration and voting at the county level in various states, marshals an impressive body of evidence for his thesis. There can be little debate about whether major changes in the mass electorate occurred during the 1850s, 1890s, and 1930s. The evidence is convincing. Less convincing is Sundquist's argument that these changes in the mass electorate "shifted" the party system on its axis. In Sundquist's model, if the new issue does not seriously divide the political parties *internally,* then "the crisis will be reached and resolved relatively quickly" and the scale of the realignment "will be relatively minor" (1983, 44–45). In other words, the severity of a realignment is a direct function of the internal divisions of the parties—if a new issue fell exactly along the current line of cleavage, no realignment would occur.

In Sundquist's model, the mass electorate and professional politicians are part and parcel of the same process. Sundquist's evidence comes from changes in the *mass electorate.* We draw our evidence from changes in the behavior of professional politicians. Specifically, the purpose of this essay is to examine the "standard position" in the realignment literature (as represented by Sundquist) by analyzing all recorded roll call votes of the members of Congress from 1789 to 1985.

In subsequent sections, we state a simple model of realignment based upon the spatial model of party competition and offer evidence that the realignments of the 1890s and the 1930s occurred along the line of cleavage that solidified in the 1870s. We find only one realignment since 1830. This was the 1850s realignment over the extension of slavery to the territories. The *late* 1930s or early 1940s witnessed the birth of a second realignment focused on the issue of civil rights for blacks. But as this second realignment proved to be less intense than the first (and only temporary), we describe it more appropriately as a perturbation.

Realignment in the Context of the Spatial Model of Voting

In previously published work (Poole and Rosenthal 1985, 1987, 1988, 1989a, 1989b, 1991b) we have laid out in detail a spatial theory of roll call voting and shown a method, D-NOMINATE, for estimating our model. Since our model is a simple application of standard spatial theory, we will only briefly review it here and then turn to a discussion of realignment within the model.

We represent each legislator with an ideal point in a multidimensional policy space, and each roll call by two points—one representing the policy outcome corresponding to a yes vote and one representing the policy outcome corresponding to a no vote. We place both the legislators and the roll calls in the space using the D-NOMINATE procedure, which is blind to the party affiliation of the legislators, the content of the roll calls, and, in fact, to any information other than the actual yes or no choices. The space turns out to be, at most, two dimensional. Even the most casual inspection of the results suggests that the main (graphically horizontal) dimension is almost always economic, involving redistribution. Contemporary liberals are on the left, redistributive side, of this dimension, conservatives on the right. The first dimension briefly switches to the slavery conflict in the 1850s. The second dimension is, *grosso modo,* slavery in the 1830s and 1840s, agrarian versus urban from 1870 through 1936, and civil rights from 1937 through the early 1970s.

A legislator's vote is determined by utility maximization. Utility functions consist of a deterministic component and a stochastic component. The deterministic component is represented by a monotonic function of distance from the ideal point, whereas the stochastic component picks up nonspatial factors and idiosyncratic spatial dimensions.[2] Dynamics are captured by letting the legislator ideal points be simple polynomial functions of time.

We found little evidence that legislator positions in the space changed dramatically at any point in U.S. history. Allowing for quadratics and higher order polynomials did not permit a notably better fit to the data than the model where legislator positions were restricted to simple linear functions of time. In addition, annual linear movement was in itself small, never averaging more than 1 percent of the space. We also found that, with critical exceptions noted below, roll call voting could be captured by a two-dimensional model.

Consistent with the Sundquist view, roll call voting is, in fact, largely unidimensional for most of U.S. history, with a second dimension becoming relevant at times when realignment is incipient. Adding a third dimension is never useful to our understanding of the evolution of the political process. The results we report here are based on a dynamic, two-dimensional estimation for 1789–1985 with legislator positions constrained to linear functions of time. This estimation places considerable constraint on the positions of each legislator. In particular, the reader should note that, whenever we display legislator positions and their votes on a specific roll call, the legislator positions are based on the legislator's voting record throughout his or her career.

---

2. More precisely, the symmetric distribution is a simple transformation of the unit normal, and the stochastic component is distributed as the log of the inverse exponential (i.e., the logit distribution).

As defined by Sundquist, realignment is easily accommodated with the context of the spatial model we estimated. For example, well before a realignment, congressional voting should be stable and organized around the cleavage of the last realignment. In a spatial model, this means that the policy space is stable—the same dimension(s) account for voting over time, and legislator ideal points should show little change from Congress to Congress. A new issue then emerges that splits the political parties internally and begins the process of polarization. This can be modeled as a new dimension, orthogonal to the stable set from the last realignment, across which both political parties become increasingly polarized. We should see this polarization occur in two ways within our two-dimensional framework. First, newly elected representatives from the same party should take relatively polarized positions on the new dimension. Second, incumbents, through the linear terms, should exhibit movement that, relative to their earlier positions, resulted in polarization. As the process continues, more and more of the voting is concerned with the new issue, so that the old, stable set begins to wither away. Figure 1 illustrates the process.[3]

Figure 1 shows the realignment process at three stages—early, middle, and late. Two political parties are shown as contour maps over a space of two dimensions. The first dimension is the original line of cleavage, and the second is the new, realigning issue. Early in the process, as shown in figure 1a, we observe a bimodal distribution that shows party polarization on the first dimension and little differentiation on the second dimension. Because the new, second dimension has only recently emerged, members typically have not had to take positions on the issue that show internal party differentiation. As the issue heats up in the electorate and becomes more salient, the legislators begin reacting more forcefully, and the process of polarizing on the second dimension begins (fig. 1b). Figure 1c shows the process in its later stages. Both political parties are now polarized. The new dimension is the primary focus of voting and the legislators are bimodally distributed across it. The stage shown in figure 1c may be followed by the creation of a new party system where the second dimension becomes the first dimension. This is what happened in what we claim is the one real realignment, the 1850s realignment over slavery. Alternatively, if the new dimension becomes an important but not primary focus of voting, the issues represented by the new dimension may be resolved within the existing system, resulting in the collapse of the second dimension and the reemergence of the dominance of the preexisting first dimension. The latter scenario describes the conflict over civil rights in the twentieth century. Once formal segregation was ended and blacks received

---

3. See also Aldrich 1983.

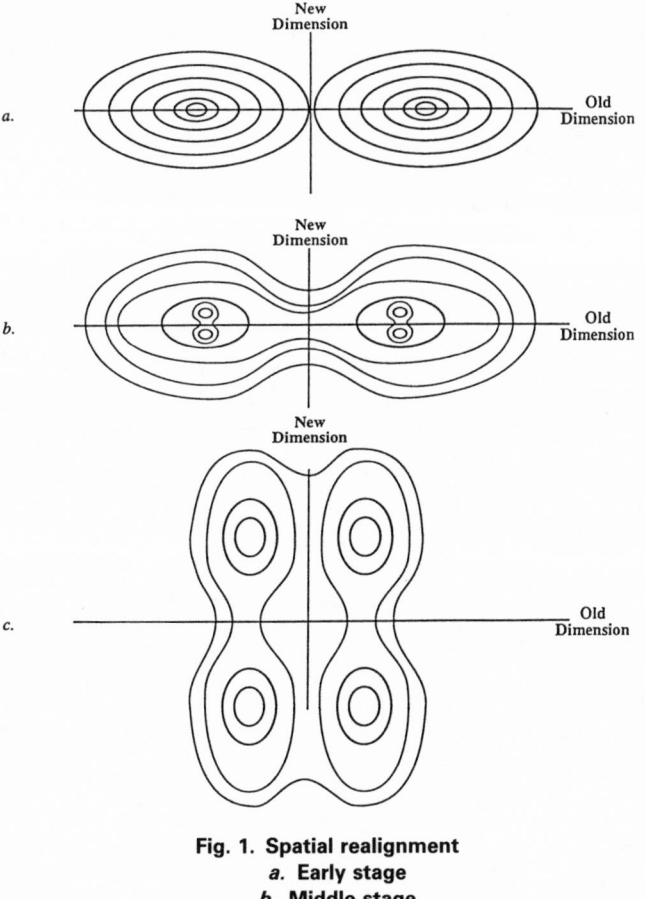

Fig. 1. Spatial realignment
a. Early stage
b. Middle stage
c. Late stage

voting rights in the 1960s, conflict over race became entwined with other aspects of redistribution captured by the first, economic dimension.

Below we test this model with our two-dimensional, D-NOMINATE scaling. Earlier, in Poole and Rosenthal 1991b, we discussed estimation and statistical issues. Our aim here is to apply the results of our scaling to the analysis of the model of realignment outlined above.

In the third section, we discuss our scaling results for the 1850s, 1890s, and 1930s. For these three periods, we find evidence for only one realignment—the 1850s. We also discuss our scaling results for the late 1930s

to the 1970s and show that an important perturbation of the space—as distinct from a dimensional realignment—began in the second New Deal. In the fourth section, we turn to a discussion of issue change more generally, namely, how new issues are accommodated within an existing spatial structure. We conclude in the fifth section.

Evidence for Realignments?

As part of our larger research project, we coded every roll call vote cast in the House of Representatives from 1789 to 1985 for three sets of categories of issues.[4] First, we coded each roll call using the coding scheme developed by Clausen (1973) and Clausen and Van Horn (1977).[5] Second, we also coded each roll call using a modified version of a coding scheme developed by Peltzman (1984).[6] We also coded each roll call by specific issue categories that we developed.[7] The flexibility and detail of this coding allow us to select all roll call votes cast on almost any issue of importance in U.S. history.

To analyze realignments and issue change, we select all roll calls on the relevant issue and examine the spatial voting patterns over the issue across time. In particular, we focus on how well voting on each roll call is accounted for by the first dimension of our estimation as well as the increase in fit from adding the second dimension. In all of this we control for the margin of the roll call. To control for the margin, we focus on how well we do in accounting for the *minority* vote by computing the proportional reduction in error (PRE) as our measure of fit. The PRE is equal to the minority vote minus the number

---

4. The accuracy of our coding depends upon the accuracy of the descriptions of the roll call votes in the ICPSR codebooks. The codebook descriptions can be misleading. For example, a key vote on the Wilmot Proviso (August 8, 1846) was actually a vote on foreign affairs appropriations. The codebook description does not mention slavery. Whenever, from *other* sources, we know of such instances, we have coded the roll calls and corrected the codebooks appropriately. (Our thanks to Barry Weingast for alerting us to this example.)

5. The codes are: government management, social welfare, agriculture, civil liberties, foreign and defense policy, and miscellaneous policy.

6. The categories are: budget general interest, budget special interest, regulation general interest, regulation special interest, domestic social policy, defense policy budget, defense policy resolutions, foreign policy budget, foreign policy resolutions, government organization, internal (to Congress) organization, Indian affairs, and the District of Columbia.

7. We used 98 categories ranging from Iran and Central America to slavery, the national bank, presidential impeachment, school prayer, voting rights, public works, disputed elections, and price controls.

of classification errors, with the difference being divided by the minority vote. That is:

$$\text{MINORITY} = \min \{\text{Number voting Yea, Number voting Nay}\},$$

$$\text{PRE} = 1 - \frac{\text{Classification errors}}{\text{MINORITY}} = \frac{\text{MINORITY} - \text{Classification Errors}}{\text{MINORITY}}$$

This measure is 1 if there are no classification errors and 0 if the spatial model is not doing better than the marginals of the vote. For example, suppose the roll call is 65 to 35 and the first dimension classifies 75 percent of the legislators correctly and adding the second dimension results in 88 percent of the legislators being correctly classified. The PRE would equal $(35 - 25)/35$ or 0.29 for one dimension and $(35 - 12)/35$ or 0.66 for two dimensions.

Comparing the PRE for one dimension (PRE1) with the PRE for two dimensions (PRE2) gives a good indication of the spatial character of the roll call. If PRE1 is high and PRE2 − PRE1 is small, then the vote is concerned primarily with the first dimension. If PRE1 is low and PRE2 − PRE1 is large, then the vote is along the second dimension. In our figures, we focus on these sorts of differences by issue areas. The analysis is restricted to roll calls with splits less than 80-20, that is with at least 20 percent of those voting on the minority side.[8] The aim here is to exclude "hurrah" votes and nonspatial protest votes.

Note that it is possible for PRE2 − PRE1 to be negative for two reasons. First, our scaling maximizes a likelihood function, *not* classification.[9] Second, the legislator coordinates are chosen as a function of all the votes and not just the vote on one roll call; therefore, two-dimensional coordinates can improve the fit overall while decreasing the fit on some individual roll calls.

Slavery and the Realignment of the 1850s

A total of 857 roll calls concerning slavery were included in our scaling of the House. In figure 2 we plot 20-roll-call moving averages of PRE1, PRE2 −

---

8. In contrast, every roll call with at least 2.5 percent in the minority was included in the estimation of legislator positions. This is because lopsided votes provide us with information about the relative positions of extremists, even though the votes themselves typically fit the spatial model relatively poorly and are substantively uninteresting. For details, see Poole and Rosenthal 1991b.

9. Consequently, it might be preferable to focus on changes in probabilities rather than classifications (Poole and Rosenthal 1991b). But because the results are similar, we use the more interpretable PRE measure.

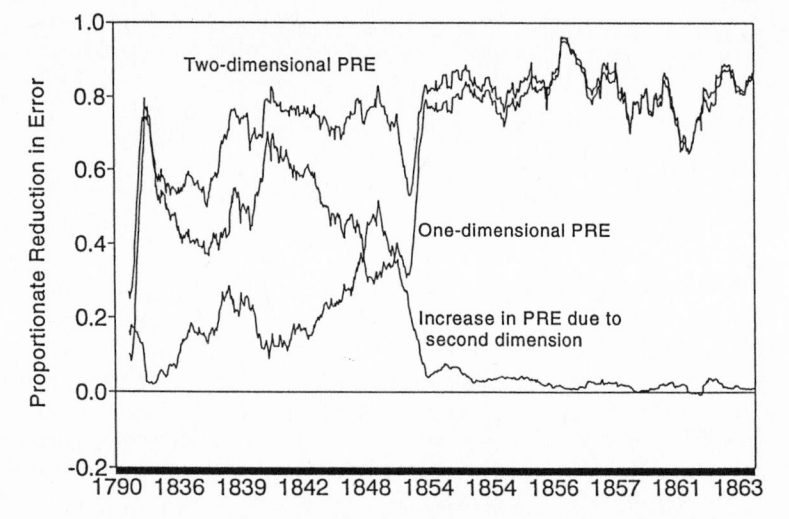

Fig. 2. Twenty-roll-call moving averages in votes on slavery, 1790–1867

PRE1, and PRE2 for the 822 roll calls having at least 20 percent voting in the minority.[10] Since there is one point per roll call, the horizontal axis is not evenly divided in units of time. In particular, note that 1854 appears twice— showing the large number of roll calls on slavery during the middle 1850s.

Only 68 of the 857 roll calls occurred before 1831; the great bulk of the roll calls were cast in the 1830s, 1840s, and 1850s, during the Whig-Democrat political party system. Beginning in the 1840s, voting on slavery occurred primarily along the second dimension. In line with the scenario shown in figure 1, the 20-roll-call moving average of PRE2 − PRE1 trends upward from 1830 until the late 1840s and then drops to nearly zero after 1852. In addition, PRE1 falls steadily from 1840 to 1852 and then climbs dramatically, indicating that the first dimension is now the slavery dimension. The scenario is clear: as the conflict within the country grew, the Whig and Democratic parties split along North-South lines on the *second dimension,* while the first dimension continued to divide the Whigs from the Democrats along traditional economic issues (e.g., tariffs, internal improvements, the

---

10. The graphs in this figure result from computations based on more than eight million individual voting decisions in the first 99 Houses. A typical legislator's position is estimated from some 900 choices. In modern times, a typical roll call's parameters are estimated from more than 400 choices. Evidence in the figures reflects aggregations of these parameters. Poole and Rosenthal (1991b) conduct statistical significance tests for statements similar to those made in the text. They generally significant at p levels several orders of magnitude below conventional levels. Basically, anything of interest displayed in the figures is statistically significant.

national bank, homestead acts). By 1853, the economic dimension collapsed and was replaced by the slavery dimension.

The 32d Congress was pivotal. By then the conflict had become so intense that it destroyed the spatial structure of congressional voting. The 32d is the second-worst-fitting House in U.S. history. (The worst occurred when the Federalists collapsed and gave way to one-party government in the Era of Good Feelings.) But by the 33d Congress, spatial structure began to reform, and slavery became the primary dimension. The scatter diagrams presented in figures 3 through 6 illustrate this process. In scatter diagrams throughout this chapter, each legislator is represented by a letter token, coded for the political party identifications assigned by Martis (1989).

Figure 3 shows a vote on whether to accept a petition concerning slavery in the district of Columbia on December 10, 1844. The legislator positions are those for the 28th Congress. The vote of each legislator is shown by the letter case of the token. Lower case corresponds to an antislavery vote, upper to proslavery. The first (horizontal) dimension separates the Whig and Democratic parties; the second (vertical) dimension separates the representatives into southerners (on top) and northerners (on bottom). Since proslavery voters are at the top and antislavery voters at the bottom, this second dimension accounts for the almost perfect spatial separation on this roll call; only 9 of 188 votes are misclassified in the D-NOMINATE estimation.[11] The spatial structure shown in figure 3 held from approximately 1832 to 1849.

Figure 4 shows a motion to adjourn made on May 11, 1854, during the debate on the Kansas-Nebraska Act.[12] Like the District of Columbia slavery vote, this roll call is spatially structured with only 3 of 147 votes misclassified. But in the period between the vote on District of Columbia slavery and the Kansas-Nebraska Act, the spatial structure changed completely. The first dimension is now a slavery dimension, and the Democratic and Whig parties are mixed together in the center of the space.

Figure 5 shows a vote concerning appropriations for the Kansas legislature taken on the last day of the 34th Congress, March 3, 1857.[13] Only one of the 171 votes is misclassified. In contrast to figure 4, there is little mixture in the center of the space, and the pro- and antislavery blocs are well separated. By this time, the Whig party was all but dead, and the party identification "opposition" best describes the ex-Whigs (Martis 1989, 34). The second

---

11. Roll call number 433 in the 28th House. The division on the roll call was 107 yea and 81 nay.

12. Roll call number 175 during the 33d Congress. The division on the roll call was 64 yea and 83 nay.

13. Roll call number 719 in the 34th Congress. The division on the roll call was 85 yea and 86 nay.

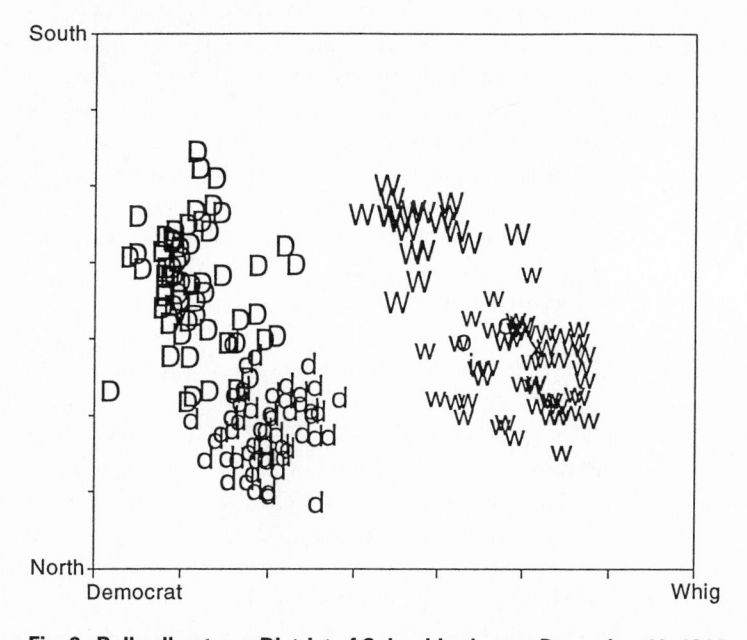

Fig. 3. Roll call vote on District of Columbia slavery, December 10, 1844.
(Each token represents a legislator; lower case = antislavery vote; up-
per case = proslavery vote. Party affiliation is shown with the following
symbols: D = Democrat; I = Independent and Democrat; O = Law and
Order; X = Independent Whig; V = Van Buren Democrat; W = Whig.)

dimension is very weak but appears to capture the nativist sentiment of the
time, because it tends to separate members of the American (Know-Nothing)
party from the rest of the House.

Finally, figure 6 shows an early vote in the 36th House on a procedural
motion regarding slavery during the battle over the speakership.[14] Only one of
the 232 votes is misclassified. The Republican party was now in the House in
force, and the spatial separation between the pro- and antislavery blocs is very
clear.

What figure 2 and figures 3 through 6 show is that the realignment of the
1850s within Congress was sudden and occurred *before* the Republican party
became a real force in U.S. politics. This result throws into question some
recent work by political economists and historians.

Fogel (1990) studies the realignment that produced Lincoln's electoral
victory by comparing the elections of 1852 and 1860. At least in Congress,
we see that the old Whig system had largely disintegrated by the time of the

14. Roll call number 3 in the 36th House. The division on the roll call was 116 yea and 116
nay.

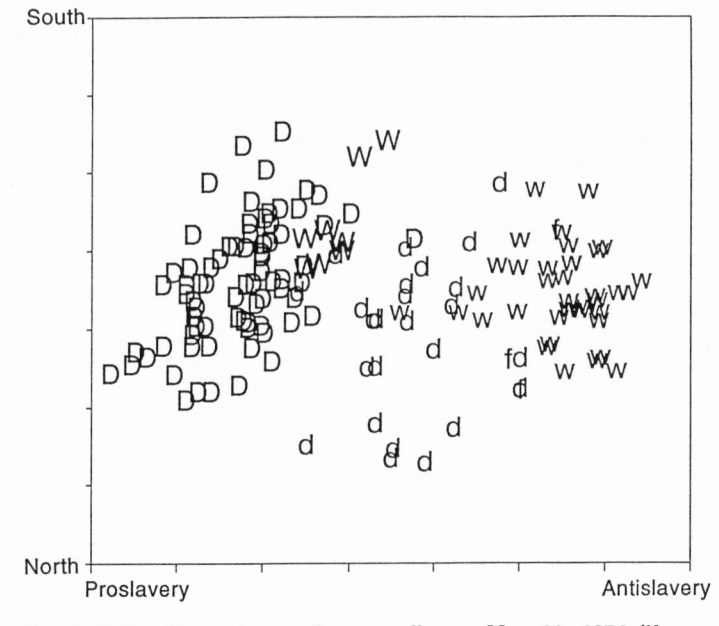

Fig. 4. Roll call on the motion to adjourn, May 11, 1854 (Kansas-Nebraska Act). (Each token represents a legislator; lower case = anti-slavery vote; upper case = proslavery vote. Party affiliation is shown with the following symbols: D = Democrat; F = Free Soil; W = Whig.)

elections of 1852. To compare the old system to the new, 1848 would appear to be a better benchmark.

Weingast (1991) correctly identifies 1850 as a crucial date in the slavery conflict. The old spatial alignment collapsed in the 1851–52 House (and Senate). But Weingast attributes the sudden change to a single event—the destruction of a credible commitment to slavery in the South by breaking the North-South balance in the Senate with the admission of California as a free state in 1850. What we show is that the tension over slavery had built gradu-ally over time, as shown by the steadily rising importance of the second dimension in the 1840s. The realignment of the 1850s was more a matter of a process that gradually increased stress until a breaking point was reached than one of a single, overwhelming event.

This pattern does fit Sundquist's model rather nicely. A new issue (actu-ally a version of a very old issue), the extension of slavery into the territories, emerged. It cut across the existing line of cleavage (conflicts over economic policy) and caused the two political parties to polarize, with one being de-stroyed in the process. A new party system then formed around the new issue. In spatial terms, a stable, two-dimensional two-party system becomes un-

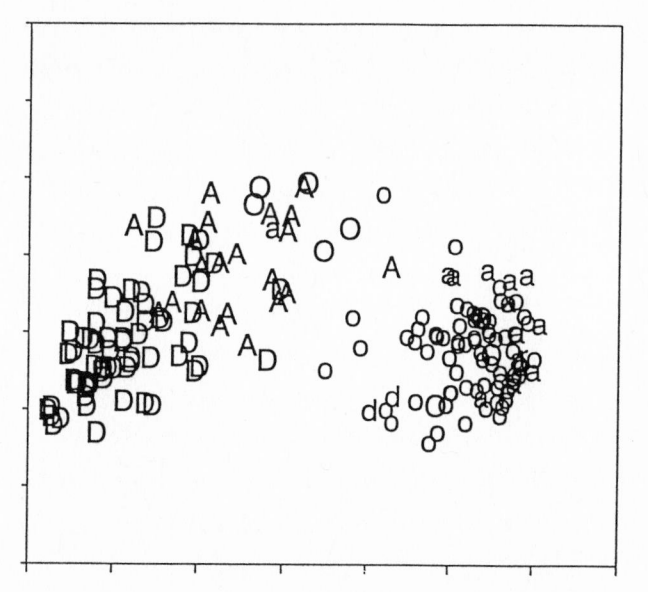

Fig. 5. Roll call on appropriations for the Kansas legislature, March 3, 1857. (Each token represents a legislator; lower case = antislavery vote; upper case = proslavery vote. Party affiliation is shown with the following symbols: A = American; D = Democrat; O = Opposition; R = Republican.)

stable. The first dimension disappears, and its place is taken by the old second dimension.

Gold and Silver and the "Realignment" of the 1890s

In Sundquist's narrative, in the aftermath of the Civil War, the main dimension of conflict was concerned with reconstruction, secession, Negro rights, and related issues. Neither party was attentive to the farmers and the emerging labor movement. The period from 1866 to 1897 was marked by a long-run, persistent deflation with accompanying falling commodity prices. This was the driving force behind the inflation issue, which, according to Sundquist's narrative, represented a new line of cleavage that led to the realigning election of 1896. The Gold Democrats deserted the Democratic party for the Republican party; the Silver Republicans were not able to overcome their aversion to the Democrats because of the Civil War and remained in the Republican party. Consequently, the Republicans were the majority party until the 1930s.

During the period from 1866 to 1908, a total of 179 roll calls with a minority of at least 20 percent were cast in the House on the gold and silver

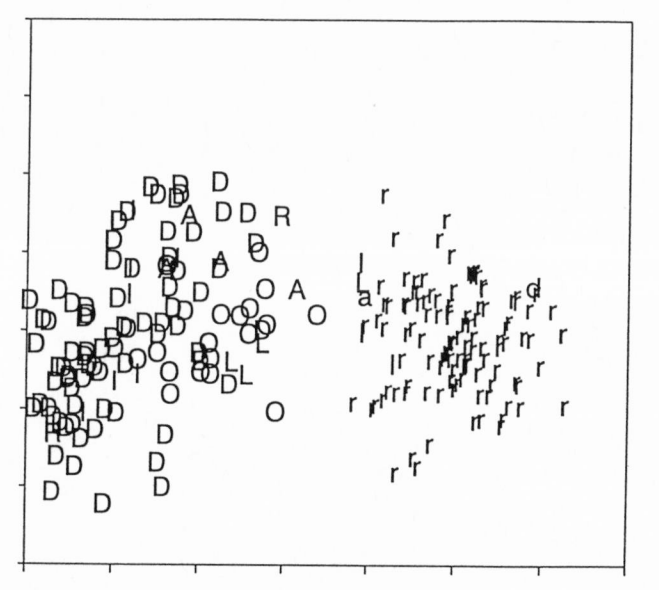

Fig. 6. Roll call to elect the Speaker without discussing slavery, December 6, 1859. (Each token represents a legislator: lower case = antislavery vote; upper case = proslavery vote. Party affiliation is shown with the following symbols: A = American; D = Democrat; I = Independent and Democrat; L = Anti-Lecompton Democrat; O = Opposition; R = Republican.)

issue (see fig. 7). In addition, we show the PRE increase for the actual roll calls as well as the moving average. The level of variability is similar to that which could be shown for the other issues considered in this essay. We also show MAJORITY = 1 − MINORITY to indicate that the average voting on the winning side is not a factor that warrants special attention. Again note that the horizontal axis is not evenly divided in units of time.

The pattern for the gold and silver issue is quite different than that for slavery. There is evidence that the gold and silver issue was a new line of cleavage in that a persistent but low-level effect can be seen for the second dimension. Indeed, an examination of the spatial maps for Congresses through this period shows that the second dimension tended to separate westerners from easterners, especially within the Republican party. In addition, this separation was *maintained* after the 1896 election.

Moreover, gold and silver is only *weakly* a second-dimension issue. Note that the increase in PRE from the second dimension peaks in the late 1870s, well before the "realigning" election of 1896. By the middle of the 1880s, members of Congress saw the gold standard and the monetization of silver as

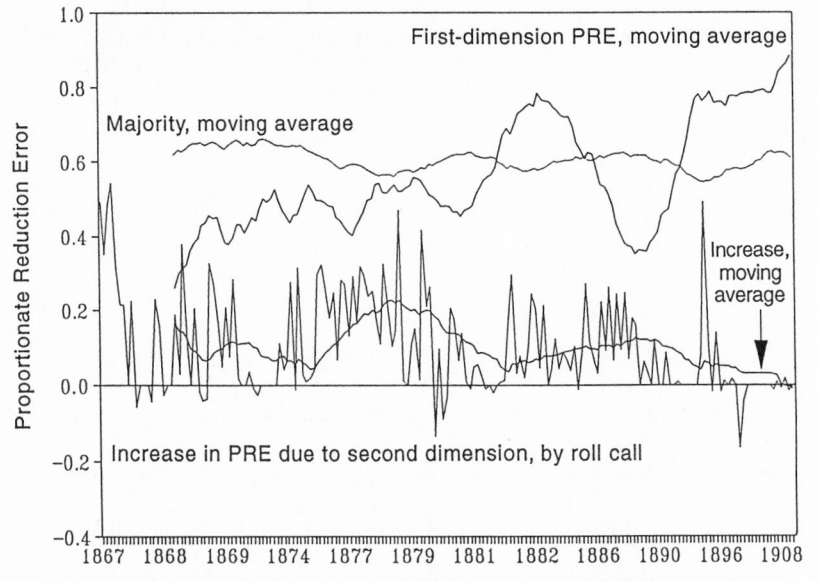

Fig. 7. Twenty-roll-call moving averages in votes on gold and silver issues, 1866–1908

part of set of issues, including the regulation of railroads and antitrust laws for industrial monopolies, that were defined along a "procommercial/anticommercial" axis (Poole and Rosenthal, 1991a). From 1890, well before the "critical" election of 1896, through 1908, the first-dimension PRE on gold and silver is always above 0.75. Although the first-dimension PRE's for gold and silver were lower prior to 1890, the first dimension was *never* replaced, in contrast to the 1850s. Rather, by the early 1890s, gold and silver as an issue was absorbed by the first dimension.

In sum, the evidence indicates that gold and silver *as an issue* realigned. That is, the basic configuration of the members of Congress was fairly stable throughout this period, but the *mapping* of gold and silver changed. That is, gold and silver slowly changed from a weakly two-dimensional issue to a strongly one-dimensional issue over the period. The realignment at the level of congressional voting did not change the basic structure of voting, rather, as an issue, gold and silver evolved until voting on it lined up along the first dimension.

The Great Depression and the "Realignment" of the 1930s

The collapse of the stock market in October, 1929, was followed by the economic slide into the Great Depression of the 1930s. By the summer of

1933, industrial production was down 50 percent, commodity prices were down 50 percent, and unemployment was around 24 percent. The consequences for the Republican party were equally severe. The elections of 1930, 1932, 1934, and 1936 resulted in a thoroughgoing replacement of Republicans by Democrats in Congress. By 1937, the Democratic party held a 333 to 89 margin over the Republicans in the House (13 members of Congress belonged to minor parties) and a 75 to 17 lead in the Senate (4 in minor parties). This massive replacement is the "realignment" of the 1930s. Since the Civil War, never before or after this time were the two parties so imbalanced in Congress.

The economic catastrophe changed the agenda of Congress. Providing relief for the destitute, formerly the function of private and religious organizations, became the province of the federal government. Moreover, the New Deal altered forever the role of the federal government in regulating the economy. Sinclair argues that the New Deal agenda "increased the ideological content of American politics" and produced "a much clearer ideological distinction between the congressional parties" (Sinclair 1977, 952). Ginsberg argues that "changes in policy after 1933 are in keeping with voter choices favoring alterations in the economic system and redistributions of opportunities in favor of urban working class elements" (Ginsberg 1976, 49).

There is no question that the Congressional agenda radically changed during the 1930s. The central question concerning realignment is: did the change in content bring with it a change in the spatial structure of voting? The answer is no. The change in agenda was accommodated within the existing framework. What *did* change was the ratio of Democrats to Republicans. This point is illustrated by figures 8 and 9, which show the estimated positions of representatives for the 71st (1929–30) House and 73d (1933–34) House, respectively.[15] Individual spatial positions are largely unchanged. Note that, in both figures, southern Democrats (S tokens) are at the left edge of the Democratic party. The depression did not lead to an immediate repositioning within the Democratic party, but simply to an expansion of the Democratic "cloud" through the addition of numerous northern Democrats. Similarly, the shape of the Republican cloud changed, but largely as a result of the elimination of a part of the cloud.

The spatial structure of figures 8 and 9 is essentially the same. In addition, the fit of the two-dimensional dynamic model to the roll call data through the "realigning" period is quite good (Poole and Rosenthal 1991b). The second dimension through this period picked up a weak western-versus-eastern-states effect along with voting on the "social" issues of the day—prohibition and immigration.

The stable spatial structure shows that the legislation of the *First* New

---

15. For similar results for the Senate, see Poole and Rosenthal 1989b.

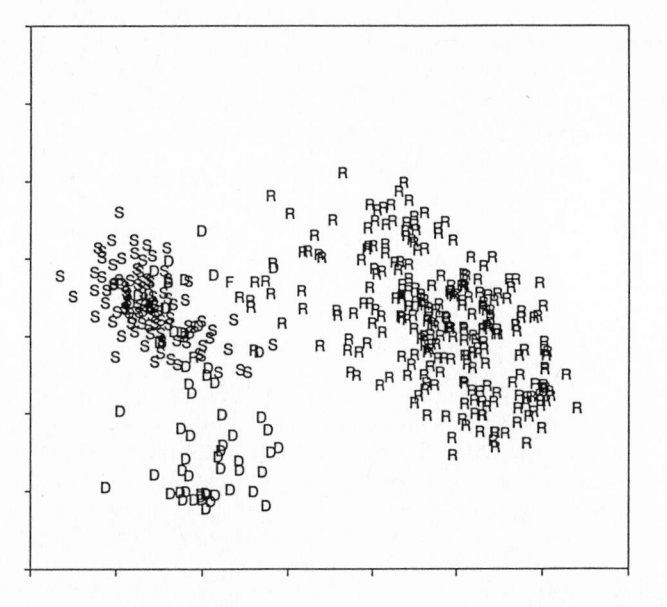

Fig. 8. Estimated positions in the 71st House, 1929–30. (Party affiliation is shown with the following symbols: D = Northern Democrat; F = Farmer-Labor; R = Republican; S = Southern Democrat.)

Deal was largely accommodated within the spatial structure that had prevailed since the end of Reconstruction. The legislation reflected either new issues that mapped readily onto the old lines of conflict or old issues, latent during the Democrats' prolonged minority status, that could be brought to the floor and passed with the new Democratic majorities.

A good illustration of the nonrealignment of the Depression is illustrated by roll call voting on labor issues, shown in figure 10. Not until the battle over the Fair Labor Standards Act—the original minimum-wage bill—in 1937–38 did the second dimension play any role in labor legislation. When the second dimension did come into play, it closely tracked the North-South division within the Democratic party over race (see below).

Another illustration of the nonrealignment of the depression is roll call voting within Clausen's social welfare category, shown in figure 11. We removed voting on liquor regulation and immigration from the category because they were strongly two-dimensional *before* the depression (see figs. 15 and 16; these issues will be further discussed in the next section). Figure 11a shows all roll calls from 1900 to 1977. The bottom line shows the increase in PRE brought about by adding a second dimension. It is essentially at a zero level since the mid-1970s; consequently, we have not graphed the large number of roll calls since 1977. It can be seen that social welfare has been largely

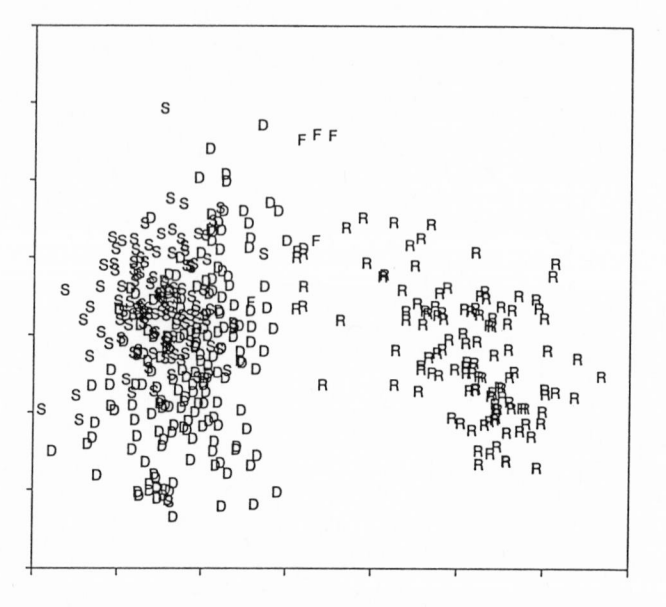

Fig. 9. Estimated positions in the 73rd House, 1933–34. (Party affiliation is shown with the following symbols: D = Northern Democrat; F = Farmer-Labor; R = Republican; S = Southern Democrat.)

a first-dimensional issue throughout the century, with occasional minor increments from the second dimension. These increments occurred in the late 1930s, the 1950s, and the 1960s. There is no evidence of a realignment brought about by the depression.

The result is emphasized by figure 11b, which enlarges the 1900–1964 portion of figure 11a. The increments to PRE brought about by the second dimension all occur after the beginning of Roosevelt's second administration. Since the social welfare category also contains the labor roll calls, the pattern in figures 11a and 11b is very similar to that in figure 10.

Civil Rights and the Perturbation of the Space

In perhaps a classic illustration of Riker's (1962) size principle, the sweeping Democratic victories in 1932 and 1936 were too good to last. Northern Democrats embarked on the Second New Deal. Many of the new programs were not to the liking of the South, and the conflict is most evident in the area of civil rights for blacks.

Roll calls on civil rights issues are shown in figure 12. During the Civil War and Reconstruction, civil rights votes had high first-dimension PRE's. During the war, there were many votes on the role of negroes in the military.

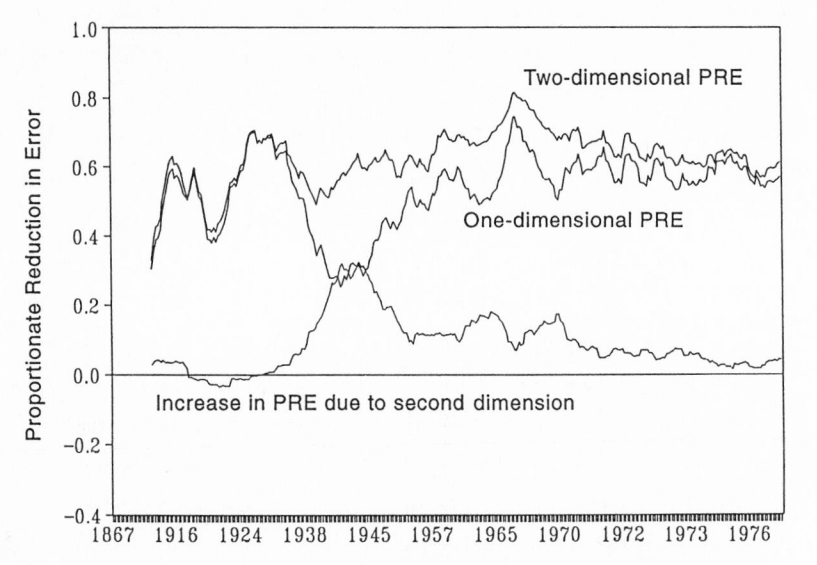

Fig. 10. Twenty-roll-call moving averages in votes on labor issues, 1867–1976

Reconstruction saw votes on the Bureau of Freedmen and civil rights bills. Between Reconstruction and the New Deal, votes on civil rights had some- what lower PRE's, but voting alignments on civil rights continue to be along the first dimension. This is largely because being left on economic issues meant favoring redistribution from richer whites in the Northeast to poorer whites in the South. The split on economic issues happened to match, with reverse logic, the split on a host of antilynching roll calls in 1921 and 1922.

Between 1922 and 1937, there were only two civil rights roll calls, with only one falling in the first Roosevelt administration. By the time votes on lynch laws recurred, in 1937 and 1940, and were joined, during World War II, by roll calls on the poll tax and voting rights in the armed forces, there was a horde of Northern Democrats who aligned themselves on the left on economic issues. A second dimension became necessary to differentiate Northerners and Southerners on civil rights votes.

The economic agenda itself became infused with the conflict over race. Although the opposition of the South to the minimum-wage legislation intro- duced in 1937 and passed in 1938 might have been motivated from the economic interest of a low-wage area,[16] Southern white congressmen also

---

16. Sinclair argues that "Southerners feared that a nationwide minimum wage would nullify their region's advantage in attracting industry" (1977, 948). Sinclair also argues that the North-South split on minimum wage was also due in part to the fact that it was a *permanent* measure as opposed to *temporary* measures such as work relief (949).

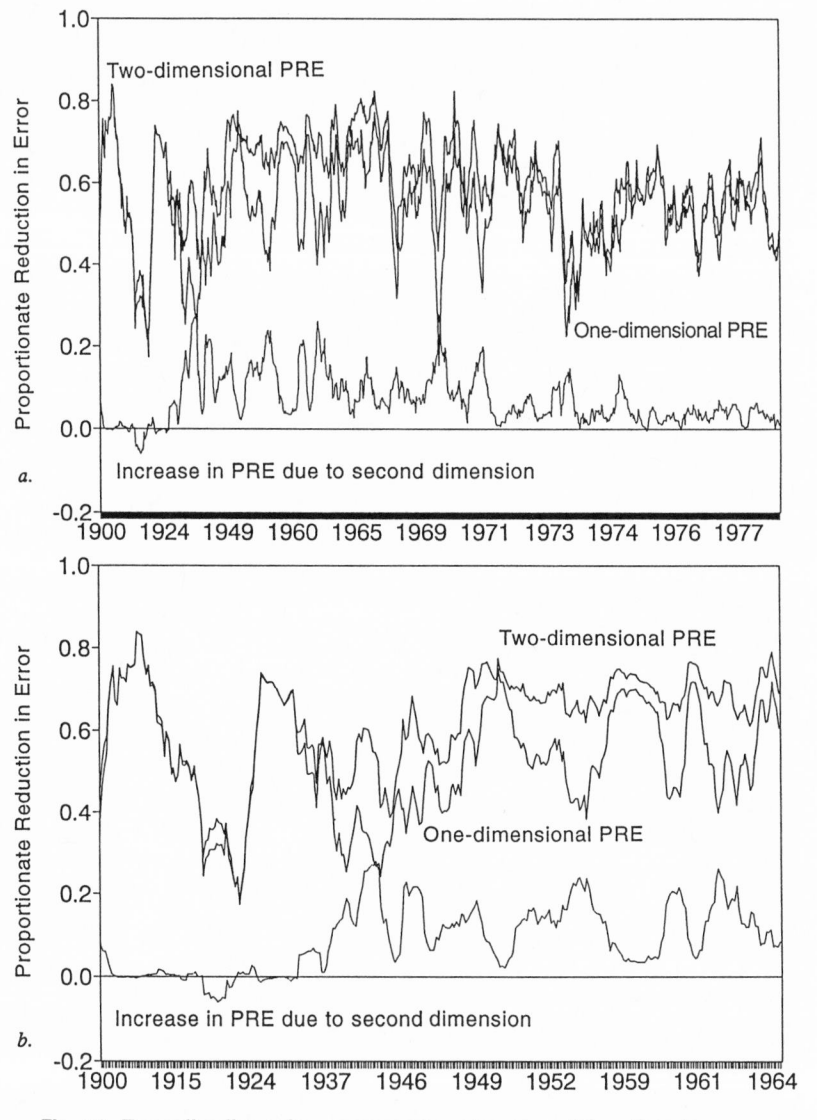

Fig. 11. Ten-roll-call moving averages in votes on social welfare issues
***a.* All roll call votes, 1900–1977**
***b.* Roll calls from 1900 to 1964 only**

explicitly opposed minimum wages as favoring Southern blacks (Poole and Rosenthal 1991c). Even though the position of the South was accommodated by keeping sectors of the economy concentrated in the South (and where competition with the North was not an issue), such as tobacco, out of the

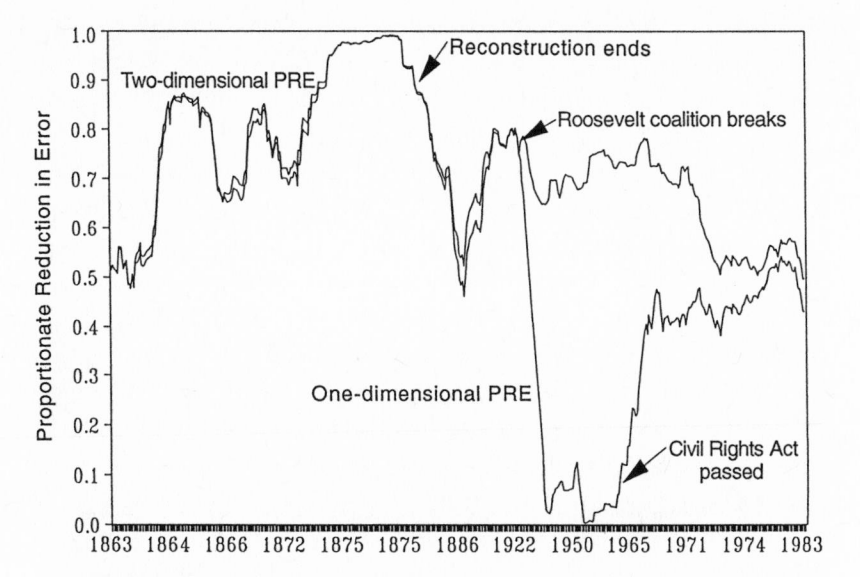

Fig. 12. Twenty-roll-call moving averages in votes on civil rights for blacks, 1862–1985

initial coverage, Southerners largely opposed the labor legislation of the Second New Deal. Consequently, labor also had an important second-dimension component from the late 1930s onward (see fig. 10).

As economic issues also turned from redistribution between whites to redistribution from whites to blacks, particularly in the South, Southerners became more conservative on the first dimension in addition to defining a pole on the second dimension. Most of the increase in classification accuracy on economic issues available from a second dimension was thus eliminated by the late 1950s. Voting on labor issues increasingly lined up on the first dimension. By 1970, first-dimension PRE levels returned to those found in the 1920s and 1930s (see fig. 10).

Civil rights remained a second-dimension issue longer than labor. But after economic conservatives in the Republican party joined Northern Democrats to pass the Civil Rights Act of 1964 and the Voting Rights Act of 1965, civil rights could increasingly be accounted for by the first dimension. In signing the legislation and "delivering the South to the Republicans for 50 years," Lyndon Johnson signaled a realignment in mass voting behavior, particularly in presidential elections. But this did not lead to a spatial realignment in Congress. Rather, it ended the perturbation of the space by the civil rights issue. Unlike the 1920s, there is now a consistent position, personified by Jesse Helms, of a "right" position on economics and race. Similarly, as

Southern Democrats sought black support, they became increasingly like Northern Democrats. Not a single Southern Democratic senator failed to vote to override President Bush's veto of the Civil Rights Bill of 1990. The veto was sustained by conservative Republicans, North and South. Indeed, the impact of the bill is nationwide, and there is a heavy component of economic redistribution inherent in the bill.

The vote to override Bush's veto is shown in figure 13. The configuration of senators was produced by running NOMINATE on the 100th Senate; only the 88 senators who served in both the 100th and 101st Senates are shown in the figure. What is striking about the configuration is the nearly complete disappearance of the second dimension. The most "extreme" Southern Democrats are now indistinguishable along the main dimension from such "liberal" republican senators as Bob Packwood of Oregon. Indeed, our animation work (Poole and Rosenthal 1989a) shows the gradual disappearance of the second dimension from the middle 1970s through 1985. Figure 13 suggests that this trend continued through the late 1980s, producing a true "unidimensional Congress."

The civil rights episode, lasting roughly from 1940 to 1966, is very instructive about spatial realignment. Although race and economics are substantively quite distinct, only one dimension was needed before 1940. This outcome was just fortuitous. Conservative positions on race and economics just happened to be strongly, albeit negatively, correlated. The breakup of the oversized Roosevelt coalition and the subsequent enfranchisement of Southern blacks took place in a framework of spatial perturbation. A second dimension was needed to capture the resolution of this conflict, but the conflict never managed to dominate the basic economic conflict inherent in democracy. Voting never became chaotic, as in 1851–52. The perturbation ended with legislation that induced a strong positive correlation of conservative positions on race and economic policy. Converse's view of constraint in ideology (1964) is now reflected in a basically one-dimensional political space in Congress.

Incorporation of Substantive Issues
Into the Basic Space

Most of the galaxy of policy issues that confront Congress are neither as intense nor as enduring as the question of race, which led to the realignment of the 1850s and the perturbation of the 1950s. How are these issues accommodated in the basic space?

If an issue is to result in sustained public policy, we hypothesize that the policy must eventually be supported by a coalition that can be represented as a split on the first, major dimension. Policy developed by coalitions that are

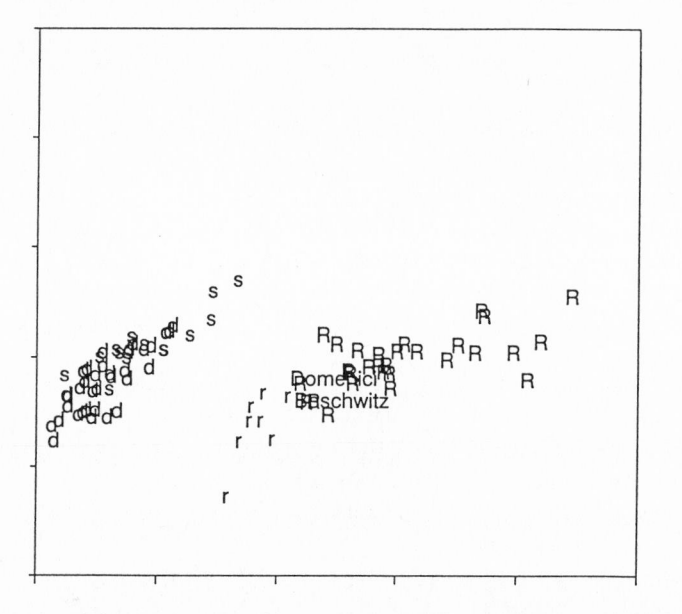

Fig. 13. Roll call to override the veto of the Civil Rights Bill of 1990. (Each token represents a legislator; lower case = vote to override; upper case = vote to sustain. Party affiliation is indicated with the following symbols: D = Northern Democrat; S = Southern Democrat; R = Republican. Names indicate classification errors.)

nonspatial or built along the second dimension is likely to be transient and unstable.

To investigate this hypothesis requires us to sharpen our focus and look at issue areas that are relatively narrowly defined, permitting us to hold substance relatively constant. Our first effort of this type was a detailed study of the history of minimum-wage legislation (Poole and Rosenthal 1991c). We found that, before World War II, minimum wage was relatively poorly mapped into the space. Even if two dimensions are used, the classifications were much worse than after the war. After the war, minimum wage became a first-dimension issue with a high degree of classification accuracy.

Abortion is an example of an issue in the initial, ripening phase. As shown in figure 14, when abortion first came onto the agenda shortly after the Supreme Court's *Roe v. Wade* ruling, the issue was quite variable in its fit to the existing spatial dimensions. It basically falls along the first dimension but with a low level of PRE. But the PRE has gradually and significantly ($t = 5.12$) increased with time. Part of this increase has resulted from well-known flip-flops, such as Richard Gephardt's conversion to a pro choice position. It

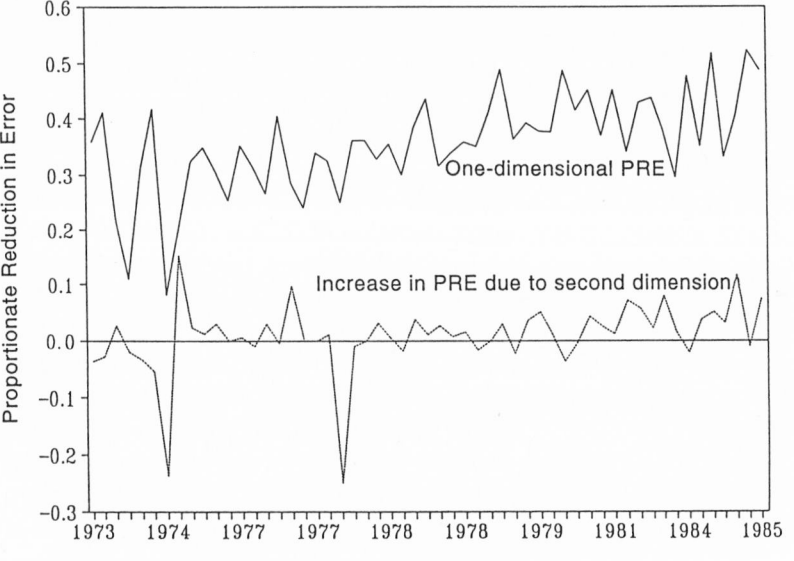

Fig. 14. Votes on abortion issues, 1973–85. (PRE regressed on time; R^2 = .331; t = 5.12.)

no longer seems possible that abortion policy can be decided by single-issue politics.

Prohibition is a nice counterpoint to abortion. The temperance movement was a classical example of single-issue politics. As figure 15 shows, voting on the passage of prohibition and its repeal did not map at all into the first dimension and had a moderately high level of PRE on the second dimension. The special-interest coalition was strong enough to amend the Constitution, but it did not produce a lasting element of public policy.

Finally, immigration is a more complex issue, as shown in figure 16. Free immigration (of Europeans) was a permanent element of public policy throughout the eighteenth and nineteenth centuries. There was a conflict, a classical economic conflict, between those who wanted cheap labor and those who did not. Through 1910, votes on immigration were, as we would expect, on the first dimension with a very high level of PRE. But, in the early twentieth century, the immigration issue took on an added element of conflict. Northern and western Europeans wanted to keep eastern and southern Europeans out. In a large number of roll calls just before World War I, the first dimension failed to classify votes on immigration. An enduring policy of restricted immigration was enacted only when the issue had been substantially "remapped" onto the first dimension and the immigration acts of 1920 and

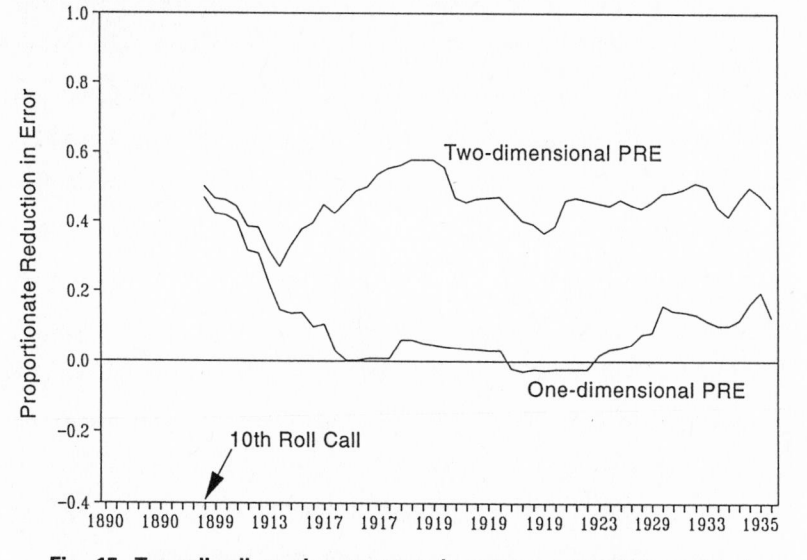

Fig. 15. Ten-roll-call moving averages in votes on prohibition-related issues, 1890–1937

1924 were passed. Subsequently, in the 1930s through the 1970s, the second dimension was more relevant, but the substance changed. The basic policy of restrictive immigration was not changed, but votes took place on the admission of political refugees. When a systematic policy change was introduced in the 1980s, there was no longer an effect from a second dimension.

Although much more work is required on how specific issues map into the basic unidimensional structure of congressional voting, the results from minimum wage, abortion, prohibition, and immigration, and, in an earlier period, monetary policy, provide support for our hypothesis that stable policy coalitions are built on the first dimension.

Conclusion

Major changes in the mass electorate occurred during the 1850s, 1890s, and 1930s. But only in the 1850s is there evidence that these changes produced a corresponding shift in the structure of congressional roll call voting. The changes of the 1890s and 1930s were largely massive replacements of one party by the opposing party. These replacements did not change the basic structure of congressional voting.

Beginning in the late 1930s, however, a realignment did perturb the structure of congressional voting. The unwieldy Roosevelt coalition broke up

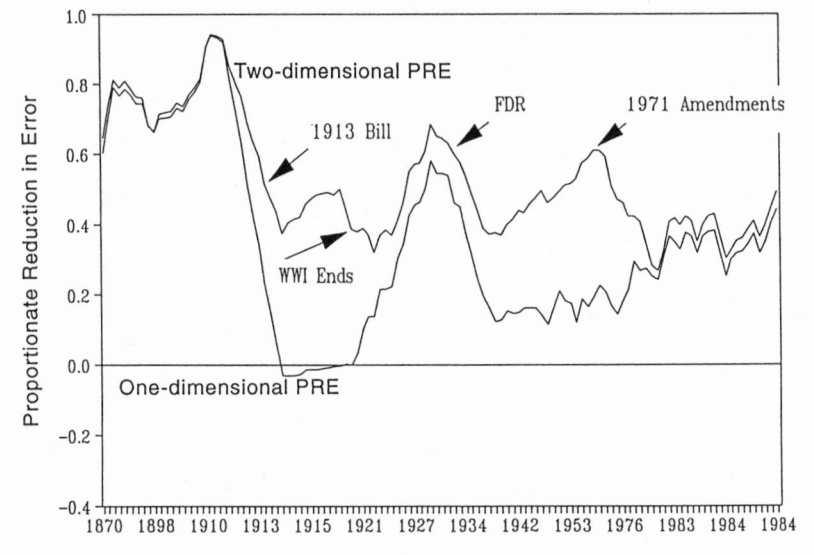

Fig. 16. Ten-roll-call moving averages in votes on immigration issues, 1870–1984

because of North-South conflicts over the old issue of race. This division peaked in the 1960s and has slowly faded away. Southern Democrats are now to the left of "liberal" Republicans.

Our finding of only one major realignment rather than the three commonly described in the literature may be a simple consequence of our focus on professional politicians as opposed to previous analyses of national election results. We speculate that this difference in data is not the source of the disparity in the findings. Whereas we estimated spatial positions and were thus able to study dimensional realignment directly, the literature focuses on how shifts in voter allegiances influence presidential election winners and congressional majorities. But sometimes these shifts in voter allegiances may be no more than a remapping of ideal points on the long-run first dimension. For example, it is well known, at least since Kramer 1971, that economic conditions are strongly related to electoral outcomes, with the incumbent's party being punished in bad times. It has also been established (Alesina, Londregan, and Rosenthal 1991) that electoral gains have long-run lagged effects that dampen only slowly. Consequently, the "realignment" of the 1930s may have been only a powerful shock on the dimension as a result of the depression. Because the shock was massive, Democratic majorities persisted for several decades, but there was no dimensional realignment. Similarly, Republican ascendence in the late 1890s may have reflected the vast

discoveries of gold in South Africa and the Klondike that vitiated the inflationary agenda of the Democrats.

Our results on realignment suggest a general model for issue change. We have found that the first dimension throughout most of U.S. history has captured the main economic conflicts between the two major political parties. During normal periods, one typically finds a weak second dimension that captures the "social" issues of the day. New issues that have staying power will eventually be drawn into the exiting one- or two-dimensional alignment because it is easier to build stable coalitions within the existing stable structure of voting.

REFERENCES

Aldrich, John H. 1983. "A Spatial Model with Party Activists: Implications for Electoral Dynamics." *Public Choice* 41:63–100.

Alesina, Alberto, John Londregan, and Howard Rosenthal. 1991. "A Model of the Political Economy of the United States." Graduate School of Industrial Administration, Carnegie-Mellon University, paper #1990-27.

Brady, David W. 1982. "Congressional Party Realignment and Transformations of Public Policy in Three Realignment Eras." *American Journal of Political Science* 26:333–60.

Burnham, Walter Dean. 1970. *Critical Elections and the Mainsprings of American Politics.* New York: Norton.

Clausen, Aage R. 1973. *How Congressmen Decide: A Policy Focus.* New York: St. Martin's Press.

Clausen, Aage R., and C. Van Horn. 1977. "The Congressional Response to a Decade of Change: 1963–1972." *Journal of Politics* 39:624–66.

Converse, Philip E. 1964. "The Nature of Belief Systems in Mass Publics." In *Ideology and Discontent,* ed. David E. Apter, 206–61. New York: Free Press.

Fogel Robert. 1990. "Modeling Complex Dynamic Interactions: The Role of Intergenerational, Cohort, and Period Processes and of Conditional Events in the Political Realignment of the 1850s." Historical Working Paper no. 12. Cambridge, Mass.: National Bureau of Economic Research.

Ginsber, Benjamin. 1972. "Critical Elections and the Substance of Party Conflict: 1844–1968." *Midwest Journal of Political Science* 16:603–25.

Ginsberg, Benjamin. 1976. "Elections and Public Policy." *American Political Science Review* 70:41–49.

Kramer, Gerald. 1971. "Short Term Fluctuations in U.S. Voting Behavior, 1896–1964." *American Political Science Review* 65:131–43.

Martis, Kenneth C. 1989. *The Historical Atlas of Political Parties in the United States Congress: 1789–1989.* New York: Macmillan.

Peltzman, Sam. 1984. "Constituent Interest and Congressional Voting." *Journal of Law and Economics* 27:181–200.

Poole, Keith T., and Howard Rosenthal. 1985. "A Spatial Model for Legislative Roll Call Analysis." *American Journal of Political Science* 29:357–84.

Poole, Keith T., and Howard Rosenthal. 1987. "Analysis of Congressional Coalition Patterns: A Unidimensional Spatial Model." *Legislative Studies Quarterly* 12:55–75.

Poole, Keith T., and Howard Rosenthal. 1988. "Roll Call Voting in Congress 1789–1985: Spatial Models and the Historical Record." In *Science at the John von Neumann National Supercomputer Center: Annual Research Report Fiscal Year 1987*, 111–16. Princeton, N.J.: John von Neumann Center.

Poole, Keith, T., and Howard Rosenthal. 1989a. "Color Animation of Dynamic Congressional Voting Models." Graduate School of Industrial Administration, Carnegie-Mellon University, paper #64-88-89.

Poole, Keith, T., and Howard Rosenthal. 1989b. "Political Realignment in American History: Results from a Spatial Scaling of the Congressional Roll Call Record." In *Science at the John von Neumann National Supercomputer Center: Annual Research Report Fiscal Year 1988*, 157–62. Princeton, N.J.: John von Neumann Center.

Poole, Keith, T., and Howard Rosenthal. 1991a. "The Enduring 19th Century Conflict Over Economic Regulation: The Interstate Commerce Act Reconsidered." Manuscript, Graduate School of Industrial Administration, Carnegie-Mellon University.

Poole, Keith T., and Howard Rosenthal. 1991b. "Patterns of Congressional Voting." *American Journal of Political Science* 35:228–78.

Poole, Keith T., and Howard Rosenthal. 1991c. "The Spatial Mapping of Minimum Wage Legislation." In *Politics and Economics in the 1980s*, ed. Alberto Alesina and Geoffrey Carliner, 214–46. Chicago: University of Chicago Press.

Riker, William. 1962. *The Theory of Political Coalitions*. New Haven: Yale University Press.

Schattschneider, E. E. 1940. *Party Government*. New York: Holt, Rinehart and Winston.

Sinclair, Barbara. 1977. "Party Realignment and the Transformation of the Political Agenda: The House of Representatives, 1925–1938." *American Political Science Review* 71:940–53.

Sinclair, Barbara. 1981. "Agenda and Alignment Change: The House of Representatives, 1925–1978." In *Congress Reconsidered*, 2d ed., ed. Lawrence C. Dodd and Bruce I. Oppenheimer, 221–45. Washington: CQ Press.

Sundquist, James L. 1983. *Dynamics of the Party System*. Rev. ed. Washington: Brookings Institution.

Weingast, Barry. 1991. "Political Economy of Slavery: Credible Commitments and the Preservation of the Union, 1800–1860." Paper presented at the Seventh International Symposium in Economic Theory and Econometrics, St. Louis.

Issues, Dimensions, and Agenda Change in Postwar Democracies: Longterm Trends in Party Election Programs and Newspaper Reports in Twenty-three Democracies

Ian Budge

Almost by definition, election issues play a key role in setting and defining the political agenda in contemporary democracies. This is because major problems do not go away easily and almost inevitably last more than one election. There is thus a strong incentive for some political party to inject them into the campaign: if the issues are sufficiently pressing, it is likely to win votes and enter government in a coalition system or to win outright in two-party competition. Under most accounts of the democratic process, it is then likely to confront the issue in office, either because its ideology and support groups demand it or because it hopes to consolidate its vote for the next election. Theories of the "party mandate," of course, make carrying through electoral commitments a central feature of representative democracy.

The election process thus tends to pick up and winnow out issues with staying power that then feature centrally during the next legislative and government term. As stated in the Introduction, most of the essays in this volume are concerned with saying what the issues are or have been, a concern that leads naturally into how they have or might originate, which often also involves the question of how they have been presented and possibly manipulated by political parties or media according to their own views and interests.

While answering these last two questions is essential if we are to get a theoretical grasp on the agenda formation process, a first step is to list and describe the issues that have actually dominated the postwar agenda. These are important in themselves because they constitute and define the issue-spaces within which parties locate themselves in elections and parliaments. Formal models of election competition and coalition formation need a specification of substantive issues to supplement their general utility assumptions with more specific ones on what precisely produces utility for the main actors.

For further studies of the processes of agenda setting we need to specify postwar issues in order to track them back to their determinants and origins.

This essay, therefore, concentrates primarily on the question of what issues have been important in democracies since World War II. I try to be as comprehensive as possible in examining issues across large numbers of democracies, partly to see if there are tendencies for the same agenda to emerge in all of them and partly to provide a framework for evaluation of any one country's peculiarities. I start by considering problems in the definition and measurement of political issues—in particular, whether issue creation involves all parties and both political leaders and electors or whether issues can be "created" by only one of these. Confrontational approaches to the handling of issues are contrasted with saliency theories. The choice of a conceptual approach affects the way issues and change are measured and represented, whether this is done through typologies or by the spatial analysis of party movements.

Spatial analysis presents two possibilities in regard to issue change: parties may change positions over time within the space, but the space itself (defined in terms of issues relevant at each time point) may change. Both are considered on the basis of codings of sentences in party election programs across a number of democracies since the war. This is supplemented by trends in newspaper reports of campaign issues over the same period. These seem to indicate that, in the long term, issues are generated by the objective problems facing governments at the time. The discussion ends by briefly considering consequences of issues for government formation and action and how far commitments to take action on issues are put into effect, as party mandate theory would imply.

The question of issue change is so vast, extending from party competition and government change through media and communication studies to election studies and voting behavior, that it is narrowed down here to comparative research done over the last 15 years on party interrelationships in elections and governments, in roughly the same group of democracies—Western Europe, North America, Australasia, Japan, and Israel. Within these constants a variety of data sources—surveys, documents, reported events—have been used and analyzed by various techniques, including spatial analysis. The distinction between party leaders and electors has always been central and, where possible, their mutual influence on each other has been examined.

The use of different sources, techniques, and subjects for analysis throws into relief questions usually neglected at a purely abstract level, such as how do we identify issues in the first place and how do we put them into the same frame of analysis for comparative purposes. These are the first questions I take up, before going on to more theoretical points (which still affect measurement and operationalization however).

Defining Issues

While it is possible to think of issues being defined and discussed independently of political parties (in the media, for example), they are, for the purposes of political analysis, usually related to what the parties say and do. What do we mean by parties, however? Are they the leadership or electoral base or both? Bearing in mind this potential ambiguity, we could define an issue variously as:

a) a point "at issue" or any way discussed by all parties, so that, in terms of a spatial analysis, the concurrence of all is necessary to define the space,

b) a point or topic emphasized by only one of the parties (each can contribute independently to defining any space, so that a dimension of concern to one may not interest another—this has consequences for the kind of metric one might want to use in measuring distances within a space),

c) a point or topic or "position," whether or not stressed by leaders, important in

(1) defining party support among electors (in which case it could presumably include the "permanent issues" of class, religion, ethnicity, or urban-rural divisions stressed in Lipset and Rokkan 1967), or

(2) moving support between the parties—a narrower and more dynamic concept, within which issues are more likely to be short term.

These are very different concepts with strong bearings on what one might identify as issues and, therefore, how one might identify change in relation to them. There is little basis for deciding, in the abstract, which definition is better: presumably it all depends on one's research purposes. As my interest has been primarily in the interaction of issues as defined by the party leadership with those important in consolidating party support among electors (and sometimes in moving electors between parties), I would want to be as inclusive as possible and define issues as topics raised by one or more party leaderships and/or important among electors. Part of the research interest then lies in estimating the extent to which issues defined in each of these ways coincide, not simply assuming that they do, as in most theories of the Downsian tradition (Downs 1957). In discussing issues in this sense it is important, obviously, to specify their provenance and source (in which party leadership and/or electorate do they originate or exert influence, for example).

Documenting Issues and Tracking Change

In tracking issues one may draw on various data sources. Again, what one discovers is fairly heavily dependent on the source used, so it is worthwhile to comment briefly on these in passing.

  a) By far the commonest source for identifying issues are election surveys—indeed, so common are they that many analysts use surveys with the implicit assumption that their questions define the universe of issues that existed for a given election. While these questions usually represent the best guesses of the investigators about what would be issues at a point two or three months before the election, they are informed guesses by experts using polls and similar sources as evidence. Surveys have two other features. One is that certain questions get carried on from previous years because of a long-term interest in electors' reactions to them, not because they were necessarily prominent in that particular election. The other is that electors are often invited to talk about politics generally, in response to open questions, though as far as I know no one has ever used this issue material to check on the closed questions included by the designers of the questionnaire.

  b) An alternative source for tracing issues are media descriptions and analyses, especially as summarized in such compendiums as "Keesing's Contemporary Archives" or in such retrospective accounts of campaigns as the Nuffield General Election Series in Britain; the *Making of the President* or the Enterprise Research Institute series in the United States. Media accounts are clearly biased by the position of the observers and are unlikely to be based on any very systematic sampling of opinions. Nevertheless, they do comprehend the whole campaign and reflect opinions and events both at elite and electoral levels in a way no other source does.

  c) One can also trace issues through party documents, particularly the election programs (in the United States, the platforms) of the parties. Though these are directed at electors, they clearly originate with the leadership and reflect its opinions or strategies. They are also written at various times before the campaign opens and, in many countries, are read by few electors. As against this they are read by commentators and media people, who use them as a basis from which to begin their discussions. In this indirect way they reach the general public and shape many of the themes of the campaign. They thus constitute a major source for the analysis of issues change.

  d) One should also mention legislative sources and proceedings, such as

roll calls, bills, and other outputs and debates. These differ from the sources mentioned previously in that they are nonelectoral, falling generally between campaigns. They tell you a lot about the questions that preoccupy party leaderships at a particular time: these often, of course, precipitate the fall and rise of governments and could provide issue information highly relevant to coalition formation. In theory, such information could also be related to polling information about electoral opinions.

Clearly, the different source materials may give rather different pictures of what issues are relevant at any one time. An attempt at comparing judgments based on surveys, media, and party documents for the 1960 presidential election in the United States and the 1964 General Elections in Britain is made in tables 1 and 2.

Obviously themes culled from each of the sources often coincide: when they do they are listed on the same line, parallel to the corresponding issue among electors as ascertained from survey sources (col. 4). Some themes stressed by politicians were not asked in surveys (presumably because their resonance among electors was not apparent). Some survey questions that divided electors very effectively into partisan groups were not stressed at all by politicians according to our sources (e.g., in Britain in 1964, the question of entry to the Common Market). These are listed in column 5 of the tables. It will be noted that only one trivial issue appears in this column for the United States in 1960, as compared to three issues of some weight for Britain in 1964. This contrast holds generally for British and U.S. elections. Generally in the United States for all elections examined, all issues could be seen as originating with leaders. For Britain most do, but there are usually two or three questions, important and divisive among electors, about which leaders seem to have said nothing.

Two additional aspects of leaders' influence on electors need to be noted. First, politicians must be credited with putting up particular presidential and prime ministerial candidates, who have some impact on electors. Candidate reactions are therefore listed in both tables at the top of column 4. Second, leaders can, at times, give considerable weight to long-standing issues (such as nationalization in Britain) that are not very prominent among electors.

In spite of discrepancies between leaders and electors and between sources, there is perhaps more convergence on characterizations of issues in tables 1 and 2 than one might have expected. So far as I know, no one has done a systematic comparison of this kind over an extended series of elections. This simple validation is obviously a first step to be undertaken in a more comprehensive study of issue change. The encouraging results of the limited comparisons for 1960 and 1964 encourage some substitution of one

TABLE 1. Correspondence between Issues Emphasized by Leaders and Issues Important among Electors, 1960 U.S. Presidential Election

Campaign Issues[a] (1)	Platform Topics[b] (2)	Media Topics[c] (3)	Survey Issues[d] (4)	Elector Issues[e] (5)
			Reaction to Kennedy	Attitude to union-endorsed candidate
			Reaction to Nixon	
			Most important problem facing the government	
Kennedy's Catholicism			Catholic question	
		Freedom	School integration	
Civil rights	Civil rights	Minority groups	Equality for blacks	
Peace		Peace	Likelihood of war	
Prosperity	Economic growth	Economic stability	Personal financial prospects	
Foreign policy Formosa General U.S. standing vs. USSR	Foreign policy	Internationalism	Isolationism	
Federal tax role			Government role in housing and power	
			Government guarantee for employment	
Farm policy	Agriculture	Agriculture		
	Social policy	Social services	Medicare	
	Overseas aid		Foreign aid	
	Science	Technology		
	Education		Government aid to education	
	Government administration	Government		
	Fiscal policy	Efficiency		
	Natural resources	Conservation		
	Labor groups	Labor groups		
	Defense	Military	Retaining troops overseas	
		Regionalism		
		Social justice		

Source: Budge and Farlie 1977, 436.
[a]Campaign issues as noted in White 1961.
[b]Topics selected because of emphasis in platforms.
[c]Topics selected on the basis of the number of media references.
[d]Issues stressed in election survey instruments.
[e]Issues stressed by electors but not stressed by political leaders.

source for another in the general tracking of issues, though it also appears from the tables that leaders are likely to nominate many more issues than electors actually take up.

How Electors and Parties React to Issues:
Confrontation Versus Saliency

The way in which parties and electors react to issues has considerable implications for the way we measure them. The conventional picture of party competition is one in which the parties endorse opposing positions on the same set of issues, and electors estimate the agreement between their own position and those of the parties and vote for the alternative that is closest. This kind of picture is very familiar from Downs's classic treatment (Downs 1957) and from many spatial analyses in the Downsian tradition.

However, when one actually studies electoral programs it is hard to find much evidence for confrontation, at least at the leadership level. If one examines the number of references to other parties, it is on average about 10 percent of all sentences in the documents, and party-related issue references are even lower—about 5 percent. Clearly, this minority of sentences does not contain the main thrust of what is being said—which we must take as the party leaderships' attempt to attract electors to vote for them (Budge, Robertson, and Hearl 1987, 389–91).

What do these documents contain? For the most part, assertions of the importance of various problems (unemployment, social services, strong defense, law and order, the erosion of freedom, the environment) in the form of rather rambling analyses of history and of the current state of affairs, with a view to stressing the urgency of action in the particular area. These analyses do not give great prominence to other parties or what they have done. But they do talk a lot about the originating party's record and attitudes.

The importance of party documents of this kind is that, unlike survey questionnaires or media reports, they come directly and unmediated from participants in the struggle for votes. They must therefore be taken as direct evidence for the way parties handle issues and for the way in which the leadership, at any rate, thinks electors will react.

How do they think of issues in this context? Clearly not primarily as direct confrontation, since so few of their references are dedicated to contrasting party policies. Rather, they seem to be engaged in stressing the priority of certain topics, which they discuss at great length, in comparison with others, which they discuss in passing or hardly at all.

Why should parties present themselves in this way? It seems that party leaders have a picture of the way electors react to parties that differs somewhat from the one prevalent among survey analysts. Party leaders stress certain

TABLE 2. Correspondence between Issues Emphasized by Leaders and Issues Important among Electors, 1964 British General Election

Campaign Issues[a] (1)	Manifesto Topics[b] (2)	Media Topics[c] (3)	Survey Issues[d] (4)	Elector Issues[e] (5)
Defense	Defense	Military	Reaction to Wilson Reaction to Hume Differences between parties Nuclear deterrent	Common Market Importance of monarchy Death penalty
Balance of payments and nationalization			Closeness of party policy to own preferences on nationalization	
Trade unions			Trade union ties to Labour	
Housing (land prices)	Housing Social Security			
Pensions	Social services	Social services	Closeness of party policy to own preferences on social services spending	
Health	Health			
Education	Education			
Immigration		Immigration policy		
	Disarmament		Nuclear deterrent	
	Commonwealth			
	Prices			

Government Waste

Economic planning
Redundancy and retraining
Regions
Transport
Taxes
Leisure and Recreation
Overseas Aid
Agriculture

Economic planning

Culture

Internationalism
Technology
Economic stability
Peace
Productivity

Ties with United States
Personal prosperity

Attitude to strikes

Source: Budge and Farlie 1977, 437

[a] Campaign issues as noted in Butler and King 1965.
[b] Topics selected because of emphasis in party manifestos.
[c] Topics selected on the basis of media references.
[d] Issues stressed in election survey instruments.
[e] Issues stressed by electors but not stressed by political leaders.

issues more than others because they think they would benefit if those they favor become prominent in the campaign. This, in turn, seems to assume an almost automatic linkage between the prominence of a certain type of issue and party advantage (in terms of votes).

The most plausible explanation of why politicians present themselves in this way is that they endorse a "saliency" rather than a confrontational theory of voting. They think that the majority of electors see different parties as having the obviously "correct" policy for particular areas. Thus, "left" or reformist parties will expand social services; right-wing parties will be tough on offenders in the field of law and order; left or reformist parties will generally intervene more where intervention is needed, while right-wing parties are more likely to reduce government activity and implement tax cuts.

There seems little doubt in politicians' minds about most electors endorsing one "obvious" course of action in each area and clearly identifying the party most likely to carry it through. In view of this, they seem to think that elections will be won by the party most of whose proprietary issues assume prominence in the election. So, much party effort seems to be devoted to making "their" issues prominent and downplaying those of the opposition. (For a similar interpretation of issue effects, which is called the dominance principle, see the discussion in Riker, in this volume).

These tendencies are reinforced by the difficulty parties have in dissociating themselves from their own history and actions in government, which give them an indelible association with certain policy stances. This implies, in turn, that they are able to shift their policy positions only gradually, so they are far from enjoying unlimited mobility over the entire policy field. Clearly again they must find it difficult to leapfrog as it would be quite impossible for a Labour party to pretend it was more conservative than the Conservatives. They would lose many long-standing supporters to no avail as nobody would believe they had changed radically in any case.

All this has considerable implications for the way one defines and codes issues, pointing to the importance of the space or attention devoted to a topic, rather than the nuances of what is said about it. And, in fact, one striking empirical finding in coding party documents is that remarks about any area are usually of one kind. One does not discuss defense, for example, to attack military expenditure but only to support it. The same goes for social services.

Proof for the assertions of saliency theory comes above all from the very plausible results, including spatial maps, obtained when one applies it to documentary data (see Robertson 1976; Budge and Farlie 1977, chap. 12; Budge, Robertson, and Hearl 1987). This supports the general impression you have from reading party documents or following political discussions in the media, that party spokesmen rather than discussing a problem (say crime) on some common ground, will switch: the more right-wing emphasizes conven-

tional law and order, the more reformist the fact that crime breeds in poor social conditions that call for more intervention and services.

One further piece of specific evidence, apart from the low rate of programmatic references to other parties and their issue positions, is the fact that specific commitments and pledges are so limited in party documents and confined almost exclusively to marginal areas (Rallings 1987). One simply cannot code an election platform in terms of specific stands without throwing away most of the material. But surely, everything that is written has some purpose. If so, saliency theory is the only explanation that makes sense of 90 percent of the sentences in the election programs.

Characterizing Issue Positions: Scores and Typologies

It is possible to characterize party and electoral positions by simply recording stances on every conceivable issue. For most purposes, however, one needs to summarize and estimate the overall issue position. This is particularly necessary when one wants to estimate distances between parties, and between parties and electors, and to define voting and coalition theories.

Again, there are a number of ways of doing this. It is salutary to reflect that many—perhaps most—summary characterizations are not spatial in nature. I review these here, going on in the next section to consider the spatial characterizations that may be applied.

A first, heroic solution is to concentrate only on the most important issue and characterize parties and electors in regard to that. (In terms of a saliency characterization, this would be the contrast between each party's leading topics.) A specific example of this is where Budge and Keman (1990, 83)—partly from paucity of data as well as from a desire to simplify—hypothesize that parties agreeing on the most important issue would be more likely to enter into a governmental coalition with each other than those that did not, where no obvious structural impetus to coalition existed. Given the difficulty of getting data from newspaper accounts, the hypothesis had a fair degree of success: 58 percent of relevant cases.

From the point of view of trying to predict the direction of voting in elections, summary scores for each party may do very well. The simplest solution was suggested by Kelley and Mirer (1974). For elegance and parsimony it has never been bettered. They simply took advantage of the "open" questions about issues and candidates included in practically all national election surveys and added up positive and negative references to each candidate algebraically (each counting one). Electors were then postdicted to vote for the party with the highest score—a characterization that seemed to fit the data for the United States very well.

More directly related to the discussion of issues as such, rather than vote

prediction, is the idea of typing specific issues into long-term "clusters" or "areas," as shown in table 3. The advantage of doing so is that the "types" are relevant over all elections, whereas specific issues appear and disappear. In line with saliency ideas, one can assign most of these types to one party or another (in terms of their prominence in an election causing a net inflow of votes to one of the parties). Election failure or success can then be explained in terms of more of one parties' issues than another's predominating at an election.

The advantage of such a characterization is that it can be applied over all elections for which newspaper accounts of prominent issues are available (i.e., in practice, over all elections in democracies since World War II). Not only that, it can be used to *predict* election results in advance on the basis of such accounts. Predictions on this basis have had a fair degree of success (Budge and Farlie 1983, 84–114). The advantage of this approach in the present context is that it can be used to survey the incidence of issues of the various types in elections since the war: tables drawn from Budge and Farlie 1983 form, in fact, the centerpiece of a subsequent section (see table 10).

Summarizing Issue Positions: Dimensions and Spatial Analyses

The power and flexibility of nonspatial analyses are much greater than is commonly credited. But spatial analyses have well-known advantages of direct, intuitive representation and openness to mathematical analyses and formal modeling that render them very appealing. This is even truer of one-dimensional representations, which have the advantage, usually, of avoiding cyclical voting problems. A pervasive problem with many analyses, however, has been that, in their eagerness to utilize the power of a spatial approach, they have been unself-critical—even unconscious—of the operational assumptions necessary to produce them and on which their results depend just as much as on the highly refined mathematical postulates that they use explicitly (cf. Budge and Keman 1990, 21–30). This is even more true when theoretical analysts have availed themselves of empirically derived spaces, for there it is even clearer that what goes in determines what comes out—and that is not always an issue-space! I illustrate these points in the following paragraphs.

The commonest type of space used to explain and predict government coalitions is a judgementally derived Left-Right space, where country specialists have been asked to order and space out parties along a continuum between (usually undefined) Left and Right ends. Usually this puts Communist and radical left parties as well as extreme right parties way out at each end of the line, so it is not hard to predict that the coalition will form from those parties of the center that are closest to each other. This kind of judgmental placement

TABLE 3. Broad Groupings for Newspaper Accounts of Issues

Broad Grouping	Specific Campaign Issues within Each Broad Grouping	General Topics in Party Document Analysis found in Each Broad Grouping
Civil Order	Law and order, measures against crime, death penalty, rioting, strikes and demonstrations, anti-system parties and problems caused by their strength	Law and order, defense of the way of life
Constitutional	Questions involving established institutions (e.g., monarchy, presidency, parliament, and relations between them), democracy, civil rights	Constitutionalism, democracy
Foreign relationships	Membership in NATO and other foreign alliances, détente, attitude to communist powers, entry to EC, colonies and decolonization, overseas aid, attitudes to war and peace (Vietnam)	Foreign special relationships, colonies, decolonization, peace, internationalism, isolationism.
Defense	Military spending increases, reduction importance vis-á-vis other policy areas, nuclear arms	Defense, military
Candidate reactions	Likes and dislikes about candidates, leading candidates' performance	
Government record	Current financial situation and prospects, expectations, economic prosperity, depression; incidence of inflation and unemployment; government corruption, inefficiency; satisfaction with government in general and in any specified areas in ways not stipulated in other categories; is tax money spent wisely? desire for majority government, strong government	Government efficiency, government corruption, economic stability
Moral-religious	Support of traditional/Christian morals and church, abortion and birth control, temperance, anticlericalism—danger from clergy/church, religious schools and education	Support of morality, national effort
Ethnic	Immigration and foreign workers, attitudes to minority groups and their advancement, discrimina-	Underprivileged minority groups, culture

(continued)

TABLE 3—*Continued*

Broad Grouping	Specific Campaign Issues within Each Broad Grouping	General Topics in Party Document Analysis found in Each Broad Grouping
	tion, school and housing integration, language questions	
Regional	National unity	Regionalism; national
Urban-rural	Farmers and rural interests, agricultural subsidies	Agriculture
Socioeconomic redistribution	Social service spending, importance of social welfare, housing as a problem, housing subsidies, rent control, food subsidies, health and medical services, social reform, pensions, aid to other services such as education, action in regard to unemployment, employment guarantee	Social justice, social services, labor and other underprivileged demographic groups
Government control and planning	Nationalization, state control of the economy, general governmental power and control, management and regulation of environment	Controlled economy, economic planning, conservation
Government regulation in favor of the individual	Action against monopolies, big business power, trade union power, protectionism and free trade	Regulation, protectionism, and free trade
Initiative and freedom	Closed shop and action in relation to it, incentives, level of taxation, support for free enterprise economics	Freedom, enterprise, incentives, productivity, technology, economic orthodoxy

Source: Budge and Farlie 1983, 28–30.

often leads to an implicit tautology. It is difficult for specialists making this kind of judgment to confine themselves to pure issue stands (which they are often not very conscious of anyway). So quite naturally, one of the most important factors entering into estimates of closeness is parties' previous experience in government together. Distances at least partly based on this are then used to predict future coalitions. The specialists might just as well have been asked directly to say what parties would join in government, without going through elaborate intervening procedures.

The other disadvantage of such "judgmental" spaces, particularly relevant for the current discussion, is that specialists cannot be retrospectively asked to reconstruct party locations over a period of time, as judgments about one set of positions tend to contaminate others. If experts have themselves been asked to make estimates at different time points and these were recorded,

then of course this objection would not hold, though one would like to know that they had the same understanding of Left and Right at each point.

Much the same objections apply to the kinds of space commonly obtained by survey analysts in the early 1970s, based on electors' rank orderings of the parties in terms of closeness to them. First, these are not clearly issue-spaces, since who knows what may have influenced the judgments of closeness? And, second, since the nature of the dimensions is inferred from the positioning of parties on them rather than from independent evidence, any movement by the parties changes the inferred nature of the dimensions, rendering it impossible to trace party change within the same space (Budge and Farlie 1978).

In the 1970s, Farlie and Budge experimented with a "party-defined" space, derived either from issue responses or social characteristics of party supporters or both. This was based on Bayesian likelihood ratios and produced a space varying in dimensionality with the number of parties (one-dimensional with two parties, two-dimensional for three, etc.). The ends were "pure party positions" that actual parties could approach more-or-less closely but never attain. The space was used for relating party positions, as defined by British manifestos and U.S. platforms, to survey data on electors, with a view to checking Robertson's (1976) hypothesis on party competition (Budge and Farlie 1977, chap. 11). There are obvious problems in applying this representation to multiparty systems, however, as the space cannot be represented directly with more than three parties. The demonstration that the odds against the nearest Democratic and Republican platforms being mistaken for each other are 200 to 1 does lend some force to the idea that parties rarely leapfrog and keep close to their own segment of issue-space, in contradiction to Downsian ideas of unlimited free movement.

The natural technique to apply to any scoring or issue positions, whether survey or content analytic in nature, is factor analysis. Provided that the input relates to issues, this will give you a policy-space as assumed by most theoretical models. However, the resulting space will differ from the pure issue-space of free party movement, assumed by most theories, as it will be one in which parties do not and cannot venture into certain areas: it will be a policy-space with certain parts reserved to particular parties (Budge and Farlie 1977). This should be borne in mind with the factor-analytic spaces examined below.

Although the more-or-less straightforward factor-analytic spaces are the main ones I use to trace issue change, two other approaches have been used, particularly to examine coalition formation and relationships between party and coalition policy (Laver and Budge 1992, chap. 2).

A "forced" left-right dimension: having drastically reduced our original 54-category coding of party programs, by leaving out thinly populated categories, we combined those we thought intuitively belonged together as a

left-right dimension and checked this by factor analysis. Subsequently, we put the "left-right" variable in factor analyses with the remaining ones to see if any "fitted" with it across 12 countries. This was, in a sense, a "forced" dimension as we were using it to mop up all of the variation in the data set that we possibly could, being guided rather than determined by the factor analysis.

The dimension that we obtained opposed right-wing emphases on "capitalist economics," "social conservatism," "freedom and domestic human rights," and "support for military" to left emphases on "state intervention," "peace and cooperation," "democracy," "support for social services," "support for education," and "support for labor." Left-right positions of parties were computed by subtracting percentages of "leftist" references from percentages of "rightist" references.

No other general comparative dimension emerged from these data. This meant that the forced left-right dimension was, in some ways, our best summary representation of party positions (on a comparative basis). To catch the other tendencies present in the data there was no alternative to using our (reduced) 20-variable coding framework as a whole—in effect a 20-dimensional representation of the parties in issue-space. This lost the advantage of concise presentation but did allow us to form alternative estimates of distance between parties, which is all that is necessary, for some theories at any rate, to make predictions of coalition membership and policy. However, the best metric for these measurements turned out to be city block rather than Euclidian, a point that has considerable relevance for the formal modeling of issue-spaces.

Party Movement within (Leadership) Issue-Spaces
Obtained by Factor Analyses of Party Programs

If we were concerned only with changes of party position within issue-spaces that we could assume to be invariant for the whole postwar period, I would present estimates of this, based on party electoral programs, in terms of the last two spaces described, as these are the latest to be evolved from our continuing analysis of the programmatic data.

However, change within a given space is not the only type of change with which we should be concerned. There is also the question of whether the relevant dimensions of the space are stable or themselves change at some point. It is not unreasonable to think they do, given the political record of most countries in the 1960s and early 1970s: the growth of new social movements since then; and the impact of environmental considerations and détente in the 1980s. This can be illustrated through table 4, taken from an unpublished secondary analysis of the election programs by Hofferbert and

TABLE 4. Regression and Correlation Analysis of Postmaterialism Trends in Party Programs and Public Values, by Country

Country and Party	Time Trend	r-Values vs. Programs
Belgium		
Socialist	.29*	.28
Christian Social	.26*	.73*
Liberal	.34*	.61*
Denmark		
Communist	−.39*	−.70
Social Democrat	.15	−.53
Conservative	−.07	−.71*
Radical Liberal	.15	.51
Agrarian Liberal	.37*	−.54
France		
Communist	−.01	−.62*
Socialist	.27*	.56
Gaullist	.22*	.41
Germany		
Social Democrat	.31*	.08
Christian Democrat	.40*	−.46
Free Democrat	.60*	.47
Great Britain		
Labour	.26*	.42
Conservative	.19*	−.41
Liberal (all)	.32*	.47
Ireland		
Fine Gael	.40*	.85*
Fianna Fail	−.01	−.53
Labour	.32*	.92*
Italy		
Communist	−.34*	.48
Socialist	−.21*	−.44
Christian Democrat	−.32*	−.28
Luxembourg		
Communist	.49*	−.23
Socialist	.27	−.24
Christian Democrat	.49*	.24
Democrat	.41*	−.05
Netherlands		
Labor	.42*	−.31
Christian Union	.15*	−.32
Catholic People	.67*	−.31
Anti-Revolutionary	.72*	−.25
Liberal	−.04	−.15

Source: Hofferbert and Inglehart 1990.
*p = .10.

Inglehart (1990) that shows interesting correlations between postmaterialist issues and time. Use of the right-left dimension or of an original coding frame, both made invariant by definition, confines us to examining party changes of position within definitionally fixed parameters. So I shall base my discussion on the original two-stage factor analyses, based on 54 categories, into which were counted all sentences of all available electoral programs for all significant parties in 19 democracies for the postwar period. The categories (Budge, Robertson, and Hearl 1987, app. B) are based on the saliency ideas (described previously), rather than on coding directly opposing positions of parties. Saliency ideas in turn gain some validity from the plausible results produced by the factor analyses.

The major findings (Budge, Robertson, and Hearl 1987, chap. 18) were as follows.

1. The optimal spaces for each country were never less than three-dimensional, and sometimes four- or five-dimensional. Generally, the leading dimension, and less often the second, were generalizable across countries; the others were country specific.
2. In 14 out of 19 countries, the leading dimension that emerged was interpretable as a left-right one, broadly along the lines of the "forced" dimension described previously.
3. In 9 countries, of the 14 that generated a leading left-right dimension, a second dimension emerged that could be interpreted in broad terms as a "New Politics" dimension, where some concern with "new issues," particularly the environment and democracy, is contrasted with older emphases. Although we forced orthogonality on the dimensions, an inspection of the two-dimensional figures produced in these cases shows that collapsing the space to one dimension still gives a reasonable representation of the major parties' relative positions. This explains the success of our "forced" left-right dimension that, in some ways, combines these two sets of concerns. (A summary of these findings over all countries analyzed is given in table 5.)
4. Although the nature of the dimensions is important to the interpretation of what kind of change is taking place, it is change itself we are concerned with—in this case, the movement of the parties over various points in these dimensions. For predicting alliances or coalitions, what is needed of course are the exact scores at each point in time, which can hardly be presented here. A general interest is in the general convergence or divergence of parties over the postwar period, particularly in view of theses of the "end of ideology" (Bell 1962) or of the emergence of the totally pragmatic "catch-all" party (Kircheimer 1966). In part, of course, judgments of convergence and divergence rest on arbitrary decisions about which years to compare.

An inspection of individual graphs of party movement on the main dimension shows that, in most countries, there is no steady movement to convergence or divergence; parties come together and move apart presumably in response to imperatives of party competition, not to secular trends toward deideologization.

TABLE 5.   The Two Leading Dimensions from Factor Analyses over Twenty Postwar Democracies

Country	First Dimension	Second Dimension
United Kingdom	Left vs. Right	Liberalism vs. class conflict concerns
New Zealand	Left vs. Right	Internationalism and welfare vs. isolationism
Australia	Left vs. Right	Discipline and restraint vs. free pursuit of goals
United States	Left vs. Right (in a modified sense of conservatism vs. interventionist liberalism)	Interventionism vs. new interventionism
Canada	New Leftism	Old Leftism
Sri Lanka	Urban vs. Rural	Old Left vs. Right
Israel	Nationalism and technological progress	Modernization vs. democracy (associated with new issues)
Ireland	Authoritarianism vs. ability to govern	Capitalist economics and Irish unity
Northern Ireland	Pro– and anti–status quo	Socioeconomic concerns vs. sectionalism
Sweden	Left vs. center	Left vs. Right
Denmark	Old Left vs. Right	New Left vs. Right
Finland[a]	Socialist vs. capitalist organization of the economy	Contrast between group norms and individual values
Netherlands	Left vs. Right	New Left issues vs. social conservatism
Belgium	Left vs. Right (but left includes francophone orientations)	Progressive vs. clerical conservatism
Luxembourg	New issues vs. isolationism	Social justice and freedom
Austria	Socioeconomic Left vs. Right	New issues and interventionism vs. social conservatism
West Germany	Organization of (World) society	Degree of concern with the social market economy
France	Left vs. Right (economic, social, and foreign affairs)	Populism vs. bourgeois liberalism
Italy	Left vs. Right	Social harmony (subsume Catholicism)
Japan	Left vs. Right	New issues vs. concentration on economic growth

Source: Budge, Robertson, and Hearl 1987, 390–91.

[a]Based on Borg's study of Finnish election programs, 1945–66. This was a first-stage rather than a second-stage analysis, based on programs to the mid-1960s, and on a somewhat different categorizaton than ours, but seems generally compatible with our approach.

Taking party positions in the first postwar election and comparing it with the last for which we have data (the early 1980s), we get the results summarized in table 6. In the limited sense used here, most countries experienced convergence. The extreme case is Italy (see fig. 1)—curiously, as it is so often described in terms of "polarized pluralism" with irresistible "centrifugal" tendencies (Sartori 1972). In fact, in the latter period the tendency to convergence is so strong that it even produces some leapfrogging that (exceptionally) goes against some of the points made earlier. The results also illustrate the point that Communist parties are often close, in policy terms, to the other parties in the system, even though permanently excluded from government coalitions. There are two footnotes to these findings that must be stressed. One is that the factor analysis is of emphases on issues (as measured by percentages of sentences falling into the categories). Thus, convergence must be interpreted as putting less stress on traditional issues, not taking up the same positions on them. And, of course, these stresses are the party leaderships', addressed to electors certainly, but not emanating from them and therefore not necessarily reflecting their thinking. In the absence of more direct information, one might of course wish to use these documents as a surrogate indicator of electoral opinion, but it is only a surrogate.

TABLE 6. Convergence or Divergence of Parties in the Left-Right Dimension and Two Leading Dimensions of Second-Stage Factor Analysis

Country	Left-Right Dimension	Two Leading Dimensions
United Kingdom	D	Little change
New Zealand	D	Little change
Australia	C	C
United States	D	Little change
Canada	C	C
Sri Lanka	D	D
Israel	—	Little change
Ireland	—	C
Northern Ireland	—	Irrelevant (two parties ceased to exist)
Sweden	D	Little change
Denmark	D	D
Netherlands	C (in 1970s)	C (in 1970s)
Belgium	C	C (in 1970s)
Luxembourg	—	C (all parties but Communist)
Austria	C	C
West Germany	—	C
France	Limited C	Limited C (within but not across tendencies)
Italy	C	C
Japan	C	—

Source: Budge, Robertson, and Hearl 1987, 397.
Note: C = convergence; D = divergence.

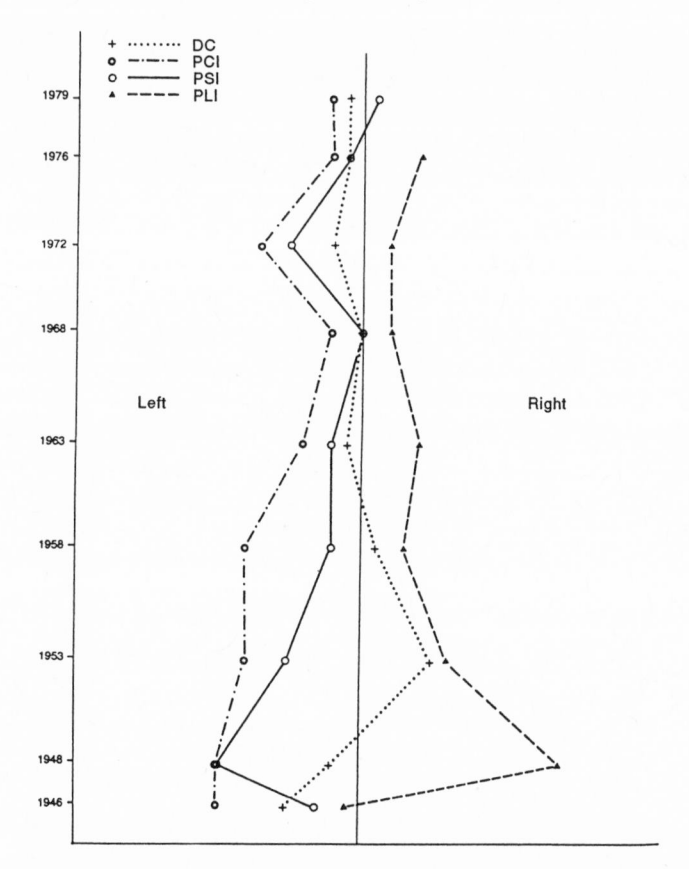

Fig. 1. Movement of Italian parties on the leading (Left-Right) dimension produced by an analysis of the party programs. (Fig. from Mastropaolo and Slater 1987, 364. Parties are indicated as follows: DC = Christian Democrat, PCI = Communist, PSI = Socialist, and PLI = Liberal.)

New Dimensions and Structural Change in the Space of Party Competition

The findings presented in the preceding section rest on the assumption of an invariant issue-space over the postwar period, within which party emphasis and deemphasis of the issues take place. What if the space itself changes over this period, in terms of its politically important dimensions, however, making different issues relevant to party relationships at different times? There are dramatic turning points in most countries' political history that at least point to this possibility: the Bad Godesberg conference and renunciation of Marxism

by the SPD in Germany (1959), the Schools Pact in Belgium of roughly the same date, and the dramatic influx of new parties to parliament in Norway and Denmark in 1972–73. In terms of my data, the prevalence of the New Politics dimension may be a covert indicator of change over time, as these issues become prevalent in the late 1960s and 1970s. Of course, we can show it as a dimension over the whole postwar period, but it might be more accurate to represent it as creating a different space.

To test this possibility, separate factor analyses were run of the documentary material before and after a break-point (identified for each country in terms of historical events). The results are summarized in table 7. Obviously, some caution needs to be exercised, since breaking the postwar into two periods attenuates the number of cases for factor analysis quite seriously: some simply cannot be done. However, a general impression is that the Left-

TABLE 7. Comparison of the Two Leading Dimensions in the Earlier and Later Postwar Periods in Selected Countries

Country	Earlier Period		Later Period	
	Dimension 1	Dimension 2	Dimension 1	Dimension 2
Canada	Old Left vs. Right	New Leftism	New vs. Old Left	New Left vs. Old Right
Netherlands	Secular vs. religious traditional values	Social interests vs. Government Efficiency	Secular Left vs. religious Right	Left vs. Social Christian values
Belgium	Political vs. social concerns	Secular vs. religious traditional values	Nationalism vs. economic infrastructure	Modernization vs. decentralization
Luxembourg	Secular vs. religious traditional values	Left vs. Right	Left vs. Right	International vs. national concerns
France	Left vs. Right	National populism vs. sectional interests	National vs. international values	European vs. French nationalism
Italy	Secular Left vs. traditional right	Religious vs. sectional values	—	—
Sweden	Left vs. Right	New Leftism	New Right vs. New Left	Old Left vs. New Left
Denmark	Left vs. Right	New Leftism	Old Left vs. New Right	Old Left vs. Old Right
Austria	Defense of nation vs. sectional interests	Right vs. Left	Defense of postwar settlement vs. nationalism	Left vs. Right
Germany	Degree of concern with social market economy	Organization of society	Social market economy vs. New Politics	Interest groups vs. New Politics

Right dimension is the leading one in most countries both in the earlier and later periods. It emerges explicitly in the earlier postwar period in seven out of ten countries shown in the table. One also has the impression from examining the analysis in detail that it would take very little to "tip" dimensions given other interpretations (for example, the secular vs. religious clash in Belgium and the Netherlands) into a Left-Right confrontation, which is presumably what happened in these countries anyway.

With the later period, we find that the dimension emerges in some form in six out of nine countries (very unstable solutions emerged for Italy, which caused the second period to be excluded from the table). No other general dimension emerges to challenge it in the table. It is certainly clear that there is no "end of ideology" in the later period. On the contrary, the entry of the New Politics, whether of the New Left or Green variety, make for a reassertion of ideological conflict rather than a diminution of it.

The basic finding from the methodological point of view is that we are justified in condensing these data into a single left-right dimension. This emerges spontaneously as the leading, and only generalizable one, from the nearest we can get, statistically, to a purely inductive approach, whether for the whole postwar period or for its earlier and later periods. Breaking the whole period into two substantially increases the possibility of idiosyncratic and time-bound dimensions emerging, as they can predominate over a shorter period whereas, over the long term, they are likely to give way to the more enduring and stable organization of conflict underlying them. This is not, of course, to say that using one or the other time period is wrong. Each is a summary that leaves out certain aspects of these quite complex data. I have already noted that the Belgian dimensions could easily tip over into a left-right form: this is what, indeed, happened when the whole postwar period was analyzed.

The Old Left and New Politics dimensions are reasonably related to each other. The old left-right distinction opposes peace and disarmament, social welfare and government economic intervention to economic freedom and orthodoxy, traditional values and support for military alliances. The New Left puts less emphasis on welfare and more on participation, democracy, and rights of noneconomic groups. The Greens add to this their concern with environmental issues. None of these are incompatible with Old Left positions, and, indeed, might positively call for more government intervention and welfare support. So we can envisage a consolidation of left-right opposition in the future rather than its replacement, and, indeed, this seems to have happened in the 1980s after most of my data were collected.

An interesting additional point that emerges from table 7 is that the New Politics of environmental concern, protection of minorities, and greater participation was already making its way in the first part of the postwar period.

These concerns were often carried by the New Left parties, particularly in Scandinavia. Issue change was certainly not absent in the earlier postwar period as compared to the second. We can examine this at a more specific level in the next section.

Specific Issue Change over the Postwar Period

Changes in Programmatic Issues

Whether or not one thinks of issue change primarily in terms of parties changing position within the same space or of the dimensions of the relevant space themselves changing and, in that sense, imposing a qualitative change in relationships, it is relevant to ask, at a more detailed level, what specific issues are changing and how. This is also of concern to some of the nonspatial approaches summarized previously. Table 8 summarizes overall results in terms of change in specific issues, from the same comparison of countries before and after a crucial turning point in their postwar history.

The table not only gives an overall judgment on whether change in specific issues had taken place (in 6 out of 11 it had, up to the beginning of the 1980s), it also identifies most of the issues that are rising or declining in prominence or remaining stable. This gives us an opportunity to see if some issues share the same fate across developed democracies and, thus, to get some clues about the factors that make for their entry onto the political agenda. (*Agenda*, however, may be a misleading term for issues, as one gets the impression, both from party tryouts in their programs and from the way in which issues bob up and down in elections, that they are never fixed enough to be on a definite agenda: it is rather a process of constant change, and party competition to push others' issues out and yours in.)

It is difficult to generalize very much on the basis of the data in table 8. The same broad topics clearly appear among leading issues in all countries, for example, social issues, economic orthodoxy, and so forth. However, they do not show the same pattern of rise and decline. In the Netherlands and Britain, the attention paid to social services (up to the early 1980s) was stable; in Belgium it was declining, as also in Sweden (but from a very high base there). Economic orthodoxy and free enterprise, which in retrospect one might have expected to be consistently rising, were instead declining in Denmark, Belgium, and the Netherlands, but certainly rising in Australia and Denmark.

The few general tendencies that emerge are the following.

> *a)* Questions connected with traditional morality (which in party programs is more the virtues of the family and Christian values rather

than the minefields of abortion and divorce) are in general decline. This may reflect deconfessionalization, particularly in the Netherlands.

b) Attention to agriculture is generally declining, reflecting the migration from country into town that has taken place in practically all of these countries.

c) Attention to the military seems to be declining to the early 1980s (apart from the United States), running in parallel with the reduction of international tensions. The difference between the United States, where the attention the topic gets is stable, and other countries is interesting because of course the United States *was* more heavily involved in military ventures during the later period than its allies.

d) Along with the military and defense, there seems a general decline in attention to international affairs in the later period, again perhaps reflecting the more reassuring atmosphere as détente proceeded.

Issues to which more attention was paid in the later period are the following.

a) Technology: rising in the United States, United Kingdom, and Italy and stable elsewhere.

b) A cluster of New Politics issues—democracy, decentralization, social justice, and environment—not always the same in every country but recognizably related. The most consistent issue to enter is the environment, although only in Sweden does it jump to almost the most prominent role. Mostly the entry of new issues is signaled by modest increases in attention to a topic, which brings it to the bottom of the leading ten.

There is a hint from the evidence on party programs that issue change is a function of economic, social, and external political changes, particularly in international affairs. This would be a reassuring conclusion as it would demonstrate that parties do function as transmitters and debaters of real problems, which governments may then be stimulated to take action on. It would be nice if it were so, since it would buttress our faith in the ability of democracy to cope with contemporary problems. There is, however, one piece of counterevidence from the programs that we ought to consider and two general points to make on the way in which the real world gets reflected in issues.

The counterevidence is the general absence of references to the European Community in most of the countries directly affected by it. Only in Italy and Belgium does it appear as a rising issue. Perhaps, however, this is because it

TABLE 8. Change and Stability in Leading Issues between the Earlier and Later Postwar Periods

Country	Great Change	Issues that Change		Issues that Stay the Same
		Decline	Rise	
Australia	Yes	Military Social services	Economic orthodoxy Government effectiveness Specific economic goals	Labor groups Agriculture Social harmony Free enterprise Technology Incentives Education
Canada	No	Social services Agriculture Decentralization Military	Technology Specific economic goals	Noneconomic groups Social Justice
United States	No	Military Decolonization	Technology Law and order Education	Noneconomic goals Internationalism Agriculture Labor Economic orthodoxy Environment Foreign relations Social services
United Kingdom	No	Internationalism Peace Agriculture	Social justice Decentralization Government efficiency Law and order Environment	Social services Specific economic goals Education Economic orthodoxy Planning

Netherlands	Some	Traditional morality Free enterprise Communalism Agriculture	Education Democracy Noneconomic groups Technology Economic orthodoxy Freedom	Social services Social justice Noneconomic groups Technology Economic orthodoxy Freedom Labor
Belgium	Yes	Communalism Social justice Social services Free enterprise Traditional morality Agriculture Economic orthodoxy	Noneconomic groups Decentralization Specific economic goals Arts, leisure Environment European Community	Nonlabour groups Economic groups
Luxembourg	Yes	Traditional morality Agriculture Labor groups Social justice	Education Arts, leisure Technology Environment	Nonlabor groups Economic groups Democracy Freedom
France (Fifth Republic)	—[a]	National way of life Social justice Freedom Education Constitution Labor peace	Minorities	Controlled economy Democracy Regulation of capitalism
Italy	Yes	Democracy Labor groups Peace Agriculture Government effectiveness Productivity	Specific economic goals European Community Government efficiency Technology	Freedom Social services Economic planning

(continued)

TABLE 8—*Continued*

Country	Great Change	Issues that Change		Issues that Stay the Same
		Decline	Rise	
Sweden	Yes	Social services	Social justice	Economic orthodoxy
		Agriculture	Democracy	Education
		Free enterprise	Environment	Freedom
		Incentives	Decentralization	
Denmark	Yes	Noneconomic groups	Social justice	Traditional morality
		Antimilitary	Economic orthodoxy	Social services
		Education	Specific economic goals	Free enterprise
		Regulation of capitalism		
		Foreign special relations		
		Peace		
Austria	Yes	Freedom	Economic orthodoxy	Democracy
		Incentives	Technology	Social justice
		Constitution	Noneconomic groups	Free enterprise
		National effort	Social services	Agriculture
		Foreign relations	Education	Quality of life
		National way of life	Environment	

is not controversial in many places—though this would not be true for Britain and Denmark in the 1970s.

The reflection I want to add on the genesis of issues is how far the environment is really an objective problem creating immediate difficulties for people, and how far it is an issue created by some scientists and the media. Objectively, in the countries considered, most people probably suffer less, directly, from pollution than in the smoke- and smog-shrouded cities of 50 years ago. Yet it is clearly a rising issue. Declining international tension is also not experienced directly, though it is true that, in the earlier postwar period, wars were actually being fought. And environmental change also seems to be a real process happening "out there," as well as a subject of concern for scientists and media. Do the media, most of the time, reflect the real world?

Another general aspect of issue generation at the international level is the effect of imitation and transmission. Although they may be insulated to some extent, no national politics takes place entirely in a vacuum. In particular, what is said and debated in the United States has an enormous impact elsewhere—probably it is an asymmetric relationship. Thus it may be that the environment issue *was* touched off by objective conditions in the United States, where the big cities probably *are* more polluted than 50 years ago, and then spread as an issue to Western Europe even though the cities are cleaner than they were. Whatever the plausibility of this particular speculation, there is no doubt that imitation and transmission effects need to be reckoned with.

Changes in Newspaper Accounts of Campaign Issues

Further evidence on the processes behind issue change comes from study of campaign issues mentioned by newspapers in 23 countries during the postwar period up to 1980 (Budge and Farlie 1983, 35–41). Codings here were made on a different (though broadly compatible) categorization to those of electoral programs (also based on saliency ideas) into 14 broad categories, including candidate reactions (see table 3). They are not directly comparable with the programmatic issues discussed earlier, but they do give an alternative estimate of postwar trends to compare with them.

Table 9 first of all gives an overall summary of the issues that emerged in elections over the whole postwar period within each country. From this we can see (always constrained by the type of classification made) that the most widespread type of issue that enters into the great majority of elections in all countries, in newspaper terms, is government records. This is hardly surprising, since elections are designed to choose a government and the most immediate ground for choice is how well the contestants have performed in the past or seem likely to perform in the future. The record has always been assessed

TABLE 9. Issue Salience over All Postwar Elections in Twenty-Three Democracies

Country	Number of Elections	Civil Order	Constitutional	Foreign Relationships	Defense	Candidate Reactions	Government Record and Prospects	Moral-Religious	Ethnic	Regional	Urban-Rural	Socioeconomic Redistribution	Government Control and Planning	Government Regulation in Favor of Individual	Initiative and Freedom
Australia	13	4	2	3	2	11	13	1	0	2	2	11	2	2	4
Austria	9	2	1	1	1	5	7	1	6	0	1	11	2	0	3
Belgium	10	1	6	1	2	3	6	6	6	3	0	3	0	0	2
Canada	13	3	3	5	3	10	13	1	0	6	0	1	2	0	2
Denmark	13	0	2	2	3	3	13	0	0	0	0	7	2	0	6
Finland	11	1	1	8	0	3	11	0	0	0	1	0	0	3	0
France	7	3	4	3	0	5	6	0	0	1	4	5	2	3	2
Iceland	12	0	2	6	0	3	10	0	0	0	0	1	4	0	0
India	7	2	1	3	1	7	7	0	1	0	0	4	1	1	0
Ireland	10	1	1	3	0	9	9	0	0	3	0	3	0	0	3
Israel	10	2	4	6	3	9	10	0	3	0	0	2	3	2	1
Italy	8	3	1	4	0	3	6	4	0	0	5	5	0	0	0
Japan	9	2	2	6	3	4	9	0	0	1	0	1	1	0	0
Luxembourg	6	0	1	0	1	1	6	3	0	0	2	2	0	0	1
Netherlands	11	2	0	3	1	2	11	2	0	0	2	5	5	3	4
New Zealand	10	2	0	4	0	6	8	0	1	0	0	2	1	1	3
Norway	8	0	0	6	0	1	8	0	0	1	2	2	3	0	2
Sri Lanka	5	1	2	1	0	5	4	2	1	1	0	1	0	0	2
Sweden	11	0	0	2	0	4	8	0	0	0	0	5	4	1	5
Switzerland	8	0	0	0	0	1	3	0	0	0	0	0	0	0	0
U.K.	10	1	1	6	3	10	10	0	0	2	0	7	7	4	3
U.S.	9	2	0	7	1	6	9	1	1	1	0	5	0	1	3
W. Germany	7	3	1	5	1	7	6	0	0	0	0	2	1	0	0
Total	217	33	35	85	25	118	193	16	16	20	12	81	40	20	45

Source: Budge and Farlie 1983, 35.

Note: Entries in table cells are the number of elections in which an issue was salient, based on newspaper accounts.

primarily in economic terms, but there is an increasing concentration on this in the later postwar period.

In most countries, government record is as predominating a concern as it is overall. In Belgium, however, it enters into only six out of ten elections—buried very often by the disruptive linguistic divisions of the 1970s. Switzerland is the other country where government record is not prominent, but this is a reflection of the absence of national issues in many Swiss elections rather than a downgrading of government record in relation to other types of issues.

The personal characteristics of candidates (usually for the chief executive office) enter into slightly more than half the elections. Again it is not surprising that the qualities of potential leaders should form such a widespread basis of assessment. Being less widespread than government record, however, there is more room for variation between countries. The United Kingdom, West Germany, India, and Sri Lanka have candidates entering as a major consideration into all elections, followed by Australia (11 out of 13), Canada (10 out of 13), Ireland and Israel (9 out of 10), and the United States (6 out of 9). On the whole, it seems that countries with a broadly Anglo-Saxon parliamentary tradition and tendencies to a two-party system tend to focus attention on candidates (however, West Germany does not follow the Anglo-Saxon tradition and Israel has not, until very recently, had anything like two-party competition). Democracies with the least stress on candidates are Denmark, Finland, Iceland, Italy, Japan, Norway, Switzerland, and the Low Countries. There are, on the whole, the smaller North European countries, with the significant exceptions of Italy and Japan. Perhaps the factionalism of the dominant party in the last two countries prevents national leaders appearing as more than nominees of special interests. The institutionalization of the parties and traditions of collective leadership in the smaller North European democracies may inhibit assessment through individual personalities.

Foreign relations appears as an important issue in rather less than half the elections. It is particularly important in the United States—naturally, in a country at the center of a world system of alliances that has been engaged in two major conflicts within the last 30 years. The United Kingdom (6 out of 10) and France (3 out of 7) have been in a similar situation. Foreign relations are also important to smaller countries next to a powerful, threatening neighbor, such as Finland vis-à-vis the USSR (8 out of 11 elections), West Germany 5 out of 7), Japan (6 out of 9), India (3 out of 7), and Norway (6 out of 8). Iceland (6 out of 12) and Canada (5 out of 13) have been particularly concerned over relations with the United States.

The last leading issue type, again cropping up in nearly half the elections, is socioeconomic redistribution, at the core of which stand welfare policies. In Australia, these were debated in 11 out of 13 elections, attaining almost similar prominence in the United Kingdom (7 out of 10). They were raised also in more than half the elections held in Italy, India, and, rather

surprisingly, the United States. Elsewhere they appeared in a significant number of elections, except in Canada (1 out of 13), France (2 out of 7), Sri Lanka (1 out of 5), and Switzerland (no elections at all). Possession either of a Socialist party or strong two-party competition appears to contribute to the raising of this issue, although the exceptions indicate that the relationship is not strong.

All remaining issue types appear in the range between 14 and 45 elections (i.e., between about 8 percent and 20 percent of the total). In all cases, low general representation stems from their uneven distribution within different countries. All are raised frequently in one or two countries, but do not appear at all elsewhere. Thus, civil order has been a recurring concern in France and West Germany (three out of seven elections) and peculiarly—because of fears about communist subversion—in almost a third of Australian elections. Constitutional changes have been debated a great deal in Belgium (six out of ten elections), primarily because of the need to conciliate Flemish speakers by bestowing greater autonomy. Defense has been of particular concern in Canada, where it unleashes tensions between Francophones and Anglophones, and toward the United States; in Denmark and the United Kingdom, debate has revolved around the overall level of defense expenditures within a precarious economy. Religion has entered into politics in Italy, the Netherlands, and Luxembourg, through the Christian parties there and in Sri Lanka through the fears of the Buddhist priesthood about its position. Ethnic rivalry has dominated Belgian politics over the last ten years, and has emerged in Britain and Israel through problems of assimilation posed by recent immigration. Regional issues are related to ethnic tension in Belgium, while in Canada the position of French speakers is symbolized by the power of Quebec. Farming problems are important to Finland, not only because of the relatively greater proportion of the rural population, but because of the pivotal position of the Agrarian party. Nationalization and associated powers of government control have been particularly controversial in the United Kingdom, but also in Sweden, Norway, and the Netherlands, while its converse—an emphasis on individual freedom and initiative—was prominent in Denmark even before the dramatic emergence of Glistrop's antitax party in 1973. Government regulation has emerged in about a quarter of the elections in Finland, the United Kingdom, and the Netherlands, mainly in relation to strikes. Since these are an endemic problem in modern economies, we may expect this type of issue to become increasingly prominent in the future. Even generally underrepresented issue types thus emerge as important for the analysis of elections in at least one country.

Issue types vary not only across countries but also over time—some recurring more frequently in later elections, some declining in saliency. Table 10 traces the incidence of salient issues in each election period of the postwar years. Such periods have been selected simply to group contiguous elections,

TABLE 10. Trends in Issue Salience over Twenty-Three Democracies for Each Postwar Period

Period	Number of Elections	Civil Order	Constitutional	Foreign Relationships	Defense	Candidate Reactions	Government Record and Prospects	Moral-Religious	Ethnic	Regional	Urban-Rural	Socioeconomic Redistribution	Government Control and Planning	Government Regulation in Favor of Individual	Initiative and Freedom	Total
1945–49	14	2	1	9	1	5	13	1	0	2	1	5	6	2	2	50
1950–54	28	4	3	7	2	11	21	1	0	0	2	14	5	2	7	79
1955–59	31	3	5	12	4	16	28	4	1	1	3	10	6	1	5	99
1960–64	31	2	6	12	5	11	27	2	3	1	2	12	1	1	5	90
1965–69	34	8	6	16	4	18	30	2	3	6	0	13	3	2	6	117
1970–74	34	5	6	19	4	23	33	2	4	6	4	15	6	4	5	136
1975–79	36	7	7	9	2	24	33	4	4	6	0	10	9	8	11	131
1980–81	9	2	1	1	3	10	8	0	1	1	0	2	4	0	4	37
Total	217	33	35	85	25	118	193	16	16	20	12	81	40	20	45	739

Source: Budge and Farlie 1983, 36.
Note: Entries in table cells are the number of elections in which an issue was salient, based on newspaper accounts.

without any deeper theoretical justification. They do seem to be short enough to capture significant changes.

Government record is such a ubiquitous type of issue that no particular trend can be traced; if anything, it appears to have become an even more widely used basis of assessment in recent years than formerly. The same can be said more strongly of candidates—from a third of elections in the late 1940s to three-quarters since the mid-1970s. Foreign relations appear more sensitive, as one might expect, to the state of international affairs—relatively more prominent in the late 1940s with the cold war, then, in the late 1950s and early 1960s, with détente, then from 1965 to 1974 with Vietnam and its aftermath. Socioeconomic redistribution appears in a quarter to a half of the elections in each time period, attaining most prominence in the early 1950s, during the first wave of postwar prosperity and least prominence more recently.

Of the less generally recurring issues, civil order comes to much greater prominence in the politically disturbed periods after 1965, during the more active student demonstrations and terrorism. Constitutional issues come to prominence earlier, from 1955. Defense shows a rising trend to the early 1960s and a slow decline thereafter. Religious-moral questions remain at a low level throughout, with a slight peak in the late 1950s. Reflecting the growth of separatism and autonomist movements in Europe, and the increasing number of foreign workers in all countries, ethnic issues show a distinct rise over the postwar period. Regionalism reached a sudden peak in 1965–74, but an indication of decline is seen in the 33 elections out of 36 in which it failed to appear in 1975–79. Urban-rural questions, on the other hand, show no distinct tendencies, though they reached their highest prominence in 1970–74.

The three nonredistributive class issues all show a tendency to grow in prominence over the postwar years. The extent of government control (involving such questions as nationalization), much debated during postwar reconstruction, slipped almost out of sight in 1960–64, then returned to prominence in the 1970s with the breakdown of Keynesian approaches to economic management and the advent of neocapitalist modes of thought. A broadly similar pattern, though different in detail, can be seen for the antonym of government control—individual initiative and freedom. Regulation, increasingly discussed in relation to industrial unrest and strikes, again rises sharply to prominence in the 1970s.

Most of these tendencies are understandable in terms of a postwar history that, in most countries, involved initial reconstruction, followed by a relaxed enjoyment of restored prosperity from about 1955 to 1965, succeeded in turn by the increasing problems of a complex economy and intergroup tensions connected with this (foreign affairs proceeding, meanwhile, from a consolida-

tion of cold war alliances, through détente, to a concern with U.S. involvement in Vietnam, and further dissolution of previous alliances). That the appearance and disappearance of election issues can be related to general tendencies outside the control of politicians in any one country carries implications for analyses of campaign strategies. For if politicians have only a limited ability to emphasize or deemphasize issues that become independently salient in elections, one can attribute only a partial influence over victory or defeat to their actions. Rather than seeing their strategy as determining the outcome, we must ask, instead, whether they made the most of their appeal under given circumstances that they could not wholly (or perhaps even substantially) affect.

The inference that salient election issues relate broadly to significant events in the outside world and are not sham debating topics designed to divert attention from real problems is consistent with the evidence and is a cheering conclusion for the democrat, if somewhat daunting for ambitious politicians.

Future Research

It must be said that all the evidence reviewed here is inferential and highly circumstantial. We look at changing patterns of issues (or, more exactly, of various categorizations of issues) and interpret them in terms of changing conditions in the world around them. That is quite suggestive but can only be a first cut at the problem of issue generation. Further efforts need to be made in regard to the systematic collection of indicators of political and socioeconomic change (both national and international) in order to relate them through regressions to changes in programmatic content. This should answer more conclusively some of the questions raised by the analysis reported here.

The Consequences of Political Issues

Strictly speaking, the question of what effects issues produce is beyond the limits of this discussion, whose major focus is on the way in which one type of issue succeeds another. To leave it at that, however, is to leave many questions hanging. We should not, after all, consider issue change important if we did not think it carried further consequences for election outcomes, party strategies, and government activity. Each of these is considered briefly, in turn.

Election Outcomes

There was a great debate in the field of U.S. voting studies about the extent of issue voting compared to voting on the basis of party identification, in the

early 1970s (reviewed in Margolis 1977). This partly derived from the fact that explanations of voting have to cope with two phenomena: (1) the large number of voters who vote the same way from election to election, and (2) the smaller, but possibly increasing, number who vote differently.

In many studies, the first phenomenon is associated with voting on the basis of a basic identification with the party uncontaminated with issues, and the second phenomenon is associated with voting under the influence of issues (cf., among many others, Pomper et al. 1972). Obviously, however, one could associate both effects with issue voting. From both spatial and non-spatial perspectives, if a party makes only marginal adjustments to policy and voters do not substantially change their opinions, most of its previous supporters will end up voting for it in the next election. Explaining all voting in terms of reactions to issues is neater and more internally consistent than using one type of factor to account for stability and quite another to account for change. All rational choice accounts make issue-based assumptions.

Budge and Farlie (1983) made an attempt to develop a thoroughgoing issue-based account of voting that (unusually) generated advance predictions of ten national elections and performed reasonably well. Current predictive economic models of elections (Tufte 1975 and 1978; Sanders, Ward and Marsh 1987 and 1991) are also, of course, issue based, though emphasizing effects of only one type of issue (economic). Thus, there seem strong grounds for assuming that issues have a determining, if not exclusive, influence over election outcomes, and that election change is the effect of issue change.

Party Strategies

If this is the case, then what parties do about issues strongly affects their electoral fortunes and participation in government. The whole tradition of modeling and spatial analysis, which relies exclusively on issue-spaces and issue effects, seems to be on the right lines. I have suggested one direction that such analyses could take, in terms of saliency theory. As government record is itself a major issue, what governments do in office will affect their electoral fortunes, and vice versa.

Government Formation

Most models of coalition bargaining have moved ever closer to using pure policy factors rather than office-seeking ones to explain government formation. Recent research using election programs to measure party policy positions and government programs to represent government policy have given only limited support to the idea that policy proximity or strategic positioning in issue-space provide a basis for coalitions. Of ten different policy-based

models tested (two indirectly median-legislator ones), the most successful attained only a 50 percent success rate and 50 percent efficiency rate over postwar governments in 12 countries. Moreover, party programs related only inconsistently to government programs—only in 4 out of 8 countries were there correlations of any magnitude between the two (Laver and Budge 1992, chap. 14).

Government Outputs

These negative results could be explained, however, by government programs not being good indicators of policies actually pursued by government. Much stronger relationships are discovered between parties' programmatic stands and actual government outputs, as measured by percentage expenditures (Budge and Hofferbert 1990; Hofferbert and Klingemann 1990). Parties in coalitions may well affect outputs through their tenure of specific ministries for which they have a strong preference linked to their particular policy concerns (Budge and Keman 1990, chap. 4). Specific ministries may thus be an intermediate goal for parties as a means to affect policy outputs (Budge and Keman 1990, chap. 5). This undermines established perceptions of ministries as interchangeable coinage (Browne and Franklin 1972) in favor of certain ministries having a particular value for a party (Budge and Herman 1978).

Besides saving the idea of a reasonably pure policy-space as the venue within which coalition parties operate, the more general findings on the linkage between emphases in election programs and the expenditures made by governments support mandate theories of democracy (cf. Downs 1957) in which electors choose between parties on the basis of their alternative programs for government, and parties carry through the programs in office, thus effecting majority or at least plurality preferences.

Conclusions

We have, therefore, the promise from this line of research of a totally issue-based, empirically grounded theory of the functioning of party democracy, from party strategies through election outcomes to government functioning. Not only does this provide us with the prospect of a more exact and testable account of the processes involved, it is also in line with philosophical and popular justifications of the greater choice offered by democracy as a political system. It helps to emphasize the importance of studying the emergence of issues along the lines undertaken here, as they constitute the agenda for government action on societal problems at a particular juncture.

All this underlines the basic importance of better definitions and measures of political issues themselves, of their effects, and of the influences that

shape them and change them. It is this last aspect of issues that is currently the least studied and yet potentially the key to the ability of democratic political processes to respond to their environment and keep themselves and their populations going. It is this that makes studies of issues and agenda setting particularly valuable at the present time, when vast new populations are turning to democratic methods of tackling and resolving the major problems that threaten to overwhelm them.

REFERENCES

Bell, Daniel. 1962. *The End of Ideology.* New York: Random House.
Browne, E., and M. Franklin. 1972. "Coalition Payoffs in European Parliamentary Democracies." *American Political Science Review* 67:453–64.
Budge, Ian, and D. J. Farlie. 1977. *Voting and Party Competition.* London: Wiley.
Budge, Ian, and D. J. Farlie. 1978. "The Potentiality of Dimensional Analyses." *European Journal of Political Research* 6:203–31.
Budge, Ian, and D. J. Farlie. 1983. *Explaining and Predicting Elections: Issue-Effects and Party Strategies in Twenty-Three Democracies.* London: Allen and Unwin.
Budge, Ian, and V. Herman. 1978. "Coalitions and Government Formation." *British Journal of Political Science* 8:459–77.
Budge, Ian, and R. I. Hofferbert. 1990. "Mandates and Policy Outputs: U.S. Party Platforms and Federal Expenditures." *American Political Science Review* 84:111–31.
Budge, Ian, and Hans Keman. 1990. *Parties and Democracy: Coalition Formation and Government Functioning in Twenty Countries, 1950–1988.* Oxford: Oxford University Press.
Budge, Ian, D. Robertson, and D. J. Hearl, eds. 1987. *Ideology, Strategy and Party Change: Spatial Analyses of Postwar Election Programmes in Nineteen Democracies.* Cambridge: Cambridge University Press.
Butler, D. E., and Anthony King. 1965. *The British General Election of 1964.* London: Macmillan.
Downs, Anthony. 1957. *An Economic Theory of Democracy.* New York: Harper.
Hofferbert, R. I., and R. Inglehart. 1990. "Post-Materialist Values and Party Programs in Democratic Europe." Paper presented at the annual meeting of the Midwest Political Science Association, Chicago.
Hofferbert, R. I., and H.-D. Klingemann. 1990. "The Policy Impact of Party Programmes and Government Declarations in the Federal Republic of Germany." *European Journal of Political Research* 18:277–304.
Kelley, S., and T. Mirer. 1974. "The Simple Act of Voting." *American Political Science Review* 68:572–91.
Kircheimer, Otto. 1966. "The Transformation of the Western European Party Systems." In *Political Parties and Political Development,* ed. J. Lapalombara and M. Weiner, 177–200. Princeton: Princeton University Press.

Laver, M. J., and Ian Budge, eds. 1992. *Party Policy and Government Coalitions in Ten Democracies.* London: Macmillan.

Lipset, S. M., and Stein Rokkan. 1967. *Party Systems and Voter Alignments.* New York: Free Press.

Margolis, M. 1977. "From Confusion to Confusion: Issues and the American Voter, 1956–72." *American Political Science Review* 67:342–56.

Mastropaolo, Alfio, and Martin Slater. 1987. Italy: "Ideological Change and Party Movement." In *Ideology, Strategy and Party Change: Spatial Analyses of Postwar Election Programmes in Nineteen Democracies,* ed. Ian Budge, D. Robertson, and D. J. Hearl, 345–68. Cambridge: Cambridge University Press.

Pomper, G. M., R. A. Brody, B. I. Page, and R. W. Boyd. 1972. "Issues and American Voters 1956–68." *American Political Science Review* 66:450–69.

Rallings, Colin. 1987. "The Influence of Election Programmes: Britain and Canada 1945–79." In *Ideology, Strategy and Party Change: Spatial Analyses of Postwar Election Programmes in Nineteen Democracies,* ed. Ian Budge, D. Robertson, and D. J. Hearl, 1–14. Cambridge: Cambridge University Press.

Robertson, David. 1976. *A Theory of Party Competition.* London: Wiley.

Sanders, D., H. Ward, and D. Marsh. 1987. "Government Popularity and the Falklands Effect." *British Journal of Political Science* 17:135–61.

Sanders, D., H. Ward, and D. Marsh. 1991. "Government Popularity and the Next General Election." *Political Quarterly* 62:236–60.

Sartori, G. 1972. "European Political Parties: The Case of Polarized Pluralism." In *Political Parties and Political Development,* ed. J. Lapalombara and M. Weiner, 137–76. Princeton: Princeton University Press.

Tufte, E. R. 1975. "Determinants of the Outcomes of Mid-Term Congressional Elections." *American Political Science Review* 69:812–29.

Tufte, E. R. 1978. *Political Control of the Economy.* Princeton: Princeton University Press.

White, T. H. 1961. *The Making of the President.* New York: Atheneum.

Rhetorical Interaction in the Ratification Campaigns

William H. Riker

While detail on the debates on ratification of the Constitution in 1787–88 may seem remote from the subject of agenda formation in contemporary democratic politics, there are advantages to studying this now almost forgotten campaign. One preliminary advantage is that it is indeed forgotten, so we can look at it without partisan bias. But the main advantage is that only a modest amount of the most important material survives. We have neither tapes nor videos, no replays of programs, and no newspaper accounts of canvassing. Instead, we have only editorials and squibs from 100 or so newspapers (mostly weeklies) and a few magazines and pamphlets. Furthermore, Kaminski and Saladino (1981) have compiled a sample of the most popular of these materials, namely the squibs and editorials republished in more than one state. Thus, the editors of 1787–88 really selected the sample, not Kaminski and Saladino, and not I, so the sample represents a kind of market success for the ideas and rhetoric of that campaign. We have nothing comparable for any contemporary campaign, though I suppose that dedicated scholars could, at enormous expense, compile a similar sample for some campaign today. Fortunately, however, for the campaign of 1787–88, we do have a reasonably representative sample, which is the basis for this work on rhetorical interaction.

From the point of view of agenda formation, the most important part of this essay is the theory that leads to the two principles for the choice of rhetorical effort. One is the Dominance Principle: when one side successfully wins the argument on an issue, the other side ceases to discuss it, while the

---

The National Science Foundation supported this work under Grant SES-8410092. I am greatly indebted to my assistants, Patrick Fett, Evelyn Fink, John Huber, William Kubik, Thomas O'Donnell, and Margaret Raymond. I am also greatly indebted to seminar participants in seminars at the Universities of Iowa, North Carolina, and Rochester, especially David Austen-Smith, John Conybeare, Calvin Jillson, George Rabinowitz, David Weimer, Thomas Schwartz, and Kenneth Shepsle.

winner continues to exploit it. The second principle is the Dispersion Principle: when both sides fail to win the argument on an issue, both sides cease to discuss it and search for some other, more profitable issue. These Principles together guarantee that most of the time opponents do not talk about the same things. This means that, typically, they are not located on the same dimensions of argument of the outcome space. Of course, when they are locked in a tie on an issue they will subsequently both abandon, they are necessarily on the same dimension. But by the very fact of the dispersion principle, they do not stay there.

Given this feature of rhetorical interaction, it follows that agenda formation consists of each side carving out issues on which it is dominant. Since issues on which neither side dominates are abandoned, the equilibrium of argument must be the set of issues that one side or the other exclusively pursues. From this it follows that the winner is likely to be the side that dominates on those issues with more appeal to voters than the issues dominated by the other side.

Of course the great question for politicians is: What are those more appealing issues? This is what they are always trying to discover in their restless search for new issues as they disperse from old ones. But that is a subject I leave for a later study. Now I seek merely to understand the process of dispersion to the equilibrium of dominant issues.

In a previous paper (Riker 1991), I analyzed the content of the rhetoric of the two campaigns separately, as if two sets of rhetors were, independently, addressing separate classes of voters. Unfortunately, this form of presentation suggests a scenario of simple proselytizing, wherein sly, sophisticated rhetors convert shy, naive voters. This is a deceptive model, however, because the two campaigns were actually concurrent and entwined with each other in audience and content. While victory would ultimately come to the side that most successfully impressed and manipulated the voters and delegates, it is descriptively inaccurate to attribute the outcome, as some scholars unfortunately do and as I have perhaps previously done, to the inherent quality of the arguments.

Thus, Storing (1981, 1:71), after reviewing the debate, asked, "Why did the Antifederalists lose?" (The odd phrasing of this question probably resulted from Storing's acceptance of Main's calculation, possibly dubious, that the Antifederalists very likely got more votes for delegates than did the Federalists [Main 1961, 1973]. Hence, for Main and Storing, the puzzle was negative: "Why did the Antifederalists lose?" rather that the more natural and obvious puzzle: "Why did the Federalists win?") Storing answered that Antifederalists lost "not merely because they were less clever arguers or less skillful politicians but because they had the weaker argument." I agree that the

Antifederalists had the weaker argument, but this is not a conclusive answer. One wonders why, if they had the weaker argument, they still got more votes in the elections, or at least about the same number of votes. Of course, what constitutes a weaker or stronger argument depends as much on the auditors' or readers' predispositions as it does on an objective evaluation of the debate. So to say that Federalists had the better argument reveals more about Storing (and me) than it does about the correct answer to the question about winning and losing.

As we know from recent social choice theory, cycles of preference over alternatives are always possible and often ubiquitous. If a cycle exists, then there is no equilibrium of social choice, that is, for *any* outcome currently adopted, a majority of people prefer some other outcome(s). Thus all public opinion is flux. The fact that voters mostly agree with one side's argument does *not* imply that they select its policy alternative. Rather, the selection of one alternative in the cycle depends on a variety of both rhetorical and non-rhetorical features of the decision process.

While it is not appropriate to elaborate social choice theory here, I should point out one fundamental meaning of cycles for Federalist victory. The way parties interactively develop issues has a lot to do with which alternative ultimately wins. Of course, ratification must also have depended on a variety of heresthetical manipulations, such as agenda control, that directed the selection of the Federalist-preferred alternative from the cycle.[1] But I will leave discussion of those devices to another occasion. Here I will concentrate on the sifting of issues in rhetorical interaction, for the issues thus selected set the scene for heresthetical manipulations.

Interactive Debate

Campaigns are not like school debates or courtroom disputes. In debates and courtrooms, judges keep the disputants to the predetermined subject by scoring the arguments or by accepting only relevant ones. In trial courts, judges exercise even more control, limiting and even directing the presentation. As a consequence, disputants in these settings directly engage each other in argument, rebuttal, and surrebuttal or in complaints and answers followed by replications, rejoinders, and surrejoinders. As the vocabulary suggests, these disputes must follow rather rigid rules of relevance in response.

Campaigns are quite different because there is no judge. Each disputant decides what is relevant, what ought to be responded to, and what themes to

---

1. *Heresthetic* is a word I coined from a Greek root for choosing and voting. It refers to a wide range of devices by which political actors force outcomes they desire, even when most other actors desire some other possible outcome (see Riker 1986).

emphasize. Today, campaigners sometimes complain that the themes of the other side are "not the issue," as if there were a judge to decide what the real issues are. But of course there are no judges, and whatever a campaigner successfully emphasizes is, willy-nilly, an issue. In 1787–88, the writers, at least in my sample, did not complain about "false issues." Their silence implies recognition of the essential anarchy of the campaign forum.

In the unstructured situation of a campaign, what might we expect rational campaigners to do? Consider the situation of 1787–88, where the disputants were, for the most part, attempting to estimate the consequences of consolidation or, alternatively, of maintaining the status quo. These were fundamental features of political organization, so the campaigners could reasonably attribute a wide array of potential consequences to the alternative outcomes. From this wide array, each rhetor was entirely free to choose the consequences to emphasize. As will be apparent in tables 4 and 5, Federalists and Antifederalists chose quite different things. Federalists emphasized the crisis of the times, and Antifederalists emphasized the threat to liberty in the Constitution. Each side presumably believed that these disparate themes were to their advantage. Surely, neither side chose to emphasize themes that gave an advantage to the other.

The result of this method of choosing issues was that rhetors in two groups did not, by and large, discuss the same things. But of course they were conscious of each others' claims and, in many ways, phrased their arguments to undercut the opponents' positions. So while we have two campaigns with different themes, we also have responses and deprecations. In some degree, which I shall try to assess, these interactions affected both the course of debate and, possibly, its outcomes.

The most direct sort of response is criticism of the words and actions of an opponent. In the national campaigns studied here, as distinct from local campaigns, by far the largest amount of direct criticism centers around the works and words of prominent public figures who wrote something for or against the Constitution under their own names. The bulk of the writing in both campaigns was pseudonymous as Publius (The Federalist), Federal Farmer, Centinel, Landholder, et al. But several of the framers—Washington, Franklin, Wilson, Randolph, Gerry, Mason, Luther Martin, Yates, Lansing, Williamson, and Pierce—did write under their own names, and some of these writings were widely discussed, especially those printed early in the campaign. These were also lightening rods for criticism and, to interpret the significance of the direct interaction, I will discuss several instances, those concerning Washington, Wilson, Gerry, and Mason.[2]

---

2. I have chosen to focus on the writings of Washington, Wilson, Gerry, and Mason because they are among the most "important" in my sample, that is, they appear in table 1, which lists the number of printings of the most widely disseminated items contained in Kaminski and

Washington's Endorsement

I start with Washington, not because he wrote the most elaborate or provocative commentary, but because his endorsement of the Constitution was one of the most widely used Federalist arguments (see table 1, items 1, 2, 4, 5, 7, 8, and 13). That Washington endorsed the Constitution must have been a widely known fact. His letter transmitting the Constitution from the Federal Convention to the Congress contained the first statement of what became typical Federalist arguments on the inadequacy of the Articles of Confederation, on the consequent necessity of union and consolidation, and on the desirability of ratification. Probably his strongest remarks were that "the greatest interest of every true American" was "the consolidation of our Union, in which is involved our prosperity, felicity, safety, perhaps our national survival." The 423 words of this letter, appended to the Constitution, were printed at least 76 times (table 1, item 1, *CC* 76).[3] While I did not include this letter in my count of the campaigns, it amounts to 32,148 weighted words, which, moreover, were disseminated early enough to impress nearly everyone.[4]

Federalists utilized this endorsement immediately and extensively. In one of the first newspaper discussions of the Constitution, it was prophesied that Washington would be the first president (see table 3, item 7, *CC* 101, 45 printings). Also, the reports of Washington's accident as he returned home from the Philadelphia convention emphasized that his "dear" life was saved for the sake of his future leadership (table 1, item 2, *CC* 96, 73 printings).

On October 1, a Boston newspaper praised the Constitution and said "its acceptance, will enroll the names of the WASHINGTONS and FRANKLINS, of the present age, with those of the SOLONS and NUMAS of antiquity. . . . Illustrious CHIEFTAIN! immortal SAGE—ye will have the plaudit of the world for having twice saved your country!" (*CC* 120; seven printings). After some Antifederalist criticism of the Constitution had begun to appear, Federalists used Washington's endorsement to dispel fears: ". . . it is ushered to us

---

Saladino 1981ff. For the items listed in table 1, note that the theoretical maximum number of printings is just over 100, i.e., 97 newspapers, three magazines, and several pamphlet editions. Thus, the table, with items ranging from 30 to 76 printings, lists those items attaining from, roughly, one-third to three-fourths the theoretical maximum. Since there were more Federalist papers than Antifederalist ones, most of the widely disseminated items are Federalist. The only Antifederalist material included is Gerry's objections to the Constitution, Mason's objections, the statement of the 16 seceding assemblymen in Pennsylvania, and Clinton's speech to the New York legislature.

3. In the tables and text, the citations of Federalist and Antifederalist materials are from Kaminski and Saladino 1981ff. This work is cited as *CC* followed by the entry number or, in the case of newspaper squibs, as *CC* followed by the volume number and page number.

4. "Weighted words" are the number of words in the document itself times the number of times the document or essay was printed. For details on the calculation of weights of documents, themes, and so forth, see Riker 1991.

TABLE 1. Frequency of Printing Widely Disseminated Items
in *Commentaries on the Constitution*

Citation	Content	Times Printed
1. *CC* 76	The Constitution, with letter of transmittal to Congress	76
2. *Cc* 96A, B	Report of Washington's accident (with comments on his destiny)	73
3. *CC* 508A, B	Massachusetts' Proposed Amendments	60
4. *CC* 638A	Washington to Carter (endorsing the Constitution)	51
5. *CC* 638A	Washington to Gibbs (praising Massachusetts' ratification)	50
6. *CC* 339	Sullivan's speech to New Hampshire General Court praising the Constitution	50
7. *CC* 101, par. 6	*Pennsylvania Gazette* (Washington for President)	45
8. *CC* 2:456 Squib	Squib *Pennsylvania Gazette* (False report of Washington to represent Fairfax in Virginia Ratifying Convention)	45
9. *CC* 227A	Gerry's Objections to the Constitution	42
10. *CC* 3:565	Squib *Massachusetts Gazette* (Georgia's Ratification)	42
11. *CC* 77	Franklin's speech to the Federal Convention	40
12. *CC* 289	Wilson's speech to the Pennsylvania Convention (all versions)	40
13. *CC* 233A	Washington's comment (spurious) on signing the Constitution	39
14. *CC* 101, par. 3	Constitution wisest, etc., of any government	38
15. *CC* 134	Wilson's speech in the State House Yard	38
16. *CC* 407	An Old Man (Federalist description of Carlisle riot)	38
17. *CC* 566A	Hancock's speech to the Massachusetts General Court	36
18. *CC* 529A	Calculation of Delegates' support for Constitution	35
19. *CC* 3:559	Squib *Pennsylvania Herald* (West Indians attracted to U.S. by the Constitution)	34
20. *CC* 156A	Middle States Baptist Convention's endorsement of the Constitution	33
21. *CC* 3:558	Squib, *Pennsylvania Packet* (New Jersey ratification unanimous)	32
22. *CC* 552A	Francis Hopkinson, "A Yankee," poem celebrating Massachusetts ratification	32
23. *CC* 290B	Jay's endorsement of the Constitution	31
24. *CC* 125A	Statement of the Sixteen Seceding Pensylvania Assemblymen	30
25. *CC* 150	"Federal Constitution," rejoinder to the Seceders	30
26. *CC* 276A	Mason's Objections	30
27. *CC* 439	Clinton's Speech to the New York Legislature	30

under the respectable and illustrious signature of GEORGE WASHING-
TON. . . . [T]o suppose that any act of his, could . . . injure a people whose
freedom he has already established, . . . would be a piece of base ingratitude,
that no *honest* American can possibly be guilty of" (*CC* 220, seven printings).
Soon, some Federalist editors transformed Washington's endorsement into a
threat, attributing to him the following (uncharacteristic and of course spurious) utterance as he signed the Constitution: "Should the states reject this
excellent Constitution, the probability is, an opportunity will never again offer
to cancel another in peace—the next will be drawn in blood" (see table 3,
item 13, *CC* 233A, 39 printings; drawn from Curtius, III). Other Federalist
editors contrasted Washington and Franklin with the nonsigners: "[A]re
the gentlemen who have withheld their assent from the Federal Constitution, superior to Washington or Franklin . . . —men whose names . . . are
known throughout the world. . . . [T]he good and great of every nation have
been lavish in their panegyrick . . . —A French philosopher [scil., Mira-
beau], speaking of our illustrious Fabius, enraptured bids us to 'Begin with
the infant in the cradle: Let the first word he lisps be WASHINGTON'" (*CC*
251, 11 printings).

Federalists' use of Washington's endorsement posed a difficult problem
for Antifederalists. Most of them responded simply by ignoring the subject. A
few attempted to divert attention, usually by pointing out that "great names"
ought not to be decisive—a muted and indirect attack. Thus Cato I: ". . . the
wisest and best men may err, and their errors, if adopted, may be fatal to the
community" (*CC* 104, 6 printings). And Old Whig (possibly George Bryan)
began his third essay with "'Great men are not always wise.' They have their
seasons of inattention" (*CC* 181, 2 printings). Early in his second essay,
Centinel (probably Samuel Bryan, son of George Bryan), much more vi-
tuperative than Old Whig, more widely disseminated and much more resented
by Federalists, remarked: "What astonishing infatuation! to stake their [i.e.,
the people's] happiness on the wisdom and integrity of any set of men" (*CC*
190, 11 printings). Or again, Brutus, Junior, possibly the same author as
Federal Farmer, began his first letter: "It is an invidious task, to call into
question the character of individuals. . . . But when we are required implicitly to submit our opinions to those of others . . . [because] they are so wise
and good as not to be able to err, . . . every honest man will justify a decent
investigation" (*CC* 239, 2 printings). Altogether, the "be-suspicious-of-great-
names" argument accounted for 19,191 weighted words in 19 essays. In
contrast, Federalist advice to "follow the great names" was at least 26,089
weighted words, entirely apart from Washington's and Franklin's own recom-
mendations, which together were just about 75,000 weighted words.[5] While

---

5. Washington to Congress (*CC* 76): 32,148; Washington to Carver (*CC* 386): 15,249;
Washington to Gibbs (*CC* 638): 5,300; Franklin's speech to the Convention (*CC* 77): 22,152.

the argument from suspicion probably helped to dispel some of the framers' aura generally, it did not specifically attack the overwhelming prestige of Washington. So Centinel carried the matter further. In his first essay, he attacked directly.

> [T]he wealthy and ambitious . . . flatter themselves that they have lulled all distrust . . . by gaining the concurrence of the two men in whom America has the highest confidence [i.e., Washington and Franklin]. . . . I would be very far from insinuating that the two illustrious personages . . . have not the welfare of their country at heart; but that the unsuspecting goodness and zeal of the one, has been imposed on, in a subject of which he must be necessarily inexperienced, from his other arduous engagements; and that the weakness and indecision attendant on old age [Franklin was 81], has been practiced on the other. (*CC* 133, 19 printings, 5,440 weighted words)

Centinel himself frequently repeated this argument (see *CC* 190, 311, 410, 427, 470). But the only other writers who used the argument that Washington was misled were those, like Centinel, in the coterie around Ebenezer Oswald of the *Philadelphia Independent Gazetter,* namely An Officer of the Late Continental Army (*CC* 231 and *RCS,* Pa. 210–16),[6] Philadelphiensis IX (*CC* 507), and an unsigned note in the *Gazetteer* (*CC* 290A).

While Centinel's disparagement of Washington's judgment garnered 12,162 weighted words—mostly from Centinel's own letters, the first two of which were printed 19 and 11 times, because, I believe, of other arguments than this one—still, the disparagement did not catch on. And, I think, for good reason. It certainly excited substantial revulsion. In the next issue after Centinel I, Oswald printed a complaint about Centinel's "abuse" (*CC* 158). Similarly, Uncas (*CC* 247) remarked of Centinel's "insult" that a "Bear with a sore head will growl in the serenest weather," while a New Haven writer (*CC* 283A) denounced Centinel for saying "General WASHINGTON is a Fool from habit and Dr. FRANKLIN a Fool from age. . . ." In each case, the writer began a general attack on Centinel with an attack on his disparagement of Washington, which suggests that all three of them believed the "insult" was Centinel's most vulnerable spot. The fact that other Antifederalists outside Oswald's circle did not pick up Centinel's argument suggests that they thought so too.

Altogether, the arguments against great names and against Washington as misled were not, so it seems, successful, and most Antifederalists simply

---

6. In the text, items from Jensen 1976ff. are cited as *RCS* followed by the abbreviated state and page number.

ignored Washington's initial endorsement, which, after all, might be interpreted as an official act rather than a personal opinion. But, in December, Washington wrote a personal letter (*CC* 386A) that made his endorsement absolutely clear and, when printed 51 times in January, February, and March, probably became universally known. "There is no Alternative between the Adoption of it [i.e., the Constitution] and Anarchy" (7,395 weighted words) and "General Government . . . is really at an End" (4,386 weighted words). Again, most Antifederalists ignored it as, presumably, unanswerable. But in Massachusetts, where the state ratifying convention was in progress (January 9 through February 7), the Antifederalists seemed to think it sufficiently dangerous to require a response. Some writers denied the letter was genuine (*CC* 386C, 386H), while others (*CC* 386C, 386F) misread one phrase to brand Washington a potential man on horseback. Washington had said that no one state or a minority of states could dictate a Constitution [scil: the retention of the Articles], except by the "ultima ratio." But An American (*CC* 386F) misinterpreted this to mean that ". . . the General has declared, that this Constitution shall be supported by the ULTIMO [*sic*] RATIO, that is by force." Of course, Federalists quickly corrected this misreading (*CC* 386E, 386G) and there the matter apparently came to rest, because these articles were seldom reprinted either inside or outside Massachusetts. Furthermore, Washington wrote still another endorsement of the Constitution (*CC* 638) in the form of a letter (February 29) congratulating the "conciliatory behaviour" of Massachusetts Antifederalists in acquiescing to the state's ratification and prophesying that this ratification would be "greatly influential in obtaining a favourable determination" in the remaining states. As Kaminski and Saladino observe, the reaction to this letter was minimal (*CC* 638A), and it was printed 51 times in all but two states.

Washington's endorsement appears to have been a persuasive argument, at least on the basis of the available evidence. Of course, we do not know if there existed people who, with the endorsement, voted for ratification, but who, without the endorsement, would have voted against it. But, then, we are equally ignorant about similar puzzles in contemporary campaigns, simply because we do not know much about individual choices. We do, however, have systematic knowledge about the editors' behavior in 1787–88, which gives us some evidence about the persuasiveness of his endorsement.

Federalist editors showed that they thought it persuasive by extensively reprinting his letters (items 4 and 5 in table 1). Of course, most editors (72 or 73 out of 97 in the country) printed the Constitution with his official letter to Congress appended. But they also printed his two nonofficial letters 51 and 50 times, which is close to the maximum shown in table 1. They also widely disseminated newspaper accounts of his actions (items 2, 7, 8, and 13).

Antifederalist editors displayed a similar conviction of the persuasive-

ness of his endorsement by treating it as unanswerable. Since the "be-suspicious-of-great-names" rejoinder was apparently self-defeating and shunned by all but the Oswald circle, and since Washington's letters to Carter and Gibbs occasioned little response, it seems clear that Antifederalist editors gave up on refutation and conceded, albeit reluctantly. It seems reasonable that they should concede. Citizens were accustomed to accepting and recognizing Washington's leadership and this custom would not change because of a few editorial criticisms.

Wilson's Speech

Though Antifederalists could not effectively oppose Washington's endorsement, they could and did rebut other Federalist writers. Antifederalists directed their most intense and, very probably, their most effective attack on James Wilson, even though Publius produced a much larger volume of Federalist argument. Indeed, the first 74 *Federalist Papers*, which are the ones in my sample, constituted 771,682 weighted words, about 24 percent of my Federalist campaign. Of course, Publius achieved this by writing a lot. Most of the papers were not often printed. (Only five were printed 10 to 16 times, 29 were printed 5 to 9 times, and 40 were printed 3 or 4 times, including the book form, which was too late to influence much of the campaign.) Wilson wrote far less. But his speech of October 6 in the State House Yard (*CC* 134) was the main rhetorical event of October. Editors printed it 38 times, producing 92,118 weighted words, about 3 percent of my Federalist sample. Probably because of the interest generated by the October 6 speech, editors then printed his speech of November 24 to the Pennsylvania Convention (*CC* 289) 40 times. It is difficult to measure its weighted words, but, because it was quite long, it constituted a maximum of 386,720, or about 12 percent. Since, however, much of this weight came later in the campaign, the response to it was fairly muted.

The October 6 speech generated an intense Antifederal response. To demonstrate the intensity, I list here all those essays that responded directly, naming Wilson or referring to him clearly though obliquely. Several writers attempted a systematic refutation, point by point: Democratic Federalist (*CC* 167), Old Whig II (*CC* 170), Republican I (*CC* 196), and Cincinatus (Arthur Lee) I, II, III, IV, and VI (*CC* 222, 241, 265, 287, 307). Others devoted over half of more general essays to rejoinders to Wilson: Old Whig III (*CC* 181), Centinel II (*CC* 190), and Brutus II (*CC* 221). Still others responded with several paragraphs: Timolean (*CC* 223), Brutus, Junior, (*CC* 239), and Federal Farmer (*CC* 242), as well as many, not here counted, who referred to Wilson in passing.

Altogether, these direct responses sum to 109,813 weighted words, which is about 6 percent of the Antifederal campaign. Considering that the speech of October 6 was only 3 percent of its campaign (double the size of the Antifederalist campaign) and that the Antifederal response is thus proportionately four times as large, it appears that Antifederal editors believed they had a great advantage in attacking Wilson. Furthermore, the themes developed in this attack ultimately become a very considerable part of the Antifederalist campaign. In table 2, I list Wilson's propositions, along with the Antifederal and Federal themes and their volume (from Riker 1991) that extend or elaborate Wilson's arguments and the responses to them.

Table 2 reveals that, ultimately, the Antifederalists' responses to Wilson's arguments account for over one-fourth their campaign. On the other hand,

TABLE 2. Extentions of Wilson's Arguments and Responses to Them

Wilson's Argument	Extensions of Responses to Wilson's Arguments[a]	Extention of Wilson's Arguments[a]
1. It is proper to omit rights in a government of delegated powers	91,863	31,125
2. The Constitution does not abolish trial by jury in civil cases because state codes provide for it	50,429	25,929
3. The Constitution provides for a standing army for national safety	71,369	105,696
4. The Senate cannot be aristocratic because it can act only with the House and President	19,674	39,330
5. The Constitution does not reduce states to mere corporations because they fill national offices	149,075	181,650
6. For national safety, the Constitution provides for direct taxes with civilian collection, though the impost will be the main national tax	101,923	91,578
7. State office holders oppose the Constitution out of private interest	3,603	28,988
Total	487,936	504,296
Percentage of Campaign	28	16

[a]Entries in the table are weighted words.

Federalists' elaboration of Wilson's arguments account for less than one-sixth of their campaign. Clearly, Antifederal editors thought Wilson was vulnerable and indeed that all Federalists were vulnerable when they reiterated Wilson's points. Furthermore, though constrained to defend themselves by continuing to make arguments similar to Wilson's, Federalists obviously had less enthusiasm, as if they too sensed the vulnerability. If both sides were right about vulnerability, we can, I think, learn a lot about the interaction of the two campaigns by investigating this apparent Federal weakness.

Table 3 reveals just where the Federalists' vulnerability lay, that is, just where Antifederalists were far more eager than Federalists to discuss the subject. In volume of weighted words, the total Federalist campaign is just about double the volume of the Antifederalist campaign: 3,204,819 Federalist + 1,742,434 Antifederalist = 4,947,253 total weighted words, so that the Federalists produced 65 percent of the total and the Antifederalists 35 percent. Hence, it is expected that, if the editors on the two sides concurred on the importance and value of developing or attacking Wilsonian arguments, the Federalists would produce about twice the volume of the Antifederalists. That one side produces more (less) of the expected volume indicates that this side senses an advantage (disadvantage). The relative volume on these arguments is set forth in table 3.

Most of the ratios are easy to understand. On the fourth argument (Senate), volume is as expected. Presumably, Antifederalists hoped they could make "aristocracy" an issue, while Federalists believed that even the dullest voter would understand an upper house, which existed in most states. On the third (standing army) and fifth (states' role) arguments, volume is only moderately disproportionate. The issue of a standing army is something of an intellectual tie. Conventionally, Americans opposed it but perhaps also thought it was a military necessity in a hostile world. Similarly, the Anti-

TABLE 3.   The Relative Weight of Wilsonian Arguments
and Antifederalist Responses

Subject	Federal Volume[a]	Antifederal Volume[a]	Proportion[b]
Bill of Rights	31,125	91,893	0.33
Civil juries	25,929	50,429	0.51
Standing army	105,696	71,369	1.48
Senate	39,330	19,674	1.99
States' role	181,650	149,075	1.21
Direct taxes	91,578	101,923	0.89
State officeholders	28,988	3,603	8.04

[a]Weighted words.
[b]The proportion is derived by dividing the Federal volume by the Antifederal volume.

federalists were entirely correct that the Constitution diminished the states' role, but Federalists could also show that "mere corporations" is a demagogic exaggeration. The Antifederalist volume on the sixth argument (taxes) is relatively quite large, but that is to be expected. Supporters of the status quo (Antifederalists here) usually denounce the cost of reform, while reformers (here Federalists) usually ignore cost increases if they can. On the seventh argument (state officeholders), the Federalists obviously sensed a great advantage, though the argument is not very large in absolute terms. This sense of advantage is easy to understand. In Philadelphia and New York, where the state officials employed in the metropolis typically belonged to the faction with few urban supporters, Federalist editors could believably attribute greed for retaining a metropolitan job to such Antifederal officeholders as George Bryan in Pennsylvania and John Lamb in New York.

The truly striking ratios are the first (bill of rights) and second (civil juries). Here, the Antifederalist advantage and Federalist disadvantage are abundantly clear, so I will examine them in detail.

Wilson's argument on a bill of rights was, in his own words (*CC* 134), that in establishing state governments "everything which is not reserved is given," but in establishing the federal government

> everything which is not given, is reserved. This distinction being recognized, will furnish an answer to those who think the omission of a bill of rights, a defect in the proposed constitution: for it would have been superfluous and absurd to have stipulated with a federal body of our own creation, that we should enjoy those privileges, of which we are not divested either by the intention or the act, that has brought that body into existence.

No one can deny that Wilson here created a neat and memorable formula— "not reserved is given, not given is reserved"—a formula worthy indeed of a Philadelphia lawyer, which is exactly what Wilson was.

Wilson did not, however, invent this argument. It was accepted by the framers in the Convention and subsequently accepted in Congress at the time it sent the Constitution to the states. The first person recorded as uttering it was Roger Sherman, the Connecticut "Countryman" of the ratification campaign. According to Madison's *Notes,* on September 12 in the Federal Convention, George Mason (Va.) proposed a bill of rights, saying it might be prepared in a few hours. Elbridge Gerry (Mass.) then moved for a committee to do so. Madison recorded: "Mr. Sherman was for securing the rights of the people where requisite. The State Declarations of Rights are not repealed by this Constitution; and being in force are sufficient. . . ." Mason then responded "the Laws of the U.S. are to be paramount to State Bills of

Rights. . . ." The Convention then rejected Gerry's motion, zero to ten (Farrand 1937, 2:587–88). As Mason implied, the time constraint was probably more of an issue than Sherman's argument—though the joint sponsorship of Mason and Gerry would probably have doomed any motion at this point in the Convention. Two days later, Gerry, this time with Charles Pinkney (S.C.), tried to insert a declaration for liberty of the press. Again, Sherman was the spokesman of the opposition and this time he made his argument clearer by saying of the notion: "It is unnecessary—the power of Congress does not extend to the Press. . . ." This motion was then rejected by a much closer margin, five to six, which ought, perhaps, to have warned the framers of the tone of the forthcoming ratification debates (Farrand 1937, 2:617–18).

It does not seem likely, however, that Sherman was the sole inventor of the argument. William Pierce (Ga.), who left the Convention before the end of July, set forth a primitive version of it in a letter on September 28 (*CC* 634): ". . . the defined powers of each department of the government, and the restraints that naturally follow, will be sufficient to prevent the invasion of . . . those rights. Where then can be the necessity for a Bill of Rights?" Pierce thus has the core of the "all-not-given-is-reserved" argument and he might have learned it before Sherman's recorded utterance.

Or again Pierce might have learned it in New York, where he was on September 28, because the previous day Nathaniel Gorham (Mass.), a framer who was also a member of Congress, used it in the congressional debate over the transmission of the Constitution to the states. According to Melancton Smith's (N.Y.) notes, Gorham argued there was "no necessity of a Bill of rights, because a Bill of rights in state Govts. was intended to restrain certain powers, as ye Legis. had unlimd. powers" (*CC* 95).

Except for Mason's remark about the supremacy clause, both the Convention and Congress accepted the Sherman-Gorham-Pierce(?) rationale without question. I think it can thus be regarded as the settled Federalist response to the charge of omission of a bill of rights. It was left to Wilson, however, to encapsulate the argument in a memorable formula.

Unfortunately for Federalists, the improved argument was not much help and, possibly, much harm. Only a few Federalists used it, mainly, perhaps, because only a few Federalists talked about a bill of rights anyway. (Wilson's argument involved only 24,417 weighted words, of which 20,805 were by Wilson himself. Non-Wilsonian defenses added another 6,708 words. So Wilson's defense in one speech is much more than half of the total Federalist discussion of the issue. Note that Publius, by far the most voluminous Federalist, delayed discussion of a bill of rights until the next to last paper [84th]— not in my sample—and then barely alluded to Wilson's argument.)

I think Federalists were afraid of Wilson's formula. One Federalist sympathizer, A True Friend (*CC* 326), referred to Wilson's argument as "not

sufficient to calm the inquietude of a whole nation" and proposed a bill of rights as a compromise (see also a private letter, *CC* 249). Of those Federalists who did use Wilson's argument, only five used it unequivocally. An American Citizen IV (Tench Coxe, *CC* 183), writing at Wilson's request, only wrote one brief paragraph on this theme. Anti Cincinnatus (*CC* 354), writing against Cincinnatus I, followed Wilson closely and more extensively, but inelegantly; Hugh Williamson (N.C.), a framer, used Wilson's formula briefly in a speech in North Carolina on November 8 (not published until February 25, *CC* 560), and Marcus (James Iredell, *CC* 548) also used Wilson in a point-by-point refutation of Mason's objections, identifying it from "Mr. Wilson's celebrated speech"; finally, Aristides (Alexander Contee Hanson, *CC* 490) set forth Wilson's argument fully.

This is all—the entire Federalist use in my sample of the most famous argument in the "celebrated speech." In contrast, the Antifederalists had a field day. I have already listed the writers who attacked Wilson, most of them on his first argument, among others, because it was made to order for their attack. Even at this distance of time, one can sense their delight as they speak of his "flimsy sophistry," denounce his "specious" argument, and sneer at his formula for having "more the quaintness of a conundrum than the dignity of an argument." They devised several telling responses. Like Mason's riposte to Sherman, they pointed to the necessary and proper clause, the supremacy clause, the federal court system, and so on to show that congressional power could override popular liberties and should therefore be restrained by a bill of rights. Cincinnatus and several others argued that the states making a federal constitution were just like citizens making a state constitution, so, if a bill of rights was appropriate in the latter, then it was equally so in the former. But the Antifederalists' neatest argument, one that matches Wilson's formula in cleverness, was that the Constitution itself listed a number of prohibitions on Congress (e.g., no bill of attainder, no title of nobility, etc.). So, as Brutus II said, "If everything not given is reserved, what propriety is there in these exceptions?" Or, as Republican I said of titles of nobility, "Is this power expressly given to Congress? If it is not, then the exception must be to guard against an incidental or implied power." Thus they proved, out of the Constitution itself, the falsity of Wilson's formula. It cannot be that everything not given is reserved.

In a sense, Wilson got what he deserved: a sophistical claim invites a sophistical rejoinder. Not surprisingly, therefore, the Federalists left this particular field of battle quite shaken up, and, as previously noted, stayed well away from it thereafter.

The same thing happened in the argument over civil juries. Wilson had argued that, since the practice of the states varied quite widely on the use of juries in civil cases, the framers thought it best not to impose a national rule,

knowing, of course, that the states would continue to follow their established practices. Unfortunately for Wilson, however, the guarantee of juries in criminal cases attracted attention to the absence of a guarantee for civil cases. Cincinnatus II (*CC* 241) observed that the "reservation of trial by jury in criminal, is an exclusion of it in civil cases. Why else should it be mentioned at all?" Cincinnatus's inference is logically false—as he himself elsewhere said, civil juries are "not secured" rather than "excluded"—but "exclusion" was, perhaps, rhetorically effective. Antifederalists had a much better theoretical argument, namely that federal appellate jurisdiction on law and fact denied the finality of juries' factual determinations and thus threatened juries in a systematic way (Democratic Federalist, *CC* 167). These arguments seem to me a bit sophistical, but the Antifederalists also had a practical argument, that the federal court system jeopardized juries of the vicinage. As Federal Farmer IV (*CC* 242) pointed out, the difficulty—and here he rebuked cruder thinkers—was not so much the loss of juries of neighbors, "for in this enlightened country men may probably be impartially tried by those who do not live very near them," but rather that "the common people can establish facts with much more ease with oral than written evidence." Considering that, in a rural society, civil disputes often concern land ownership, the prospect of generating effective written testimony must have seemed daunting to owners of small holdings. Hence, Federal Farmer's argument must have seemed quite realistic. Altogether, then, Wilson's argument on juries apparently seemed to both sides to be much less impressive than the Antifederalist critique. So the Federalists left the field.

Wilson's speech of October 6 seems to me to have done the Federalists more harm than good. With all the publicity, Wilson became a whipping boy for the Antifederalist campaign. In the Carlisle (Pa.) riot, after the Pennsylvania ratification, the rioters burned him in effigy. As the Pennsylvania Antifederalists became increasingly vitupertive, Centinel began referring to "James, the Caledonian, lieutenant general of the myrmidons of power, under Robert, the cofferer [i.e., Robert Morris]" (*CC* 443), other Antifederalists published spurious letters by "James the Caledonian" in which he appeared utterly Machiavellian (*CC* 570; *CC* 2:552, 560), and Centinel (*CC* 565) interpreted the ex post facto clause as a device to allow Morris and Wilson to escape punishment for defaulting on debts to the United States.

What happened to the reputation of one man is not, however, as important as what happened to the Federalist cause. And Wilson's speech gave Antifederalists the opportunity to systematize and make memorable their attacks on the absence of a bill of rights and civil juries and on taxes and standing armies. The Antifederalists owed much of the coherence of their campaign to the chance Wilson gave them to answer his defenses. I think it may very well be that their emphasis on liberty (instead of consolidation) was

brought about by their response to this speech. Main and Storing both believe that Antifederalists were truly interested in attacking consolidation, while I have shown that they mainly attacked the Constitution as a threat to liberty (Riker 1991). Perhaps the Antifederalists went in this direction because of the opportunity Wilson afforded them.

Mason, Gerry, and Landholder

Turning now to the objections by Mason and Gerry, they served the same function in the Antifederalist campaign that Washington's persona and letters served in the Federalist campaign. Mason and Gerry were two well-known delegates to the Convention whose opinions the Antifederal editors presumably believed would be influential. Since both delegates refused to sign the Constitution and wrote clear and unequivocal objections early in the campaign, they became central figures in it.

Other nonsigners had much less influence, even though they also wrote out objections. Randolph (Va.) wrote a long but late-appearing piece (*CC* 386, January 2, 135,562 weighted words) in which, however, he equivocated, saying that if prior amendments proved impossible, he would support the Constitution. Consequently, Federalists used him as much as Antifederalists and it is hard to tell whether to assign his work to one side or the other. In the middle of the winter, Robert Yates and John Lansing (N.Y.), who left the convention on July 10, and Luther Martin (Md.), who left on September 4, published their objections (Yates and Lansing: *CC* 447, January 14, 15,400 weighted words; Martin, *Genuine Information, CC* 389, 401, 414, 425, 441, 451, 459, 467, 484, 493, 502, 516, December 28 to February 8, 201,905 weighted words). The prolix Martin's commentary was almost equal in volume to Centinel, whose volume was 268,597 weighted words.

Mason's and Gerry's commentary, 17,875 and 18,174 weighted words respectively, were each about 1 percent of the Antifederal campaign. They had little to say about personalities, tactics, or the campaign strategies, and they ignored peripheral issues as well as a few major ones (e.g., taxes). Otherwise, however, they touched on most of the important substantive Antifederalist ideological themes, themes that, taken together in all writers, amounted to 714,840 weighted words or about 41 percent of the Antifederal campaign total. So they can be regarded as epitomes of their campaign. Furthermore, the Federalist response is also an epitome of that part of the Federalist campaign. Marcus (James Iredell, *CC* 548, 571, 596, 616, 630), whose lengthy, point-by-point response to Mason was 40,735 weighted words (about 1 percent of the Federalist campaign), nevertheless touched on themes that accounted for 767,990 weighted words, or 24 percent of the Federalist campaign in my sample.

Thus, on the level of political ideas, Mason and Gerry are unremarkable because they mirror a large part of the ideological element of the campaign. On the personal level, however, they stand out because they occasioned fairly vicious criticism. Of course publicists on both sides attacked the rhetors and leaders of the other, especially so in Pennsylvania, where the campaign was notably virulent: such Federalists as Benjamin Rush and Francis Hopkinson and such Antifederalists as George Bryan (thought to be Centinel, though apparently Centinel was his son Samuel) and Benjamin Workman (Philadelphiensis). But Federalists sprayed special venom on Mason and Gerry, almost as much as Antifederalists sprayed on Wilson.

The main critic of both Mason and Gerry was Landholder (Oliver Ellsworth, a framer from Connecticut). His fourth (*CC* 295, November 26, 17,875 weighted words) and fifth papers (*CC* 316, December 3, 21,461 words) attacked Gerry, his sixth paper (*CC* 335, December 10, 43,729 words) attacked Mason, and his eighth paper (*CC* 371, December 24, 25,418 words) attacked both as well as Luther Martin. Altogether, these four Landholder papers accounted for 108,483 weighted words, or about 3 percent of the Federalist campaign. These papers circulated mainly in New England and New York and may well have neutralized the effect of Mason and even Gerry.

Though less intellectual than Publius or Wilson, Landholder was still a very important writer. After reading the fourth and sixth papers, Rufus King, a framer and one of the two or three main leaders of the ratification campaign in Massachusetts, believed that "'the Landholder' will do more service our [i.e., the Federal] way than the elaborate works of Publius" (*CC* 368). Perhaps the most practical recognition of Landholder's merit came as imitation: When Luther Martin (*CC* 460, January 18) defended Gerry against Landholder VIII, an unidentified framer, whom Kaminski and Saladino believe was Daniel Jenifer (a framer from Maryland), responded under Landholder's pen name, attacking Martin and Gerry (*CC* 580, February 29).

Landholder tried to trivialize both Gerry and Mason. Of course, he attacked their arguments whenever these seemed vulnerable. To Mason's complaints that the President lacked a council and the Senate seemed aristocratic, he responded that the states found governors' councils useless and that the Senate was not at all like the House of Lords. Furthermore, he said, the danger "is not aristocracy or monarchy, but anarchy." To Gerry's complaints about "inadequate representation" and the powers of Congress, Landholder responded that federal representation was much like Connecticut's and that Congress needed broad powers to defend freedom. But these substantive rejoinders do not convey the flavor of Landholder's prose. His main thrust was to show that, however much Mason and Gerry purported to fear for the common good, they actually wanted, instead, to satisfy the crassest of private and provincial interests.

As Landholder proceeded from his fourth to eighth papers, his portrayal of their supposed deceit moved from indirect insinuation to direct charges of greed. Initially, he simply insinuated that Gerry was personally interested in "state dignities and emoluments" and that he was a "cunning" politician "of metaphysical nicety." In the sixth paper, Landholder, probably less inhibited in denouncing a Virginian than a New Englander, launched a powerful attack on Mason's private pecuniary motives. Editors showed their appreciation by printing this paper 23 times, double the 11 printings of the fourth and fifth. Thus encouraged, Landholder blasted Gerry even more in the eighth paper.

In both cases, Landholder developed his allegations by pointing out that both framers had cooperated fully in writing the Constitution, presumably because they were then actuated by concern for the public good. Then, suddenly, at the end of the Convention, they turned against the Constitution as, presumably, they realized it would hurt their private or provincial interests. Mason had, Landholder said, "zealously supported" the proceedings, and, as for Gerry, during "almost the whole time . . . no man was more . . . conciliating." So there is a real puzzle why these enthusiastic framers turned sour in the end.[7] Having posed the puzzle, Landholder resolved it by offering a believable and discreditable reason why these two framers switched.

In the case of Mason, Landholder pointed out that Mason had moved to require a two-thirds majority in Congress to pass a navigation act (i.e., an act to cartelize the shipping trade, perhaps prohibiting foreign carriers from transporting U.S. cargoes). Presumably, Mason believed that a U.S. shipping cartel would aid eastern carriers at the expense of southern planters, and a two-thirds rule would make that kind of sectional legislation difficult. When the motion failed, Mason turned against the Constitution and this was one of his objections. Landholder's clinching argument was that northern editors omitted this objection in order to conceal the fact that "Mason preferred the subjects of every foreign power to the subjects of the United States who live in New England."[8]

---

7. Landholder was, we now know, entirely correct in identifying the puzzle. While Mason was often cited in the campaign for his dramatic pronouncement "that he would sooner chop off his right hand than put it to the Constitution," this was still the same Mason who, in the middle of the Convention, said "he would bury his bones in this city [i.e., Philadelphia] rather than expose his Country to the Consequences of a dissolution of the Convention without any thing being done" (Farrand 1937, 2:479, 1:533). Similarly, it was Gerry's and Strong's pivotal votes on July 14—contrary to Massachusetts's superficial interests as defined by King and Gorham—for equal representation in the Senate that saved the Convention from collapse and made a Constitution possible. In the summer, then, both men did indeed seem actuated by national goals, not provincial or personal interests.

8. Landholder was entirely correct that Mason rejected the Constitution because of this provincial economic interest. In 1792, Jefferson, visiting Mason's home, summarized for posterity Mason's reminiscences about the Convention.

Landholder's other charge against Mason related to an even more direct and even more discreditable pecuniary interest. Another of Mason's objections was that the Constitution restrained Congress from prohibiting the importation of slaves for 20 years. While this objection to the delay sounds humane, Landholder pointed out that, in Virginia, slaves increased in population numbers naturally and owners sold the surplus to the South in competition with the imports from Africa. Mason, as the owner "of three hundred slaves," presumably wished to minimize competition: " . . . perhaps Col. Mason may suppose it more humane to breed than import slaves . . . but his objections are not on the side of freedom, nor in compassion to the human race who are slaves, but that *such importation render the United States weaker, more vulnerable, and less capable of defenses*" (*CC* 335). Landholder concluded: "A man governed by such narrow views and local prejudices, can never be trusted." Probably many readers in New England and the middle states agreed.

Having discredited Mason, Landholder devoted his eighth paper to discrediting Gerry, who, he said, turned against the Constitution because of the failure of his motion for the redemption of the Continental money. "As Mr. Gerry was supposed to be possessed of large quantities of this species of paper, his motion appeared to be founded in . . . barefaced selfishness."[9]

Having founded the opposition of Mason and Gerry in private interests, Landholder concluded his eighth paper with a systematic attribution of private interests to other opponents. Thus, he said, Massachusetts Antifederalists were Shaysites; New York Antifederalists wanted to keep the state impost that produced about (£50,000 annually on goods bound for Connecticut, Massa-

---

The constn as agreed to till a fortnight before the Convention rose was such a one as he wd. have set his hand & heart to . . . [including] a vote of ⅔ in the legislature . . . on navigation. . . . [T]hose 2 states [South Carolina and Georgia] struck a bargain with the 3.N.Engld. states, if they would join to admit slaves for some years, the 2 . . . states wd join in changing the clause which required ⅔. . . . [I]t was done . . . & from that moment the two S. states and the 3 Northern ones joind Pen. Jers. & Del. & made the majority 8 to 3 against us. (Farrand 1937, 4:367)

9. Landholder was probably less accurate on Gerry than on Mason. Gerry responded (*CC* 419, January 5) with a specific denial, but pseudo-Landholder nevertheless repeated it (*CC* 580, February 29, Daniel Jenifer [?]). According to Madison's *Notes,* Gerry, like most framers, supported the provision (art. 6, sec. 1) declaring valid the prior debts of the United States. But there is no evidence that he made a special motion on the redemption of Continental money, although he did urge that Congress be specifically obligated to pay prior public debts. There are three possibilities: (*a*) Ellsworth (Landholder) and pseudo-Landholder (surely a framer, possibly Jenifer) heard Gerry make a special issue of Continental money, but Madison did not record it (Madison's *Notes* sometimes differ substantially from those of other careful note takers); (*b*) Ellsworth and Jenifer (?) misinterpreted Gerry's concerns about prior debts as a plea for payment of Continental money; or (*c*) Gerry did not mention Continental money and Landholder fabricated the charge that pseudo-Landholder repeated.

chusetts, and New Jersey; Virginia Antifederalists reflected the Lee faction's (Richard Henry and Arthur) "implacable hatred" of Washington, and so forth.

A Model of Debate

In order to locate these examples of interaction within an abstract framework for analysis, I construct a model of the main decision, typically a binary vote on some pair of alternatives, one of which is identified as a^+, the other as a^-. (Here I use a^+ for ratification of the Constitution and a^- for rejection.)

In this model, there is a set of N voters, $i \in N$, $i = 1, 2, \ldots , n$. There are also rhetors for each side who state positions and utter arguments to attract voters to the rhetors' sides. The positions are alternatives, x_j, $j = 1, 2, \ldots ,$ that are identified relative to one or more dimensions, d_l, $d_k \in R^m$ and R^m defines the alternative space.

(For example, on the subject of the provision of a military system, some relevant dimensions are:

size: the number of troops,
specialization: the degree of professionalization ranging from a militia of citizen soldiers to an entirely full-time army,
permanence: the period of time for which the military is mobilized, from semiannual musters to a standing army, and
centralization: the degree of control of the military forces by national rules, officers, and so forth.

The actual x_j chosen for the Constitution was: on size, the existing state militia plus a national army of unspecified size; on specialization, unspecialized militia plus national professionals; on permanence: state organization and training of the militia according to national rules, along with a national standing army; and, on centralization, a state militia nationally armed and subject to national takeover, but trained by locally chosen officers, plus a national army. Of course, many other x_j might have been chosen from only a small, unspecialized, short-time local militia to, exclusively, a large, professional, standing, national army.

A justification of x_j is an argument, σ_h, $h = 1, 2, \ldots ,$ to persuade voters that x_j is a desirable alternative. (To justify the military provisions of the Constitution, $\sigma_h x_j$ might, relative to the dimensions of permanence and centralization, defend the divided control of the militia as a means to provide a large army without depriving states of their military forces.)

A particular position x_j is thus tied to a cluster of dimensions, $d_k, \ldots ,$ d_m, by the arguments, σ_h, used to justify x_j. Identifying such clusters as d, where $d = (d_k, \ldots , d_m)$, there is a set of voters $C(d)$ for whom d is salient in

the sense that d is used in the voters' choices between a^+ and a^-. For some particular d_0, *salience* means that a voter in $C(d_0)$

1. prefers some $x_j(d_0)$ to any $x_h(d_0)$, $j \neq h$, and
2. uses $x_j(d_0)$, inter alia, to choose between a^+ and a^-.

This means that the voter thinks there is a "best argument" in d_0 and that he or she uses it, with others, to decide how to vote. Each voter belongs to a number of sets $C(d)$. While $C(d)$ may be a singleton, it may also contain most voters. Typically, a voter belongs to more than one set $C(d)$, but the human attention span limits the number of a voter's memberships in $C(d)$, perhaps to "the magic number 7 ± 2."

A voter's choice, s_i, between a^+ and a^- is an operation on the preferred x_j for all $C(d)$ to which i belongs. Thus,

1. for $i \in C(d_0)$, $0 = 1, 2, \ldots$, i prefers x_j (d_0) to $x_h(d_0)$, for all $j \neq h$, and
2. $s_i(a^+, a^-) = f[x_j(d_1), x_j(d_2), \ldots)$.

In general, no one knows just what f is or how it operates. Indeed, it may operate differently for each person, so one might properly write f_i instead of f.

The voter's calculus sets the rhetor's problem. To persuade voters to choose, say, a^+, a rhetor cannot simply extol a^+. Instead, he or she must set forth positions, x_j, defending them with those arguments, σ_h, that establish d such that $x_j(d)$ enter into $f(\bullet)$ in a way that influences $s_i(a^+, a^-) = a^+$. This is indeed a roundabout procedure, much complicated by the rhetor's uncertainty about how the d affects preferences for x_j and how f (or f_i) operates. Consequently, the rhetor works by trial and error, testing by experience what positions on what clusters of dimensions encourage voters to choose a^+.

In undertaking persuasion by trial and error, the rhetor faces many costs. First there are the costs of argument, which are, in effect, opportunity costs. Spending time and energy on one position and related arguments precludes spending time and energy on others that might indeed be more profitable. Among these costs are determining which $C(d)$ include many voters, selecting arguments, σ_h, that call forth those clusters, d, that favor the rhetor's cause, avoiding σ_h and d that give opponents an opening, and so forth. Second there are the mechanical costs of speaking, writing, printing, distributing, and so forth.

Rhetors incur these costs whether they win or not, indeed whether or not they win a single voter. I assume these costs increase, after an initial investment in writing, linearly with the number of voters persuaded, so that for any $C(d)$ the costs of persuasion range from the cost of the initial investment

to some maximum, when the rhetor persuades all the members of $C(d)$. The assumption of linearity means that the cost per person persuaded is constant. It is possible that the marginal cost of persuasion rises with the number persuaded, but I ignore that possibility because of the homogeneity of the persons in the set $C(d)$. They all think that the dimensions are salient; so an argument that is successful, with some probability, with one randomly chosen member should, with equal probability, be successful with another randomly chosen member, regardless of their positions in the queue of the persuaded.

On the other hand, the rhetor benefits from successful persuasion because the voters in $C(d)$ are thus partially encouraged to choose between a^+ and a^- in the way the rhetor wishes. I point out three features of the rhetor's benefits.

1. Benefits, like costs, increase linearly with the number persuaded. I reject the possibility of decreasing marginal benefits because the number in $C(d)$ is unknown, but probably less than half the voters. If $C(d)$ contained all voters, then the marginal value of additions would decrease after half were persuaded (in accordance with the Size Principle [Riker 1962]). But if $C(d)$ contains an unknown but minority number, then each addition is as good as each other addition.

2. Benefits exceed costs if the rhetor is completely successful, that is, if he or she persuades all members of $C(d)$. I assume that rhetors are rational in the sense that they do not offer positions and arguments if they gain nothing by complete success. Hence, benefits must exceed costs by at least the persuasion of all members of $C(d)$.

3. Benefits accrue to rhetors only when they persuade more than half the members of $C(d)$. Given two sides, if rhetors on one side persuade less than half, then the other side must have the allegiance of more than half. Since a rhetor's costs are linearly increasing with each voter persuaded from first to last and since benefits do not accrue until the number of voters persuaded exceeds $.5|C(d)|$, costs initially exceed benefits. But since a rational rhetor's benefits exceed costs at the maximum persuaded, $|C(d)|$, benefits must exceed costs at some point t^+, where $.5|C(d)| < t^+ \leq |C(d)|$. These two features lead to the following observation.

Proposition 1. Benefits for rhetors on one side exceed costs at some point t^+, where $.5|C(d)| < t \leq |C(d)|$.

A corollary is that the same holds true for the other side, using t^-, where $0 \leq t^- < .5|C(d)|$.

A second observation follows.

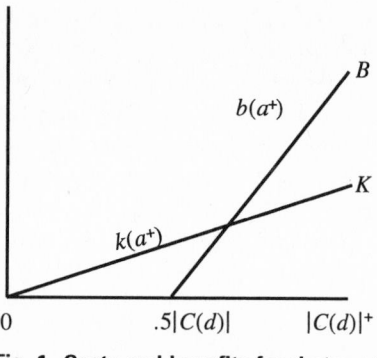

Fig. 1. Costs and benefits for rhetor a^+

Proposition 2. In the range from t^- to t^+, costs exceed benefits for rhetors on both sides.

The observations can be displayed graphically. In figure 1, the horizontal axis measures the number of i in $C(d)$ from 0 to $|C(d)|$. The vertical axis measures costs, $k(a^+)$, and benefits, $b(a^+)$. The linearly increasing line, $k(a^+)$, indicates costs from $(0, 0)$ to point K. The linearly increasing line from $(.5|C(d)|, 0)$ to point B, indicates benefits, $b(a^+)$. The mirror image for $k(a^-)$ and $b(a^-)$ is figure 2, where the measurement on the horizontal axis goes from $|C(d)|$ at the left to zero at the right. The line $k(a^-)$ from $(0, 0)$ to point K' measures costs and the line $b(a^-)$ from $.5|C(d)|$ to point B' measures benefits. In figure 3, the diagrams from figures 1 and 2 are superimposed. Although $|C(d)|^+ = |C(d)|^-$, I label them differently to indicate the direction of the horizontal axis. Figure 3 also shows the points t^+ and t^- where benefits exceed costs.

Two inferences follow from the propositions and these figures. The first is that, if a side persuades more than t^+ (t^-) members of $C(d)$, then that side profits from continued persuasion, while the other side does not. Hence, assuming rational rhetors, the successful side reiterates its arguments, while the unsuccessful side abandons its arguments. Hence, there are two equilibria: (1) 0 for a^- and $|C(d)|^+$ for a^+, and (2) 0 for a^+ and $|C(d)|^-$ for a^-. I call this feature the Dominance Principle.

The second inference is that, if neither side persuades as many as t^+ (t^-) members of $C(d)$, then neither profits. Again assuming rational rhetors, both sides abandon their arguments. Hence there is one equilibrium, at 0 for a^+ and simultaneously 0 for a^-. I call this feature the Dispersion Principle.

The rhetorical interaction so far described clearly illustrates these principles. Both sides' use of Washington's endorsement is an indisputable instance

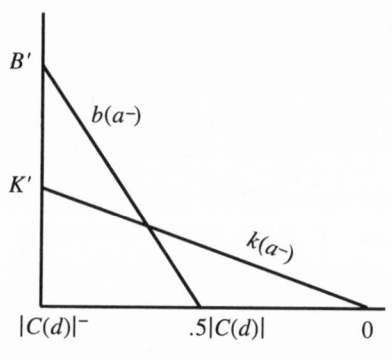

Fig. 2. Costs and benefits for rhetor a^-

of the Dominance Principle. The Federalists made much of the endorsement throughout the campaign. The Antifederalists, after some feeble, initial attempts at refutation, simply ignored the issue, leaving the field entirely free for Federalist domination. Presumably there was an equilibrium at $|C(d)|^+$. At least, nothing stood in the way of Federalists persuading all persons who took seriously the d_k clustered in this particular d.

Similarly, when Wilson exposed the Federalists to attack on the absence of a bill of rights and the issue of civil juries, the Antifederalists responded with enthusiasm, entirely and swiftly driving Federalists out of the field. Consequently, the Antifederalists dominated, so there was an equilibrium at $|C(d)|^-$ or at least nothing stood in the way of Antifederalists persuading everyone who took these d seriously.

Turning to the Dispersion Principle, the joint responses to Wilson's other arguments are instances of it, as I will show when I discuss the temporal development of rhetorical themes. Now, however, I can clearly display the motivation involved in the Dispersion Principle with the development of Landholder's letters. Landholder initially undertook to refute Mason and Gerry, but his efforts, while reprinted, were not definitive refutations. Mason and Gerry had developed the main themes of their side, so that Landholder's broad attack was diffuse and clearly did not result in a rhetorical victory. At best he achieved a rhetorical standoff, that is, some point between 0 and t^+. Then Landholder changed rhetorical tactics, attempting to trivialize his opponents' persona and interests rather than their arguments. Of course, I do not know whether or not he succeeded with the voters, but clearly he succeeded with Federalist editors, who reprinted his new themes much more than his old ones, and he infuriated Luther Martin, who replied in Gerry's (but not Mason's) defense. Landholder's change of tactics reveals the motive involved in the Dispersion Principle. Failing on the several d involved in his initial pa-

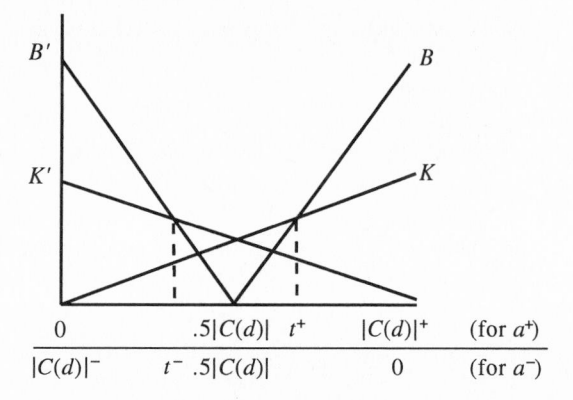

Fig. 3. Combined costs and benefits for both rhetors

pers, he switched to several new d, for example, the private pecuniary interests of the opponents of the Constitution, the provincial economic interests of Virginians, and so forth.

The Dominance and Dispersion Principles are closely related to each other, as indeed figures 1, 2, and 3 display. Consequently, they can be stated in one sentence.

> When one side has an advantage on an issue, the other side ignores it; but when neither side has an advantage, both seek new and advantageous issues.

While the formulation of these Principles is based on the study of direct interactions, they apply to the whole of both campaigns, as I will now demonstrate.

Variable Emphasis and Dispersion in the Campaign

The Dominance Principle and the Dispersion Principle refer to dynamic features of the campaigns. In order to visualize and study the changes subsumed by these Principles, I have divided the campaign into stages and summed the weighted words, by stages, on the major issues. Unfortunately, this is a rather Procrustean procedure because issues change at different rates with different apogees. Hence, the stages appropriate for one issue may not be appropriate for another. Nevertheless a division into stages demarcated by state ratifications, some of which changed the political situation dramatically, is likely to reveal significant variations on a number of themes. Thus, I have constructed tables 4 and 5 with three stages: (*a*) prior to Pennsylvania's ratification (De-

cember 15), (*b*) between Pennsylvania's ratification and Massachusetts's (February 6), and (*c*) between Massachusetts's ratification and March 31, when my sample ends.

The rationale for these stages is that the two ratifications were events that reoriented politics for the whole country. Pennsylvania's ratification, the first by a large state, gave both sides a good start. As expected, Federalists were excited by this send off, especially because they had a big majority. But Antifederalists also benefited in a back-handed way. They were able to explain the ratification away with the claim that the procedures were outrageously unfair, thereby inspiring their troops to greater effort. The Massachusetts ratification, the sixth and also the first really difficult one, clearly foreshadowed the ultimate outcome. Federalists were elated. They could easily visualize three more and thus victory, even without Virginia and New York. Antifederalists, however, were demoralized.

In tables 4 and 5 I have gathered the 178 categories from Riker 1991 into just about the same themes used there. In the following paragraphs, I comment on the main variations revealed by the separation of the data into stages.

Dominance in the Main Themes: Federalists

Each side's attention to its main theme was remarkably stable. In all three periods, the Antifederalists devoted about half their rhetoric to warning that the Constitution would, if adopted, endanger liberty. Similarly, in the first two periods, the Federalists devoted about two-fifths of their rhetoric to warning that the national crisis endangered peace, prosperity, liberty, and national existence. In the third period they decreased their warning on crisis to just over one-fourth. Part of this decrease was artifactual. While, in the first two periods, Publius mainly discussed crisis, in the last period (papers 52–75), he discussed institutions almost entirely, showing that they would enhance liberty, not endanger it. Since this emphasis accorded with his plan in the first paper, it is hard to think of this change, involving about 20 percent of the whole third-period campaign, as responding to any features of the campaign itself, except, of course, Publius could have changed his program, had it seemed appropriate to do so. This artifact of Publius's plan accounts for about half of the decline in attention to crisis. The other half derives from increased Federalists' cheering for their success. This is the positive form of the emphasis on crisis, namely, crisis averted. So, with the exceptions noted for the third period—half endogenously reflecting campaign developments and half not—the Federalists also maintained their emphasis on their main theme.

Each side thus appeared to preempt a theme. But to show that the Dominance Principle applies fully, it must also be the case that opponents ultimately ignored the issue.

TABLE 4. Themes of the Federalist Campaign

Theme	Campaign Stage						Total	
	Before Pennsylvania Ratification		Pennsylvania Ratification to Massachusetts Ratification		After Massachusetts Ratification			
	Number of Words	Percentage of Stage Total	Number of Words	Percentage of Stage Total	Number of Words	Percentage of Stage Total	Number of Words	Percentage of Stage Total
1. Ad hominem	130,491	8	107,842	10	79,393	15	317,726	10
Crisis								
2. General	203,001	13	39,495	3	27,251	5	265,749	8
3. Responses to crisis	189,750	12	138,656	13	7,346	1	335,752	11
4. Foreign military crisis	132,180	8	96,363	9	49,715	9	278,258	9
5. Economic crisis	52,083	3	70,163	7	36,736	7	158,985	5
6. Constitutional	37,483	2	74,321	7	27,784	5	139,588	4
7. Subtotal	614,497	38	414,998	39	148,835	27	1,178,330	37
8. Populist legislature	117,077	7	43,678	4	22,473	4	183,228	6
Positive Defenses								
9. On liberty	312,737	20	140,823	13	123,973	23	577,533	18
10. On consolidation	122,100	8	75,600	7	2,232	>1	199,932	6
11. Miscellaneous	36,807	2	24,462	3	2,406	>1	63,675	2
12. Subtotal	471,644	30	240,885	23	128,611	24	841,140	26
13. Response to Federalists	12,765	1	14,353	1	7,602	1	34,720	1
14. Cheers	249,794	16	242,358	23	157,523	29	649,675	20
15. Total	1,596,268	100	1,064,114	100	544,437	100	3,204,819	100

Note: To arrive at the entries in this table, I summarized each essay in Kaminski and Saladino 1981ff. in sentences of units of meaning, counting the words allocated to each unit and multiplying this number by the number of printings, thus arriving at the "weighted words" of each summary sentence. Then I categorized the sentences into 178 categories of meaning (101 for Federalists and 77 for Antifederalists) and summed the weighted words of sentences in each category. In tables 4 and 5 I further combined the categories into 15 for Federalists and 11 for Antifederalists. For more detail on the construction of categories and a list of the 177 categories, see Riker 1991.

TABLE 5. Themes of the Antifederalist Campaign

Theme	Campaign Stage						Total	
	Before Pennsylvania Ratification		Pennsylvania Ratification to Massachusetts Ratification		After Massachusetts Ratification			
	Number of Words	Percentage of Stage Total	Number of Words	Percentage of Stage Total	Number of Words	Percentage of Stage Total	Number of Words	Percentage of Stage Total
1. Ad hominem	69,086	8	60,448	9	61,549	33	191,083	11
2. Tactics	119,651	13	21,343	3	17,380	9	158,374	9
3. Miscellaneous	17,686	2	16,018	3	—	—	33,704	2
4. Subtotal	206,423	23	97,809	15	78,929	42	383,161	22
Threats to liberty								
5. General	98,854	11	130,373	20	15,493	8	244,720	14
6. Civil liberty	140,018	16	53,481	8	57,696	31	251,195	15
7. From government structures	156,694	17	79,925	12	9,888	5	246,507	14
8. From federal powers	58,880	7	62,116	9	5,800	3	126,796	7
9. Subtotal	454,446	51	325,895	49	88,877	48	869,218	50
10. Consolidation	161,939	18	187,594	28	13,534	7	363,067	21
11. Positive positions	67,917	8	53,020	8	6,015	3	126,988	7
12. Total	890,725	100	664,318	100	187,391	100	1,742,434	100

Note: See note to table 4.

It is clear that the Antifederalists gave up on the theme of crisis. It was a difficult issue for them. In 1786–87, the delegates to the Annapolis Convention, the members of the state legislatures, especially the Virginia legislature, and finally the delegates to Congress had requested the states to send delegates to Philadelphia because of the widespread belief that the defects of the Articles had brought on, at least, a constitutional crisis. Proto-Federalists of course believed that the crisis was also economic, military, and even moral. By the acts selecting delegates, twelve state legislatures, all but Rhode Island, officially acknowledged the crisis. All the acts instructed the delegates to render the federal constitution "adequate to the exigencies" of union, but Virginia spoke of "extending the revision of our federal system to all its defects" and New Hampshire spoke of the "truly critical and alarming situation" (Farrand 1937, 3:559–86). Even Antifederalists often acknowledged the crisis. In Pennsylvania, the Seceding Assemblymen (*CC* 125), Old Whig (*CC* 202, 303), the Convention Minority (*CC* 353), and even—amazingly enough—Centinel (*CC* 202, 311) and Philadelphiensis (*CC* 438), in New York Brutus (*CC* 178) and Federal Farmer (*CC* 242), and elsewhere—again amazingly—Luther Martin (*CC* 425) and Columbian Patriot (Mercy Warren, *CC* 581) conceded that a crisis existed, although they often bracketed their concessions with remarks tending to minimize its significance.

With so much official and journalistic acknowledgment, it was extremely difficult for Antifederalists to deny crisis. Some of them attempted to do so: Centinel (*CC* 133), Federal Farmer (*CC* 242), the Pennsylvania Minority (*CC* 353)—all of whom also affirmed the crisis—Governor Clinton (*CC* 439), and others. Alfred (*CC* 345), writing in Oswald's *Philadelphia Independent Gazette,* composed the most elaborate denial, though not the most widely distributed one. He pointed out that European liberals praised U.S. liberty under the state constitutions, that exports were flourishing and living was cheap, and that the rich hinterland awaited exploration. He blamed "our misfortunes" on "manners" or "our attachment to . . . foreign luxuries" and explained away the difficulties with foreign debt by civil lists that "enormously exceeded what they formerly were prior to the late revolution." He did not defuse the foreign dangers, but Federal Farmer (*CC* 242, also Brutus, Junior, *CC* 239), among others, attempted to do so, saying "we are in a state of perfect peace."

The net effect of Antifederal ambivalence on crisis is summarized in table 6. Although net denials increased in the second period, they declined in the third, and, in any event, the absolute amount is tiny compared with the Federalists' emphasis of 39 percent or 27 percent. So it seems clear that, given the Antifederalists' concession, the Dominance Principle applies to the Federalists argument on crisis.

TABLE 6. Net Effect of Antifederal Denials of Crisis

	Stage 1		Stage 2		Stage 3		Total	
	Number of Words	Percentage	Number of Words	Percentage	Number of Words	Percentage	Number of Words	Percentage
Denials	13,569	1.5	13,447	2.0	805	0.4	27,871	1.6
Acknowledgments	10,495	1.0	4,498	0.6	232	0.1	15,225	0.8
Net denial	3,047	0.5	8,949	1.3[a]	573	0.3	12,579	0.7[a]

[a]Rounding variation.

Dominance in the Main Themes: Antifederalists and the Threat to Liberty from the Structure of Government

Turning to the Antifederalists' main theme of threats to liberty, the case is somewhat more complicated. While they emphasized the theme itself about the same amount in each period, they sharply varied the emphasis among subthemes—and the Federalists sharply varied their responses.

The Antifederalists' variation appears to be opportunistic and thus endogenously determined—as required in the Dominance and Dispersion Principles—by the events of the campaign itself. For example, part of the shifting is the decrease in the second period of attention given to the two main subthemes of the first period. These initially dominant subthemes were the threat to liberty in the structure of the proposed Constitution (17 percent in the first period) and the absence of a bill of rights (16 percent in the first period). Both these rhetorical lines are more or less obvious initial criticisms. However, in the second period, beginning with the Pennsylvania ratification, they emphasized themes that seem to derive from this very ratification. The Antifederalists thought the procedure for ratification was outrageously unfair, so they emphasized the potential for despotism. In the third period, which began soon after the Post Office changed its method of delivery in such a way that Antifederalist editors failed to receive newspapers from other states, they interpreted the delays as deliberate sabotage of their campaign material and concrete evidence of the potential for despotism. The Federalists both responded and failed to respond to these shifts in emphasis in ways that show the application of both the Dominance Principle and the Dispersion Principle.

Though the persistence of the Antifederalist emphasis on liberty reflects the Dominance Principle, the internal shifts in emphasis reflect the Dispersion Principle as well. Thus, from the first period to the second, there is a striking decline, as previously noted, in the emphasis on threats to liberty from the proposed governmental structure—from 17 percent of the volume in stage 1 to 12 percent in stage 2. A good part of that decline results from a standoff in stage 1, so that Antifederalists sought out other issues, entirely in keeping with the Dispersion Principle. In the transition from stage 2 to 3, the Antifederalists substantially gave up, dropping this theme from 12 percent of the volume in stage 2 to 6 percent in stage 3. They did, however, keep the issue of the federal judiciary, which, in fact, they preempted. The fact that, on this one issue, they followed the Dominance Principle seems to me to indicate that it was no accident that they followed the Dispersion Principle on the others. Of course, when one side abandons a contested issue, it is always possible for the other side to dominate it and that is what happened here.

In the theme of governmental structure, both sides initially wrote quite a

bit about five issues, which the Antifederalists wrote much less about in the second stage and abandoned entirely in the third:

1. that the proposed system would violate the principle of the separation of powers with the Federalist response that separation ensured liberty;
2. that the President would have too much power with the Federalist response that he should be energetic and yet restrained in the ways provided;
3. that the Senate would be too powerful with the response that its power would be shared;
4. that a unicameral legislature would be more liberal than a bicameral one (which came almost entirely from Centinel [*CC* 133], and was uniquely an issue in Pennsylvania because of its radically majoritarian unicameral legislature, much admired by the state Constitutionalists who became the Antifederalists, and much despised by the Republicans, who became the Federalists);
5. that Congress would be too small and would lack rotation and annual elections, with the Federalist response that Congress was structured to guarantee liberty.

The relative volume on these five issues is displayed in table 7. In reading this table, recall that Federalist volume is about double Antifederalist volume, so the expected ratio of Federalist to Antifederalist volume on an issue is 2.0, but, as previously, I believe a ratio of 1.0 indicates a standoff in obtaining the public's attention.

Table 7 reveals that, in the first period, the ratio is one or greater on the first three issues. While it is less than one on two other issues, it rises for these issues to greater than one in the second period. So by February, there is something of a standoff. Furthermore, on *all* these issues, the Antifederal volume falls by more than the expected amount. As shown in table 5, the total Antifederal volume falls by only one-fourth from stage 1 to stage 2, but on these five issues the Antifederal volume falls by much greater amounts, as shown in table 8.

It seems clear that Antifederal writers and editors were abandoning these apparent standoffs from mid-December on. On the other hand, the Federalists, whose total volume declined by one-third from stage 1 to stage 2 (see table 4), did not so clearly abandon the standoffs. They did abandon the issues of the presidency, Senate, and unicameral legislature, but, on the issue of the separation of powers, their volume declines only by the expected amount, and, on the issue of congressional structure, their volume actually rises. This presages what happened in the third stage, where the Antifederalists are entirely silent on all five issues and the Federalists increase their volume

TABLE 7. Ratios of Federalist to Antifederalist Volume on Five Issues of Liberty and Governmental Structure, by Stages

Issue	Stage 1			Stage 2			Stage 3			Total		
	Federalist Volume	Antifederalist Volume	Ratio	Federalist Volume	Antifederalist Volume	Ratio	Federalist Volume	Antifederalist Volume	Ratio	Federalist Volume	Antifederalist Volume	Ratio
Violation of the sep- aration of powers	36,367	23,915	1.52	24,410	11,962	2.04	12,561	0	∞	77,338	35,877	2.04
President too powerful	42,429	29,719	1.43	2,420	11,890	0.20	48,898	0	∞	93,747	41,609	2.25
Senate too powerful	12,578	12,477	1.00	0	3,836	0.00	11,811	0	∞	24,389	16,313	1.49
Unicameral legislature	9,470	16,600	0.57	1,630	1,218	1.34	8,433	0	∞	19,533	17,817	1.09
Congress poorly struc- tured	23,569	32,367	0.72	23,803	18,975	1.25	29,127	0	∞	76,499	51,342	1.48

mightily on four of the five. Of course, most of the Federalist increase is from Publius, but I do not believe it should be discounted simply for that reason. He could have muted his discussion of institutions, but he did not. Evidently he sensed the Federalist advantage. Thus, the Antifederalists, who initiated the issue of the structural threat to liberty, discovered a standoff and went on to other themes in accord with the Dispersion Principle, while Federalists, who gradually realized their advantage here, seized it in accord with the Dominance Principle.

The interpretation of the data in table 7 and five issues of structure and liberty could be duplicated on several other, lesser issues, but on the issue of the judiciary, another structural issue, the story is quite different. The Antifederalists dominated it. Their volume was much higher than Federalist volume in all three periods, as set forth in table 9. While Antifederal volume declined over time, its decline on this issue was less than would be expected from the decline in total Antifederal volume (see table 10). Furthermore, the Federal response is a whisper. Had my sample included Publius's discussionof the judiciary, Federal volume in the third period would have been larger, but not by any means large enough to declare a tie. So, on this one issue of structure, the debate clearly displays the Dominance Principle and this fact increases one's confidence in attribution of the Dispersion Principle on the other issues.

Why were the Antifederalists able to preempt the Federalists on the proposition that the federal judiciary, especially as empowered by the supremacy clause, would absorb and dominate state courts, causing injustice by the complexity of law and the remoteness of courts? Other structural issues were a standoff or actually dominated by Federalists, but not this one. Why?

While the federal government of the Articles had a legislature and a rudimentary executive, it had nothing like a judiciary. Citizens were already accustomed to some national legislation and they could easily imagine a new

TABLE 8. Decline in Antifederalist Volume for the Five Issues of Liberty and Governmental Structure

Issue	Volume		Decline	
	Stage 1	Stage 2	Volume	Percentage
Violation of the separation of powers	23,915	11,962	11,953	50
President too powerful	29,719	11,890	17,739	60
Senate too powerful	12,477	3,836	3,641	70
Unicameral legislature	16,600	1,218	15,382	93
Congress poorly structured	32,367	18,975	13,392	41

federal government with a legislature and an executive modeled on those of the states. Indeed, even if the Constitution had been rejected, the states would probably have enhanced federal powers to tax, legislate, and even execute because moderate Antifederalists seemed willing to accept these reforms. So probably neither side could win the dispute about the effects on liberty from the revised legislature and executive. But the Constitutional provisions for a judiciary centralized a heretofore exclusively local part of government. Furthermore, it was just the part that nationalists, eager to enforce the peace treaty, wanted to take out of the hands of local judges and juries, who had often been unwilling to enforce the payment of debts to British subjects or to restore improperly seized property. This Federalist predisposition made Antifederalists nervous, even after ratification. It is no accident, I believe, that the first structural feature of the Constitution to be fixed was the judiciary (Eleventh Amendment). The politically delicate nature of the judiciary explains why, in accord with the Dominance Principle, the Antifederalists continued to emphasize the judicial threat to liberty. Indeed the entire 9,888 words on threats from structure in stage 3 (see table 5, item 7) concern the judiciary. Conversely, in accord with the Dispersion Principle, the Antifederalists, faced with standoffs, changed the subject in all the other issues in the structural subtheme.

Dominance in the Main Theme: Antifederalists and the Threat to Liberty from Federal Powers

For the Antifederalist subtheme of the threat to liberty from federal powers (table 5, item 8), volume increased modestly (5 percent) from stage 1 to 2 (against an expected decline of 25 percent) and then from stage 2 to 3 it declined sharply (90 percent), far beyond expectations (71 percent). This is a quite different pattern from the issue of the threat to liberty from governmental structure. This difference deserves explanation.

In part, the issues of federal powers do display the same pattern as the issues of structure. The Antifederalist assertions that the powers of Congress

TABLE 9.   Ratios of Federalist to Antifederalist Volume on the Judiciary and Liberty

	Federalist Volume	Antifederalist Volume	Ratio
Stage 1	14,460	36,450	.40
Stage 2	4,253	28,489	.16
Stage 3	4,572	13,886	.33
Total	23,285	78,825	.30

were too broad and that the proposed government would increase taxes are similar to the arguments on structure and might have been classified with them. Since, however, the Federalist responses on federal powers are wholly tied into their assertions about crisis, it is impossible to calculate ratios of volume for the two sides. Still, on these two issues, Antifederalist volume declines 60 percent from stage 1 to 2 (against 25 percent expected) and 67 percent from stage 2 to stage 3 (about like the 71 percent expected). So the pattern is about the same as in table 7.

But when we look at other issues in this subtheme a quite different pattern emerges, one that combines features from tables 7 and 9. The Antifederalists interpreted the military clauses of the Constitution as providing for a standing army and the Federalists, on the whole, did not disagree. The Antifederalists argued heatedly that standing armies threatened liberty and that the Federalists' espousal revealed sinister intentions. The Federalists responded that standing armies were necessary and would be politically controlled. The ratios of volume on those issues are set forth in table 11.

The pattern in this table is odd. In stage 1 there is a clear standoff. One expects, therefore, that one or the other or both of the sides would have abandoned the issue in accord with the Dispersion Principle. Instead, both sides intensified their arguments (see table 12), the Federalists by 40 percent (when a decline of 33 percent was expected) and the Antifederalists by 29 percent (when a decline of 25 percent was expected). How can we explain this unanticipated behavior?

Conventionally in the United States, citizens despised the idea of standing armies and Antifederalists appropriated this emotion. Philadelphiensis prophesied that despotism would be supported by a standing army composed of "profligate idle ruffians," cruel to fellow citizens but "a body of mean cowards" when "facing a foreign foe" (*CC* 320). According to the Pennsylvania Minority, the framers knew "Congress under this constitution will not possess the confidence of the people" and so they "made a provision . . . for . . . a permanent STANDING ARMY" (*CC* 353). But Federalists thought that a standing army was also a good argument on their side. Publius, espe-

TABLE 10.   Decline in Antifederalist Volume on the Judiciary and Liberty

	Volume	Decline		Expected Percentage Decline
		Volume	Percentage	
Stage 1	36,450	—	—	—
Stage 2	28,489	7,691	22	25
Stage 3	13,886	14,603	51	72

cially, repeatedly argued for "national forces" necessary for the "common defense" (*CC* 352, 355, 366), and emphasized the dangers on borders with Britain, Spain, and Indians (*CC* 364). But so convinced were Antifederalists of the persuasiveness of their position that they rejoiced that Publius and others had been trapped. An editorialist in the Philadelphia *Freeman's Journal* (*CC* 409) crowed that "the last numbers of Publius have done still more" to defeat the Constitution in New York because his "attempts to prove the expediency of supporting a standing army in time of peace have been so futile, that even the friends of the new plan are offended with them" (see also Brutus, *CC* 455 and 475). But it seems that the Antifederalist writers and editors were probably wrong, because Federalists also increased their volume substantially almost as much as Antifederalists from stage 1 to stage 2.

This Antifederal misconception explains the odd pattern. In spite of the clear standoff in stage 1 (which should have warned both—but especially the weaker Antifederalists—to try another issue), the Antifederalists, ideologically disposed to believe it was persuasive, stepped up their volume by a huge amount. The Federalists responded appropriately. By the third stage, however, the Antifederalists had apparently shaken off their ideological blinders. So both sides knew they could not dominate. In belated accordance with the Dispersion Principle, therefore, both sides almost abandoned the issue, both cutting their volume by 90 percent or more, as shown in table 12.

Dominance of the Main Theme: Antifederalists and the Threat to Civil Liberty

Continuing the analysis of the Antifederalists' vision of Constitutional threats to liberty, the two remaining themes (items 5 and 6 of table 5) seem closely related. As the subtheme of threats to civil liberties (item 6) declines in stage 2, the theme of general threats to liberty (item 5) rises; then, in stage 3 the reverse movement occurs. How can this inverse relation between these two subthemes be explained?

It is almost entirely an artifact of my classification. The themes allocated

TABLE 11.   Ratios of Federalist to Antifederalist Volume
on Standing Armies

	Federalist Volume	Antifederalist Volume	Ratio
Stage 1	41,842	20,522	2.03
Stage 2	58,503	46,986	1.24
Stage 3	5,351	3,861	1.39
Total	105,696	71,369	1.48

TABLE 12. **Percentage Change in Federalist and Antifederalist Volume on Standing Armies**

	Stage 1 to Stage 2		Stage 2 to Stage 3	
	Federalist	Antifederalist	Federalist	Antifederalist
Actual change	+40	+29	−92	−90
Expected change	−33	−25	−49	−71

to item 5 are Antifederal claims that the Constitution endangers liberty by creating an aristocratic, despotic government. In stage 1, the illustration of this general claim is the absence of a bill of rights, which I allocated to item 6. In the next two stages, the Antifederalists opportunistically derived illustrations from the events of the campaign. Since I assigned the illustrations in stage 2 to item 5 and those in stage 3 to item 6, items 5 and 6 ought properly be combined for all three periods.

In stage 2, the Antifederalists drew their main illustration from the Pennsylvania campaign: (a) Federalist haste, which Antifederalists interpreted as evidence of the Federalists' despotic intentions, and (b) the large size of the United States, which the minority in Pennsylvania (*CC* 353), followed by Luther Martin (*CC* 425 and 502), Centinel (*CC* 453 and 501) and others, asserted would more readily admit despotism than would small, loosely confederated states.[10] Since these themes clearly involved claims of despotism, I allocated them to item 5. In stage 3, however, the Antifederalists drew their main evidence of the potential for despotism from the collapse of postal delivery, especially north of Philadelphia. Postmaster General Hazard changed the method of intercity newspaper delivery from the more expensive stagecoaches to cheaper postriders who, however, often sold or destroyed the papers. By February, most northern editors were frantic about the failure of deliveries that the Antifederalists blamed on the postmaster, who they interpreted as muzzling their campaign and the freedom of the press.

Viewing items 5 and 6 as closely related in content (and therefore as appropriately combined) reveals that the Dominance Principle is at work on these themes. Together, these items are by far the most important Antifederalist argument: In stage 1, they are 27 percent of the whole Antifederal campaign; in stage 2, they are 28 percent; and in stage 3, 39 percent. Note also that the ratio of Federalist to Antifederalist words is remarkably low. Instead

---

10. This theme was initially developed in stage 1 by New York writers (Cato III, *CC* 195; Federal Farmer, *CC* 242) but Pennsylvania writers greatly increased the volume and intensity of this theme in the next period.

of the expected ratio of 2.0, the actual ratios are those shown in table 13. The danger of despotism and the loss of civil liberties are thus a mostly unchallenged theme throughout the campaign, which is exactly an instance of the Dominance Principle at work.

A Psychological Explanation of the Dominance Principle and the Dispersion Principle

My examination of several concrete themes led to the construction of a model that, at a higher level of abstraction, suggested two principles of rhetorical behavior. Then a survey of the main themes of the two campaigns confirmed that, on the whole and despite some variation, rhetors acted on these principles. A question remains, however: What psychological theory explains why these principles describe what rhetors do? As I have repeatedly stressed, we possess very little theoretical knowledge about rhetoric, but one recent investigation by Lau, Smith, and Fiske (1991) does suggest a rationale for these principles in terms of the information-processing capacities of the audience.

The overall model for this investigation consists of an alternative space, outcome space, and mappings from the former to the latter. In my application, the alternatives are ratifying, ratifying conditionally (in several ways), and rejecting the Constitution. The outcomes are states of the world produced by various choices of alternatives. While the adversaries of 1787–88 agreed that the outcome of ratification was consolidation (and the outcome of rejection, the status quo), consolidation (and the status quo) had different possible interpretations or locations in the outcome space. Consolidation might mean a free, secure, and prosperous nation or an unfree, insecure, and impoverished one. Similarly, the meaning of the status quo might be a decline into anarchy or stabilization and growth. Which outcome was to be associated with each alternative was, of course, uncertain, so this was the subject of campaign presentations. Rhetors offer interpretations of the consequences of choices among alternatives, interpretations that are mappings of each alternative to an outcome. Auditors accept or reject these mappings as bases for their choices

TABLE 13.   Ratios of Federalist to Antifederalist Volume on Despotism and the Loss of Civil Liberties

	Federalist Volume	Antifederalist Volume	Ratio
Stage 1	56,722	238,872	.24
Stage 2	22,870	184,855	.12
Stage 3	15,735	73,189	.21
Total	95,327	496,916	.19

among alternatives. If auditors accept, they are said to be persuaded; otherwise not.

In this model, the rational rhetor seeks to offer interpretations persuasive to a majority of voters. That is, he or she seeks to offer believable reasons $\sigma_h x_j$ that his or her mapping from alternatives to outcomes is correct. So the crucial question of a rhetor's mapping is whether or not a goodly number of auditors accept it as correct. We want to know what is involved in auditors' acceptance of interpretations.

Lau, Smith, and Fiske (1991) offer an elegant answer based on their investigation of auditors' processing of the messages of an interpretation. They assume that auditors are persons with preexisting knowledge stored in memories and that this knowledge is organized in schemata that are used for processing interpretations. Auditors bring schemata—which I call *d*—into play by initially accepting or rejecting key features of interpretations through entry points or "chronically accessible constructs." These entry points may be key words (e.g., party, group, or class names), issue positions (e.g., a desire for security against anarchy or foreign war, an attachment to liberty, etc.), or simply catch words (e.g., representation, separation of powers, liberty, or anarchy).

In a brilliantly conceived and conducted experiment, they showed how the processing worked. They distinguished three cases.

1. Rhetors present a single interpretation, at least marginally acceptable to auditors.
2. Rhetors present two interpretations, both marginally acceptable to auditors.
3. Rhetors present two interpretations, only one of which is marginally acceptable to auditors.

In the experiment, a sample (nonrandom) of adult Pittsburgh citizens read arguments composed by the experimenters out of sentences from Pittsburgh newspapers, arguments about alternatives on potential local referenda on widely discussed public issues. The citizens then chose between the alternatives. The experimenters correctly predicted that, in case 1, the single interpretation and, in case 3, the single acceptable interpretation (but not the unacceptable one) would significantly affect the auditors' evaluations. In case 2, they correctly predicted that an interpretation would influence evaluations when its assertions about consequences of alternatives agreed with auditors' general political beliefs.

Applying the Lau-Smith-Fiske discoveries about auditors to the rhetors' use of the Dominance Principle, assume that rhetors on both sides recognize that, for a great majority of auditors, a pair of interpretations lies in case 3.

Then, rhetors offering the unacceptable interpretation know that their effort is wasted. Appropriately, therefore, they abandon the presentation of their interpretation. On the other hand, the rhetors offering the acceptable interpretation are effectively in case 1 and so they have a motive to continue the presentation of their interpretation. This pair of actions by rhetors on the two sides is summarized by the Dominance Principle. For rhetors who want to win, this rhetorical situation is a rational response, once they discover they are in case 3. So it is entirely to be expected that rhetors, given time to observe the consequences for auditors of the presentation of mappings, would preempt (or abandon) issues, just as happened in 1787–88.

Applying the Lau-Smith-Fiske discoveries about auditors to rhetors' use of the Dispersion Principle, as in case 2, both groups of rhetors offer marginally acceptable interpretations. The success or failure of presentations thus depends on auditors' general political beliefs, which are auditors' tastes in the outcome space. In real campaigns, as in 1787–88, regardless of whether the two sides are close together on an issue or very far apart, the rhetors still are uncertain about just how auditors and voters are distributed in the space. So it behooves rhetors looking for an advantage to seek out other issues with new interpretations that can lead them into case 3 and thence to case 1. Action so taken is, of course, exactly in accord with the Dispersion Principle.

This rationale for the Dispersion Principle seems at odds with the median voter theorem, which occupies such a large place in contemporary political science. The conflict is, I believe, more apparent than real. For one thing, the median voter theorem has no time element. Action is assumed to be simultaneous and instantaneous. In the world of campaigning, however, the situations of the campaigners change. They have different amounts and kinds of resources. They have different tolerances for stalemate and different opportunities to introduce new subjects. So, in the temporal world, they do not typically waste resources fighting out the issues in exactly the same locations. If they arrive at a point near the median on some issue, they probably do not, of course, abandon it. But they do decrease the resources they put into maintaining that position and they do divert resources to a search for new issues. Thus, both sides, having initially or not, as the case may be, staked out positions in accordance with the median voter theorem, undertake to find new issues and gradually and approximately together cease to emphasize their initial positions as they take new positions on new issues. Indeed, within a temporally extended campaign, one should probably not even expect initial position taking at the median because rhetors, if they expect their opponents to have as strong a case as their own, know they will ultimately abandon their argument and need not waste resources hunting for the median. Hence follows the Dispersion Principle. For another thing, the median voter theorem applies to one-dimensional space. But a campaign space is multidimensional. The

Dispersion Principle applies to a single dimension in this space. And there is no reason to expect a median location on a specific issue. Even if the outcome on the whole set of dimensions taken together is in some more-or-less central position in the space (e.g., the yolk [McKelvey 1986]), it can easily be that the outcome is quite far from the median on at least some of these dimensions. So there is no obvious conflict between the theorem and the principle.

REFERENCES

Farrand, Max, ed. 1937. *The Records of the Federal Convention of 1787.* 4 vols. New Haven: Yale University Press.

Jensen, Merrill, ed. 1976ff. *Ratification of the Constitution by the States.* Vols. 2–12 of *The Documentary History of the Ratification of the Constitution.* Madison: State Historical Society of Wisconsin.

Kaminski, John, and Gaspare Saladino, eds. 1981ff. *Commentaries on the Constitution: Public and Private.* 4 vols. Vols. 13–16 of *The Documentary History of the Ratification of the Constitution.* Madison: State Historical Society of Wisconsin.

Lau, Richard R., Richard Smith, and Susan T. Fiske. 1991. "Political Beliefs, Policy Interpretations, and Political Persuasion." *Journal of Politics* 53:644–75.

Main, Jackson T. [1961] 1973. *The Antifederalists: Critics of the Constitution 1781–88.* New York: Norton.

McKelvey, Richard. 1986. "Governing, Dominance, and Institution-Free Properties of Social Choice." *American Journal of Political Science* 30:911–34.

Riker, William H. 1962. *The Theory of Political Coalitions.* New Haven: Yale University Press.

Riker, William H. 1986. *The Art of Political Manipulation.* New Haven: Yale University Press.

Riker, William H. 1991. "Why Negative Campaigning is Rational." *Studies in American Political Development* 5:224–83.

Storing, Herbert J. 1981. *The Complete Anti Federalist.* 7 vols. Chicago: University of Chicago Press.

Part 2
The Origin of Issues

Domestic and International Imperatives in the Specification of Foreign Policy Objectives

Bruce Bueno de Mesquita and David Lalman

An important puzzle in international affairs concerns the origin of demands, disputes, and attendant threats. In this essay we pose two variations of a sequential game of international interactions. In one variant—the realpolitik version—demands exchanged between nations originate as an endogenous consequence of the international context within which interactions take place. In the second variant—the domestic version—international demands arise through the give and take of some unspecified domestic political process. Thus, in the former case, national foreign policy agendas are set by the context and structure of the international system. In the latter case, domestic institutions and the domestic political context fix the foreign policy agenda. In either context, international interactions take place within an anarchic international environment. Therefore, the process is modeled as a noncooperative game.

We begin by assuming that national governments are the central agents of policy implementation in international affairs. They, as the metaphorical embodiment of the general welfare, are the natural unit of analysis even for a theory, such as is proposed here, that is grounded in the axioms of individual rationality. From one viewpoint, foreign policy goals grow out of the political leadership's interest in advancing the welfare of the state within the international community unencumbered by considerations of domestic affairs. This is quite similar to Waltz's (1959) "third image," in which "The requirements of state action are . . . imposed by the circumstances in which all states exist" (160) so that "the peace strategy of any one country must depend on the peace or war strategies of all other countries" (222). The other outlook indicates that foreign policy goals grow out of the give and take of domestic politics, with all its prospects for generating problems of coherence in the aggregation of individual preferences. This second perspective is akin to Waltz's "second image," in which "foreign policy is a phase of domestic policy, an inescapable phase" (Waltz 1959, 80; quoting Charles Beard).

From the first perspective—the realist perspective—foreign policy leaders—professional diplomats if you will—select policy goals by examining the external constraints and opportunities that confront their nation. Where do the goals or preferences of these leaders come from? For the realist theorist the answer is that foreign policy goals are selected strictly *within* the foreign policy context, without regard for how this or that goal might advance one or another decision maker's domestic political agenda. According to this realist viewpoint, foreign policy leaders live in a rarified world of high politics that is responsive to external pulls and tugs but is inattentive to the low politics of domestic affairs (Kaplan 1957; Morgenthau 1973; Waltz 1979; Niou, Ordeshook, and Rose 1989). For the realist, the specific policies that a state pursues are structurally constrained by the nation's endowments of power, geography, alignments, and the like. The leader, then, is the conventional unitary actor selecting policy objectives with the constraints of the international environment firmly in mind and implementing strategies to maximize those chosen objectives. Domestic political pressures, especially in the form of costs for utilizing force, may constrain actions, and leaders may be punished *after the fact* for policies that clearly have failed (Denzau, Riker, and Shepsle 1985), but it is fundamentally the leader's understanding of *international* circumstances that dictates the selection of the state's tactical and strategic actions.

The second perspective is at the heart of arguments favoring a bureaucratic politics or interest-group point of view (Allison 1971; Bueno de Mesquita, Newman, and Rabushka 1985; Putnam 1988). Domestic constituencies—whether in a democratic or authoritarian society—express preferences. Some political participants, for instance, may seek to maximize the nation's external security by accommodating the demands of rivals, while others desire to expand military capabilities to maximize jobs in local defense industries. Some may try to promote protectionist trade barriers or, alternatively, a free-trade regime, or attempt to promote pacifist policies that guarantee no use of force or policies that expand the size of the defense budget for defensive purposes (but that also may be interpreted by rivals as reflecting aggressive intentions). Each such constituency is interested in influencing the policies pursued by the national leadership. The leadership, in turn, is dependent on those constituencies for its continuation in office and so wishes to meet, to the greatest extent possible, the desires of the constituents. At the same time, leaders must be conscious of the costs they will bear if their responsiveness to domestic pressures leads to foreign policy disasters. Furthermore, foreign policy leaders confront the additional, serious problem that the foreign policy goals of competing domestic groups may themselves be incompatible and irreconcilable.

Those who subscribe to a nonrealist, "liberal" point of view note that

domestic political processes may be dominated by bureaucratic infighting, interest-group competition, and a narrow pursuit of localized interests, even at the expense of secure or stable foreign relations. The domestic political process may be characterized by Condorcet's paradox, with the attendant prospects of chaos, structure-induced equilibria, or heresthetic manipulation. When cyclical social preferences exist—and they are more and more likely as the number of relevant choosers increases and/or the number of dimensions to the issues at hand increases—they may make nonsensical any notion of the pursuit of "the national interest" (Niemi and Weisberg 1968; Krasner 1978; Bueno de Mesquita 1981). Yet this does not mean that goals are not chosen and pursued. Indeed, it does not even mean that the relevant foreign policy elite *know* that a social intransitivity exists. The structure of the domestic political process in which goals surface may mask the existence of cycles.

The domestic fabric of decision making may induce a choice that is inferior in two senses. The selection process may have eliminated an alternative that was unanimously preferred over the option finally chosen, thereby implying that the actual decision was inferior from a domestic political standpoint. Furthermore, the selection process may have led to the elimination of an alternative that was preferred by domestic groups that *are* attentive to the foreign policy environment, thereby implying that the actual decision was inferior from a foreign policy standpoint. The domestic groups may even unanimously prefer an eliminated option over a chosen policy exactly because it *is* the choice that makes the most sense in the strictly foreign policy context. In that case, the unanimously preferred, but unchosen, alternative may be equivalent (or identical) to the goal that would have been pursued if such decisions were left up to the key foreign policy elite, as is the case in the realist view. Thus, even if domestic constituencies, like "realist" foreign policy elites, give priority to alternative goals as a function of *international* circumstances, the structure of *domestic* politics may still induce an outcome that is inferior from a foreign policy perspective (Ostrom and Job 1986; Gaubatz 1991; James and Oneal 1991; Morrow 1991).

Similar problems can arise without cycles, but rather just as a function of the rules used to aggregate preferences. The Borda count method, for instance, can yield different results than does a runoff system, which in turn can yield an entirely different policy choice than would arise if a plurality system were used. These differences in policy choices can arise even though preferences are held constant across rules of aggregation and even though there is a Condorcet winner (Riker 1982). Indeed, the political structure of decision making can sometimes determine policy choices or, at least, severely constrain the set of feasible outcomes. The domestic political process can—though it need not—turn aside a goal that would have been selected in a realist context.

A fundamental objective of our investigation, therefore, is to ascertain how well the empirical record matches deductions derived from a realist and domestic perspective. We will explore how these two points of view alter predictions, given that options on foreign policy actions are the same in both perspectives, but that the demands or proposals brought forward are different.

The Game

No two interactions in international politics are likely to be exactly the same. Yet there are essential features in the development of any relationship between states. These features relate to sequences of decisions that lead to friendly or hostile relations. To describe these essential features, the scaffolding from which foreign policies are built, we begin with the common assumption that each nation can be treated as a unitary actor. We distinguish between a strong unitary actor assumption and a weaker variant. In the strong version, a single decision maker is assumed to be responsible for selecting foreign policy goals for his or her nation, as well as being responsible for selecting the tactics and strategies by which the goals are implemented. In the weaker version, the unitary actor is only responsible for selecting tactics and strategies, while the domestic political process is assumed to foster the selection of goals. In the application of these unitary actor assumptions, then, we recognize that the metaphorical unitary actor is responsive to domestic political considerations as well as to calculations of support from its allies and support for its enemies from their allies (Altfeld and Bueno de Mesquita 1979; Siverson and King 1980; Iusi-Scarborough and Bueno de Mesquita 1988). We also recognize that this is a controversial assumption, both from the perspective of systemic theorists who discount the importance of individual states and from the perspective of those who investigate bureaucratic processes. One of us has defended the unitary actor assumption when studying phenomena that threaten a state's sovereignty elsewhere (Bueno de Mesquita 1981; Bueno de Mesquita, Silverson, and Woller 1992). Here we merely note that heads of governments bear direct costs for failed foreign policies that result in unsuccessful wars and reap direct benefits from successful military campaigns (Bueno de Mesquita, Silverson, and Woller 1992). There can be little doubt that national leaders have strong incentives to act *as if* their welfare and the welfare of the state are the same when sovereignty is at risk.

Any international interaction is assumed to arise in a context that provides one or another state with an opportunity to take the initiative in shaping relations, an initiative that may govern the future development of events. Each state shapes its relationship with each other state through the selection of strategies. States may, for example, make demands or not make demands. Leaders may elect to acquiesce to a rival's demands or they may choose to try

to negotiate over their differences. And, of course, leaders may choose to use force rather than capitulate to a rival's wishes.

Different combinations of strategies result in different political outcomes. If, for instance, two states exchange demands and each state uses force to try to accomplish its demanded goal, then a war ensues. If the interaction between two states involves no demands, then each has elected to live with the status quo. The selection of strategies is a function of the value states attach to alternative outcomes and the beliefs they hold regarding how their adversary will respond to their strategic decisions.

We assume that decision makers respond to circumstances by making the choice they believe maximizes their expected utility from that stage of the game onward. They cannot precommit themselves to a future course of action—in the largely anarchic system of international relations, no binding authority exists to enforce agreements against the participants' own will—but they can act in anticipation of their opponent's choices. That is, we assume subgame perfection in which forward-looking decision makers contemplate the consequences of their current strategic choices for an entire sequence of interactions (Selten 1975).

The state, which we call state A, that has the opportunity to initiate an interaction can choose to make a demand (D^A) or not make a demand ($\sim D^A$) of another state. The demand may be about anything. We are not concerned here with the specific content of prospective disputes so much as with the *process* by which interactions evolve.

Once state A makes its move, state B has the opportunity to select a course of action by making a demand or not. Using superscripts to name the actor selecting a strategy, we can say that if the initial sequence is $\sim D^A, \sim D^B$, then the outcome is the maintenance of the status quo. If the sequence is $D^A, \sim D^B$, then state B is said to acquiesce to state A's demand. Should state A forego the opportunity to initiate a demand and allow state B to initiate ($\sim D^A, D^B$), then state A has the opportunity to acquiesce to state B's demand ($\sim D^A, D^B, \sim d^A \rightarrow$ acquiescence to state B's demand) or to make a counterdemand ($\sim D^A, D^B, d^A \rightarrow$ crisis). Similarly, if the initial sequence of strategic choices were D^A, D^B then, by state A's second move, there is also a crisis. Failure by both parties to abide by the status quo and failure by either party to acquiesce to the other's demand results in a crisis (Powell 1987; Lalman 1988).

In a crisis, a state may choose to escalate the dispute further by using force or it can attempt to defuse the situation by offering to negotiate: abiding by the status quo ante is no longer an option (Lalman 1988). If there is an offer to negotiate, the rival can reciprocate by not using force or it can exploit the offer to bargain by attacking the rival itself. Anytime a state escalates a dispute by using force it can expect one of two responses by its adversary. The

adversary can capitulate to the attacker's demands, thereby cutting its battle-field losses, or the adversary can retaliate, escalating the dispute further so that it becomes a war.

The extensive form of the international interaction game is depicted in figure 1, with the crisis subgame highlighted by brackets. In the crisis sub-game, state A offers to negotiate by not initiating the use of force ($\sim F^A$) or state A escalates the dispute by using force to back up its demand (F^A). If state A elects to escalate the dispute, then state B must choose between capitulating to A's first strike ($F^A, \sim F^B$) or striking back by using force itself (F^A, F^B). In the latter case, the strategy sequence D^A, D^B, F^A, F^B results in a war initiated by state A.

Should state A elect to offer to negotiate ($\sim F^A$) at the outset of the crisis, then B's choices can lead to negotiations ($\sim F^A, \sim F^B$) or to escalation ($\sim F^A, F^B$). If state B selects the escalatory path, then state A must make a final strategic determination: to capitulate to B's enforcement of its demand ($\sim F^A, F^B, \sim f^A$) or to retaliate ($\sim F^A, F^B, f^A$), resulting in a war initiated by state B.

As is evident from figure 1, international interactions can culminate in the following eight different generic outcomes.

Status Quo	Acquiescence by state B to A's demand (Acq_B)
Acquiescence by state A to B's demand (Acq_A)	Negotiate (Neg)
Capitulation by state A (Cap_A)	Capitulation by state B (Cap_B)
War Initiated by state A (War_A)	War Initiated by state B (War_B)

The structure of the international interaction game establishes a sim-plified view of the foundations of all international relations, but it does not provide sufficient information to make positive statements about behavior. The game requires further elaboration in the form of assumptions that estab-lish the feasible range of preferences over the game's outcomes. The value national leaders associate with each of the game's outcomes, and, therefore, the set of admissible preferences over the outcomes, is determined in accor-dance with the following assumptions.

A1. The players choose the strategy with the greatest expected utility given that they are playing subgame perfect strategies.

A2. The ultimate change in welfare resulting from a war or from nego-tiations is not known with certainty. Hence, arriving at a war node or at negotiations yields an expected value, assessed according to the subjective probabilities of gaining welfare and the subjective

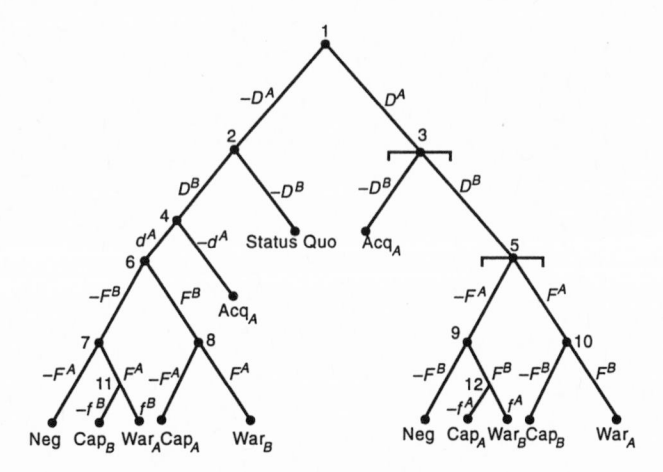

Fig. 1. International interaction game

probabilities of losing welfare. We restrict the probabilities in such lotteries: $0.0 < P < 1.0$ and we assume that the probability of gaining one's ends in negotiations is the same as in war. All probabilities are treated as subjective unless stated otherwise.

A3. In contrast to A2, capitulations result in changes in welfare that are certain rather than probabilistic. The capitulating state loses with certainty to the challenging state.

A4. All nations prefer to resolve their differences through negotiations rather than through war.

A5. Measured from the status quo (SQ) are $U^i(\Delta_i)$, the expected *gain* in utility by successfully obtaining one's demands, and $U^i(\Delta_j)$, the expected *loss* in utility by acceding to the adversary's demands. The value of these terms is restricted such that $U^i(\Delta_j) < U^i(SQ) < U^i(\Delta^i)$.

A6. Each outcome has a set of potential benefits and/or costs appropriately associated with it. We make restrictions on the various costs such that: α, τ, γ, $\varphi > 0$; and $\tau > \alpha$. $\alpha_i(1 - P^i)$ is the expected cost in lost life and property for nation i associated with fighting *away* from i's home territory; $\tau_i(1 - P^i)$ is the cost in lost life and property that i expects if it fights at home as the *target* of an attack; $\gamma_i(1 - P^i)$ is the cost in life, property, and lost face or credibility from absorbing a first strike to which the attacked party *gives in;* and $\varphi_i(P^i)$ is the domestic political cost (separate from life and property) associated with *using force* rather than diplomacy to try to resolve differences.

A7a. The Realpolitik Variant. The magnitude of i's demand ($U^i[\Delta_i]$), if any, is determined by i so as to maximize i's expected utility within the international context, without regard for the wishes or objectives of domestic political constituencies; or

A7b. The Domestic Variant. The magnitude of i's demand ($U^i[\Delta_i]$), if any, is determined by the domestic political process in i. That process is determined by internal political rules, procedures, norms, and considerations and may or may not be attentive to foreign policy considerations.

A detailed explication and justification of each assumption is contained in Bueno de Mesquita and Lalman 1992. These assumptions imply restrictions on the order in which outcomes can feasibly be preferred. Table 1 shows a summary of those restrictions.

Implications

Possible Equilibria with Perfect Information: The Realpolitik Variant

In the realpolitik interpretation of international interactions, demands are selected to maximize expected utility within the game without regard for external pressures to make alternative demands. The magnitude of any demand is, therefore, endogenous to the structure of the game. This means that demands, like actions, are chosen on the basis of a backward induction starting at the end of the game and working up to the very first move. Actor A

TABLE 1.   Possible Preference Rankings for Nation i on the Outcomes of the Game

Outcome	Ordinal Restrictions on Orderings	Possible Positions in Preference Order
SQ	$> \text{Acq}_i, \text{Cap}_i$	7-3
Acq_j	$>$ all other outcomes	8
Acq_i	$> \text{Cap}_i$	5-2
Neg	$> \text{Acq}_i, \text{Cap}_i, \text{War}_i, \text{War}_j$	7-5
Cap_j	$> \text{War}_i, \text{War}_j$	7-3
War_i	$> \text{War}_j$	5-2
Cap_i	—	4-1
War_j	—	4-1

Note: 8 is the highest ranking and 1 is the lowest.

will make a demand only if doing so yields a higher expected utility at the end of the game than is anticipated if no demand is made. And if actor A makes a demand, actor B will make a counterdemand only if doing so produces a higher expected utility than acquiescing to A's demand. Looking down the game tree, then, we can determine the size of any demands made by actors A and B if they are fully informed and if the realpolitik version of the game is germane.[1]

If actor A makes a demand, how large will it be? Actor A knows that the expected utility from a negotiation is superior for actor B to acquiescence by B to A. Therefore, actor A knows that if B can steer A toward negotiations, then there *must* be a counterdemand for B that yields B greater expected utility than will result from acquiescence. Both actors A and B have an interest in steering one another toward a terminal node that maximizes the relevant actor's expected utility. Actor B can maneuver the situation to encourage actor A to negotiate if A makes an initial demand. This generally—though not always—places actor A in a position that encourages it to make a very large initial demand.[2]

Because actor A knows that a fully informed B always has a counterdemand that improves B's welfare relative to acquiescing, A can anticipate that the crisis subgame that starts at node 5 will be reached if A makes a demand. If actor A makes a demand, then, it must pick a demand that maximizes its expected utility in the crisis subgame. By the assumptions already stated, it is known that the best that can happen to actor A in the crisis subgame is either a negotiated resolution of the dispute or a capitulation by B. It is common knowledge, then, that actor A will pursue the attainment of one of these outcomes *if* A makes a demand. Actor B strictly prefers a negotiated settlement to a situation in which it is compelled to capitulate to A. Therefore, B's counterdemand will be chosen to ensure that A's utility for negotiations is at least as large as its utility for compelling B to capitulate. Given this realization, actor A must pick a demand that will lead B to choose negotiations over the use of force if A makes a demand and offers to negotiate. What do these various restrictions look like and how do their feasible combinations affect the possible equilibria for the realpolitik variant of the game? We answer this question by stating the main realpolitik proposition that results under full information conditions in the international interaction game. A proof of the proposition can be found in Bueno de Mesquita and Lalman 1992.

---

1. Note that we assume that once a demand is made it is of fixed magnitude for the duration of the game, although actors A and B are each prepared to settle for less than their demand at the negotiation stage.

2. For a discussion of the conditions under which actor A is constrained in its choice of demands, see Bueno de Mesquita and Lalman 1992.

Realpolitik Negotiation/Status Quo Proposition. Under full information conditions and with demands being endogenous to the international interaction game, only negotiations or the status quo can be equilibrium outcomes of the realpolitik variant of the international interaction game.

The first realpolitik proposition suggests a very stable world under full information conditions. Only negotiations or the status quo prevail. These implications are similar, though not identical, to the system-stability and resource-instability results derived by Niou, Ordeshook, and Rose (1989). In our realpolitik game, resources or valued goods may be exchanged through negotiations, or the system may remain fixed through the maintenance of the status quo, but other outcomes are precluded under full information conditions. The proposition suggests several possible empirical tests. Using the measurement procedures described in detail in Bueno de Mesquita and Lalman 1992, we now enumerate and perform these tests.[3]

According to the proposition, only negotiation or the status quo can be the outcome of an international interaction if demands are endogenous to the international context and there is full information. This implies that, on average, as uncertainty diminishes, the likelihood of negotiation or the status quo should increase if the realpolitik variant of the game is an accurate description of behavior. The first test compares the frequency of negotiation or status quo outcomes in Europe between 1816 and 1970 to the degree of uncertainty. Negotiations are identified within the militarized international dispute data set of Gochman and Maoz, while dyads that maintained the status quo are a representative sample of randomly paired European nations that did not engage each other in any form of dispute during the year in question. Uncertainty is assessed as the within-year variance across the European states in their propensity to take risks (Bueno de Mesquita and Lalman 1986; Morrow 1987). The association between these variables is estimated with a logit analysis in which the dependent variable (Neg/SQ) is coded as 1.0 if the outcome was the status quo or a negotiation, and is coded as zero otherwise. The expectation for the logit analysis is that uncertainty is inversely associated with the dependent variable. Yet this is *not* the case. Rather, the weak association between Neg/SQ and uncertainty is positive, indicating that there is some tendency for the incidence of the predicted outcomes to rise as uncertainty

---

3. All indicators use only information that was readily available to the decision makers at the time they made their choices. No ex-post information is reflected in the estimation of the independent variables. All of the indicators are, of course, necessarily crude and coarse. Therefore, all tests reported here are concerned primarily with the central tendency of the data. Tests of statistical significance provide a helpful heuristic for evaluating the approximate strength of association.

increases. This calls into question the realpolitik version of the game in which Neg/SQ would always be satisfied when information was complete, with the likelihood of mistakenly arriving at some other outcome increasing as incomplete information leads to the mistaken selection of demands and counterdemands. Our test result is

$$\text{Neg/SQ} = -.660 + 0.806 \text{ Uncertainty}$$

$$\chi^2 = 1.69 \qquad p \leq .193 \qquad N = 686.$$

On the strength of this and other tests not reported here (but see Bueno de Mesquita and Lalman 1992), we conclude that the first realpolitik proposition is not supported by the evidence.

War, Acquiescence, and the Realpolitik Variant

Perhaps the doubts cast on the realpolitik version of the game are offset by successful predictions about behaviors other than negotiation or the status quo. In this section, we turn to two additional propositions implied by the development of the first realpolitik proposition. These pertain to acquiescence by actors A or B and to certain characteristics of war.

Realpolitik Acquiescence Impossibility Proposition. If demands are endogenous to the international context of the international interaction game, then, regardless of information conditions, neither actor A nor actor B ever acquiesces.

The intuition behind this proposition is that the first proposition establishes that, for any demand made by actor A, B has a counterdemand such that $U^A(\text{Neg}) \geq U^A(\text{Cap}_B)$ and for any demand made by B, A has a counterdemand such that $U^B(\text{Neg}) \geq U^B(\text{Cap}_A)$. Regardless of A's or B's belief about the other player, when confronted with an initial demand, each actor believes it has an appropriate counterdemand that will induce negotiations. Negotiation is strictly preferred by actor B to its acquiescence to A just as actor A strictly prefers to negotiate rather than acquiesce to B. Therefore, under the realpolitik variant in which demands are endogenous to the international setting, neither A nor B ever has an incentive to acquiesce to the rival.

This implication of the realpolitik version of the game, like the implications of the first proposition, does not withstand empirical scrutiny. Of the 707 observations in the data set, 101 represent acquiescence by B and 8 involve acquiescence by A. As these conditions can never arise under the realpolitik variant of the game, regardless of uncertainty or misperception, the existence

of 109 such cases is strong evidence that the realist perspective of the proposed game structure is empirically trivial or false. Indeed, this is particularly strong evidence because the realist perspective implies that acquiescence is *impossible* under any and all circumstances of the game. Thus, the only way to explain the incidence of even one acquiescence is that such cases are miscoded. All 109 cases would have to have been, in actuality, some other terminal event of the game.

> *Realpolitik War Proposition.* If actor B anticipates greater costs from a war begun by actor A than from capitulating to A, then B's subjective estimate of its probability of success in war must be greater than or equal to 0.5 for War$_A$ to arise as the equilibrium outcome in the realpolitik version of the game.[4] Proof of this proposition can be found in Bueno de Mesquita and Lalman 1992.

The war proposition and a companion condition for War$_B$ replicates a well-known realist hypothesis: that a perceived balance of power (or the misperception that one's own side is weaker than the rival's side) tends to promote peace, while war tends to follow when each side to a dispute believes its chances for success are greater than 50-50. Indeed, this is virtually identical to a hypothesis put forward by Blainey (1973). That this hypothesis follows from the realpolitik variant of the game encourages the belief that the game captures central features of the realist perspective. We provide here a preliminary test of this central realist hypothesis.

We define two dependent variables, WAR and BIGWAR, to be all of those cases of instances of reciprocated, state-directed violence that involved at least some fatalities between European states from 1816 to 1970 or that satisfied the Singer and Small (1972) criteria for an interstate war, respectively. WAR, then, includes events that did not meet the commonly used Correlates of War Project fatality threshold of at least 1,000 killed, while BIGWAR does satisfy this criterion. Using the operational definitions of WAR and BIGWAR and the measure of B's subjective estimate of its probability of success delineated in Bueno de Mesquita and Lalman 1986 and 1992, we display simple cross-tabulations of the incidence of war in relation to the frequency with which P^B is or is not greater than or equal to 0.5 in tables 2 and 3. If the proposition is supported empirically, then all (or nearly all, given measurement error) cases that became wars should have arisen when $P^B \geq$

---

4. Although our assumptions do not require that $\tau_B \geq \gamma_B$, we believe that this is the typical circumstance in reality. This condition states that the expected costs in lost life, credibility, and property from sustaining an unreciprocated first strike are generally smaller than or equal to the same costs associated with absorbing a first strike and then fighting back.

0.5, although meeting this requirement does not preclude the possibility of an outcome other than war.[5]

Neither table reflects a significant association, measured in terms of Yule's Q (a measure of one-way association) or in terms of χ^2. Thus, this most conventional realist proposition derived from the realpolitik version of the game also is not supported by the empirical record.

We have presented three critical realist propositions and failed to find support for any of them. Perhaps the general structure of the international interaction game is not a useful vehicle for investigating international affairs. Or, perhaps, the realpolitik variant of the game, with its reliance on the assumption that demands are endogenous to the international setting, does not capture an essential feature of reality. If the former explanation is correct, then the domestic variant of the game will also fail to produce propositions that prove empirically informative. If the latter explanation is correct and the domestic assumption that foreign policy demands are endogenous to a significant degree to the domestic political setting is correct, then we should expect to find meaningful implications from that version of the game. We turn now to the central full information propositions of the international interaction game in its domestic version.

Possible Equilibria with Perfect Information: The Domestic Variant

The Possibility of War with Perfect Information
The first domestic proposition shows that war is a possible equilibrium outcome of the game of international interactions under the restrictions placed on the preference orders described earlier (and including A7b, but not A7a).

> *Domestic Basic War Proposition.* With perfect information, War_A is a pure strategy equilibrium outcome if and only if we add to the restrictions on the preference orders already delineated (including A7b, but not A7a) that for actor A: $Cap_A > War_B$, $War_A > Acq_A$ and for actor B: $Cap_A > Neg$, $War_A > Acq_B$.

The proposition is proven in Bueno de Mesquita and Lalman 1991 by a simple backward induction. The proposition makes clear that if the magnitude of demands is not endogenous to the international interaction, then misperceptions of an adversary's intentions or an adversary's available options are not necessary to obtain war in equilibrium.

The puzzle of wars between nations is not a simple one. It is not neces-

---

5. We are only able to observe War_A with our data set and not War_B.

TABLE 2. WAR and P^B

	$P^B \geq 0.5$	$P^B < 0.5$
No WAR	290	228
WAR	107	82

Note: $\chi^2 = .022$; $p \leq .881$, n.s.; Yule's $Q = -0.013$, n.s.

sarily escapable by merely finding mechanisms to reveal to the players the precise values held by their antagonists. We see that mistaken beliefs or misperceptions need not reside within this game structure in order to obtain war in equilibrium. It is possible, of course, that the mistaken beliefs could reside in some supergame (such as the prior domestic political game that produces a choice of national foreign policy objectives) of which this already fairly large game is only a part. That is, that some larger game with the structure suggested here as a subgame would not produce war as an equilibrium, because the players would not play out a subgame resulting in war. Then, perhaps, misperceptions would be required to obtain war. But notice that such misperceptions as these are becoming remote from the event, and are stretching the notion of misperceptions (as generally understood by students of war) quite far.

Consider still further the preferences of the decision makers in order to see whether their preferences are intuitively reasonable. Is it difficult to imagine national leaders holding such preferences? Let us begin with actor A, the party initiating the war. While actor A is unwilling to acquiesce rather than fight a war it initiates, and as such is not such a pacifist as to forswear all violence ($War_A > Acq_A$), actor A is also unwilling or unprepared to retaliate against an initial use of force by B ($Cap_A > War_B$). Actor A, however, is confronted by an adversary who seems to hold a first strike advantage in that if B were to use force first, A would capitulate. Actor B, while fairly desirous of negotiating, prefers still more than negotiating to take advantage of the opponent and force a capitulation by actor A if given the chance.

TABLE 3. BIGWAR and P^B

	$P^B \geq 0.5$	$P^B < 0.5$
No BIGWAR	345	273
BIGWAR	52	37

Note: $\chi^2 = .214$; $p \leq .644$, n.s.; Yule's $Q = -0.053$, n.s.

What we have here is a failure by actor A to deter. Actor A's inability or unwillingness to resist the initial use of force by actor B gives B an incentive to initiate force. Should actor B not be the type that would capitalize on a capitulation by actor A, then A need not fear B's actions. But there are many potential opponents with different value systems. There are those who would exploit the opportunity to appropriate another's goods. Taken from an Arab perspective, this ordering of preferences may be a reasonable characterization of relations and expectations between the Arab states and Israel. Negotiation is difficult to attain because the Arab states fear exploitation by Israel if they offer to negotiate. They are ill-prepared to retaliate effectively if attacked by Israel's superior air and ground forces. Thus they live much of the time uncomfortably with the status quo, tacitly acquiescing to Israel's existence, or they strike first, seeking whatever advantage can be gained from seizing the initiative.

The first domestic proposition raises a troubling and, to some, surprising observation about international relations. This first result of the domestic variant of the international interaction game, however, may be a mere quirk of the structure proposed here, rather than a germane feature of international affairs. Thus far, our assessment of the realpolitik version of the game suggests that it is not an empirically useful representation of international affairs. The degree to which the domestic basic war proposition is an important starting point for evaluating war depends, consequently, upon an assessment of *its* empirical relevance. Therefore, we propose the following empirical evaluation.

We again use two dependent variables: WAR and BIGWAR. Using the operational procedures elaborated in Bueno de Mesquita and Lalman 1992, we estimate three independent variables: War_A, War_A*Uncertainty, and Uncertainty. War_A is a dummy variable that equals 1.0 if the conditions of the proposition are satisfied by our operational criteria and otherwise is coded as a zero.[6] Uncertainty is evaluated in terms of the variance in risk-taking propensities across European nations in each year (as discussed earlier). The interaction term and the Uncertainty variable are included to evaluate the effects of full information conditions on the prospects of war. Since the conditions of the proposition are necessary and sufficient for war under full information conditions, we expect War_A to be positively associated with the likelihood of

---

6. In actuality we are unable to distinguish the expected utility for actor A (or B) of the outcomes War_A and War_B. This means that we can only assess three of the four conditions of the theorem. We cannot assess whether $Cap_A > War_B$ for actor A. Therefore, the test is weakened beyond the already crude nature of many of the indicators. Consequently, in this, as in all other empirical tests, we are concerned primarily with the central tendency of the theory to provide a significant accounting of relationships.

war, the interaction term to be negatively associated with the risk of war, and Uncertainty by itself to be positively associated with the danger of war.

That War_A should be positively associated with the incidence of war follows directly from the proposition. Since the interaction term War_A*Uncertainty equals zero under full information conditions, it evaluates the impact of Uncertainty when the proposition's noninformational conditions are met but uncertainty is present. Since the proposition theoretically guarantees war when its conditions are met and there is no uncertainty, the risk of war can *only* decline as uncertainty enters the picture with the conditions otherwise being satisfied. When, however, the conditions are *not* met, then Uncertainty can *increase* the likelihood that war will result as a mistaken consequence of someone's misjudgment, misperception, or miscalculation. Therefore, the Uncertainty variable by itself should be positively associated with the danger of war while the interaction term should be negatively associated with war.

The first domestic proposition is evaluated through the use of logit analysis. As shown in table 4, the proposition is supported by the historical record. One-tailed significance levels are reported beneath the logit coefficients for their heuristic value. All signs are in the anticipated direction, with modest significance levels for the weaker WAR variable and substantial significance in the case of BIGWARs.

The first domestic proposition indicates that decision makers have a basis for fearing even those nations that are not particularly belligerent. It is a direct contradiction of the first realpolitik proposition that indicates war cannot arise under full information conditions. The evidence supports the domestic perspective over the realist outlook. Hobbes warns, perhaps correctly, that *homo homini lupus* (all men are wolves), but one need not be surrounded by wolves to see the need to prepare defenses in a world in which attentiveness to domestic affairs helps shape foreign policy objectives.

TABLE 4. Logit Results for Tests of the Basic War Theorem

Variable	WAR		BIGWAR	
	Coefficient	p	Coefficient	p
Constant	-2.29	.000	-2.93	.000
War_A	0.58	.094	0.95	.027
War_A*Uncertainty	-2.48	.065	-5.05	.004
Uncertainty	3.37	.001	4.69	.000
χ^2	11.10		19.44	
p	.015		.000	
N	625		686	

The Impossibility of Obtaining Certain Outcomes in
Pure Strategies

Domestic Secondary War Proposition. A war initiated by actor B is not a complete information equilibrium in pure strategies, given the assumptions of the domestic version of the game.

Proof. War$_B$ arises as a possible terminal event of the game in two distinct places. We show that neither of these terminal nodes can be reached in the game under the conditions of full information (and strict preferences).

The War$_B$ outcome contained in the subgame at node 9 cannot survive as an outcome. While it is possible that actor A prefers War$_B$ to Cap$_A$ at node 12 and chooses f^A, according to assumption A4, actor B prefers negotiations to War$_B$. Thus, actor B would choose $\sim F^B$ at node 9.

It is possible that the other War$_B$ could survive as far up as node 2 if it is an equilibrium outcome at node 6 and actor A prefers it to acquiescing at node 4 and B prefers it to the status quo. For the War$_B$ outcome contained in the subgame at node 8 to survive as an equilibrium at node 6, several conditions would have to be met. At node 8, actor A must prefer War$_B$ to Cap$_A$. At node 6, a choice by B of War$_B$ implies that, at node 11, B prefers Cap$_B$ to War$_A$. Otherwise, according to assumption A4, A would choose to negotiate at node 7. This, in turn, would induce a choice at node 6 for negotiation over War$_B$. So the conditions for War$_B$ at node 6 are that actor A prefer War$_B$ to Cap$_A$ and that B prefer Cap$_B$ to War$_A$. On the other hand, these preferences induce negotiations in the crisis subgame at node 5. At node 3, the only outcomes would be either Acq$_B$ (which, by assumption A5, is better for actor A than negotiations) or negotiations. Therefore, actor A can guarantee itself at least the value of negotiations by playing the subgame at node 3. By assumption A4, negotiations are preferred over War$_B$, removing it as an equilibrium outcome. Neither of the paths to a war initiated by actor B can be supported in equilibrium under full information conditions.∎

Domestic Basic Capitulation Proposition. Capitulation is not a pure strategy equilibrium outcome for fully informed players.

Proof. Begin with capitulation by actor A. It is possible for Cap$_A$ to survive as an outcome to the subgame at node 3, but actor A will not choose to play this subgame. Actor A can guarantee itself at least the value of its own acquiescence in the subgame at node 2. By choosing not

to make a demand, $\sim D^A$, actor A would face the possibilities that B responds either by making a demand or by not making a demand upon A. If actor B were to choose $\sim D^B$, the status quo would be preserved, which A prefers over capitulating. Even if actor B were to make a counter demand, A has the opportunity to acquiesce at node 4. Players would rather acquiesce to demands peacefully than have to capitulate after the use of force and suffer the additional costs from an attack. If the other Cap_A were to be the equilibrium outcome to the crisis subgame at node 6, actor A, disliking capitulation, can escape this outcome at node 4 by acquiescing. Thus, actor A has sufficient control of the game to avoid being forced to capitulate.

Capitulation by actor B also does not occur as a pure strategy outcome. If actor B understands the outcome to the crisis subgame at node 5 to be Cap_B, then, at node 3, B would choose $\sim D^B$ and acquiesce to A's demand. The other capitulation by actor B can be an outcome as far as node 4. At node 2, actor B can prevent being forced to capitulate by choosing $\sim D^B$ at node 2. By making no demand upon actor A at node 2, B terminates the game and secures the value of the status quo, which B prefers to capitulating (assumptions A5 and A6). Actor B also has sufficient control of the game to avoid its own capitulation. ■

Conditions for Pure Strategy Equilibria Leading to the Other Terminal Nodes

Conditions for Acquiescence by A

Acquiescence by A Proposition. The necessary and sufficient conditions with full information, assumption A7b (the domestic variant), and strict preferences for an acquiescence by actor A are the same as in the Basic War theorem except that for A, $Acq_A > War_A$ or Cap_A is the subgame perfect equilibrium outcome in the crisis subgames.

The proof, presented in Bueno de Mesquita and Lalman 1992, is a straightforward backward induction first upholding the conditions of the proposition to show that they are sufficient, and then relaxing them one at a time to show that they are necessary.

Acquiescence by B Proposition. Under full information conditions, assumption A7b (i.e., the domestic variant), and with strict preferences, Acq_B is a full information equilibrium outcome of the international interaction game if and only if, for actor A, $Cap_B > War_B$ and $War_A >$

Acq_A, while, for actor B, Cap_B > Neg and Acq_B > War_A or Cap_B is the equilibrium outcome of the crisis subgame.

Again, the proof is in Bueno de Mesquita and Lalman 1992. There is sufficient data to test this proposition against the record of European history during the past nearly two centuries. To do so, we define a dummy variable, *BACQ*, that satisfies the conditions of the Acq_B proposition. We define a dependent variable, ACQ_B, that equals 1.0 if actor A made a demand and B did not respond and the incident ended without fatalities according to the Gochman and Maoz coding criteria. Uncertainty is again used as a control variable, although the interaction between *BACQ* and Uncertainty is dropped because of collinearity. According to the proposition, *BACQ* should be positively associated with actual acquiescence and Uncertainty should be negatively associated with the dependent variable. The results are reported as a logit analysis, with one-tailed significance levels reported below the coefficients.

$$ACQ_B = -1.48 + 0.47\ BACQ - 2.32\ \text{Uncertainty}$$
$$(.00)\quad (.02)\qquad\qquad (.01)$$

$$\chi^2 = 12.57 \qquad p < .01 \qquad N = 686.$$

Given the difficulties inherent in measuring the concepts here, the logit analysis provides strong encouragement for the domestic variant of the game. Acquiescence by actor B is substantially more likely when the conditions of the proposition are approximated in reality. What is more, the evidence for the proposition represents a contradiction of the realpolitik acquiescence proposition that states that acquiescence cannot arise under *any* circumstances in the realist interpretation of the game.

Conditions for the Status Quo
In order to reach the status quo, actor A must initiate the game by making no demand and actor B must respond by making no demand. The necessary and sufficient full information conditions for the status quo to be the outcome in equilibrium are stated as a proposition and then evaluated empirically.

Domestic Basic Status Quo Proposition. With complete information and domestic assumption A7b, the status quo is the equilibrium outcome of the game if and only if actor A prefers the status quo to negotiation and A and B satisfy one of the following four cases of additional restrictions on their preferences over outcomes.

Case 1. A: $Cap_A > War_B$;
        B: $War_A > Cap_B$, Neg $> Cap_A$, SQ $>$ Neg.
Case 2. A: Neg $> Cap_B$, $Cap_A > War_B$;
        B: $Cap_B > War_A$, Neg $> Cap_A$, SQ $>$ Neg.
Case 3. A: $War_B > Cap_A$;
        B: $War_A > Cap_B$, SQ $>$ Neg.
Case 4. A: Neg $> Cap_B$, $War_B > Cap_A$;
        B: $Cap_B > War_A$, SQ $>$ Neg.

Once again, the lengthy proof is in Bueno de Mesquita and Lalman 1992.

Since there are four different sets of restrictions and numerous pairs of complete orderings can meet any one of them, there are many ways to arrive at the status quo. Indeed, with uniformly distributed preferences, there are 232 possible pairings of preference orders (or 8.6 percent of all possible orderings on outcomes) that lead to the status quo. But, as with each other proposition thus far, we must wonder whether these particular conditions, when approximated in the empirical world, disproportionately increase the prospect that nations will abide by the status quo. We turn to an empirical assessment of the Basic Status Quo theorem to evaluate its usefulness.

We define a dummy variable, SQ, coded 1.0 if, by the operational procedures delineated in Bueno de Mesquita and Lalman 1992, actor A preferred the status quo to negotiation and A and B satisfied one of the four cases of the theorem that support the status quo as the equilibrium outcome. Otherwise, SQ is coded as zero. Likewise, we define a dependent variable, STATUS QUO, that is coded as 1.0 if actors A and B made no demands on each other, and coded zero otherwise. That is, STATUS QUO is coded 1.0 for the subset of cases in the data set that represents randomly paired European nations in years that they did not engage each other in an event in which at least one of them made a demand of the other accompanied by a threat.

$$STATUS\ QUO = -0.74 + 0.64SQ$$

$$\chi^2 = 5.76 \qquad p < .016 \qquad N = 707.$$

Again, the evidence supports the domestic version of the game.

Negotiation as an Equilibrium

We have described the conditions on the preference orders of the players that lead to outcomes of the game other than negotiation. Any pairing of orderings not meeting one of these sets of restrictions will lead the players to negotiate

their differences rather than settle them in some other way. Whether actual behavior is consistent with the expectations of the game, as with each other outcome that is feasible under full information conditions, is an empirical question. Here we offer tests of the predictions regarding the advent of negotiation. In one test we define a dummy variable, PredNeg, which is coded 1.0 when the conditions of the game lead to the prediction that an interaction will culminate in negotiations, and is coded zero otherwise. We undertake a logit analysis with the dependent variable, NEG, which equals 1.0 when the interaction did lead to negotiations, and equals zero otherwise. The results of the first logit analysis are:

$$NEG = -3.17 + 1.14PredNeg$$

$$\chi^2 = 7.21 \qquad p < .007 \qquad N = 707.$$

In a second test, we conduct a logit analysis that relates NEG to the previously specified dummy variables $BAcq$, War_A, and SQ, as well as a dummy variable coded 1.0 if the conditions for an acquiescence by actor A are satisfied. This independent variable is called $AAcq$. Since these four variables each predict an event other than negotiations as the equilibrium outcome under conditions of full information, each should be inversely related to the likelihood that an interaction culminates in a negotiated settlement.

The test results, along with one-tailed assessments of statistical significance, are shown in table 5.

Once again, the direct evaluation of the conditions identified in the game provides substantial support for the belief that the domestic version of the

TABLE 5.   Negotiation and the Basic
Theorem of the International
Interaction Game

	PredNeg	
Variable	Coefficient	p
Constant	-2.22	.000
War_A	-0.79	.037
$AAcq$	-0.85	.068
$BAcq$	-1.20	.010
SQ	-0.11	.421
χ^2	6.00	
p	.10	
N	707	

international interaction game represents a meaningful structural scaffold for understanding relations among nations. Negotiations were three times more likely when the theory's full information conditions were met for such an outcome than when they were not satisfied. Even without controlling for incomplete information, nearly 30 percent of the actual negotiations turn out to be expected to have ended in that way.

Only the status quo variable in the final test does not meet or approximate normal standards of statistical significance. The status quo, of course, is the political circumstance in the international interaction game that is closest in its promotion of peace and harmony to the outcome of negotiations. All of the other variables appear to be significantly associated with the likelihood of resolving a dispute through negotiations. Each variable has the predicted direction of impact, with most also having a statistically strong influence on the prospects for a negotiated settlement.

Conclusion

Several fundamental, full information propositions have been set out and evaluated empirically. Each one represents the full information conditions that are necessary and sufficient for each possible outcome of the international interaction game under the two principle interpretations of the game: the realpolitik perspective and the domestic perspective. We have found that, in either version of the game, three events—Capitulation by actor A or by actor B and a war started by actor B—*cannot* arise without some imperfect information or uncertainty on the part of at least one actor. We have also seen that five events—negotiation, the status quo, acquiescence by actor A or by actor B, and a war started by actor A—can each arise under full information conditions (as well, of course, as under conditions of imperfect information) in the domestic variant of the game. Only negotiation or the status quo are possible with full information from the realpolitik perspective.

Some of the domestic deductions, most notably those concerned with war, represent a significant departure from perspectives previously stated by students of international affairs. The significant empirical support for the domestic explanation of international interactions and the absence of such support for the realpolitik version of the game suggests that international demands do *not* arise strictly within the international context of interactions, but rather are a product of other, possibly domestic, political considerations. As such, the evidence here represents a challenge to the dominant realist view of international affairs.

Having said that, we are mindful that the basic propositions discussed here are restricted by a very demanding condition—the presence of full information. That such conditions are often violated in reality almost goes without

saying and certainly is reflected in the empirical results reported here. Many of these propositions are expanded upon under conditions of incomplete or imperfect information elsewhere. The empirical assessments in those cases also support the domestic version, with many counterintuitive and highly demanding propositions finding significant support in the historical record from Europe during the past two centuries. Of course, all of these results are highly tentative, pending improved measurement procedures and replications for other time periods and in other geographic domains.

REFERENCES

Allison, G. 1971. *The Essence of Decision.* Boston: Little, Brown.
Altfeld, M., and B. Bueno de Mesquita. 1979. "Choosing Sides in Wars." *International Studies Quarterly* 23:87–112.
Blainey, G. 1973. *The Causes of War.* New York: Free Press.
Bueno de Mesquita, B., D. Newman, and R. Rabushka. 1985. *Forecasting Political Events: Hong Kong's Future.* New Haven: Yale University Press.
Bueno de Mesquita, B. 1981. *The War Trap.* New Haven: Yale University Press.
Bueno de Mesquita, B., R. Siverson, and G. Woller. 1992. "War and the Fate of Regimes." *American Political Science Review* 86:638–46.
Bueno de Mesquita, B., and D. Lalman. 1986. "Reason And War." *American Political Science Review* 80:1113–31.
Bueno de Mesquita, B., and D. Lalman. 1992. *War and Reason.* New Haven: Yale University Press.
Denzau, A., W. Riker, and K. Shepsle. 1985. "Farquharson and Fenno: Sophisticated Voting and Home Style." *American Political Science Review* 79:1117–34.
Gaubatz, K. 1991. "Election Cycles and War." *Journal of Conflict Resolution* 35:212–44.
Iusi-Scarborough, G., and B. Bueno de Mesquita. 1988. "Threat and Alignment Behavior." *International Interactions* 14:85–93.
James, P., and J. Oneal. 1991. "The Influence of Domestic and International Politics on the President's Use of Force." *Journal of Conflict Resolution* 35:307–32.
Kaplan, M. 1957. *System and Process in International Politics.* New York: Wiley.
Krasner, S. 1978. *Defending the National Interest: Raw Materials Investments and U.S. Foreign Policy.* Princeton: Princeton University Press.
Lalman, D. 1988. "Conflict Resolution and Peace." *American Journal of Political Science* 32:590–615.
Morgenthau, H. 1973. *Politics among Nations.* 5th ed. New York: Knopf.
Morrow, J. D. 1987. "On the Theoretical Basis of a Measure of National Risk Attitudes." *International Studies Quarterly* 31:423–38.
Morrow, J. D. 1991. "Electoral and Congressional Incentives and Arms Control." *Journal of Conflict Resolution* 35:245–65.
Niemi, R., and H. Weisberg. 1968. "A Mathematical Solution for the Probability of the Paradox of Voting." *Behavioral Science* 13:317–23.

Niou, E., P. Ordeshook, and G. Rose. 1989. *The Balance of Power.* Cambridge: Cambridge University Press.

Ostrom, C., and B. Job. 1986. "The President and the Political Use of Force." *American Political Science Review* 80:541–66.

Powell, R. 1987. "Crisis Bargaining, Escalation, and MAD." *American Political Science Review* 81:717–35.

Putnam, R. 1988. "Diplomacy and Domestic Politics: The Logic of Two-Level Games." *International Organization* 42:427–60.

Riker, W. 1982. *Liberalism Against Populism.* San Francisco: W. H. Freeman.

Selten, R. 1975. "Reexamination of the Perfectness Concept for Equilibrium Points in Extensive Games." *International Journal of Game Theory* 4:25–55.

Singer, J. D., and M. Small, 1972. *The Wages of War, 1816–1965: A Statistical Handbook.* New York: John Wiley.

Siverson, R., and J. King, 1980. "Attributes of National Alliance Membership and War Participation, 1815–1965: *American Journal of Political Science* 24:1–15.

Waltz, K. 1959. *Man, the State and War.* New York: Columbia University Press.

Waltz, K. 1979. *Theory of International Politics.* Reading, Mass.: Addison-Wesley.

On the Evolution of Political Issues

Edward G. Carmines and James A. Stimson

Where do issues come from? Why, when most do not matter, are some the leading themes to the story of a polity? Some last when most do not. Why that too? Some issues, like lines drawn in the dust, define what it means to be a party to political conflict. Most are easily stepped over.

To speak of politics is to speak of political issues, almost invariably. We speak of them as if we knew of them. But we truly do not. We do not know why they arise, why one question rather than another comes to seem important, why it happens at a particular time, rather than another, why some last, why most do not. These are familiar sorts of questions in the worlds of biology, geology, or paleontology. There we ask about species. But the questions are much the same. Why do they arise in one rather than another form? Why do some persist, others not? Why do whole groups of similar species thrive and then die out? These are all questions about change, organic change.

The preeminent theoretical problem addressed in this essay is the explanation of change—specifically, the evolution of political issues. We have turned to the biological theory of natural selection because it addresses that problem. It carries with it a powerful system of reasoning, and the analogy directs our thinking to certain kinds of questions and leads us to look for distinctive patterns. It is a useful organizing framework for considering the question of organic change. We discuss the uses—and abuses—of grafting such a metaphor to our purposes below.

That large numbers of potential issues compete with one another for the highly limited attention of the public in an ever changing political environment leads us to think of issue evolutions as biological evolutions.[1] The life

This is a revised version of a chapter that was originally published in Edward G. Carmines and James A. Stimson, *Issue Evolution: Race and the Transformation of American Politics* (Princeton: Princeton University Press, 1989). Used by permission.

1. Issues, of course, do not compete. Nor in fact do animals in evolutionary theory. Individual organisms behave as if they intended to survive. What we observe, then, looks like "competition" for survival among species. But the "competition" comes from our outside, human vantage point. So too issues, which more obviously lack intent, appear to compete for public

cycles of political issues are determined by the selective pressure of competition—in this case for public attention—in an environment that is itself always in flux.

Issues, like variations of species, arise in great abundance. A complex governmental environment produces policy questions, problems, and conflicts in far greater number than can ever be the subject of public discussion. Of these, most are not suited to the opportunities offered by the political environment at any given time and never gain a place on the public agenda. Some are the subject of unseen administrative decisions, some are nonsalient acts of Congress, and some are the issue platforms of aspiring politicians that never quite strike a sensitive public response.

Some issues—a minute proportion of the potential—are well fitted into new niches provided by an evolving political environment. New environmental opportunities can emerge from unsatisfied constituencies, from political leaders in search of electoral leverage, or from exogenous shocks to the system. Darwinian "fitness," biologists agree, is not absolute but relative to the evolving ecological niche. "Most fit" then comes to mean "best adapted" to an available niche. And so it would seem with issues. Adaptation to the niche is readily understandable after the fact. But the evolution of the niche itself is but one of a nearly infinite number of possible outcomes dependent upon a long series of events in which chance plays a major role. Particular issues come to influence the life of a political system, not so much because they are fundamental to the system but because they fundamentally fit well to an opportunity provided by the evolving political environment.

The political environment that evolves to create new issue opportunities just as surely dooms most issues to a temporary existence. Creation and extinction are two sides of the same coin of system change. However, we shall argue that issues, like species, can evolve to fit new niches as old ones disappear. But, unless they evolve to new forms, all issues are temporary. Most vanish at birth. Some have the same duration as the wars, recessions, and scandals that created them. Some become highly associated with other, similar issues or with the party system and thereby lose their independent impact. And some last so long that they reconstruct the political system that produced them; these are obviously the most important for the long-term development of the political system and are the principal focus of our inquiry.

In sum, we wish to know where issues come from, why some thrive in the competition for limited public attention and others do not, and how the origin and development of new issues is capable of transforming the organic

---

attention. That appearance is created by the human actors on the stage who employ them—just as Dawkins (1976) argues that genes may be best understood as behaving as if they employed their host organisms to perpetuate themselves.

system in which that development occurs. We turn first to a discussion of the sources of issue competition, then to the outcomes of issue competition, and finally to the processes of issue competition that link sources to outcomes. We conclude with a comparison of our notion of issue evolution to the more traditional concept of realignment theory.

Sources of Issue Competition

Accounting for "ultimate" issue origins is not a difficult explanatory problem. Like the origins of species, we can readily postulate the interaction of a complex environment and chance processes as the source of more numerous raw material in issue innovations than can ever develop. Just as natural variation in gene pools is filtered by chance processes to produce a plenitude of variations in species, so a complex governmental environment superimposed upon a disparate social order can be counted upon to raise new issues in abundance. The regulation, distribution, and redistribution of governed acts, multiplied by the number of spheres of social and economic activity, in turn multiplied by time and interaction at the boundary of government and governed is an engine for the production of new, unresolved questions of such power that we need never fear it will fail to produce enough new material to supply our need for diverse possibilities.

The more important question is how issues are selected for development. Why do some thrive against the heavy odds of competition for scarce attention? If far more issues are generated than can ever gain space on the small stage of issue competition, we must know what processes filter the possibilities from the many potential issue conflicts to the few that can command significant public attention, what mechanisms promote some and not others.

Four mechanisms will command our detailed attention: (1) the promotion of particular issues by strategic politicians as effective leverage in the struggle for power, (2) issues moved to the center of public discourse when highlighted by external disruptions to the established order, (3) new issue species that are old issues transformed by isolation and specialization in a new context to something quite different than their origins, and (4) cybernetic issues selected for importance because internal contradictions and imbalances in the political system generate corrective needs.

Strategic Politicians

Strategic politicians play the most obvious and perhaps most influential role in determining the relative competition among political issues. All successful politicians instinctively understand which issues benefit them and their party

and which do not. The trick is to politicize the former and deemphasize the latter.

Every party alignment embodies a more-or-less explicit issue agenda— the set of policy conflicts around which the struggle for power has been fought (Carmines 1991; Johnston n.d.). The winning party naturally seeks to maintain the salience and centrality of the current agenda, not only to preserve but also to perpetuate the distribution of power emanating from those salient political conflicts. After all, the exploitation of those issues has resulted in success in the first place. Of course, one way of exploiting is to continue to emphasize the original aligning issues; another is to treat all new issues as logical outgrowths of the original agenda. In both cases, the idea is to fight current political battles within the framework of old ones. The existing majority, in short, has an obvious incentive to keep winning; the equally obvious strategy for victory is emphasizing the original aligning issues. Because these issues contributed to its current majority status, it sees no reason to deemphasize or discard them. Just as genes behave as if they seek to perpetuate themselves by becoming attached to viable species, so strategic politicians attempt to maintain their power by being associated with winning issues. For politicians of the existing majority, these are issues of the past.

Not so with the existing minority. Its ultimate goal is to upset the dominant party alignment, including the issue basis on which it has been constructed. Losing politicians naturally turn to new issues to improve their political situation. New issues—if they can split the majority coalition and sufficiently attract the electorate—offer the opportunity for converting old losers into new winners (and old winners into new losers); they are, thus, the stock-in-trade of successful politicians. This does not mean, of course, that all new issues will have this effect. On the contrary, the vast majority of new issue proposals are bound to fail, striking an unresponsive cord in the mass public and leaving the current majority party's coalition intact. Political losers may occupy an even more disadvantageous position than they did before introducing the proposal. Nor are new issues the only mechanism for undermining the majority coalition. The minority may also emphasize performance on old issues or attempt nonissue appeals, such as candidate personality. Be this as it may, sponsoring new issue proposals is one of the few strategies that losers have for permanently improving their political position. And on those rare occasions when losing politicians provide exactly what the public is seeking, the issues, as Riker observes, "flourish, even to the point of completely reshaping the environment in which they arose" (Riker 1982, 210).

Dissatisfied political losers, in sum, have an ever-present motive to unseat the governing status quo. Generating new issue conflicts is a natural vehicle for this purpose. The natural selection of issues thus reflects the dominant strategy of losing but rational politicians and their parties.

External Disruptions

Potential issues always exist on the periphery of awareness. Some are called to the center when the world outside a particular political system intrudes upon it. The external world causes disruptions and shocks, raises challenges and opportunities, and, in general, prevents any organic system from being driven entirely by internal imperatives. Most evident in the case of crises, wars, depressions, terrorism, and invasions of the economic sort, the external world is always a source of problems to be solved, opportunities to be exploited. Matters requiring public discussion generate issue conflicts over how best to deal with them. Thus, the relevant set of potential issue conflicts in the domain of intrusion is selected for greater attention, greater debate, and greater conflict.

Local Variations

The thesis of local variation is a leading account of the origin of new species. When an interbreeding population and common gene pool are physically divided by distance, geologic events, or whatever, we reasonably expect that the local populations that continue to interbreed will adapt more readily to the specialized local environment than to the common environment of the original population. After a few generations of isolated adaptation and sufficient variation in environmental conditions, the isolated population may diverge quite substantially from the ancestral population. Given enough time and variation, the divergence may create a new species (no longer capable of interbreeding with the old) and a closed gene pool.

We can readily imagine similar developments in political issues. A common issue (whether, for example, government ought to intervene in the market economy) applied in diverse, specialized settings over a long time may produce offspring issues (e.g., the regulation of airline fare structures) so adapted to the new, specialized context that they take on an identity and developmental path distinct from the ancestral issue.

Cavanagh and Sundquist argue that this is precisely what happened with respect to economic issues in the 1980s.

> The debate between the parties on the old role-of-government and economic policy issues has been placed in such a new ideological context in the 1980s by the radicalized Republican party of Ronald Reagan that the distinction between the parties may have taken on quite new meanings. . . . To that extent the line of party cleavage can be seen as having shifted, with much the same impact on the party system that a new line born of wholly new issues might hypothetically have had. (1985, 37)

Internal Contradictions

The world of systems in perfect balance and harmony is inspired more by theology than empirical observation. In the real world of politics, harmony is partial, balance often nonexistent. Thus, problems arise from the internal contradictions and imbalances. Issues associated with those problems and their solutions may then move to the fore from their tie to a growing consciousness of policy problems in need of solution.

Thus by their very nature, all party alignments contain the seeds of their own destruction. The various groups that make up the party may be united on some issues, particularly on those that gave rise to the alignment in the first place. But lurking just below the surface, myriad potential issues divide the party faithful and can lead to a dissolution of the existing equilibrium. In politics, as Riker notes (1982, 197–212), disequilibrium may only be one issue away because of the inevitability of internal contradictions.

A sense of predestination or inevitability is not to be found in any of these paths to issue development. That is a central theme of the literature on natural selection and is equally true, we believe, of the evolution of political issues. We see developmental paths as sensible and explainable after the fact. But given a world dependent upon context, variation, and chance, any possible outcome, including the one that did in fact occur, has a prior probability so low as to be all but unpredictable. That view of history and evolution, in marked contrast to much theorizing on party systems and realignment, is central to our treatment of issue evolution.

Outcomes of Issue Competition

We have suggested that four sources determine the differential salience of issues in their competition with one another through time. But, in addition to understanding the pattern of competition among issues, we also want to understand the outcomes of this competition, to model the impact that evolving issues have on the larger party system of which they are the most dynamic part. We see three distinct outcomes—associated with three respective issue types—of this competition for public attention and influence.

Organic Extensions

The first is perhaps the most easily understood. Some new issues fit into the same niche that has previously existed. These are genuinely new issues; their content is novel. But because they continue already existing conflicts or at least become interpreted in that way, their capacity for moving the political system in a novel direction is sharply curtailed. Federal aid to education, for example, an issue that occupied a prominent place on the political agenda of

the early 1960s, posed the same kind of questions and invoked the same sort of reactions as did Roosevelt's New Deal. At most, these "organic extensions" are likely to reinvigorate old issues and old conflicts, to redefine them in the direction of more current issue debates.

Unsuccessful Adaptations

Unsuccessful adaptations are of two subtypes, issues that never capture public attention at all, by far the largest in number, and those that do receive attention but cannot hold it very long. Even the former may have important objective consequences. They are, however, too complex, technical, and nonsalient to form an effective communication link between citizens and elites. For this reason, they ultimately tend to be resolved by the political elites themselves with little guidance from the public. Perhaps the best illustration of this issue type is the host of conflicts involved in national energy policy. Genuine policy disputes of unquestioned importance, these conflicts have so far failed to exert substantial influence on electoral politics for lack of shared referents between masses and elites.

Some issues have great impact in the short term but do not leave a permanent mark on the political system. These issues are typically linked to political events that cause disturbances in the existing political environment. The public may become aroused about them, even to the point of decisive electoral impact. These issues do not, moreover, reinforce the bases of the existing party system; instead, they may cut across the natural development in one or both political parties.

But their effects are short term. They may influence system outcomes, but they do not change the system. These issues have the important limitation of being unable to sustain themselves beyond the events that brought them into being. Thus, as the events fade in public memory, the issues lose their salience and, with it, their ability to shape public opinion. The dramatic, short-term electoral importance of these issues is thus more than counterbalanced by their inconsequential long-term effects on the political system. Vietnam and Watergate are two recent examples of this policy type.

Issue Evolutions

We define issue evolutions as those issues capable of altering the political environment within which they originated and evolved. These issues have a long life cycle; they develop, evolve, and sometimes are resolved over a number of years. The crucial importance of this issue type stems from the fact that its members can lead to fundamental and permanent change in the party system.

Issue evolutions possess the key characteristics absent from each other

issue type. Unlike organic extension issues, they do not merely continue the existing party system. They cut across the direct line of evolutionary development. They emerge from the old environment, but, having once emerged, they introduce fundamental tensions into the party system, inconsistent with the continued stability of old patterns. These issues capture the public's attention for more than a short span of time; they tend to be salient for a number of years. They are distinctive, finally, in their unique combination of short- and long-term effects.

Thus, they may result in voting defections among partisans, but, more important, they also alter the fundamental link between citizen and party. They have the ability to alter the party system from which they emerged. Only issues of this type have the capacity to reshape the party system, replacing one dominant alignment with another and transforming the character of the parties themselves.

We have discussed how much cognitive processing is required to deal meaningfully with an issue elsewhere (Carmines and Stimson 1980). This is a critical dividing point between issues that may or may not lead to issue evolutions. "Easy" issues have the attribute that they may be responded to, indeed even understood in a fundamental sense, at the "gut" level. They require almost no supporting context of factual knowledge, no impressive reasoning ability, no attention to the nuances of political life. Thus, they produce mass response undifferentiated with respect to knowledge, awareness, attentiveness, or interest in politics; none of these is a requisite of response.

"Hard" issues, by far the more common type, require contextual knowledge, an appreciation of often subtle differences in policy options, a coherent structure of beliefs about politics, systematic reasoning to connect means to ends, and interest in and attentiveness to political life to justify the cost of expensive fact gathering and decision making. Accordingly, hard issues are the special province of the most sophisticated and attentive portion of the electorate as well as of issue publics who have special reason to be concerned about particular sets of, but not all, public policies. Hard issues are not the stuff of issue evolutions, for they can generate neither large nor sustained public response.

Models of Issue Evolution

Thus far we have discussed two typologies: the first focuses on the sources of issue competition, the second on the outcomes of this competition. But, to picture the full system, we need a further typology of processes or models that link sources to outcomes. Without it, the story has a beginning and end but no middle.

We postulate three basic models of issue evolution. The first, undoubtedly the most familiar to students of party realignment, is the critical election realignment or, stated in terms of its biological analogue, cataclysmic adaptation. The fundamental characteristics of change in this model are rapidity and discontinuity. Not only does the issue lead to a transformation of the system, but it does so dramatically and permanently. A long period of stability is followed by a sudden burst of dramatic change that shifts the party system to a new level of stability. The party system is stationary before the critical election—an intervention that leads to a radical and profound alteration of the system. The earthquake is an often used, appropriate metaphor for such change (see, for example, Burnham 1970).

To say that cataclysmic adaptation is rare in the biological world is an understatement. It is a category without any cases unless one treats biblical creationism as a serious theory.[2] Indeed, Darwinian reasoning literally rules it out as a plausible model of biological change. Although it is clearly the dominant paradigm for thinking about political change, we doubt, in fact, if it is any more common in the political world.

A second type of issue evolution is based upon Darwinian pure gradualism. The change effected through this transformation is permanent; it leaves an indelible imprint on the political landscape. And the change can be quite substantial, fundamentally altering the complexion of the system over a long time. But the process is slow, gradual, incremental. This noncritical, wholly gradual model of partisan change is consistent with Key's (1959) notion of secular realignment.

"Punctuated equilibrium" notions in biology are the origin of our third, "dynamic growth," model of political change. It is dynamic because it presumes that, at some point, the system moves from a fairly stationary steady state to a fairly dramatic rapid change; the change is manifested by a "critical moment" in the time-series—a point where change is large enough to be visible and, perhaps, the origin of a dynamic process. Significantly, however, the change—the dynamic growth—does not end with the critical moment; instead it continues over an extended period, albeit at a much slower pace. This continued growth after the initial shock defines the evolutionary character of the model. Gould puts the case for a punctuated equilibrium model of evolution as follows.

> Exciting discoveries in molecular biology and in the study of embryological development have reemphasized the integrity of organic form and hinted at modes of change different from the cumulative, gradual

---

2. The one possible exception is the passing of the dinosaurs, which some controversial interpretations view as the result of cataclysmic adaptation (Raup 1986).

alteration emphasized by strict Darwinians. Direct study of fossil sequences has challenged gradualistic biases (the "punctuated equilibrium" pattern of long-term stasis within species and geologically rapid origin of new species) and asserted the idea of explanatory hierarchy in identifying species as discrete and active evolutionary agents. (1983, 14)

On the Use and Abuse of Evolutionary Reasoning

Metaphor, it is well known, is no stranger to scientific reasoning of all kinds. Quite explicit in Burnham's *Critical Elections and the Mainsprings of American Politics,* the explanation of change by physical analogy has a long history in U.S. political science and a very long history in U.S. political thought.[3] It has no need of a defense. But organic metaphors are considerably less common in social science. And because their abuse is associated with the political and ideological use of "science" to justify common prejudices, we feel some need to be explicit about our intent and usage.

The evolution of species by natural selection is a powerful theoretical system; its postulates are simple, its reasoning elegant. Its generality is much greater than the problem it was designed to explain, important though that is. Thus, we find merit in exploiting this system of reasoning to model a different phenomenon, the evolution of political issues.[4] We believe that it offers purchase on the organic world of politics unavailable in the prevailing, more mechanical modes of thinking about political systems and institutions.

Although we are enthusiastic about the heuristic value of natural selection as a means of coming to terms with issue evolution, we have a certain reticence about open exploitation of biological theory because the social use of biology has a disreputable history. More often exploited to justify politics and policy than to explain them, the social use of biology is littered with fraud, pseudoscience, and the abusive use of "science" to justify social and racial prejudices. Beginning with "social Darwinism," an absolutist misunderstanding of natural selection used in praise of the social status quo—the rich and well born are obviously fittest (just look how well they survive and prosper), while poverty is "nature's" way of weeding out the unfit—the pseudoscience continues in the present day to assert genetic dominance of behavior, minus any empirical evidence for the case, and to claim genetic superiority for white male Northern Europeans (Gould 1981). Modern "biopolitics" lacks these abusive pseudoscientific elements, but, as a field, it is notably reluctant to test many of the theses that so readily spill out of fertile imaginations.

---

3. But the earthquake, not the mainspring, is the physical analogy central to much reasoning about electoral realignment.

4. The evolutionary perspective is beginning to gain attention and find application in areas far removed from its origins in biology. Indeed, Burnham's recent defense of critical realignment theory (1991) couches it in terms of a model of punctuated equilibrium.

We differ fundamentally from all these schools; we do not assert a biological basis to behavior. For us, natural selection is a key to understanding the organic competition among issues, a powerful analogy used to draw insight from the great theoretical achievement of Darwin and his followers to explain what seems to us a fundamentally similar situation. We are simply not interested in "nature versus nurture" and similar sorts of controversies from the application of biology and genetics to society; they are quite irrelevant to issue evolution. Pursuit of a biological (or any other) metaphor sometimes leads one to ask certain kinds of questions and not others. It probably shapes, in part, what answers are found to be satisfactory. In some cases, the application is so limited that it has little effect at all. Some of it is conscious and intentional, some not. Certain principles are conscious and can be abstracted and advertised. Among these, three are worthy of particular note.

Although structured by human reason and calculation, sometimes self-consciously strategic, and constrained by social structure, chance is the fundamental driving force in producing change. That does not imply that change is either chaotic or unknowable but, most explicitly, that it is neither determined nor inevitable. We are intellectually at war here most particularly with any notion of inevitability, which, unlike other Marxist notions, is not at all foreign to U.S. social theory. We do not assume that any particular issue evolution could only have happened as it did. Instead, scenarios of issue evolutions are more akin to Tolstoy's battle scenes, where calculation, force, confusion, and chance commingle to produce an outcome, the appearance of which is orderly only after the fact.

Second, we assume that issue change is dynamic—a process, not an event. That implies subtle movements over time. That does not commit us to gradualism; the punctuated equilibrium model we draw from Gould and others allows for bursts of rapid change, at least on the appropriate time scale. The notion of subtle dynamics is openly in conflict with the earthquake metaphor that so dominates much thinking on political change in the critical realignment tradition.

Finally, we borrow the notion that resultant change is neither unindirectional nor permanent. The species succeeds by being well adapted to a niche but not in any absolute sense superior to its ancestor. Change represents not a process of perfection but, rather, a randomly driven tryout of new survival possibilities, each successful or unsuccessful relative to the niche only. If the niches themselves are impermanent, from externally induced change, from competition from new species, even perhaps from competition with the same species, then the adaptations are not absolutely good or helpful; they are good only insofar as the conditions to which they were a lucky adaptation persist.

These assertions—that change is driven by randomness, that its form is dynamic, and that its result is impermanent—are not essentially biological. Highly consistent with Darwinian sorts of reasoning, they can be stated,

nonetheless, as abstractions without organic content. But this raises the question of whether issue evolution is merely a species of realignment theory, a question to which we now turn.

Issue Evolution: A Species of Realignment Theory?

Realignment is a dichotomous notion. Elections, or sequences of elections, are either realigning or they are not. There is no middle ground. Thus, to explain change in these terms, one must either assert realignment or deny the change. In fact, the natural critical response is the inevitable question of whether it is really a realignment.

We find the "is it or is it not" debate unhelpful in coming to terms with changes in the party system. First, scholars can choose their favorite reputable set of definitions of realignment and come to either conclusion; this definitional confusion we address subsequently. Second, and more important, neither conclusion satisfactorily fits the evidence. Most issue evolutions are not of a magnitude comparable to the better known realignments of U.S. history— for example, the Civil War or the New Deal. Most are a considerably more subtle phenomenon. Calling them a realignment seems to be stretching their impact beyond what the evidence will support. But denying the change is equally awry. Thus, the conclusion that an issue evolution is a "nothing," the only alternative to "realignment," is troublesome. Realignment notions, put another way, allow us to assert political change when the magnitude of that change is overwhelming, so obvious that it need not be documented, and deny that anything more subtle can matter. That is a formula for a simplistic science of politics. Documenting the obvious is the first task of a primitive science. It is time now to move on to matters of greater interest.

The prominent escape from this intellectual trap is amending the theory to make it speak to the evidence. Indeed, realignment theory has so often been amended when the evidence it purported to explain was not so much in conflict with its original terms but extraneous to them that the amendments are far more weighty than the original core of the theory. Because those amendments are also complex and confusing, further additions to the list are unlikely to produce scientific progress. Most scholars, we suspect, have stopped cataloging the too numerous amendments because continuing that cataloging gives the matter more the feel of theology than of scientific theory. To move to a more explicitly scientific conceptualization is the wiser course.

What Is Realignment Theory, and Why Is It So Confused?

Electoral realignment can be an appealing notion. It imbues with drama the often too routine world of politics. The realignment produces an immediately

visible change that promises permanency, as well. Where the normal channel of communication between governed and governors is clogged with noise, the realignment provides a clean, crisp signal of electoral intent. The stark drama of electoral realignment appeals to both the scholarly and the popular imaginations. This appeal is important, for it accounts for the resilience of the idea. It accounts, in particular, for the resilience of the idea of realignment in its simplest form. That resilience is indeed part of the problem.

To read the literature about realignment is to be impressed with how often scholars have searched for simple and dramatic realignments and how rarely they have found them. If simplicity is often the first casualty of scientific research, that is even more the case in realignment research: the simple and dramatic model of critical realignment, the one that so readily captures our attention, finds no supporting evidence.[5] Scholars search for evidence of realignment and find it, but the nature of the realignments found bears notably little likeness to the simple and resilient concept.

Starting with the simple concept of realignment, it seems reasonable to ask: when realignments happen, who does the realigning, how does it occur, and what is the result. On the "when" question, it is natural to look for a date. Was 1980 a realignment seems to be a sensible question from this point of view. But researchers find that dating can be accomplished only by ignoring such evidence. The closer we look, the more these "simple" realignments become movements over time, taking decades or multiples of decades to achieve their final form. When precursors and aftershocks are added, the multiple decade processes overlap, and the continuing effects of old movements are still manifested while new and different movements toward a still newer alignment are underway. There is no "normal" period left, no time when the reshaping of loyalties and behaviors is absent. From the fully developed time scale of realignment, such as in Sundquist 1983, to ask whether a particular election was a realignment is a senseless question. All elections are part of realigning progressions, and none are realigning in themselves. It is akin to asking whether a particular wave rearranged the sand on a beach; the answer is always Yes, and so did every other.

When we ask "who" shaped a new alignment and "how" that new shape was forged, the evidence is sparse, for the classic realignments occurred before serious survey research allowed us to track individual movements. The drama of the simple, resilient notion implies conversion from one party to another on a notable scale. The evidence here is controversial, but a fair summary would be that enough conversion can be found to document that the process existed, but nowhere near enough to account for observed changes in

---

5. The work of Burnham (1970) and others who rely heavily on aggregate election outcomes data comes closest to being an exception. The outcomes data are not rich enough for complex interpretations, however.

party strength. When we relax the time scale, then other processes, principally the mobilization of new voters (Andersen 1979), become more plausible accounts of "who" formed the new alignment. And even that more complex portrait would appear strikingly simple in contrast to the survey-based explorations of party movement (cf. Norpoth and Rusk 1982) in the modern electorate.

If we ask "what resulted from" a realignment, we are tempted to search for coherent sets of programs dealing with the challenge of the events provoking the new electoral structure. As is so often the case in realignment research, one historical sequence—the Great Depression and New Deal—is the prototype for thinking about the policy consequences of realignment.[6] If we allow a simplistic dating of realignment, that is, that the New Deal realignment "occurred" in 1932, then event, realignment, institutional change, and policy change (Brady 1978) can all be connected. Alas, we can also find realignments without notable policy changes and notable policy changes without realignments.

Although we can treat realignment as a unified concept, two major strands or emphases can be seen in the literature. Some authors—for example, Key (1955 and 1959), Schattschneider (1960), and Sundquist (1983)—emphasize the "alignment" aspect of party realignment. For them, a party realignment is an overlaid new issue cleavage along party lines. New issue cleavages may or may not have other consequences for party systems, policy outcomes, control of government, and so forth. The second strand—seen in Campbell et al. 1960; Pomper 1968; and Burnham 1970—emphasizes changing party fortunes at the polls as the essence of realignment. For this approach, and for popular use of the term, realignments are manifested when reversals of the majority and minority party status result from sharp and largely permanent movements of the electorate from one party to the other.

We may avoid conflict between the two uses by assuming them to be two sides of the same coin, in effect by assuming that movements of cleavages produce changes in majority party status or that changes in majority party status must include underlying changes in the lines of party conflict.[7] But this common assumption is dangerous; it is theoretically possible that the two sorts of changes may occur independently. And, in our judgment of the historical evidence, they in fact do. This bifurcated connotation, the roots of which are

---

6. A skeptical view of the realignment literature would see that much of it is tailored to "explain" this single, discrete historical event. Realignment scholars are not to be faulted for working with only five or so cases in the U.S. context, for that is the universe of evidence. The fault lies in failing to demand that general concepts fit and empirical assertions hold true for all the cases. Many a list of requisites or defining characteristics of "realignment" fail such a test; they are, instead, historical particulars of the New Deal case.

7. See Clubb, Flanigan, and Zingale 1980 for an explicit treatment of this issue.

as old as serious scholarly attention to realignment, causes confusion at the beginning. In addition to this conceptual discord, the realignment literature may be seen as a long string of amendments by typology, as successive scholars have applied the concepts to the raw materials of (usually U.S.) political history and found the empirical materials too complex to be subsumed by the initial concept.[8]

We have already seen some amendments in the conflicts over conversion versus mobilization as causal process and gradual versus cataclysmic (or secular versus critical) accounts of the pace of change. Some accounts emphasize social cleavages (Petrocik 1981), where others see issue cleavages (Flanagan and Dalton 1984) as the central phenomena of party conflicts; sometimes the two are seen as the same, sometimes different. More recent accounts distinguish between realignments as overlays on old alignments and realignments as exclusive cleavages, between the sort of national realignment implied by the simple account and realignments as sectional phenomena, occurring at different times, in different manners, and even for different reasons in different sections of the nation (Bensel 1984). More recent still is the distinction between structural and performance-based realigning processes (MacDonald and Rabinowitz 1987).

If all these distinctions (and this is by no means an exhaustive list of the possibilities or of the election outcome typologies) are to be taken seriously, then the number of possible types of realignment exceeds the number of cases by a considerable order of magnitude. That we have far more types and categories than cases to sort into them is not wholly indefensible, but it does suggest a considerable lack of theoretical power. And realignment theorists seem unnaturally eclectic about accepting this ever-growing number of distinctions. One might imagine, for example, that those who defined alignment as if it implied cataclysmic change would reject assertions that realignments might be secular or regional or performance based, all of which would appear inconsistent with the notion of change by an electoral uprising. There is, instead, a considerable tolerance for the introduction of new forms and types.

Tolerance is a good thing in politics, but it can be quite another in theory building. Its effect is to make genuine, unresolved conflicts appear instead to be only minor disagreements about details. The refinement of the realignment notion to square it with empirical reality, most notably in Sundquist 1983, is a good thing. Troublesome is that this good thing is strikingly inconsistent with the simple, resilient notion: event causes conversion causes new party system. And if the simplistic notion is a straw man, it is a straw man often and enthusiastically articulated; more than any contender it is the standard meaning of the term *realignment*.

---

8. For the most recent attempt to refine alignment theory so that it can accommodate contemporary U.S. political developments, see the essays in Shaffer 1991.

That the concept of realignment has been refined is not troublesome. The difficulty is that the original, unrefined idea is still current. If one were to ask for the best work on realignment, we think most would point to the refinements. But if one were to ask most political scientists for a definition, the answer almost invariably would be the simple, original notion. How can a concept fundamentally modified by theoretical speculation and empirical investigation remain unaltered in much professional discourse and absolutely dominant in public discussions of politics? Part of the answer may be that realignment theory, as refined, lacks most of the drama and theoretical power that first stimulated interest in the concept. Another part, we suggest, is that political scientists and other scholars do not "own" the concept and so cannot mold its usage.

We would suggest realignment belongs to that class of prescientific concepts (along with, for example, power and democracy) that predate the scientific study of politics and whose connotation is essentially in the public domain. All these concepts are difficult to deal with, not just because of the confusion of established usage but, more important, because of their resistance to scientific redefinition. Thus, just as nonspecialists speak of power in much the ordinary, prescientific connotation (in textbooks, for example), so too does the original, popular connotation of realignment remain relatively secure from scientific redefinition. It "belongs" to the popular political culture from which it derived. This is in considerable contrast to concepts of political science origin—of which "party identification" is a good example—which, though relevant to politics, remain scientific concepts. Although the authoritative source on the meaning of political science concepts is work in monographs and professional journals, such prescientific concepts as realignment are more likely to be redefined, if at all, by the *New York Times* or the *Washington Post*.

It is thus a safe prediction that the next decisive election in U.S. politics—and decisive elections are not by any means rare events—will produce a debate, both public and scholarly, about whether it was or was not a realignment. And both the question itself and the terms of the debate will be the original, simplistic idea of realignment. The matter is beyond scholarly control.

We are left with a scholarly morass. To take up the question of our section title, we cannot know whether issue evolution is a species of realignment because we cannot know what realignment means. Works on realignment invariably deal at length with definitional problems—in itself evidence of the morass—but none ever settle the matter; no connotation becomes consensually held. The research on realignment has both weaknesses and strengths. But if our analysis is correct, no additional work on the concept is called for, because no additional work will extricate us from the morass. In

other words, issue evolution—whatever its other strengths and weaknesses—can at least be scientifically defined and controlled. It allows us to proceed to the business of theory, model, and empirical analysis without the burden of a contentious and uncontrollable concept. This is surely a sign of scientific progress.

REFERENCES

Andersen, Kristi. 1979. *The Creation of a Democratic Majority, 1928–1936.* Chicago: University of Chicago Press.
Bensel, Richard Franklin. 1984. *Sectionalism and American Political Development, 1880–1980.* Madison: University of Wisconsin Press.
Brady, David. 1978. "Critical Elections, Congressional Parties and Clusters of Policy Changes." *British Journal of Political Science* 8:79–99.
Burnham, Walter Dean. 1970. *Critical Elections and the Mainsprings of American Politics.* New York: Norton.
Burnham, Walter Dean. 1991. "Critical Realignment: Dead or Alive? In *The End of Realignment? Interpreting American Electoral Eras,* ed. Byron Shafer, 101–39. Madison: University of Wisconsin Press.
Campbell, Angus, Philip E. Converse, Warren E. Miller, and Donald E. Stokes, 1960. *The American Voter.* New York: Wiley.
Carmines, Edward G. 1991. "The Logic of Party Alignments." *Journal of Theoretical Politics* 3:65–80.
Carmines, Edward G., and James A. Stimson. 1980. "The Two Faces of Issue Voting." *American Political Science Review* 74:78–91.
Carmines, Edward G., and James A. Stimson. 1989. *Issue Evolution: Race and the Transformation of American Politics.* Princeton: Princeton University Press.
Cavanagh, Thomas E., and James L. Sundquist. 1985. "The New Two-Party System." In *The New Direction in American Politics,* ed. John E. Chubb and Paul E. Peterson, 33–68. Washington, D.C.: Brookings Institution.
Clubb, Jerome M., William H. Flanigan, and Nancy H. Zingale. 1980. *Partisan Realignment.* Beverly Hills, Calif.: Sage Publications.
Dawkins, Richard. 1976. *The Selfish Gene.* New York: Oxford University Press.
Flanagan, Scott C., and Russell J. Dalton. 1984. "Parties Under Stress: Realignment and Dealignment in Advanced Industrial Societies." *West European Politics* 7:7–23.
Gould, Stephen Jay. 1981. *The Mismeasure of Man.* New York: Norton.
Gould, Stephen Jay. 1983. *Hen's Teeth and Horse's Toes: Further Reflections in Natural History.* New York: Norton.
Johnston, Richard. N.d. "Issues and Party Alignments: A Review with Canadian Examples." *European Journal of Political Economy.* Forthcoming.
Key, V. O., Jr. 1955. "A Theory of Critical Elections." *Journal of Politics* 17:3–18.
Key, V. O., Jr. 1959. "Secular Realignment and the Party System." *Journal of Politics* 21:198–210.

MacDonald, Stuart Elaine, and George Rabinowitz. 1987. "The Dynamics of Structural Realignment." *American Political Science Review* 81:775–96.

Norpoth, Helmut, and Jerrold G. Rusk. 1982. "Partisan Dealignment in the American Electorate: Itemizing the Deductions Since 1964." *American Political Science Review* 76:522–37.

Petrocik, John R. 1981. *Party Coalitions: Realignments and the Decline of the New Deal Party System.* Chicago: University of Chicago Press.

Pomper, Gerald M. 1968. *Elections in America: Control and Influence in Democratic Politics.* New York: Dodd, Mead.

Raup, David M. 1986. *The Nemesis Affair.* New York: Norton.

Riker, William H. 1982. *Liberalism Against Populism.* San Francisco: W. H. Freeman.

Schattschneider, E. E. 1960. *The Semi-Sovereign People: A Realist's View of Democracy in America.* New York: Holt, Rinehart and Winston.

Shafer, Byron E., ed. 1991. *The End of Realignment? Interpreting American Electoral Eras.* Madison: University of Wisconsin Press.

Sundquist, James L. 1983. *Dynamics of the Party System.* Rev. ed. Washington, D.C.: Brookings Institution.

Agenda Formation and Cabinet Government

Michael Laver and Kenneth A. Shepsle

Cabinet government is a private practice carried on between appointed adults.

—Peter Hennessy, *Cabinet*

There is a large and growing body of work on the institutions and processes of agenda formation. Approaches found in this literature include highly abstract formal models of majority rule (McKelvey 1976; Shepsle and Weingast 1984; Banks 1985); less abstract formal models employing "stylized facts" about institutions (Gilligan and Krehbiel 1987; Shepsle and Weingast 1987); analytical treatments of specific historical cases (Riker 1982, chap. 9 and 1991; Weingast 1990); and analyses emphasizing nonrational, incremental processes (Kingdon 1984). Almost without exception, however, these treatments of agenda formation are based on U.S. political institutions and historical experiences.

In this essay, in contrast, we explore aspects of agenda formation in the systems of parliamentary government more characteristic of continental Europe. In the first section, we summarize a model of government formation in parliamentary democracies that we have elaborated elsewhere. We define what we mean by government in a parliamentary setting and model the process by which governments are formed and sustained in office.[1]

In the subsequent three sections, we describe some extensions of this general approach that we believe throw some light on the formation of the political agenda and the determination of policy outcomes in parliamentary democracies. The first of these focuses on the role of cabinet ministers as agenda setters. The second explores the impact of bargaining, within a gov-

The authors gratefully acknowledge the financial support of the National Science Foundation (SES 89-14294).

1. This model is based on our earlier work; see Laver and Shepsle 1990a, 1990b, 1991a, 1991b. It also bears a familial resemblance to the recent work of Austen-Smith and Banks (1990).

ernment, among members of the cabinet. Finally, we examine the impact of intraparty politics.

Each of these perspectives on agenda formation revolves around the role of cabinet ministers as the political bosses of the important departments of state. In general terms, we see cabinet ministers in parliamentary systems as the gatekeepers who winnow down the alternatives and then make the decisions that produce policies and affect outcomes. How cabinet ministers are selected, and how they are subsequently constrained in the exercise of their authority, are critically important elements in the agenda formation process.

A Model of Cabinet Formation

In this section we present a brief sketch of a model elaborated much more extensively elsewhere. In many respects our approach resembles the conventional spatial model of government formation in parliamentary democracies. Issues or policy dimensions are given exogenously as the basis vectors of an n-dimensional Euclidean space.[2] The policy positions of parties are specific points in this space.[3] These points may be determined by the policy manifestos that parties issue for instrumental reasons during an election campaign, by the intrinsic tastes of autocratic party leaders, or by the collective decisions of party conventions or executive committees. For now, we do not worry about their origins. Parties are also endowed with preferences over points in the space, defined here in terms of Euclidean distance from each party policy position. Finally, after each election, every party, i, is given a weight, w_i, equal to the proportion of parliamentary seats that it controls.

In our first substantial departure from the conventional spatial model, we assume that the institutional context of cabinet decision making gives a politically meaningful structure to the set of salient policy dimensions. Let $E = (e_1, \ldots, e_n)$ be the exogenous basis vectors of the policy space, $\Re^n$. We define a jurisdictional structure as a partition of these dimensions into policy jurisdictions, $(J_1, \ldots, J_m)$. That is, policy dimensions are grouped into mutually exclusive and collectively exhaustive subsets of E; thus, each salient policy dimension $e_i \in E$ is in exactly one jurisdiction $J_k \in J$. Each of these jurisdictions defines the authority of a particular cabinet portfolio, held by a particular government minister. There is no requirement whatsoever that jurisdictions are unidimensional, though many of our illustrations have this feature for descriptive convenience.

A government is defined as any allocation of the m portfolios among the

---

2. Thus, our approach does not incorporate the creation of new issues, the heresthetical maneuver elaborated by Riker (1982 and 1986).

3. We subsequently relax this unitary treatment of parties.

legislative parties with positive weight. Thus, a single party, t, may hold all the portfolios. If it has majority weight—$w_t > 1/2$—it is a single-party majority government. If it has less than majority weight—$w_t \leq 1/2$—it is a single-party minority government. Alternatively, more than one party may hold portfolios, in which case there is a coalition government; it is a minority coalition government if government partners, between them, command less than majority weight, and is a majority coalition government otherwise. If there are T parties with positive weight, then there are T^m feasible governments.[4] Of special significance, because it distinguishes our approach from the mainstream of coalition theory, is the fact that our definition of government is confined to the executive, or cabinet. The government consists of those parties (or politicians) holding ministerial portfolios.

We assume that a specific policy forecast is associated with each particular allocation of portfolios among parties. This forecast is a belief, commonly held by all actors, about subsequent policy choices in each jurisdiction. In our earliest work (Laver and Shepsle 1990a) we assume, along with Austen-Smith and Banks (1990), that actors forecast that each government minister will implement the ideal policies of his or her party on policy dimensions within his or her jurisdiction. For example, if there are three jurisdictions, and the first two of these are two-dimensional while the third is one-dimensional, and if ministers come from parties A, B, and C, respectively, then the common-knowledge policy forecast for this government is the point $x = (A_1, A_2, B_3, B_4, C_5)$, where X_i is the ith component of party X's ideal point.

A key feature that distinguishes our approach from mainstream coalition theory is, therefore, that there is more to a government than its party composition. The *distribution* of jurisdiction-specific authority is central to our argument. Two coalitions with the same party composition may allocate key portfolios in different ways. They will, therefore, be forecast to have different policy outputs, and thus are different governments in our terms.[5]

There are thus T^m feasible portfolio allocations, and a different policy forecast associated with each one of these. We identify this collection of forecasts as the feasible set of policy outcomes in the game of government formation. In conventional spatial models, the feasible set consists of all of $\mathfrak{R}^n$. In our approach, in contrast, the feasible set is a finite *lattice, L,* defined

---

4. Presumably, no member of parliament may hold more than one portfolio, so that, if a party has fewer than m members of parliament, then the number of feasible governments is smaller than T^m.

5. It should be noted that, on the (extreme) assumption of no subsequent intragovernmental bargaining, these policy forecasts constitute rational expectations inasmuch as each minister's choice to implement jurisdiction-specific ideal point component(s) in his or her policy domain comprises a Nash equilibrium. (Note that this conclusion also depends on the jurisdictional separability of preferences.)

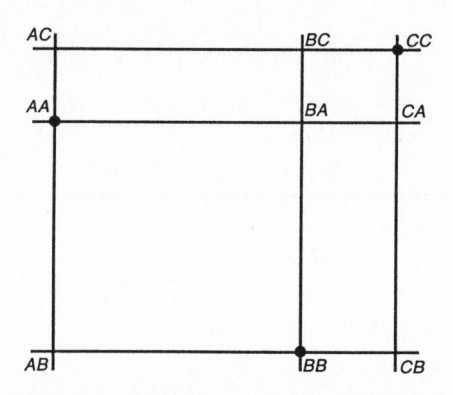

Fig. 1. The finite lattice for two unidimensional jurisdictions and three parties

by the ideal points of the actors on salient policy dimensions. Figure 1 displays the lattice, L, for an example with two unidimensional jurisdictions and three parties. The three party ideals are the single-party governments. The six additional lattice points are coalition governments, where IJ means that party I receives the horizontal portfolio and J the vertical portfolio.

We employ the conventional win-set machinery to examine equilibrium. Let $P_i(x)$ be the set of points in $\Re^n$ preferred to x by party i. We say that y is an element of the win-set of x if the combined weight of the parties for which $y \in P_i(x)$ exceeds one-half. That is, $y \in W(x)$ if $\Sigma_i w_i > 1/2$ for those parties for which $y \in P_i(x)$. We say further that the portfolio allocation leading to policy x is an empty win-set equilibrium (EWE) if and only if $x \in L$ and $W(x) \cap L = \emptyset$. Thus, prospective equilibria, and policies that upset such equilibria, are restricted to L, since only points on the lattice are the policy forecasts for feasible alternative governments.

In effect, EWEs in our approach are conventional spatial equilibria restricted to L. It is necessary, however, to extend this notion of equilibrium in order to capture a behavioral fact of life, namely, a party cannot be forced into an actual or prospective government against its will. Each participant in an actual or prospective government may veto it if it does not wish to participate in it. We define a veto-generated equilibrium (VGE) as an $x \in L$ for which every $y \in W(x) \cap L \neq \emptyset$ is vetoed by some participant. In figure 2, the government BA is a EWE and BB is a VGE, since the former's win-set has an empty intersection with L and, while the latter's does not, party B can (and will) veto any element of it (since it is a participant of each and prefers neither to its own ideal).

From our restriction of policy outcomes to the lattice L of forecasts of feasible government outputs, it follows that empty win-set equilibria are far more common than an application of chaos theorems to the full policy space

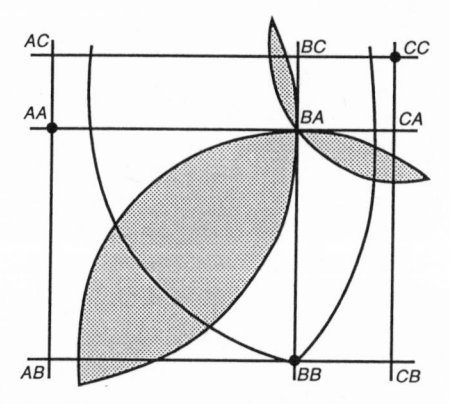

**Fig. 2. Graph of an empty win-set equilibrium (EWE) for government *BA*
and a veto-generated equilibrium (VGE) for government *BB***

$\mathfrak{R}^n$ (as in conventional spatial analysis) would suggest. In particular, such knife-edge distributional assumptions as radial symmetry are not required. In the case in which there are only unidimensional jurisdictions—the "simple" jurisdictional structure (Shepsle 1979)—we can be more specific. Notice that *BA* in figure 2 is the dimension-by-dimension median (DDM). As a corollary of the famous proposition by Kadane (1972) on the division of the question, we note that, under the simple jurisdictional structure, the DDM is a unique EWE, or no point is.

The analysis of VGEs in our early work centered on particular "proposal games" that we took to characterize the government formation process. In particular, we described a potential "standoff" between two alternative equilibria, one of these an EWE, the other the ideal point of some party participating in the EWE who exercised a veto over the EWE. Ongoing work is concentrating on what we call "strong" actors, actors in a position to veto every point in the win-set of their ideal point. Initial analysis suggests that strong actors are quite common under a range of plausible party configurations, and that these play a key role in the emergence of VGEs.

Having briefly summarized our approach to government formation in parliamentary settings, we devote the remainder of this essay to the theme of agenda formation. Let us reiterate that what follows is not a set of polished results, but, rather, an informal consideration of how agenda-related issues may emerge in cabinet government.

Ministers as Agenda Setters

As already noted, a key attraction of the Laver and Shepsle and Austen-Smith and Banks approach is the restriction of attention to the finite lattice, *L*. This lattice is generated by the assumption of complete ministerial discretion, an

assumption that must be acknowledged as a limitation of the approach in general. In its defense, it should be emphasized that much of cabinet government is *not* about the politics of legislating, but, rather, is about the politics of coordinating, administering, and implementing. Aside from a consideration of the annual budget, the key role of the legislature in a parliamentary government system is to generate and maintain the executive in office. To exaggerate somewhat, parliaments make and break governments, while governments rule. And they rule through their cabinet ministers.

Nevertheless, even this stylization of parliamentary government does not amount to an assumption of ministerial dictatorship. True, ministers do have considerable discretion. According to Churchill's *Miscellaneous Questions of [Cabinet] Procedure,* a slim volume of fourteen paragraphs outlining the rules and regulations of British cabinet government, "Matters which fall wholly within the Departmental responsibility of a single minister and do not engage the collective responsibility of the Government need not be brought to the Cabinet at all." Much of the day-to-day business of government is thus conducted between ministers and their senior civil servants.

However, important decisions on policy are likely to cross jurisdictional lines or to engage the collective responsibility of the government as a whole. And, as noted, even those decisions that do not must still pass muster with the civil servants who have various devices at their command to constrain, channel, or delay ministerial initiatives. All of these considerations lead us to consider relaxing the assumption of ministerial dictatorship in order to offer an alternative view of ministerial agenda power.

Imagine a jurisdictional status quo, $x^0 \in J_i$. If x^0 is identical to the minister's ideal, then this is an equilibrium. If not, then we need to specify the range of discretion available to minister i. Without being very specific, we define a set of points in J_i that, at the end of the day, cannot be blocked, delayed, or undone by official recalcitrance. Call it the *Whitehall set* of minister i, $WH_i(x^0) \subset J_i$. Likewise, define the set of points unblockable by the cabinet; call it the ith minister's *cabinet set,* $C_{iG}(x^0) \subset J_i$ when G is the government. The minister's feasible set, or range of discretion, is $F_i(x^0) = WH_i(x^0) \cap C_{iG}(x^0)$. Knowing a prospective minister's preferences, the status quo, and this feasible set ex ante, any agent can *still* make a government policy forecast in this jurisdiction, namely the minister's optimum when restricted to $F_i(x^0)$. That is, a minister in this formulation is much like a congressional committee operating under the closed rule, controlling the agenda in a given jurisdiction, but by no means free to do whatever he or she wishes.

On these assumptions, the original lattice, L, is no longer operative. Recall that L consists of the policy forecasts of every possible government, based on the hypothesis of absolute ministerial discretion. In our revision,

ministers operate under constraints. But there is still a commonly known policy forecast for each government. Calling this revised set of forecasts, one for each possible allocation of portfolios, L^*, the logic of our initial formulation, as applied to this alternative collection of points, holds; we can now specify EWEs and VGEs in terms of L^*.

One interesting difference emerges immediately. In the initial, unconstrained formulation, the policy forecast of ministerial behavior in each jurisdiction is implementation of the minister's ideal point. In the more restrictive formulation, the forecast is the minister's constrained optimum. But the opportunity set, $F_i(x^0)$, now depends on the government which minister i has joined. Different governments generate different cabinet dynamics and, as a consequence, different $C_{iG}(x^0)$ sets. Jurisdictional policy forecasts for a particular minister, therefore, are no longer invariant across every government of which the minister is a member.

Another interesting difference involves the status quo. In the unconstrained formulation, the status quo has no effect on policy forecasts (though it obviously affects the equilibrium analysis of government formation). Whatever x^0 is, if a specific party is awarded the ith portfolio, all agents know precisely what it will do, and this knowledge is invariant with respect to x^0. In the restricted-discretion formulation, in contrast, each jurisdiction-specific policy forecast is intimately related to x^0, inasmuch as it is the solution to a minister's constrained maximization problem, the feasible set of which depends on x^0.

We currently have no further suggestions with which to flesh out this revised approach. But this "reduced form" agenda model, similar in spirit to agenda institutions in committee-based legislatures under the closed rule, does have the virtue of suggesting a way to work around one especially restrictive feature of the earlier approach while still preserving some degree of ministerial discretion and a clear notion of a common-knowledge policy forecast associated with every prospective government.

Intragovernmental Bargaining

In figure 2, government *BA* is an EWE, but the policy forecast is not Pareto optimal for the winning coalition. There are unexhausted gains from trade in which minister *B* could make concessions in his or her jurisdiction in exchange for concessions from minister *A* in his or hers. The obvious question here concerns how the two ministers can commit to implementing a policy point off the lattice, given the extent of their discretion to "defect" from such a commitment.

But governments stay in office over quite an extended period of time. In this repeat-play setting, as the long history of the Prisoner's Dilemma game

suggests, Pareto improvements are possible, even in a world without binding commitment or third-party enforcement. Thus, even when ministers have complete discretion, the question is whether intragovernmental bargaining can generate gains from trade for government members and, if so, how rational expectations about this will affect government formation ex ante.

Consider once more the intragovernmental bargaining situation suggested by figure 2. If A and B form a government, with A getting the vertical portfolio and B the horizontal, then BA may be taken as the status quo. In effect, this is the reversion point if subsequent intragovernmental bargaining fails. The feasible set for subsequent bargaining between government members is defined by the AA-BB contract curve, the coalition's Pareto surface. Thus, the feasible set is given by the triangle with vertices AA, BB, and BA. Points in this triangle contain Pareto improvements on BA.[6]

This description shares a close resemblance to the Nash Bargaining game, which is also based upon a status quo and a feasible set. Recent scholarship on this may provide some insight into intragovernmental bargaining, though there is an additional "parameter" associated with Nash bargaining—the so-called threat point. The threat point for a player is what he or she can threaten to do if bargaining breaks down. But what can A and B threaten aside from reverting to the status quo BA, in which each minister sets policy in his or her jurisdiction according to his or her ideal point?

In this context, either coalition partner can threaten to bring down the government and enter into negotiations with C. But what does this mean? Frankly, it is not clear. Suppose B initiates a threat against A by withdrawing support, that is, voting no confidence in the BA government, and approaches C about forming a new government. Given an initial reallocation of portfolios between B and C, negotiations could commence between these new government partners. The initial portfolio assignments establish a status quo for this new government, and, as above, the BB-CC contract curve defines a feasible set. The outcome of bargaining between B and C, whatever it might be, constitutes B's threat against A in the original government. Likewise, the outcome of a potential negotiation between A and C constitutes A's threat against B.

In this way the intragovernmental bargaining problem between A and B is a Nash Bargaining game—a status quo, a feasible set, and a threat point for each of the bargainers. But the threat points are not well defined. The negotia-

---

6. It might be suggested that point AB, reflecting the circumstance in which A and B exchange portfolios, as well as all the points in the complementary triangle defined by vertices AA, BB, and AB, should also be treated as feasible bargaining outcomes. For us, however, the swapping of portfolios is indistinguishable from, say, A and C forming a government. Points AB and BA represent altogether *different* governments (even though they happen to involve the same coalition partners). Consequently, the feasible set for *intragovernmental* bargaining is the triangle described in the text.

tions between *B* and *C* and between *A* and *C,* the outcomes of which serve as threat points for the *A-B* negotiations, themselves depend upon threats. And these latter threats depend upon the bargainers, *A* and *C* or *B* and *C,* walking away from the table and taking up with the excluded third party (*B* and *A,* respectively). Thus, the outcome of the original *A-B* bargaining depends upon the threats of *A* and *B,* which depend upon the outcomes in the *A-C* and *B-C* negotiations, which in turn depend upon the threats in the *A-C* and *B-C* negotiations, which, to complete the circle, depend upon the outcome of the *A-B* bargaining. In short, the intragovernmental bargaining game is a Nash bargaining problem with *endogenous* threats.

There is a recent literature on Nash bargaining with endogenous threats (Binmore 1985; Bennett 1987; Binmore, Osborne, and Rubinstein, 1990; Chatterjee et al. 1990; Moldovanu 1990), though most of its roots are in cooperative game theory. And, as the preceding discussion suggests, there is a close resemblance between the intragovernment bargaining problem and the "competitive solution" (McKelvey, Ordeshook, and Winer 1978). Each of these literatures may prove useful in trying to understand the prospects for intragovernmental negotiations after an initial portfolio assignment. There are, however, added difficulties that need to be emphasized.

Most theories of bargaining characterize an outcome and its associated payoff distribution as the *terminal* state. In effect, when a bargaining problem is solved, the world ends. Government formation, on the other hand, is the *beginning* of politics, not its end. Even after intragovernment bargaining, there are ample opportunities for ministers to exercise discretion. Thus, any bargained outcome must not only be feasible, it must be self-enforcing as well, in the sense that parties to the bargain must have the incentive to carry out the deal that was cut despite having the discretion to depart from it. This, in turn, raises a host of incentive and monitoring problems that are often suppressed or ignored in discussions of Nash bargaining.

Finally, we must not forget that even if a "deal struck stays stuck," it must also be compatible with rational expectations and be an equilibrium of the government formation game. That is, the deal must have been anticipated ex ante by all agents, and it must have the property that no other deal, associated with some alternative allocation of portfolios, is preferred both by its participants and a parliamentary majority. The deal struck must constitute an EWE or VGE. The strategic setting is clearly complicated, but analytical progress seems possible.

Intraparty Bargaining

In most of our work to date, with the exception of Laver and Shepsle 1990b, we are as guilty as almost all other coalition theorists of the anthropomorphic fallacy of modeling political parties as unitary actors. Yet substantive intu-

ition, along with some systematic research (Luebbert 1986), suggests that parliamentary politics is influenced as much by what goes on inside parties as by what goes on among them.

As we have already shown (Laver and Shepsle 1990b), however, the fact that our approach concentrates upon the role of individual government ministers means that it can be adapted to take account of intraparty politics. Indeed, in its most comprehensively developed form, our approach is fundamentally about intraparty politics. As we have seen, a party establishes the credibility of its position in a particular policy jurisdiction by naming a party spokesperson whose "ideal" position on the policy dimensions in question is well known in advance. By appointing this person to the cabinet portfolio concerned, the party can guarantee a particular set of policy outputs.

Thus, a party cannot establish a credible claim that it will pursue a dovish military policy, for example, simply by saying that this is what it will do. Such talk comes cheap, and everyone knows this. Nor will the party inspire confidence in this claim if it keeps Attila the Hun as its defense spokesperson. No matter how much poor Attila proclaims his newfound, dovish ways, his hawkish reputational baggage will not be ignored. If, on the other hand, the party could boast the likes of Mahatma Ghandi, Ramsey Clark, or Jane Fonda among its well-known, senior members, then by naming one of them as spokesperson and prospective defense minister, the party will have credibly signaled its intention to pursue a more dovish course in military matters.

Thus, the policy position of a party is determined by the policy positions of its *stable of cabinet-caliber politicians,* and the *decision-making regime* that it uses to select spokespersons for key policy jurisdictions. The party's senior politicians have reputations that are solid enough to enable others to make reliable policy forecasts about their behavior in government.[7] The party's decision-making regime is the mechanism by which it assigns spokespersons to jurisdictions and makes tactical decisions about whether to join or support various governments.[8] Instead of representing a party by an ideal point in the policy-space, we now represent it by the *distribution* of ideals of its cabinet-caliber politicians and by a utility function summarizing the preferences induced by its decision-making regime.

For example, suppose there were three parties, each with four cabinet-caliber politicians, in a policy-space consisting of two, one-dimensional jurisdictions. There are 12 different ways in which each party could form a single-party government—namely, by assigning the first portfolio to one of their four

---

7. We assume that each party stable is given exogenously. We assume further that its composition is commonly known.

8. In Laver and Shepsle 1990b, we suggest two model types: the autocratic leader and the "national executive." The former is a single politician who makes decisions about spokespersons and about government participation in accord with his or her own policy preferences. The latter is a committee of policy-oriented politicians.

senior politicians and the second portfolio to one of the three remaining senior politicians. By a similar calculation, there are 16 different ways in which each of the three pairs of parties could form a coalition government. Thus, there are 36 feasible one-party governments and 48 feasible coalition governments—a feasible set consisting of 84 points. In contrast, our original lattice, *L,* with a unique point for each party, would have had 3 feasible single-party governments and 6 feasible coalition governments, or 9 points.

In addition to the modified feasible set produced by taking account of intraparty politics, the optimization problem is also changed. In the unitary-actor formulation, the components of a party's ideal serve not only to indicate policy forecasts associated with different portfolio allocations, but the ideal also anchors party preferences among alternative governments. One government ranks higher than another in the (Euclidean) preferences of a party if the "location" of the former is closer to the party's ideal than that of the latter. Taking account of intraparty politics, however, a party's policy position and its reference point for strategic decisions are no longer the same thing. Once a party spokesperson is appointed for each jurisdiction, their respective ideal point components determine the party *position.* However, comparisons between alternative governments are made by the party's decision-making regime. If that regime is a single autocratic leader, for example, then the *leader's* ideal point becomes the relevant reference point. If the regime is an executive committee, then there is no single reference point. In this event, tactical decisions about support for alternative governments are the result of interactions among members of the executive committee.

With this machinery, we can model government formation among non-unitary parties that takes account of intraparty politics. There are several different directions this modeling exercise can take. The most interesting, in our opinion, and also the most challenging direction involves the following sequence of choices for each party.[9]

1. Choose a decision-making regime.[10]
2. Contingent on the choices in (1) by each party, the party regime selects spokespersons from among its stable of cabinet-caliber politicians.
3. An election is held with voters expressing preferences based on the party position arrived at in (2). This determines each party's weight.
4. Government formation proceeds according to the (now) fixed position

---

9. In each stage, all the parties make simultaneous choices that are then commonly known before the beginning of the next stage.

10. Obviously, we run the risk of an infinite regress when we ask how a party chooses this regime. We assume that there is a prior "constitutional" agreement on this question, so that, at the beginning of any cycle, the method for choosing the decision-making regime is exogenously given.

of each party and its weight. Voting on various prospective governments by each party is determined by its decision-making regime. An EWE is defined as before. A VGE is one in which prospective alternatives in the win-set of a proposed government are vetoed by the decision-making regime of at least one of the participants in each alternative.[11]

This sequence describes a strategic setting in which, in principle, backward induction may be employed in the spirit of Austen-Smith and Banks 1988. The virtue of this approach is the virtue of the original Austen-Smith and Banks paper: it links electoral and legislative politics, making policy positions and weights endogenous. The obvious problem is its extremely ambitious scope.

A halfway house is to take each party's decision-making regime and weight as exogenous and model only legislative politics. In this setting, we might assume that a party's decision-making regime is free to set policy positions at any stage in the game by nominating the appropriate spokesperson from its stable of cabinet-caliber politicians. If this is the case, then the enlarged feasible set comes into play directly in the government equilibrium analysis. An EWE is any government in this enlarged set to which no other element in this enlarged set is preferred by any collection of decision-making regimes comprising majority weight. A VGE is one for which any element from the enlarged set falling in its win-set is vetoed by a participant.

Some examples of the approach are provided in Laver and Shepsle 1990b. While the approach strikes us as quite plausible and promising, systematic results are not yet available.

Discussion

We have suggested, in the context of a model of government formation in a parliamentary setting, several dynamic elements that affect both the political agenda and the choices made from it. These elements are ministerial discretion, intragovernment bargaining, and intraparty bargaining. The first, emphasizing the absence of commitment institutions and the more-or-less constrained discretion of ministers, places agenda formation squarely on members of the cabinet. The second, emphasizing the coalitional inefficiency of lattice points, suggests that policy-making need not stop with the investiture of a government— that bargaining inside the government continues the policy-making process by offering an expanded agenda of alternatives. The third, emphasizing political

---

11. The senior politicians selected to "represent" the party, both as a spokesperson and as a prospective minister, are assumed to serve if chosen. If party discipline means anything at all, then this assumption is plausible.

pluralism inside parties, expands the agenda of possible governments by enlarging the feasible set of implementable parties.

We have hardly made much of a dent in the systematic work that this kind of approach suggests. And we certainly have not broached the set of bold, Rikerian heresthetical maneuvers involved in the creation of new issues, new dimensions, or new jurisdictions. Indeed, in taking all of these things as fixed, the dynamics on which we have focused might more accurately be described as short-term adjustment processes—essentially normal, everyday politics— to be contrasted with the longer-term structural changes in politics associated with the emergence of new social cleavages, partisan realignments, and trans- formations of political practice. What we hope to have done, however, is to illustrate some of the processes of agenda formation that arise when politics is primarily driven by the need to select and maintain an executive, the essential force at work in parliamentary politics.

REFERENCES

Austen-Smith, David, and Jeffrey Banks. 1988. "Elections, Coalitions, and Legisla- tive Outcomes." *American Political Science Review* 82:405–422.
Austen-Smith, David, and Jeffrey Banks. 1990. "Stable Governments and the Alloca- tion of Policy Portfolios." *American Political Science Review* 84:891–906.
Banks, Jeffrey. 1985. "Sophisticated Voting Outcomes and Agenda Control." *Social Choice and Welfare* 1:295–306.
Bennett, Elaine. 1987. "Nash Bargaining Solutions of Multiparty Bargaining Prob- lems." In *The Logic of Multiparty Systems,* ed. M. J. Holler, 67–78. Dordrecht: Martinus Nijhoff.
Binmore, Ken. 1985. "Bargaining and Coalitions." In *Game-Theoretic Models of Bargaining,* ed. A. E. Roth, 269–93. New York: Cambridge University Press.
Binmore, Ken, Martin J. Osborne, and Ariel Rubinstein. 1990. "Noncooperative Models of Bargaining." Working Paper Series. Department of Economics, McMaster University.
Chatterjee, Kalyan, Bhaskar Dutta, Debraj Ray, and Kunal Sengupta. 1990. "A Non- cooperative Theory of Coalition Bargaining." Department of Economics, Penn- sylvania State University. Mimeo.
Gilligan, Thomas W., and Keith Krehbiel. 1987. "Collective Decision Making and Standing Committees: An Informational Rationale for Restrictive Amendment Procedures." *Journal of Law, Economics, and Organization* 3:287–337.
Hennessy, Peter. 1986. *Cabinet.* Oxford: Basil Blackwell.
Kadane, J. B. 1972. "On Division of the Question." *Public Choice* 13:47–54.
Kingdon, John W. 1984. *Agendas, Alternatives, and Public Policies.* Boston: Little, Brown.
Laver, Michael, and Kenneth A. Shepsle. 1990a. "Coalitions and Cabinet Govern- ment." *American Political Science Review* 84:873–90.

Laver, Michael, and Kenneth A. Shepsle. 1990b. "Government Coalitions and Intra-party Politics." *British Journal of Political Science* 20:489–507.

Laver, Michael, and Kenneth A. Shepsle. 1991a. "Divided Government: America is not 'Exceptional.'" *Governance* 4:250–69.

Laver, Michael, and Kenneth A. Shepsle. 1991b. "A Theory of Minority Government in Parliamentary Democracy." University College, Galway. Mimeo.

Luebbert, Gregory. 1986. *Comparative Democracy: Policy Making and Governing Coalitions in Europe and Israel*. New York: Columbia University Press.

McKelvey, Richard D. 1976. "Intransitivities in Multidimensional Voting Models and Some Implications for Agenda Control." *Journal of Economic Theory* 12:472–82.

McKelvey, Richard D., Peter C. Ordeshook, and Mark D. Winer. 1978. "The Competitive Solution for *N*-Person Games without Transferable Utility, with an Application to Committee Games." *American Political Science Review* 72:599–616.

Moldovanu, Benny. 1990. "Sequential Bargaining, Cooperative Games, and Coalition-Proofness." Department of Economics, University of Bonn. Mimeo.

Riker, William H. 1982. *Liberalism Against Populism*. San Francisco: Freeman.

Riker, William H. 1986. *The Art of Political Manipulation*. New Haven: Yale University Press.

Riker, William H. 1991. "Rhetorical Interaction in the Ratification Campaigns." University of Rochester. Mimeo.

Shepsle, Kenneth A. 1979. "Institutional Arrangements and Equilibrium in Multidimensional Voting Models." *American Journal of Political Science* 23:27–60.

Shepsle, Kenneth A., and Barry R. Weingast. 1984. "Uncovered Sets and Sophisticated Voting Outcomes with Implications for Agenda Institutions." *American Journal of Political Science* 28:49–75.

Shepsle, Kenneth A., and Barry R. Weingast. 1987. "The Institutional Foundations of Committee Power." *American Political Science Review* 81:85–104.

Weingast, Barry R. 1990. "The Political Economy of Slavery." Hoover Institution Working Paper.

Agreement, Defection, and Interest-Group Influence in the U.S. Congress

Richard A. Smith

In this essay, I investigate how interest groups influence outcomes in the U.S. Congress. I develop and test a theory of how the political and lobbying resources and activities of an interest group increase the probability that members of Congress will take public positions on a legislative proposal that agree with the position of the group. My focus is on the time after a legislative proposal has been approved by a committee of the House or Senate but before it actually comes to a vote on the floor. This is a critical period for interest groups to influence the formation of the decision agenda of the House or Senate. A proposal may never be scheduled for a vote, and hence never really be on the decision agenda, if the proposal is judged to have insufficient support in the House or Senate. Alternatively, a pending vote on a proposal may be postponed indefinitely, and thus the proposal may be removed from the decision agenda, if substantial opposition to the proposal develops. Consequently, an interest group can help put a proposal on the decision agenda and help keep it there by influencing the probability that members of Congress will support the proposal. An interest group can also help keep a proposal off the decision agenda by influencing the probability that members of Congress will oppose the proposal.

I present theory and evidence that are relevant to two of the three major themes about agenda formation that structure this volume. First, I provide insights about the ability of interest groups to control the origin of issues. One central argument and finding is that interest groups can create situations in which members of Congress will rarely, if ever, publicly oppose the position of the group. These situations are not easy to construct. They require that

My research was supported, in part, by grants from the National Science Foundation (SES-8607299) and Carnegie Mellon University. I wish to thank Paul Janaskie, Paul Cohen, and especially Amy Ulrich for their research assistance. I also owe special thanks to the lobbyists and officials of the American Federation of Teachers and the National Education Association, particularly Dale Lestina of the NEA.

groups develop and maintain strong relationships with members of Congress; in turn, this requires groups to possess substantial political and lobbying resources. But the evidence I present indicates that interest groups, such as the National Education Association, can develop these relationships with enough members of Congress that they appear capable of placing and keeping issues and policies on the decision agenda, especially when the relationships are with members of Congress that include key party leaders and members of the committees with jurisdiction over the issue.

Second, I provide insights into how interest groups can influence the success of efforts to manipulate issues. A recurring argument in this volume is that the rise and fall of issues and policies on an agenda depends importantly on the success of heresthetical campaigns that are designed to manipulate the dimensions of judgment on which the issues and policies are evaluated. Lobbying campaigns are, at their core, heresthetical campaigns in which opposing advocates invent and then disseminate competing interpretations of the consequences of enacting a legislative proposal. The aim of each interpretation is to emphasize one or more dimensions of judgment that will lead members of Congress to prefer one legislative proposal over another. One of my principle arguments is that efforts to influence the public positions of members of Congress through the manipulation of dimensions of judgment are likely to be most successful when defection conditions are present and least successful when defection conditions are absent. Whether defection conditions are present or absent is determined by the political and lobbying resources and activities of the interest groups. Defection conditions then become one way to understand how interest groups can influence the success of heresthetical campaigns designed to manipulate dimensions of judgment and, hence, the rise and fall of issues and policies.

Imagine a legislative proposal on which two interest groups are the primary advocates—one group supports the proposal and the other group opposes it. Each group is politically active, endorsing and providing campaign assistance to hundreds of the members of Congress in the last election. Each group has a large membership distributed across many states and House districts. The officials and lobbyists of both groups are intensely interested in the proposal. The proposal has just been approved by a House committee and has not yet been considered on the floor of the House of Representatives. The lobbyists of each group are planning and will execute major lobbying campaigns. They will repeatedly contact all House members about the proposal and will organize major, grass roots lobbying efforts, in which thousands of the members of their groups will write, call, or visit their House members about the proposal. Yet, despite the intensity of the lobbying campaigns, the proposal will generate little public interest. The proposal also will not provoke

an ideological response; many liberals and conservatives will support the proposal and many others will oppose it.

Now consider the following questions. Which House members will support the position of which group? How will the political and lobbying resources and activities of each interest group influence the decisions of House members? Will the lobbying campaign of each group change the positions of some House members? If so, which ones and why? Can the interest groups create situations in which some, perhaps many, House members will rarely, if ever, oppose the positions of the groups? If so, how?

Most answers to these questions would be based on the prevailing models in the literature: access (e.g., Truman 1971; Bauer, Pool, and Dexter 1972); exchange (e.g., Chappell 1982; Kau and Rubin 1982; Welch 1982), or pressure (e.g., Drew 1984). Yet all these models have a common shortcoming. They ignore the central decision processes of members of Congress. As a result, the models do not provide complete or accurate explanations of how the political and lobbying resources and activities of an interest group influence the decisions of members of Congress. They also do not provide precise predictions about which House members will support the position of a group or which House members will be most influenced by the lobbying campaign of the group.

In this essay, I examine how interest group influence depends on the basic decision processes of members of Congress. On every legislative proposal, members of Congress either formulate their public positions themselves or rely on others, typically colleagues whose expertise and judgment they trust, to formulate public positions for them (Matthews and Stimson 1975; Kingdon 1981). When members formulate their own public positions, those positions are the outcome of two decision processes: interpretation and explanation. Members develop private positions based on their interpretations of the consequences of taking various positions on the legislative proposal (Smith 1984; Fenno 1986).[1] Members generally make these private positions public if the positions do not conflict with the positions of important audiences, or, when the positions do conflict, if they believe they can successfully explain their private positions to those audiences (Fenno 1978; Kingdon 1981).

I will develop and test several hypotheses about the influence of an interest group over the public positions of members of Congress on a legislative proposal. The hypotheses describe how the level of influence depends

---

1. Riker has also written about the interpretation process, first calling it rhetoric (Riker 1984) and later including it as a category of heresthetics, called the "manipulation of dimensions" [of judgement or evaluation] (Riker 1986).

upon the extent to which the political and lobbying resources and activities of the interest group affect the interpretation and explanation processes of members. The hypotheses are tested with data from the lobbying campaigns to create a separate Department of Education that occurred in the House of Representatives in the spring and summer of 1979. These campaigns represent rare opportunities to construct strong tests. They have most of the features of the hypothetical campaigns described above. Moreover, extensive and unusual data are available about the positions of members of Congress and the political and lobbying activities and resources of the interest groups involved.

The essay is divided into four parts. The first part presents a theoretical discussion of the relationships between the political and lobbying activities and resources of an interest group and the interpretation and explanation processes. It concludes with the statement of several hypotheses. In the second part, I describe the lobbying campaign to create a separate Department of Education and discuss how it can be used as the basis for strong tests of the hypotheses. The third part presents an empirical analysis in which key theoretical concepts are defined and the hypotheses are tested. In the final part of the paper, I discuss some of the implications of the results for existing and future research on interest-group influence.

Interpretations, Explanations, and Defection Conditions

The extent to which the lobbyists of an interest group can influence the public positions of members of Congress during a lobbying campaign depends upon the extent to which they can influence the interpretation and explanation processes of members of Congress. Lobbyists try to influence the interpretation process by formulating and presenting arguments for their group's position. These arguments are designed to advance interpretations of the consequences of the group's position that the lobbyists believe members of Congress will find more appealing than the interpretations for alternative positions, thereby resulting in members developing private positions that agree with the position desired by the interest group. (For a description of these efforts and an analysis of their effects, see Smith 1984 and 1989).

The lobbyists of an interest group try to influence the explanatory process by making those members of Congress who view the interest group as an important audience believe that they would have to explain to the officials and members of the interest group any public position contrary to the position advocated by the group. The intent of the lobbyists is to get members of Congress to conclude that they cannot successfully explain an opposing position and must, instead, publicly support the position of the interest group. Lobbyists influence beliefs about the need to explain by emphasizing the

intensity of their group's interest in the legislative proposal, typically by asserting how important the proposal is to the officials and members of their group and by mounting a major lobbying campaign that includes extensive grass roots participation by the membership of the group.[2]

The actual impact of these efforts to influence the interpretation and explanation processes during a lobbying campaign can vary enormously across members of Congress. The level of influence is likely to be highest among those members who were endorsed by the interest group in the last election. Endorsed members are likely to have two characteristics that unendorsed members do not have. They are likely to share (or at least feel committed to supporting) many of the legislative objectives of the interest group. They are also likely to perceive the members and officials of the interest group as part of their primary or reelection constituencies. As a result, when members of Congress who were endorsed by an interest group are compared to those who were not, endorsed members are more likely to be accessible to the presentations of interpretations and are more likely to find those interpretations appealing. They are also more likely to view the interest group as an important audience for explaining. Endorsed members are, therefore, more likely than unendorsed members to agree with the position of the endorsing interest group and are more likely to be influenced by the efforts of the lobbyists of the endorsing group during the course of a lobbying campaign.

Yet even endorsed members will sometimes find the interpretations offered by an endorsing group to be unappealing and will, therefore, develop private positions that conflict with the position expected by the endorsing group. Whether members make those private positions public depends on whether they believe they can explain their defections from the position expected by the endorsing group in ways the endorsing group will accept. In particular, members of Congress must believe that they can convince the members and officials of an endorsing group that they had sound reasons for opposing the group this time, that their opposition does not reflect a general hostility toward the legislative objectives of the group, and that members and officials of the group should therefore not question whether they should continue to support the members of Congress in the next election.

---

2. As noted in the introduction, many House members do not directly formulate private and public positions on many legislative proposals. Instead, they rely on others, typically their colleagues whose judgment and expertise they trust, to process the information necessary to develop interpretations and explanations of various positions, and indicate to them through conversation, memo, or voting cues in the chamber what position is best (Matthews and Stimson 1975; Kingdon 1981). As a result, on most legislative proposals, the lobbyists for an interest group only have to concentrate on influencing the private and public positions of a relatively small number of members of Congress, since those members will largely influence the decisions of their less-informed and less-interested colleagues.

A major determinant of whether members of Congress believe they can formulate explanations that would be accepted by the endorsing group is the presence or absence of defection conditions. Defection conditions indicate relative weak spots in the relationship between the endorsing group and the member of Congress. The conditions concern the constituency, communication, and contribution resources of the endorsing group. The constituency defection condition is present when the group has only a small number of members in the district. The communication defection condition is present when the members of the group, regardless of their number, generally do not participate in grass roots lobbying campaigns or otherwise communicate with their member of Congress. The contribution defection condition is present when the members and officials of the endorsing group give little (if any) money to the election campaigns of the member of Congress.

The presence of defection conditions structure the opportunities for explaining defections in the following ways. The presence of either the constituency or communication defection condition allows members of Congress to claim that little or no support exists for the group's position and, therefore, they cannot publicly support it. Members of Congress can say to the officials and members of the interest group: "I know you really wanted me to support your position on this proposal, but I never got the sense your position had much support back in the district, even among your members. I never heard much in support of your position and I heard much against it. I'm sorry, but I just had to oppose you on this one. I had no other choice." The presence of the contribution defection condition influences the opportunities for explaining defection in a different way. Unlike the constituency and communication conditions, which provide the content for defection explanations, the presence of the contribution defection condition indicates the absence of an important obstacle to defection. Its presence means that members of Congress who want to defect from the position favored by the interest group do not have to explain their opposition to an interest group that gave them much-needed assistance in a recent election. Members of Congress do not have to consider how to explain their opposition when officials and members of the interest group say: "We helped you all we could when you needed it; why didn't you help us on this one issue that was so important to us?"

If these defection conditions are absent, then members of Congress whose private positions conflict with the position of an endorsing group will find it difficult to defect publicly from the position expected by the endorsing group. Indeed, when the endorsing group is perceived by the member as the most important audience on a legislative proposal, the member should rarely, if ever, publicly defect when defection conditions are absent. If one or more defection conditions are present, then members of Congress whose private positions conflict with the position expected by the endorsing group may begin to see opportunities to explain successfully public defections and will

thus sometimes publicly oppose the position of the endorsing group. As the number of defection conditions increases, members of Congress are more likely to perceive opportunities for successful explanations and, hence, are more likely to defect publicly.

In summary, the relationships among interpretations, explanations, and defection conditions suggest the following hypotheses about the probabilities of public agreement and public defection.

- The efforts by the lobbyists of an interest group to influence the interpretation and explanation processes during the lobbying campaign on a legislative proposal are likely to be most effective with the members of Congress that the group endorsed in the last election. As a result, the public positions of endorsed members of Congress are more likely than unendorsed members to agree with the position desired by the interest group. The level of agreement will be highest when the endorsed members perceive that the endorsing group is the most important audience on the proposal.
- When endorsed members view the endorsing group as the most important audience on the proposal, endorsed members will typically defect only if one or more defection conditions are present. As the number of defection conditions that are present increases, the probability of public defections will also increase.

Testing the Hypotheses: The Department of Education and the U.S. House of Representatives

Testing these hypotheses requires examining legislative proposals where interest-group participation in the lobbying campaign has the following characteristics.

- Interest groups are the primary proponents and opponents of the legislative proposal and dominate the planning and execution of the lobbying campaigns for and against the proposal.
- The interest groups that dominate the lobbying campaigns are politically active, endorsing hundreds of members of Congress in the past election.
- The members and officials of the interest groups that dominate the lobbying campaign are also viewed by many members of Congress as the most important audiences on the proposal.

Testing the hypotheses also requires the availability of extensive data about the lobbying activities and resources of the interest groups that dominate the lobbying campaigns on the proposal and the responses of members of

Congress to those activities and resources. At a minimum, for each of the politically active interest groups lobbying the proposal, enough data must be available to determine whether they endorsed the member of Congress and, if they did, whether the constituency, communication, and contribution defection conditions were present or absent. Sufficient data must also be available to indicate whether the positions of members of Congress on the proposal were influenced by the lobbying efforts of the interest groups in ways consistent with the hypotheses about the importance of endorsement status and defection conditions. The best data would consist of repeated measures of the positions of members of Congress throughout the lobbying campaign for the proposal. Such data would allow the strongest inferences about the impact of the lobbying efforts of interest groups on the positions of members. They would permit examining the relationship between changes in the lobbying efforts of the interest groups and changes in the positions of members of Congress.

Few of the lobbying campaigns for the legislative proposals that are considered in Congress have the interest-group participation characteristics outlined here. Even fewer also meet the necessary data requirements. However, one lobbying campaign comes close. It concerned the proposal to create a separate Department of Education by the House of Representatives in the spring and summer of 1979. A proposal to create a separate Department of Education first passed the Senate in the summer of 1978 but died in the House when the 95th Congress adjourned. The proposal was reintroduced into the 96th Congress and passed the Senate again in April, 1979, by a vote of 72 to 21. It narrowly passed the House in early July, 1979, by a vote of 210 to 206. In September, the House and Senate passed the conference report and President Carter signed the bill into law in October, 1979. The new department as proposed and approved did not create any new programs. Rather, it was a bureaucratic reorganization that consolidated education programs in HEW and some programs in other departments, the largest of which was the overseas schools for military personnel run by the Defense Department. Some education-related programs were not included, notably Head Start and Indian education.

Education interest groups dominated the lobbying campaigns for and against the proposal to create a separate Department of Education. The two largest, most politically active, public education membership groups—the National Education Association (NEA) and the American Federation of Teachers (AFT)—took opposing sides, despite a long history of working together on all proposals of common interest.

The NEA was the dominant group in a large coalition of interest groups that supported the creation of a separate Department of Education. It was the largest education group, and one of the largest membership groups, in the

country, with 1.7 million members distributed across all fifty states (representing about 70 percent of all public school teachers). Moreover, it was the only education group supporting the department that was politically active, endorsing 195 House members of the 96th Congress and providing over $500,000 in campaign contributions and thousands of volunteers to their campaigns in the 1978 elections. Furthermore, the NEA was the only group to try to develop an extensive grass roots lobbying network, with representatives, called contact team members, in every House district. Finally, the NEA was viewed as the prime instigator of the department by both members of Congress (in speeches recorded in the *Congressional Record*) and by columnists and editorialists in the major newspapers of the nation. Creating the department was the most important legislative priority of the NEA during the 96th Congress.

The AFT was the major public education interest group in the coalition against the department. The AFT represented about 500,000 public school teachers, primarily in large city school districts. About a third of its membership was concentrated in New York state. The AFT was politically active, endorsing 105 House members of the 96th Congress and contributing over $100,000 to their campaigns in the 1978 election. The AFT worked closely with private and parochial school groups, notably the U.S. Catholic Conference. The U.S. Catholic Conference represented the parochial school opposition to the department (the conference does not endorse or contribute to candidates).

In addition to the interest groups, President Carter, the White House, and especially Vice President Mondale, lobbied actively for the creation of a separate Department of Education. The Democratic party congressional leadership also supported it, but with less enthusiasm than the administration. The Republican congressional leadership opposed it. There was little apparent public interest in the department. The department was perceived by both observers and participants as an interest-group conflict, generating little interest among citizens who were not members of the groups involved in the fray.[3]

As for the data requirements, substantial data are available about the resources and activities of the AFT and the NEA. They are described in the next section, where the defection conditions for the NEA and AFT are defined. Extensive data are also available about the public positions of all the members of the House of Representatives on creating a separate Department of Education for the two-month period prior to the first vote. The data consist of "head counts" compiled by the NEA from the reports of its lobbyists and its coalitional allies, beginning on May 10 (just after the House Government

---

3. See Smith 1989 for evidence on this point. A national sample was asked their opinion about a separate Department of Education only once in the two years the issue was under active consideration by the Congress. In the fall of 1977, Gallup reported that the public was about evenly divided on the issue: 40 percent in favor; 45 percent opposed; and 13 percent don't know.

Operations Committee approved the department and sent it to the full House) and ending on July 11 (just before the House voted to approve the department).

Table 1 reports the head counts at about two- to three-week intervals over this two-month period. On May 10, the NEA held a substantial advantage, with 236 House members reporting that they were either "for" or "leaning for" creating the department. Over the next month, support for the department dwindled to 220 House members, while the opposition increased from 119 to 182. In the next month, support for the department held fairly steady, while the opposition continued to grow and deepen. By July 11, 219 House members reported that they supported the department with 206 of them expressing unqualified support and 216 House members reported opposition to the Department, 193 of whom were firmly against.[4]

The availability of these reported positions is especially significant because the lobbying efforts of the opponents to the department changed substantially over this two-month period, thereby providing opportunities to examine the influence of changes in the lobbying activities of interest groups on the formation of the reported positions of House members. In contrast to the lobbyists for the NEA and its allies who began lobbying the entire House membership around the first of the year, the lobbyists for the AFT, the U.S. Catholic Conference, and their allies did not begin lobbying the full House until the middle of May. Before that, they had concentrated their efforts on members of the House Government Operations Committee, hoping to defeat the department in committee. When the department passed the committee by one vote in early May, they were forced to mount a Housewide lobbying effort. That effort was in full operation by early June. For the remainder of the period, each side vigorously lobbied the entire House membership, repeatedly contacting those members who were not firmly for or against the department.

Testing the Hypotheses: Results

The Probability of Agreement

Recall the hypotheses about the probability of agreement that were developed in the theoretical discussion of the relationship among interpretations, expla-

---

4. The NEA and its coalitional allies took great care to insure that the head counts were accurate assessments of congressional sentiment at the time they were taken. Just how accurate, of course, is impossible to determine except for the last count, taken prior to the vote on final passage. That count was extremely accurate. Of the 426 House members who voted, paired, or announced a position, only three took positions contrary to the position reported in the last head count. The House approved the department 210 to 206 with 10 House members not voting, 4 House members pairing or announcing yes, and 5 House members pairing or announcing no.

TABLE 1. **Reported Positions of House Members of the 96th Congress on Selected Dates in 1979**

Position	May 10		May 25		June 7		June 29		July 11	
	N	Percentage	N	Percentage	N	Percentage	N	Percentage	N	Percentage
For	182	42	204	47	192	44	201	46	206	47
Leaning for	54	12	27	6	28	6	13	3	13	3
Undecided	80	18	49	11	33	8	5	1	—	—
Leaning against	33	8	30	7	34	8	24	6	23	6
Against	86	20	125	29	148	34	192	44	193	44
Total	435	100	435	100	435	100	435	100	435	100

nations, and defection conditions. They were as follows. The probability that members of Congress will agree with the position of an interest group on a legislative proposal depends importantly on whether the members were endorsed by the interest group in the past election. Endorsed members are more likely to attend to and find persuasive the interpretations offered by the lobbyists of the interest group and are more likely to view the members and officials of the interest group as an important audience. The more members perceive the interest group as the most important audience on a legislative proposal, the more likely their public positions will agree with the position of the interest group. Conversely, the less members perceive the interest group as the most important audience, and the more they see the opponents of the interest group (e.g., other interest groups, party leaders, presidents, and constituents) as the most important audiences, the less likely their public positions will agree with the interest group.

In the case of the Department of Education and the U.S. House of Representatives, the audiences that House members might see as important were the members and officials of all the education groups that lobbied the proposal, but especially those of the AFT and the NEA since they were the only politically active groups involved; President Carter, Vice President Mondale, and, more generally, the White House staff; and the House leaders of the Democratic and Republican parties. Just who House members actually perceived as important among these audiences probably depended primarily on the party/interest-group situations of the House members. These situations were defined by the party affiliation of the House members and whether the NEA or the AFT endorsed them in the 1978 election. Hence, a Democrat endorsed by the NEA probably viewed the White House, the House Democratic leaders, and the NEA as the important audiences. A Republican endorsed by neither the NEA or the AFT probably saw only the Republican House leadership as an important audience.

Yet many House members were in party/interest-group situations in which the important audiences advocated opposing positions. These members included Democrats endorsed by the AFT, Republicans endorsed by the NEA, and Democrats and Republicans endorsed by both the NEA and the AFT. These House members obviously could not satisfy all their important audiences. They needed to decide which audiences they considered to be most important and, hence, which position they considered to be dominant.

I used two rules to determine which position House members probably perceived as dominant. First, when the both AFT and the NEA endorsed the same House member, the position of the group that also agreed with the position advocated by the party of the House member was assumed to prevail. Second, when a House member was endorsed by only one of the interest groups, and the interest-group and party positions conflicted, the position of

the endorsing group was assumed to dominate. The application of these two rules produced the following expected positions for House members in each party/interest-group situation. House members expected to support the department were Democrats endorsed only by the NEA (NEA Dem), Republicans endorsed only by the NEA (NEA Rep), Democrats endorsed by both the AFT and the NEA (AFT/NEA Dem), and Democrats endorsed by neither the AFT or the NEA (No End Dem). House members expected to oppose the department were Democrats endorsed only by the AFT (AFT Dem), Republicans endorsed only by the AFT (AFT Rep), Republicans endorsed by both the AFT and the NEA (AFT/NEA Rep), and Republicans endorsed by neither the AFT and the NEA (No End Rep).

While the public positions of House members will generally agree with the dominant positions of their party/interest-group situations, the level of agreement can be greatly influenced by the nature of the lobbying campaign. High levels of agreement require well-planned and well-executed lobbying campaigns. The level of agreement is likely to be influenced the most in the early stages of the lobbying campaign by the party and interest groups that define the party/interest-group situation of House members. These early stages largely consist of contacting House members for the first time about the proposal. These initial contacts greatly increase the likelihood that House members will, for the first time, process and find persuasive the interpretations for the dominant position of their party/interest-group situation. The contacts also increase the probability that House members will realize that they will have to explain any positions that oppose the dominant position of their party/interest-group situation.

The later stages of a lobbying campaign consist of recontacting House members. Repeated contacts are likely to be less effective, because repeated exposures to the same interpretations are not likely to persuade House members who were not initially persuaded. Repeated lobbying contacts are also unlikely to change substantially the beliefs of members about the need to explain if the initial contacts were not sufficient. Instead, repeated contacts help maintain the influence that the lobbyists have already established. The contacts demonstrate to House members that the party's or interest group's position on and interest in the legislative proposal has not changed. These demonstrations are particularly important when opponents of the party and interest groups are also repeatedly contacting House members.

Hence, the initial efforts of a lobbying campaign are likely to produce the greatest increases in the number of House members who will take public positions that agree with the position of the interest group, especially among those members who view the group as an important audience. However, the rate of increase is likely to decline as the lobbying campaign continues.

Dominant positions and lobbying efforts had a major impact on the

development of public positions on the Department of Education by House members. Table 2 shows the probability that House members agreed with the dominant positions of their party/interest-group situations for selected dates. Agreement occurred when House members reported leaning toward or supporting a position that agreed with their dominant position. As expected, most House members agreed with the dominant positions of their party/interest-group situations, with nearly three-quarters of them having expressed agreement by July 11.

Of greater interest, however, are the changes in the probability of agreement over time. As hypothesized, the probabilities of agreement increased substantially for House members who were in party/interest-group situations where the position of the AFT or the Republican party leadership dominated (i.e., AFT Dem, AFT Rep, AFT/NEA Rep, and No End Rep), with the largest proportion of the increase having occurred by June 7. These increases corresponded closely to the substantial increase in the lobbying efforts of the AFT, the U.S. Catholic Conference, members of the Republican party, and other opponents of the department during the month of May. After June 7, the increases in the probabilities of the agreement began to decline and, by June 29, no more increases occurred.

In contrast, the probabilities of agreement were high and quite stable over the entire two-month period for House members who were in party/interest-group situations where the position of the NEA or the Democratic party leadership dominated (i.e., NEA Dem, NEA Rep, AFT/NEA Dem, and No End Dem). The high levels of agreement suggest that the lobbying efforts of the NEA and its allies had already had their major impact by May 10. Apparently, if the lobbying efforts over the next two months had any effect, it was the maintenance of the high levels of agreement.

TABLE 2. The Probability of Agreement by Party or Endorsement Situation on Selected Dates in 1979

Party/Interest-Group Situation	N	Probability of Agreement				
		May 10	May 25	June 7	June 29	July 11
NEA Dem	98	.79	.79	.78	.78	.79
NEA Rep	10	.70	.70	.80	.80	.80
AFT/NEA Dem	84	.77	.76	.74	.74	.75
AFT Dem	17	.47	.71	.65	.71	.71
AFT Rep	1	.00	.00	.00	.00	.00
AFT/NEA Rep	4	.00	.50	.50	.50	.50
No End Dem	76	.57	.54	.46	.49	.49
No End Rep	145	.55	.63	.71	.82	.82
All House Members	435	.64	.68	.68	.73	.73

The Probability of Defection

When the lobbyists of an interest group set out to build a winning coalition for a position on a legislative proposal, they must do more than just increase the probabilities of public agreement for those House members who are in party/ interest-group situations where the position of the lobbying group dominates. Often, insufficient numbers of House members are in those party/interest-group situations and so, even if the group's lobbyists were able to increase the probabilities of public agreement to one, they would still fall short of a winning coalition. For example, the opponents of the Department of Education could have counted on only 167 House members opposing the department if the positions of all House members agreed with the dominant positions of their party/interest-group situations. Of course, the probabilities of agreement rarely (if ever) approach one and thus the lobbyists of a group cannot depend upon a winning coalition forming, even if a majority of House members are in the party/interest-group situations where the group's position dominates. For example, 268 House members were in party/interest-group situations where the dominant position was support for the Department of Education, but only 185 of them actually reported positions of support. Hence, if the lobbyists of an interest group want to win, they need to do more than just increase the probabilities of public agreement. They also need to increase the probabilities of public defection for House members who are in those party/interest-group situations where the position of the lobbying group does not dominate.

However, as I argued in the theoretical discussion about the relationship among interpretations, explanations, and defection conditions, the success of lobbyists in increasing the level of public defection depends critically on the presence of the constituency, communication, and contribution defection conditions. In the case of the Department of Education, the constituency defection condition was defined by the number of members that the NEA and AFT had in the district of the House member and the number of children enrolled in private schools in the district in 1980. The latter was included to indicate the districts in which the U.S. Catholic Conference and the other organizations representing parochial schools had a strong constituency presence. The communication defection condition was defined by the strength of the NEA's grass roots lobbying network in each district, as indicated both by the assessments of NEA lobbyists and the actual number of grass roots contacts. The contribution defection condition was defined by the size of the campaign contribution that the AFT and the NEA made to House members in the 1978 election.

The precise definitions of the defection conditions depended upon the party/interest-group situations of the House members. The conditions were defined one way for all House members in the NEA Dem, NEA Rep, AFT/NEA Dem, and No End Dem situations, and in a different way for all

TABLE 3. Definitions of Defection Conditions

Group	Condition	Variable Definition
	Constituency Defection	
AFT Dem, AFT Rep, NEA/AFT Rep, No End Rep	PROPAFT < .50	PROPAFT = proportion of public school teachers in each House district who were members of AFT in 1980–81
NEA Dem, NEA Rep, NEA/AFT Dem, No End Dem	PROPNEA < .50, or PRIVEDUC ≥ .15	PROPNEA = proportion of public school teachers in each House district who were members of the NEA in 1980–81
		PRIVEDUC = proportion of children in each House district who attended private schools in 1980
	Communication Defection	
AFT Dem, AFT Rep, NEA/AFT Rep, No End Rep	CCTQUAL = 0, and CONTAC81 ≥ 10	CCTQUAL = quality assessments of NEA's Congressional Contact Team program in each state during the 96th Congress (1979–80)[a]
NEA Dem, NEA Rep, NEA/AFT Dem, No End Dem	CCTQUAL = 1, or CONTAC81 < 5	CONTAC81 = number of times an NEA member who resided in the House member's district lobbied the member in Washington during the 97th Congress (1981–82)
	Contribution Defection	
AFT Dem, AFT Rep	AFTMONY < $1,000	AFTMONY = AFT campaign contributions to each House member during the 1978 election campaign
NEA Dem, NEA Rep	NEAMONY < $1,000	NEAMONY = NEA campaign contributions to each House member during the 1978 election campaign
NEA/AFT Rep	(AFTMONY − NEAMONY) < $1,000	
NEA/AFT Dem	(NEAMONY − AFTMONY) < $1,000	

[a]Quality assessments were made by members of the NEA's Government Relations staff; coded 1 if quality was below average and 0 if average or above average.

House members in the AFT Dem, AFT Rep, AFT/NEA Rep, and No End Rep situations. For example, the constituency defection condition was present for NEA Dem House members when fewer than 50 percent of the public school teachers in their districts were represented by the NEA in 1980 or more than 15 percent of the children in their districts in 1980 were enrolled in private and parochial schools. The constituency defection condition was present for AFT Dem House members when fewer than 50 percent of the public school teachers in their districts were represented by the AFT. All defection conditions are defined in table 3.

The presence of one or more of these conditions is related to the probability of defection because the conditions provide House members who would like to defect with opportunities to develop explanations for their public defections. House members can emphasize to the leaders and members of the party and interest groups that define their party/interest-group situations that the dominant position appears to have little support in their districts, and, as a result, they cannot publicly support it.

If the link between explanations and defection conditions is strong and pervasive, then the circumstances of public defection by House members are highly predictable. House members will publicly defect only if: (1) their private positions disagree with the dominant positions of their party/interest-group situations, and (2) defection conditions exist that enable House members to formulate explanations of their public defections. This hypothesized pattern of public defections is depicted in table 4. The entry "0.00–1.00" indicates that the presence of defection conditions is necessary but not sufficient for public defection. The actual probabilities or public defection depend on the willingness of House members to explain their public positions, which in turn depends on many variables other than the presence of defection conditions, such as the personalities and the home styles of House members (Fenno 1978).

Unfortunately, tests for this pattern are not feasible. While data about defection conditions and the public positions of House members are available, data about the private positions of House members generally are not. The measurement of private positions largely depends on the self-reports of House members, which makes measurement infeasible for more than a few House

TABLE 4.   Predicted Probability of Public Defection

Private Position	No Defection Conditions Present	Defection Conditions Present
Conflicts	.00	0.00–1.00
Agrees	.00	0.00

members on a few proposals. Moreover, the accuracy of the reports would always be in some doubt, since House members might feel quite uncomfortable revealing a private position that conflicted with the position of important audiences.[5]

As a result, hypotheses about the importance of defection conditions must be tested more indirectly. The tests consist of observing the extent to which the pattern of public defection and agreement conforms to the one predicted in table 5. The predictions take the following form. When defection conditions are present, House members may or may not publicly defect. However, if they do publicly defect, House members will only do so when one or more of the defection conditions are present. Or, to put it another way, the presence of defection conditions is predicted to be a necessary, but not sufficient condition for public defection and the absence of defection conditions is predicted to be a sufficient, but not necessary condition for public agreement.

These predictions about necessary and sufficient conditions are tested in table 6. Contingency table presentations are the best way to model the relationships shown in table 5. More powerful, multivariate, polytomous dependent variable, statistical models, like logit and probit, are simply unable to represent this relationship.

Consider, for example, a bivariate model in which the dependent variable is whether the House member publicly defected and the independent variable is the presence of defection conditions.[6] The problem is that logit and probit coefficients are sensitive to the proportion of House members who publicly defect when the defection conditions are present. If a large proportion of House members defect when the defection conditions are present, then the coefficient for the presence of defection conditions will be large with small standard errors. If only a small proportion of House members defect when the defection conditions are present, then the coefficient will be small with large standard errors. Yet the proportion of House members who defect when

---

5. Private positions are also difficult to estimate indirectly. Sometimes clever reasoning and deduction by a scholar can persuasively reconstruct what the private positions of some House members must have been on a legislative proposal (for examples of this technique, see Riker 1984 and 1986, esp. chap. 11). Sometimes measures of the ideology of the House members or the characteristics of their geographical constituencies are used to estimate their private positions (as examples, see Chappell 1982; Kau and Rubin 1982). Of course, the success of this approach depends on the level of correlation between these measures and the representatives' private positions—a correlation that can only be established by assumption. In the case of the Department of Education, an assumption of high correlation is inappropriate. See Smith 1989 for evidence.

6. Alternatively, the department variable could be the presence of the defection conditions and the independent variable could be whether the House members publicly defected. The model would still be unable to represent the pattern predicted in table 5.

TABLE 5. Predicted Probabilities of the Absence or Presence of Defection Conditions, Given Public Positions that Defect or Agree

Private Position	No Defection Conditions Present	Defection Conditions Present
Defects	0.00	1.00
Agrees	0.00–1.00	0.00–1.00

defection conditions are present is largely irrelevant for testing the defection predictions. Instead, the key test is whether any House members publicly defect when the defection conditions are absent. That is not captured well in logit or probit analyses.

In table 6, the rows are defined by the reported positions of House members on May 10 and July 11 compared to the dominant positions of their party/interest-group situations. Defection is defined as a reported position that deviates from the expected positions (e.g., an AFT Dem who supports the department). Agreement is defined as a reported position that is consistent with the expected position (e.g., an AFT Dem who opposes the department).[7] The row entries indicate whether the reported positions of House members on May 10 and July 11 agreed with or defected from the expected position of their party/interest-group situations. Agreement/Defection, therefore, indicates all those House members who reported positions on May 10 that were consistent with the dominant position of their party/interest-group situations, but who reported positions on July 11 that were inconsistent with that position.

Three sets of comparisons are shown in table 6. The comparisons are structured by the endorsement status of the House member and the presence or absence of defection conditions. The category of All Endorsed House Members includes all those members who were endorsed by the NEA, the AFT, or both in the 1978 election. The second All Endorsed House Members category includes the set of endorsed members for whom the contribution defection condition was always present (e.g., an NEA Dem who received less than $1,000). The All Unendorsed House Members category includes all those members who were not endorsed by either the NEA or the AFT. The defection condition categories refer to the absence or the presence of the constituency, communication, and contribution defection conditions. The Contribution Defection Condition Present and Additional Defection Conditions Present categories are necessary because the contribution defection condition is present for some endorsed House members and all unendorsed House members.

---

7. The expected positions were consistent with the May 10 positions 64 percent of the time (280 of 435) and the July 11 positions 73 percent of the time (318 of 435).

Table 6. The Probability of Agreement or Defection by Endorsement Situation and the Presence of Defection Conditions

Reported Positions on May 10 and July 11	All Endorsed House Members			All Endorsed House Members[a]				All Unendorsed House Members	
	N	No Defection Conditions Present	One or More Defection Conditions Present	N	Contribution Defection Condition Present	Additional Defection Conditions Present	N	Contribution Defection Condition Present	Additional Defection Conditions Present
Defection/Defection	18	.000	1.000	16	.188	0.812	35	.086	.914
Undecided/Defection	18	.000	1.000	16	.063	0.937	13	.077	.923
Agreement/Defection	16	.000	1.000	13	.154	0.846	17	.118	.882
Total	52	.000	1.000	45	.133	0.867	65	.092	.908
Agreement/Agreement	141	.142	0.858	91	.462	0.538	106	.198	.802
Undecided/Agreement	17	.176	0.824	12	.500	0.500	32	.219	.781
Defection/Agreement	4	.000	1.000	4	.000	1.000	18	.056	.944
Total	162	.142	0.858	107	.449	0.551	156	.186	.814

[a] Includes only those endorsed House members for whom the contribution defection condition was always present.

The patterns of agreement and defection reported in table 6 are strongly consistent with the predictions about the impact of defection conditions. By July 11, House members *never* defected from the position of their party/ interest-group situation when all three defection conditions were absent and rarely defected when only the contribution defection condition was present. In contrast, the House members who agreed with the position of their party/ interest-group situation on July 11 were more evenly distributed across the defection categories. Indeed, the distribution pattern for those who agreed was so different from the pattern for those who defected that it was unlikely to have occurred by chance.[8] Clearly, the presence of defection conditions was necessary for public defection and the absence of defection conditions was sufficient for public agreement.

When defection conditions are present, the lobbyists of an interest group can also significantly increase the probability of public defection. Their major tactic is to formulate and present interpretations of the position of their group that they believe will appeal to all House members, not just the House members of the party and interest-group situations where the position of their group is dominant. One way to observe the success of this tactic is to compare the probabilities of defection for House members in different party/interest-group situations on May 10 and July 11.

Recall that, on May 10, the AFT, the U.S. Catholic Conference, and the Republicans had not yet mounted a Housewide lobbying campaign; thus, potentially appealing interpretations for opposing the department were probably not yet widely disseminated. In contrast, the NEA and its coalitional allies had been lobbying the entire House for several months; thus, the interpretations for supporting the department had been repeatedly presented to most House members. House members were therefore more likely to be aware of the interpretations for supporting the department and less likely to be aware of the interpretations for opposing the department.

Hence, as of May 10, House members who were in party/interest-group situations in which the dominant position was support for the department were likely to develop private positions that agreed with the dominant position. They were therefore unlikely to defect publicly. House members who were in the party/interest-group situations in which the dominant position was opposition to the department were likely to form private positions that conflicted with the dominant position. They were likely to defect publicly when defection conditions were present.

---

8. Assuming the distributions were generated by a Bernoulli process, the probabilities that the two proportions for the row entries, All Defections on July 11 and All Agreements on July 11, are equal are: .0062 for All Endorsed House Members; .0000 for the second category of All Endorsed House Members; and .0748 for All Unendorsed House Members.

However, once the AFT and its allies mounted a Housewide lobbying campaign, House members were more likely to be aware of appealing interpretations for opposing the department. House members who were in party/interest-group situations in which support for the department was the dominant position were more likely than before to formulate private positions that conflicted with their dominant positions and, thus, were more likely to defect publicly when defection conditions were present. By July 11, then, the probabilities of public defection should be similar for all House members regardless of their party/interest-group situation.

Table 7 presents the probabilities of public defection for the Department of Education by the party/interest-group situations of the House members and the number of defection conditions present. The probabilities reported for May 10 are highly consistent with the hypothesized relationships. Since the opponents of the department had yet to mount their Housewide lobbying effort, the probabilities of defection were higher for House members who were in the AFT Dem, AFT Rep, AFT/NEA Rep, and No End Rep situations than for the House members who were in the NEA Dem, NEA Rep, AFT/NEA Dem, and No End Dem situations. As the lobbying efforts of the opponents of the department increased, the probabilities of defection became more even. The defection probabilities reported for July 11 show that the probabilities increased substantially for the House members in the NEA Dem, NEA Rep, AFT/NEA Dem, and No End Dem situations, while the probabilities for House members in the other situations stayed the same or declined. Taken together, these two patterns of probabilities clearly indicate that the lobbying efforts of a group can have a substantial influence on the probabilities of defection by House members.

Conclusions

I have sought to develop and test a theory of how the political and lobbying resources and activities of an interest group increase the probability that members of Congress will take public positions on a legislative proposal that agree with the position of the group. The theory explained how political and lobbying resources and activities influence the interpretation and explanation processes of members of Congress, and I showed that the presence or absence of defection conditions were important determinants of whether members of Congress took public positions that agreed with or defected from the position of the interest group. I also demonstrated that the lobbying campaigns of an interest group had a major influence on the probabilities of public agreement and defection.

My results make several important contributions to the literature on

TABLE 7. The Probability of Defection by Party/Interest-Group Situation and the Number of Defection Conditions Present

Party/Interest-Group Situation	Defection Conditions Present							
	0		1		2		3	
	Probability	N	Probability	N	Probability	N	Probability	N
				May 10				
NEA Dem, NEA Rep, NEA/AFT Dem	.00	19	.04	75	.13	52	0.11	46
AFT Dem, AFT Rep, NEA/AFT Rep	.00	4	.20	10	.57	7	1.00	1
No End Dem	—	—	.12	25	.26	23	0.25	28
No End Rep	—	—	.10	10	.21	121	0.71	14
All House Members	.00	23	.08	120	.21	203	0.26	89
				July 11				
NEA Dem, NEA Rep, NEA/AFT Dem	.00	19	.12	75	.29	52	0.43	46
AFT Dem, AFT Rep, NEA/AFT Rep	.00	4	.20	10	.71	7	1.00	1
No End Dem	—	—	.24	25	.52	23	0.75	28
No End Rep	—	—	.00	10	.17	121	0.36	14
All House Members	.00	23	.14	120	.26	203	0.53	89

Congress and interest groups. First, they indicate that interest groups can strongly influence the extent to which members of Congress will publicly oppose an interest group. Indeed, they provide the first evidence that interest groups have the capacity to construct situations in which members of Congress will rarely (if ever) publicly oppose the position of the group.

Second, my results indicate that more attention needs to be given to the suitability of statistical approaches for analyzing interest-group influence. Clearly, the standard statistical approaches used to study interest-group influence, such as regression, logit, or probit models, do not capture well the influence relationships described here. They cannot represent the hypothesized relationships in which the presence of defection conditions is necessary for public defection and the absence of defection conditions is sufficient for public agreement. Indeed, they would understate the actual level of influence that an interest group has.

Third, I offer the first evidence of how lobbyists can influence the evolution of the public positions of members of Congress by documenting the existence of substantial short-term changes in the public positions of members of Congress. In so doing, I suggest that efforts to influence the public positions of members of Congress through the formulation and presentation of appealing interpretations are likely to be most successful when defection conditions are present and least successful when defection conditions are absent.

Fourth, my results suggest that serious thought needs to be given to how to represent the relationship between the level of influence of an interest group and the level of its political and lobbying resources and activities. Existing analyses assume that the relationship is linear and continuous: the greater the number of members in the districts of the House members or the larger the campaign contributions, the greater the influence (providing resources have any effect at all). The concept of defection conditions, however, assumes that the relationship is discontinuous and conditional on whether the interest group is viewed by the member as an important audience. Ultimately, assumptions are justified on theoretical grounds. The assumption of a discontinuous, conditional relationship is grounded in a theory of congressional decision making that emphasizes the centrality of the interpretation and explanation processes. In contrast, the theoretical rationale for a continuous relationship is unclear.

Finally, I have shown how interest-group influence is strongly structured by the interpretation and explanation processes. Therefore, my results indicate how the public positions of members of Congress and their reactions to the lobbying efforts of an interest group can be responses to both argument and pressure; to both the desire to make good public policy and the need to be politically expedient.

REFERENCES

Bauer, Raymond A., Ithiel De Sola Pool, and Lewis Anthony Dexter. 1972. *American Business and Public Policy: The Politics of Foreign Trade.* 2d ed. Chicago: Aldine-Atherton.

Chappell, Henry W., Jr. 1982. "Campaign Contributions and Congressional Voting: A Simultaneous Probit-Tobit Model." *Review of Economics and Statistics* 62:77–83.

Drew, Elizabeth. 1984. *Politics and Money: The New Road to Corruption.* New York: Macmillan.

Fenno, Richard F., Jr. 1978. *Home Style: House Members in their Districts.* Boston: Little, Brown.

Fenno, Richard F., Jr. 1986. "Observation, Context, and Sequence in the Study of Politics." *American Political Science Review* 80:1–15.

Kau, James B., and Paul H. Rubin. 1982. *Congressmen, Constituents, and Contributors: Determinants of Roll Call Voting in the House of Representatives.* Boston: Martinus Nijhoff.

Kingdon, John W. 1981. *Congressmen's Voting Decisions.* 2d ed. New York: Harper and Row.

Matthews, Donald R., and James A. Stimson. 1975. *Yeas and Nays: Normal Decision Making in the U.S. House of Representatives.* New York: Wiley.

Riker, William H. 1984. "The Heresthetics of Constitution-Making: The Presidency in 1787, with Comments on Determinism and Rational Choice." *American Political Science Review* 78:1–16.

Riker, William H. 1986. *The Art of Political Manipulation.* New Haven: Yale University Press.

Smith, Richard A. 1984. "Advocacy, Interpretation, and Influence in the U.S. Congress." *American Political Science Review* 78:44–63.

Smith, Richard A. 1989. "Interpretation, Pressure, and the Stability of Interest Group Influence in the U.S. Congress." Paper presented at the annual meeting of the American Political Science Association, Atlanta.

Truman, David B. 1971. *The Governmental Process: Political Interests and Public Opinion.* 2d ed. New York: Knopf.

Welch, William P. 1982. "Campaign Contributions and Legislative Voting: Milk Money and Dairy Price Supports." *Western Political Quarterly* 35:478–95.

Part 3
The Manipulation of Issues

Agenda Setting and Beyond: Television News and the Strength of Political Issues

Shanto Iyengar

In democratic societies, the selection of political leaders and the formation of public policy is dependent, in large measure, upon the political values and preferences of ordinary citizens. Accordingly, the characteristics and anteced-ents of individuals' opinions may be treated as important determinants of public choice. Most research on voting suggests that the sense of party identi-fication (whether voters consider themselves Democrats or Republicans) is the dominant psychological antecedent of electoral behavior. This "dispositional" model of choice relegates contextual factors to a trivial role. The impact of campaign debates and televised advertisements on voting preferences, for instance, is typically discounted. Campaigns are thought to matter only inso-far as they reinforce or activate voters' "natural" (e.g., partisan) preferences.

Contrary to the dispositional view of electoral choice, in this essay, I suggest that political opinions and choices are subject to significant circum-stantial (and short-term) influence. In particular, I argue that voters' attention span is limited to the small subset of relevant political issues that are high-lighted by the news media. In addition, I argue that the manner in which political issues are framed by the media has important consequences for the likelihood that incumbents (or challengers) stand to gain (or lose) by discuss-ing these issues. As a result, there exists a significant potential for campaigns to persuade voters.

As a practical matter, most people are unable or unwilling to monitor the course of public affairs carefully. Therefore, they attend selectively to a few issues that, for some reason, seem important; these issues become the princi-pal dimensions for evaluating and judging candidates or parties (see Krosnick 1988; Iyengar 1990). Because public opinion is based on narrow and issue-specific considerations, changes in the salience of issues are likely to shift the distribution of preferences and, thereby, to alter political outcomes. For exam-ple, the candidate whose positions are most preferred when voters consider

the issues of poverty and tax reform might not be the candidate of choice when crime and tax reform are substituted as the focal issues. Accordingly, a great deal of political rhetoric and campaign strategy consists of efforts to capitalize on this "disequilibrium of tastes" (Riker 1980) by bringing forward particular issues at the expense of others. Naturally, candidates prefer to be evaluated on the issues that place them at a relative advantage.

In contemporary U.S. politics, the mass media—and especially television news—are vital components of the process by which issues achieve public salience. For most people in the United States, the world of public affairs exists primarily in the imagery of television news shows. Here, I summarize the effects of television news coverage on the salience of political issues. I begin by proposing a general explanation of the impact of television news on public opinion, an explanation rooted in the concept of information accessibility. I then describe studies showing that those issues that are made more accessible by television news coverage are accorded higher priority by viewers and become especially influential as criteria for choosing between political candidates. I also present evidence that the manner in which television news frames political issues influences the extent to which issues that have already "hit" the public agenda become politicized in the sense of determining electoral outcomes. In concluding, I discuss the factors affecting editorial discretion and their implications for the evolution of political issues.

The Psychology of Media Influence: The Accessibility Bias

The influence of television news stems from its power to make information "accessible" or more retrievable from memory. In general, the "accessibility bias" argument stipulates that information that can be more easily retrieved from memory tends to dominate judgments, opinions, and decisions, and that, in the area of public affairs, more accessible information is information that is more frequently or more recently conveyed by the media.

Obviously, any number of factors could be considered when forming an impression of a person, purchasing a product, or choosing between political candidates, vacation tours, or job offers. The accessibility bias assumes that individuals tend to retrieve only a tiny sample of information from long-term memory. Rather than ransacking their memories for every item of relevant information, individuals select information that happens to be more conveniently "located" or accessible.

There are several competing accounts of the memory structures and processes giving rise to the accessibility bias. Wyer and Srull, for example, propose a model of long-term memory in which pieces of information are categorized and stored in a series of "referent bins" (bins containing subject-

matter information about particular politicians, issues, events, groups, etc.). A critical postulate of the Wyer and Srull model is that those items of information that have been more frequently (or recently) used are stacked at the top of the referent bins and are, therefore, encountered first when individuals locate the appropriate bin (see Wyer and Srull 1986).[1]

The accessibility bias appears primarily in the weights individuals assign various considerations when expressing attitudes or making choices. Considerations that were made more accessible (by a variety of experimental methods) have been found to exert significantly greater effects on attitudes and choices than equally relevant but less accessible considerations.

Well-known manifestations of the differential-weighting-by-accessibility principle include the tendency to overestimate the frequency of sensationalized events (such as fires and traffic accidents) as causes of death and to underestimate the frequency of "quiet" risks such as heart disease and stroke (see Slovic, Fischhoff, and Lichtenstein 1982). Parallel results have been obtained with respect to interpersonal impressions—people typically evaluate their friends or colleagues according to traits or features that are momentarily prominent (for a review of these studies, see Wyer and Hartwick 1980; Higgins and King 1981). Researchers have also shown that attitudes, like information, may be made more-or-less accessible and that the more accessible the attitude, the higher the degree of attitude-behavior consistency (for a review of this work, see Fazio and Williams 1986; Fazio 1990).[2]

In the world of politics, where people must rely heavily on the media for information, it goes without saying that patterns of news coverage are critical contextual determinants of accessibility.[3] Typically, what comes to mind when

---

1. Although Wyer and Srull do not make this point themselves, it is likely that information considered particularly valuable or important (e.g., a candidate's stand on the budget deficit for a staunchly conservative voter) is also accorded preferential location in long-term storage, thus accounting for "chronic" accessibility effects.

2. Parallel accessibility effects have been detected in studies of survey responses. Public opinion researchers have demonstrated that the wording, format, and ordering of questions produce dramatic variations in reported beliefs or opinions. Thus, people describe themselves as disinterested in politics if they are first asked a series of difficult factual questions concerning the identity and activities of various public officials. On the other hand, if they are asked about their political interest before being confronted with the factual knowledge questions, they describe themselves as substantially interested (see Bishop, Oldendick, and Tuchfarber 1982). Similarly, the proportion of respondents favoring more generous federal financial assistance is markedly higher if the recipients of such assistance are described as "poor people" rather than "people on welfare" (Smith 1987; for a general review of accessibility effects in surveys, see Zaller and Feldman 1988).

3. I do not mean to deny the importance of motivational or other dispositional determinants of information accessibility. Some voters may consider the candidates' positions on abortion when choosing, while others are drawn toward their positions on civil rights irrespective of how much media play these issues are accorded. Such "chronic" differences in accessibility may be

the citizen thinks about public affairs are the images and information that flash across the television screen. In the subsequent discussion, I describe how this type of accessibility bias affects the status of issues in U.S. politics.

Television News and Issue Salience

Issues enter and leave the center stage of U.S. politics with remarkable speed. When President Bush was elected, the problem of illegal drug use was foremost in citizens' minds and the new administration was prompted to announce a major initiative to deal with this problem. One year later, however, illegal drug use was mentioned by too few people to even warrant inclusion in pollsters' lists of "major problems" facing the country. The most plausible explanation of such dramatic shifts in political priorities is couched in terms of patterns of news coverage. In particular, the amount of news coverage accorded political issues is thought to dictate the degree of issue salience. This argument is referred to as "media agenda setting."

Early agenda-setting studies (conducted in the 1960s) were plagued by a number of methodological difficulties, including, most notably, confusion between cause and effect. Did the convergence of newspaper readers' political concerns and newspaper content mean that news coverage had set the audience agenda, or did it mean that editors and journalists had tailored their news coverage to appeal to the political concerns of their readers? In response to such ambiguities, communications researchers began to track the evolution of public concern for particular issues and events in relation to changes in the pattern of news coverage. With few exceptions, these time-series studies uncovered evidence of significant media agenda-setting effects.[4]

The time-series analyses further defined the agenda-setting paradigm by incorporating indicators of events (i.e., "real world cues") that might be directly experienced in addition to the level of media coverage as potential determinants of the public agenda. When events were relatively obtrusive (such as energy shortages, rising prices, or widespread crime), the evidence indicated that they affected public opinion directly. When the level of unemployment increased significantly, for instance, more people mentioned unemployment as a major national problem independently of how much news coverage the media provided (MacKuen 1981; Behr and Iyengar 1985). In addition to the course of events, the level of presidential rhetoric was also found to influence the public's issue agenda. When the president addressed

caused by various personal experiences or motives—party affiliation, socioeconomic status, cultural values, religious upbringing, or the intensity of particular attitudes (for an analysis of accessibility effects in political opinion associated with individuals' level of political information, see Iyengar 1990).

4. These studies are reviewed in Rogers and Dearing 1986.

the nation on a particular problem and the address was televised nationwide, he was able to boost public concern independently of the amount of other news coverage accorded that problem (Behr and Iyengar 1985). Finally, in a further elaboration of the interrelationships between events, network news, and public opinion, Behr and Iyengar (1985) demonstrated that agenda setting was generally unidirectional—news coverage affected the level of public concern, but public concern did not, in turn, affect the focus of television news.

Agenda-setting effects have been captured for all forms of mass media coverage, in both experimental and survey-based studies, and with open-ended indicators in which respondents identify the "most important problems facing the country" as well as with closed-ended items in which they rate the importance of particular issues. These effects have been observed for both local and national "problems." In all these areas, research has shown that individuals habitually refer to issues or events "in the news" when diagnosing current social and political ills.

In addition to documenting the effects of news coverage on the emergence of public issues, researchers have also investigated specific elements or mechanisms of agenda-setting. In the case of television news, these mechanisms concern particular characteristics of news stories, variations in the composition of the audience and the nature of the issue.

Television news stories may be classified according to several features. Two features that influence the agenda-setting power of news are position within the newscast and vividness. Lead stories are especially strong cues. Behr and Iyengar's longitudinal analysis (1985) found that lead stories exerted much stronger agenda-setting effects than stories appearing in the middle of the newscast. This difference was also detected in Iyengar and Kinder's experimental studies (see Iyengar and Kinder 1987, chap. 4).

In addition to questions of position, it is generally assumed that "vivid" news items are particularly persuasive. Iyengar and Kinder tested this assumption by comparing television news stories that focused on people and their problems (vivid coverage) with stories that focused on abstract concepts and collectivities (nonvivid coverage). In the case of unemployment, for instance, Iyengar and Kinder compared stories that provided close-up coverage of an unemployed worker and his family with stories describing the latest unemployment statistics and trends nationwide. Their results suggested that vivid coverage was, in fact, *less* likely to alter viewers' political priorities than nonvivid coverage (Iyengar and Kinder 1987, chap. 4).

Of course, the media agenda is not adopted uniformly by all members of an audience. The progressive refining of agenda-setting research has included efforts to identify segments of an audience that are likely to be more or less vulnerable to agenda-setting. In Iyengar and Kinder's experiments, individ-

uals with lower levels of education, political interest, and political participation were especially susceptible to influence (see Iyengar and Kinder 1987, chap. 6). The less-educated, -interested, and -involved segments of the audience are, presumably, less able to retrieve independently derived information that might cast doubt on the message contained in news reports. The availability of information that permits critical analysis of media presentations is an important factor affecting ability to resist media influence, either in the form of agenda setting or persuasion (see Petty, Ostrom, and Brock 1981).

Erbring and his collaborators (Erbring, Goldenberg, and Miller 1980) were the first to suggest that individuals differed in their receptivity to news about particular issues. Elderly people may be more attentive to news about crime, while people working for defense contractors may be first to respond to news coverage of impending layoffs and unemployment. Iyengar and Kinder's experiments confirmed that news coverage and the personal circumstances of the audience interactively shape perceptions of national issues. Retired viewers were more likely than other members of the audience to mention social security as a pressing problem following exposure to news reports on social security; blacks cited racial discrimination as a significant problem more frequently than whites after watching news coverage of the issue (Iyengar and Kinder 1987; for additional evidence concerning the joint effects of news coverage and the personal relevance of news reports, see Tyler 1980; Zucker 1978).

Television News and Differential Weighting of Issues in Candidate Evaluation

In addition to affecting the sheer salience of issues, television news coverage also influences the degree to which issues are used as criteria to evaluate political leaders. The so-called priming effect, an extension of agenda-setting, addresses the impact of news coverage on the weight individuals assign to their opinions on particular issues when they make political evaluations. In general, the more prominent an issue is in the national information stream, the greater the impact of opinions regarding that issue on political evaluations.

In the context of election campaigns, priming means that an individual voter's choice between political candidates is likely to be based on an analysis that provides greater weight to preferences on issues that receive heavy news coverage than to preferences on less newsworthy issues. For example, in a study of the 1982 election in the third congressional district of Connecticut, researchers found that voters who felt more optimistic about national economic conditions were more supportive of the Republican incumbent. However, when exposed to news coverage of the economy, the effect of voters' optimism on evaluations of the candidates was more than tripled. An even

stronger priming effect emerged with respect to participants' perceptions of the personal traits of the candidates. Viewers generally preferred the candidate in whom they saw more positive personal characteristics. But following exposure to news reports about the candidates' personal background, the weight accorded trait ratings was increased nearly fivefold (Iyengar and Kinder 1987, chap. 11).

Priming by television news has been established in several experiments, for evaluations of both presidents and members of Congress and across a wide range of political judgments, including evaluations of political performance and assessments of political leaders' personal traits. In general, news coverage of political issues induces stronger priming effects in the area of performance assessments and weaker priming effects in the area of personality assessments (for details, see Iyengar and Kinder 1987).

The evidence demonstrating the existence of priming is not drawn exclusively from laboratory experiments. In a recent study based on national survey data, Krosnick and Kinder found that the public's support for U.S. intervention in Central America became twice as influential as a determinant of President Reagan's popularity in the period immediately following the disclosure that funds from the sale of arms to Iran had been used to finance the Contras (Krosnick and Kinder 1990).

Priming is especially important in the context of primary election campaigns.[5] Recent analyses have centered specifically upon the effects of "horse race" coverage in the making and unmaking of U.S. presidential candidates. As countless studies of campaign journalism have shown, stories detailing the candidates' electoral prospects—their poll standings, delegate counts, fundraising efforts, and related campaign indicators—have become the staple of campaign reporting and frequently dwarf coverage of more relevant facets of the campaign. As Robinson and Sheehan summed up their exhaustive comparison of CBS News' and United Press International's treatment of the 1980 campaign, "Horse race coverage permeates almost everything the press does in covering elections and candidates" (1983, 148).[6] The prominence of viability in the news stream virtually guarantees that perceptions of the candidates' electoral viability will provide a strong evaluative impetus. Bartels has demonstrated not only that voters prefer the candidate who is deemed more viable, but that voters with positive feelings toward a particular candidate are espe-

---

5. In general, primaries provide an ideal ground to explore the effects of information accessibility since the major "long-term" influence on voters—party identification—is silenced.

6. While the tide of horse race coverage naturally tends to boost front-runners, there is also a bonus for candidates who exceed journalistic expectations, that is, candidates who perform better than expected in the race. Gary Hart, for instance, ran third in the 1984 New Hampshire Democratic primary; since he was quite obscure at that time, this outcome itself induced a tremendous outpouring of media attention.

cially likely to vote accordingly if they consider the candidate viable (see Bartels 1988, chap. 6).

Because horse race coverage is so prevalent, primary voters are likely to be heavily primed with information about the candidates' electoral viability. Brady has provided striking experimental evidence documenting the impact of news coverage on perceptions of candidate viability. By providing his respondents with either "encouraging" or "discouraging" news about the standing of various candidates for the 1984 Democratic presidential nomination, Brady was able to induce significant shifts in perceptions of viability (Brady 1984). These experimental results were corroborated by Bartel's survey analyses of both the 1980 and 1984 presidential campaigns, in which voters who were more attentive to the media were found to be the first to assimilate information about candidate viability (see Bartels 1985 and 1988).

Just as the ability of news coverage to set the public agenda depends on characteristics of news stories and the composition of the audience, the ability of the news to prime political evaluations is tempered by qualitative features of news reports themselves and characteristics of the audience. Most important, priming is significantly strengthened when news reports explicitly link politicians' actions or statements with the state of national problems. For example, among individuals who watched news stories suggesting that Reaganomics was the principal cause of rising unemployment, evaluations of President Reagan's overall performance and competence were more strongly colored by assessments of his performance concerning unemployment than were the evaluations by a control group who watched news stories that suggested alternative causes of unemployment (for further discussion, see Iyengar and Kinder 1987, chap. 9). The mediating effects of "presidential responsibility" in strengthening the priming effect were detected for news coverage of both political accomplishments and failures. Overall evaluations of President Carter, for example, were equally primed (i.e., equally influenced by assessments of Carter's performance in foreign affairs) by news coverage of the Carter administration's major foreign policy debacle—the Iranian hostage crisis—and by news coverage of the administration's major foreign policy success—the Camp David Accords. Depending upon the circumstances, therefore, priming can either help or harm incumbent officials (see Iyengar and Kinder 1987, chap. 11).

As is the case with agenda setting, individuals differ in their susceptibility to priming. Iyengar and Kinder found that Democrats and Republicans differed sharply in the issues with which they could be primed. Democrats tended to be most susceptible to priming when the news covered such traditional Democratic issues as civil rights or unemployment while Republicans were most receptive when the news focused on such traditional Republican issues as national defense and inflation. Iyengar and Kinder also found that

individuals with built-in "schemas" or theories of responsibility that imply a high level of presidential blame for particular issues were most likely to be primed by news coverage of these issues (Iyengar and Kinder 1987, chap. 10).

Television News and Attributions of Responsibility for Political Issues

Most political issues are capable of being viewed as the creations of government and/or appropriate targets of governmental intervention or treatment. Naturally, people vary in their willingness to attribute "causal" and "treatment" responsibility to governmental factors than to alternative factors (for discussions of attribution theory in social psychology, see Fincham and Jaspars 1980; Brickman et al. 1982).[7] Social psychologists have demonstrated that attitudes and actions within a wide variety of areas are altered by the manner in which individuals attribute responsibility (for a review of this research, see Iyengar 1991).

Television news coverage powerfully influences the manner in which individuals attribute responsibility for political issues. More specifically, research has investigated the connection between alternative television news "frames" for political issues and the resulting attributions of causal and treatment responsibility to various political actors and institutions.[8]

Typically, the networks frame issues in either "episodic" or "thematic" terms. The episodic frame depicts public issues in terms of concrete instances or specific events—a homeless person, an unemployed worker, an oil spill, a victim of racial discrimination, the bombing of an airliner, or an attempted murder. Visually, episodic reports make "good pictures." The thematic news frame, in contrast, places public issues in some general or abstract context. Reports on reductions in government welfare expenditures, changes in the nature of employment opportunities, the social or political grievances of groups undertaking terrorist activity, changes in federal affirmative action policy, or the backlog in the criminal justice process are examples of thematic coverage. The thematic news frame typically takes the form of a "takeout" or

---

7. To illustrate with the issue of poverty, causal responsibility concerns the processes by which people become poor while treatment responsibility would seek to establish what could be done to alleviate (or perpetuate) poverty.

8. The concept of framing has both psychological and sociological pedigrees. Psychologists typically define framing as changes in judgment engendered by alterations to the definition of judgment or choice problems. The psychological evidence on framing can be found in Kahneman and Tversky 1982, 1984, 1987; Kahneman, Tversky, and Slovic 1982. The sociological perspective on framing derives from work by Goffman (1974), and tends to focus on the use of "story lines," symbols, and stereotypes in media presentations. This literature typically defines news frames in terms of ideological or value perspectives (for illustrations, see Gitlin 1980; Gamson and Lasch 1983; Gamson and Modigliani 1986).

"backgrounder" report directed at general outcomes or conditions and frequently features "talking heads."[9]

The effects of the episodic and thematic news frames on viewers' attributions of responsibility for various political and social issues (including poverty, unemployment, crime, terrorism, racial inequality, and the Iran-Contra affair) were investigated in a series of experimental studies (see Iyengar 1991). Under conditions of thematic framing, viewers tend to assign responsibility to general societal factors, including the actions or inactions of public officials. Thus, when television news coverage presents a general or analytic frame of reference for national problems, the public's reasoning about causal and treatment responsibility is political in focus. Following exposure to news reports about increases in malnutrition among the U.S. poor, subjects discussed poverty in terms of inadequate social welfare programs; confronted with news accounts of the shrinking demand for unskilled labor, subjects described unemployment as a result of inadequate economic policies or insensitive public officials; and provided with news reports on deteriorating conditions in the inner cities, subjects cited improved economic opportunities for the underprivileged as the appropriate remedy for crime.

Under conditions of episodic framing, on the other hand, viewers attributed responsibility not to societal or political forces, but to the actions of particular individuals or groups. For example, when poverty, crime, and terrorism were depicted in episodic terms, viewers attributed causal and treatment responsibility primarily to poor people, criminals, and terrorists. In response to news stories describing particular illustrations of national issues, viewers focused on individual and group characteristics rather than on historical, social, political, or other general forces. Episodic framing thus seems to encourage reasoning by resemblance—people settle upon causes and treatments that "fit" the observed problem.[10]

The importance of episodic and thematic news frames is not limited to

9. In practice, very few news reports are "purely" episodic or thematic. Even the most detailed, close-up look at a poor person, for instance, might include lead-in remarks by the anchorperson or reporter on the scope of poverty nationwide. Conversely, an account of the legislative struggle over budgetary cuts in social welfare might include a brief scene of children in a day care center scheduled to shut down as a result of funding cuts.

10. While television news frames play an important role in shaping attributions of political responsibility, the impact of the alternative frames was far from uniform across the various issue areas investigated. For certain issue areas, such as poverty and terrorism, episodic coverage tended to produce individualistic attributions without regard to the particular subject matter focus of the news stories. On the other hand, for the issue of crime, episodic framing proved secondary in its effect on attributions to the particular subject matter under discussion. Stories dealing with the issue of illegal drugs were likely to produce individualistic causal attributions, no matter how framed, while stories dealing with white crime were likely to produce societal causal attributions, no matter how framed. For details, see Iyengar 1991.

attribution of political responsibility. In each of the framing experiments (and in replications with national survey data), individuals who attributed responsibility for national issues to general societal factors were found to be significantly more critical of the performance of elected officials than individuals who attributed responsibility to nonsocietal factors. In the context of campaigns, television news is a significant asset for incumbents; the predominance of event-oriented and case-study news coverage effectively insulates them from any rising tide of disenchantment over unemployment, poverty, the Savings and Loan debacle, or other such problems. In contrast, when television casts its coverage in thematic terms, issues are more likely to become campaign ammunition with which to attack incumbents.

As a very rough gauge of the degree to which thematic coverage fuels dissatisfaction with government performance, I tabulated the proportion of thematic reports on network television between 1982 and 1986 directed at the issues of civil rights, poverty, and crime.[11] This proportion was then compared with the proportion of the public stating that the government was doing "too little" about the issue in question.[12] In all three issue areas, after controlling for the effects of secular trend, the higher the degree of thematic framing, the greater the public's dissatisfaction with governmental performance.[13]

Conclusion

The impact of news coverage on issue salience, the weighting of opinions as criteria for evaluating public officials, and attributions of political responsibility can all be traced to the common psychological mediator of information accessibility. When the networks give extensive coverage to a particular issue, viewers tend to give their preferences concerning that issue greater weight when thinking about the performance of politicians. During election cam-

11. The coding of each news story was based on the number of lines devoted to thematic or episodic coverage in the transcribed *Abstracts* of the nightly newscasts. This coding is therefore *textual* and not a direct measure of the amount of news time. In order to assess the validity of this method, every story related to the issue of poverty broadcast by CBS News between January, 1981, and December, 1986, was viewed and classified on the basis of actual air time. The results of this more precise "visual" coding corroborated the coding based on the *Abstracts*.

12. The NORC General Social Survey features differing forms of the "is the government spending enough" question. In 1982 and 1983, the questions were directed at "halting the rising crime rate," "improving conditions of blacks," and "welfare." In 1984, 1985, and 1986, questions were also asked about spending on "law enforcement," "assistance to blacks," and "assistance to the poor." In 1984, still another set of questions were included that asked about "reducing crime" and "caring for the poor." In those years in which two or more questions were available, I averaged across questions. I should warn the reader that these changes in wording often induced prominent shifts in responses.

13. Given the crudity of this analysis, it is striking that all three regression coefficients for thematic framing were more than double their standard errors in magnitude.

paigns, when news reports are heavily laden with information on the candidates' prospects, the public tends to evaluate candidates in terms of their prospects rather than their policy positions, character, or other relevant factors. Finally, protracted exposure to episodic news tends to make the behavior of public officials less accessible when individuals think about causal or treatment responsibility.

The demonstrated power of television news to influence public opinion means that the "fit" between news coverage and the real world (or even the world as defined by elected representatives and political parties) is of considerable importance. If the fit is close, the rhetoric of political elites and the course of meaningful public events will be accessible to the public. On the other hand, if the fit is loose, the accessibility of particular themes and issues will depend more upon bureaucratic, commercial, or cultural influences on editorial judgment than on actual political developments. In general, the accessibility bias means that the ability to predict the actions of the public will require a theory of news coverage. In the absence of such a theory, I now focus on two "stylized facts" concerning the determinants of the agenda of the news media in the United States.

"Official Journalism"

As practiced by the U.S. press, the routines of news gathering place a premium on governmental sources (both individual and institutional). In Sigal's words, "a good deal of the news is a product of the coupling of two information-processing machines: one the news organizations, the other, the government" (Sigal 1973, 4). The president and other prominent officials exercise powerful leverage over the focus and content of public affairs reporting (see Boylan 1986; Bennett 1990). What politicians and bureaucrats say, journalists report.

Not only do government officials enjoy favored status as news sources, but they also increasingly use the media as an arena for advancement of their policy objectives (Lang and Lang 1983; Kernell 1986). The use of press conferences, staged events, news leaks, and the timing of policy proposals to coincide with publicized events are all elements of this strategy of "going public." Since news coverage consists largely of the statements of politicians, it necessarily tends to boost the accessibility of partisan values. "Waste in government," for instance, was a prominent theme in media coverage of the Reagan administration's social welfare proposals during the early 1980s (see Moss 1987).

The inherent newsworthiness of elite rhetoric and the increasing use of the news media for partisan ends suggests that diffusion or leadership models will be increasingly important to the study of public opinion. People accept or

reject incoming partisan messages depending upon the credibility of the source, the complexity of the message, their individual level of political awareness, and a host of related factors (for a comprehensive review of these models, see Petty and Cacioppo 1981). Page and Shapiro (1991) have shown, for example, that the public's policy preferences tend to follow those expressed by media commentators and other "experts" who appear in national network newscasts. And Zaller, in a series of studies, has demonstrated that the public's acceptance of partisan messages in a nonmonotonic function of political awareness with the moderately involved being most receptive (see Zaller 1992).

Of course, the ability to make news or to use the news media as a forum differs depending upon the personal characteristics of particular incumbents and other circumstances. Ronald Reagan was generally more skilled in controlling the tone of news coverage of his administration than was Jimmy Carter. However, President Reagan discovered during the Iran-Contra affair that events can suddenly transform the press from a dutiful mouthpiece to an aggressive adversary.

Candidates as well as elected officials enjoy privileged treatment by the press. Candidates attempt to campaign over issues they "own" (Petrocik 1990), and their "handlers" have developed the appropriate methods of injecting these preferences into campaign reporting. (For discussion of the influence of political candidates over news coverage, see Arterton 1978; Grossman and Kumar 1981; Hart 1987; Ansolabehere, Behr,and Iyengar 1991.) That attention focused on Willie Horton during the 1988 campaign is testimony to the power of "media management."

Organizational Incentives

While public officials can promote the accessibility of particular political issues through their rhetoric and actions, the political consequences of this power are influenced by such qualitative features of the news as framing. In particular, thematic framing politicizes issues by encouraging viewers to hold political leaders accountable.

Television news is subject to a plethora of editorial influences, including organizational norms and commercial pressures that together produce a strong demand for episodic reporting (see Arlen 1976; Tuchman 1978; Bagdikian 1983). Such basic journalistic values as "objectivity" place a premium on the reporting of "hard" news, such as specific events. Thematic, "subsurface" reporting is much more vulnerable to charges of bias and editorializing (see Roshco 1975; Gans 1979). Moreover, within the constraints of a 22-minute "headline service," in-depth, analytic, or interpretive reports on national issues would leave little room for other news items. A heavy dose of episodic

reporting is, therefore, commercially imperative; episodic reporting, which typically features "good pictures," is likely to attract and keep viewers' attention. Thematic reporting, on the other hand, tends to be dull and slow paced, characteristics that are not likely to strengthen viewer interest. In short, there are powerful organizational pressures that lead television news reporters and editors to seize upon specific events and particular episodes to portray political issues.

The premium placed on episodic framing means that many significant issues will fail to receive the news coverage necessary to enter the public's agenda. Problems that lack immediate or readily traceable symptoms are deemed less newsworthy by journalists hungry for "good pictures." The deficiencies in U.S. public education, the emergence of a large and seemingly permanent underclass, and gradual environmental degradation do not typically manifest themselves as specific events, and stories on these issues appear infrequently.

While the nature of television assures the predominance of episodic framing, there is considerable variability across issues in the use of thematic and episodic reporting. Between 1981 and 1986, network news coverage of crime and terrorism was uniformly episodic (more than 70 percent of all news reports).[14] Crime and terrorism both received much more coverage than such domestic issues as poverty, unemployment, or civil rights. The combination of extensive coverage and the predominance of episodic framing meant that crime and terrorism were consistently accessible to the public, but that public officials were rarely implicated. With the appropriate rhetoric and posturing, therefore, incumbents could use both issues to their advantage.

In contrast to crime and terrorism, the networks consistently framed unemployment in thematic terms. The issue was thus a distinct liability for incumbents, especially in 1982 when the share of network news reports allocated to unemployment was considerable (accounting for nearly 25 percent of total issue coverage). In general, however, the course of economic events, elite rhetoric, and other factors combined to produce relatively weak editorial demand for news relating to unemployment and thus reduced the relative accessibility of the issue.

As the examples of crime, terrorism, and unemployment reveal, issues differ in the degree to which they elicit episodic and thematic reports. Which issues are particularly likely to be framed thematically and what circumstances increase the supply of thematic news? In the absence of substantial evidence, I offer a few reasonable guesses.

The case of unemployment suggests that the existence of a well-

---

14. The figures on network news coverage between 1981 and 1986 are taken from Iyengar 1991.

developed system of social (statistical) recording facilitates thematic news framing. Economic outcomes are extensively recorded in the United States, and, in fact, the monthly release of the unemployment rate has become a routine news event. Reporters covering economic issues thus have easy access to statistical information. Moreover, there is no shortage of economists and other "experts" willing to interpret and analyze the implications of the latest economic figures. In addition, current economic theory posits that levels of unemployment are key indicators of the health of the national economy, and the presumed "macro" effects of unemployment may induce the networks to provide thematic rather than episodic coverage of the issue.

Just as some issues are subject to thematic coverage because of the ready availability of national indicators, other issues command thematic coverage because of their intrinsically collective nature. National defense, the budget deficit, and taxation would seem typical of this category. With the exception of military conflicts, most news about national defense deals with policy debates. Similarly, with the exception of a few well-publicized tax evasion cases (e.g., Leona Helmsley or Pete Rose), news about taxes tends to be primarily impersonal and thematic in nature. In short, certain issues are difficult to reduce to the level of individual victims or beneficiaries and news coverage thus tends to have a strong collective or institutional focus. While the inapplicability of the episodic news frame to such issues as defense and taxation would seem to enhance the ability of news presentations to serve as political catalysts, these issues are also characterized by high "built-in" levels of structural or governmental responsibility. It is difficult, for example, not to blame politicians for particular levels of taxation. For these issues, therefore, merely penetrating the media agenda is a sufficient condition for politicization. The volatility of the public's voting preferences in 1990, and the sudden drop in President Bush's popularity following the injection of the "fairness" issue into news coverage of the budget deficit negotiations, is illustrative of this "mere exposure" effect. Given the nature of the political culture and the associated stereotypes of Republican and Democratic politicians, some issues have only to be covered in the media for them to weigh heavily in voting choice.

Thematic framing is also likely to vary with the phases of an issue's history. When issues first surface, television news coverage tends to be primarily episodic. If the issue lingers, the networks are more apt to air "in-depth" feature reports (which are the staple of thematic coverage). In the case of AIDS, for example, Rogers and his colleagues have found that initial coverage in the national press was aimed at specific events, including protest activities by gay groups and such prominent individual victims as Rock Hudson and Liberace. Over time, however, news coverage of the problem became more complex and topical in focus (Rogers and Dearing 1986). The longer the

life span of an issue, the greater the probability that the issue will receive thematic coverage.

Finally, widely shared cultural values may contribute to editorial decisions on framing. The U.S. commitment to the work ethic and related individualistic values may enhance the newsworthiness of particular instances of poverty (i.e., as deviations from the norm). Conversely, news coverage of racial inequality may be more thematic than episodic because close-up coverage of individual blacks may prompt charges of racial stereotyping in the news.

In conclusion, there is considerable evidence that Americans march to the drum of television news when they think about public affairs and their elected representatives. Issues or events that receive little news coverage will be conspicuously absent in political campaigns. Issues or problems that receive extensive coverage will, as a minimum, rank high on the public's agenda and will count for more than less-publicized issues when it is time to vote. Finally, the direction in which voters assign responsibility for issues can be influenced by media framing. When issues are framed in thematic terms (which is the exception rather than the rule for television), the public is more likely to hold public officials responsible (thus increasing the potential for anti-incumbent voting). These effects of television news cry out for more theorizing and research into the gatekeeping and selection processes by which some issues are propelled into the public view while others are left unseen.

REFERENCES

Ansolabehere, Stephen, Roy L. Behr, and Shanto Iyengar. 1991. "Mass Media and Elections: An Overview." *American Politics Quarterly* 19:109–39.
Arlen, Michael J. 1976. *The View from Highway 1: Essays on Television*. New York: Farrar, Strauss and Giroux.
Arterton, Christopher F. 1978. "The Media Politics of Presidential Campaigns." In *Race for the Presidency: The Media and the Nominating Process*, ed. James D. Barber, 26–54. Englewood Cliffs, N.J.: Prentice-Hall.
Bagdikian, Ben H. 1983. *The Media Monopoly*. Boston: Beacon Press.
Bartels, Larry M. 1985. "Expectations and Preferences in Presidential Nominating Campaigns." *American Political Science Review* 79:804–15.
Bartels, Larry M. 1988. *Presidential Primaries and the Dynamics of Public Choice*. Princeton: Princeton University Press.
Behr, Roy L., and Shanto Iyengar. 1985. "Television News, Real-World Cues, and Changes in the Public Agenda." *Public Opinion Quarterly* 49:38–57.
Bennett, W. Lance. 1990. "Toward a Theory of Press-State Relations in the U.S." *Journal of Communication* 40:103–25.
Bishop, George F., Robert W. Oldendick, and Alfred J. Tuchfarber. 1982. "Political

Information Processing: Question Order and Context Effects." *Political Behavior* 4:177–200.

Boylan, James. 1986. "Declarations of Independence." *Columbia Journalism Review* 24:29–46.

Brady, Henry E. 1984. "Chances, Utilities and Voting in Presidential Primaries." Paper presented at the annual meeting of the Public Choice Society, Phoenix, Arizona.

Brickman, Phillip, James Karuza, Jr., Dan Coates, Ellen Cohn, and Louise Kidder. 1982. "Models of Helping and Coping." *American Psychologist* 37:368–84.

Erbring, Lutz, Edie Goldenberg, and Arthur Miller. 1980. "Front-Page News and Real-World Cues: A New Look at Agenda-Setting." *American Journal of Political Science* 24:16–49.

Fazio, Russell H. 1990. "Multiple Processes by which Attitudes Guide Behavior: The MODE Model as an Integrative Framework." In *Advances in Experimental Social Psychology,* ed. Mark P. Zanna, 23:75–109. New York: Academic Press.

Fazio, Russell H., and C. J. Williams. 1986. "Attitude Accessibility as a Moderator of the Attitude-Perception and Attitude-Behavior Relations: An Investigation of the 1984 Presidential Election." *Journal of Personality and Social Psychology* 51:505–14.

Gamson, William A., and Kathryn E. Lasch. 1983. "The Political Culture of Social Welfare Policy." In *Evaluating the Welfare State: Social and Political Perspectives,* ed. Shimon E. Spiro and Ephraim Yuchtman-Yaar, 398–415. New York: Academic Press.

Gamson, William A., and Andre Modigliani. 1986. "Media Discourse and Public Opinion on Nuclear Power." Boston College Social Economy Program. Photocopy.

Gans, Herbert, 1979. *Deciding What's News.* New York: Vintage Books.

Gitlin, Todd. 1980. *The Whole World is Watching.* Berkeley: University of California Press.

Goffman, Erving. 1974. *Frame Analysis: An Essay on the Organization of Experience.* Cambridge, Mass.: Harvard University Press.

Grossman, Michael B., and Martha J. Kumar. 1981. *Portraying the President: The White House and the News Media.* Baltimore: Johns Hopkins University Press.

Hart, Roderick P. 1987. *The Sound of Leadership.* Chicago: University of Chicago Press.

Higgins, E. Tory, and Gillian King. 1981. "Accessibility of Social Constructs: Information-Processing Consequences of Individual and Contextual Variability." In *Personality, Cognition, and Social Interaction,* ed. Nancy Cantor and John Kihlstrom, 60–121. Hillsdale, N.J.: Lawrence Erlbaum Associates.

Iyengar, Shanto. 1990. "Shortcuts to Political Knowledge: Selective Attention and the Accessibility Bias." In *Information and the Democratic Process,* ed. John Ferejohn and James Kuklinski, 160–85. Urbana: University of Illinois Press.

Iyengar, Shanto. 1991. *Is Anyone Responsible? How Television Frames Political Issues.* Chicago: University of Chicago Press.

Iyengar, Shanto, and Donald R. Kinder. 1987. *News That Matters.* Chicago: University of Chicago Press.

Kahneman, Daniel, and Amos Tversky. 1982. "The Psychology of Preferences." *Science* 246:136–42.

Kahneman, Daniel, and Amos Tversky. 1984. "Choices, Values, and Frames." *American Psychologist* 39:341–50.

Kahneman, Daniel, and Amos Tversky. 1987. "Rational Choice and the Framing of Decisions." In *Rational Choice: The Contrast Between Economics and Psychology,* ed. Hillel Einhorn and Robin Hogarth. Chicago: University of Chicago Press.

Kahneman, Daniel, Amos Tversky, and Paul Slovic. 1982. *Judgment Under Uncertainty: Heuristics and Biases.* New York: Cambridge University Press.

Kernell, Samuel. 1986. *Going Public.* Washington, D.C.: Congressional Quarterly Press.

Krosnick, Jon A. 1988. "The Role of Attitude Importance in Social Evaluation: A Study of Policy Preferences, Presidential Candidate Evaluations, and Voting Behavior." *Journal of Personality and Social Psychology* 55:196–210.

Krosnick, Jon A., and Donald R. Kinder. 1990. "Altering the Foundations of Popular Support for the President through Priming." *American Political Science Review* 84:497–512.

Lang, Gladys E., and Kurt Lang. 1983. *The Battle for Public Opinion: The President, the Press, and the Polls During Watergate.* New York: Columbia University Press.

Lemkau, James, F. B. Bryant, and Phillip Brickman. 1982. "Client Committment in the Helping Relationship." In *Basic Processes in Helping Relationships,* ed. T. A. Mills. New York: Aldine.

More Than News: Media Power in Public Affairs. MacKuen, Michael, and Stephen Coombs, eds. Beverly Hills: Sage Publications.

Moss, Michael. 1987. "The Poverty Story." *Columbia Journalism Review* 25:43–54.

Page, Benjamin I., and Robert Y. Shapiro. 1991. *The Rational Public.* Chicago: University of Chicago Press.

Petrocik, John R. 1990. "The Theory of Issue Ownership: Issues, Agendas, and Electoral Coalitions in the 1988 Election. Department of Political Science, University of California, Los Angeles. Photocopy.

Petty, Richard E., and John T. Cacioppo. 1981. *Attitudes and Persuasion.* Dubuque, Iowa: William C. Brown.

Petty, Richard E., Thomas M. Ostrom, and Timothy C. Brock. 1981. *Cognitive Responses in Persuasion.* Hillsdale, N.J.: Lawrence Erlbaum.

Riker, William H. 1980. "Implications from the Disequilibrium of Majority Rule for the Study of Institutions." *American Political Science Review* 74:432–46.

Robinson, Michael J., and Margaret A. Sheehan. 1983. *Over the Wire and on TV.* New York: Russell Sage Foundation.

Rogers, Everett M., and James W. Dearing. 1986. "Agenda-Setting Research: Where Has It Been and Where Is It Going?" In *Communication Yearbook,* ed. James A. Anderson. Beverly Hills: Sage Publications.

Roshco, Bernard. 1975. *Newsmaking.* Chicago: University of Chicago Press.

Sigal, Leon V. 1973. *Reporters and Officials.* Lexington, Mass.: D. C. Heath.

Slovic, Paul, Baruch Fischhoff, and Sarah Lichtenstein. 1982. "Response Mode,

Framing, and Information-Processing Effects in Risk Assessment." In *New Directions for Methodology of Social and Behavioral Science: Question Framing and Response Consistency,* ed. Robin Hogarth, 21–36. San Francisco: Jossey-Bass.

Smith, Tom. 1987. "That Which We Call Welfare by Any Other Name Would Smell Sweeter." *Public Opinion Quarterly* 51:75–83.

Tuchman, Gaye. 1978. *Making News: A Study in the Construction of Reality.* New York: Free Press.

Tyler, Tom R. 1980. "Impact of Directly and Indirectly Experienced Events: The Origins of Crime-Related Judgments and Behaviors." *Journal of Personality and Social Psychology* 39:13–28.

Wyer, Robert S., Jr., and Jon Hartwick. 1980. "The Role of Information Retrieval and Conditional Inference Processes in Belief Formation and Change." In *Advances in Experimental Social Psychology,* ed. Leonard Berkowitz, 13:241–85. New York: Academic Press.

Wyer, Robert S., Jr., and Thomas K. Srull. 1986. "Human Cognition in Its Social Context." *Psychological Review* 93:322–59.

Zaller, John, and Stanley Feldman. 1988. "Answering Questions vs. Revealing Preferences." Paper presented at the fifth annual meeting of the Political Methodology Society, Los Angeles.

Zaller, John. 1991. *Elite Discourse and Public Opinion.* New York: Cambridge University Press. Forthcoming.

Zucker, Harold G. 1978. "The Variable Nature of News Media Influence." In *Communication Yearbook,* ed. Brent D. Ruben, vol. 2. New Brunswick, N.J.: Transaction Books.

Free Trade in Canadian Elections: Issue Evolution in the Long and the Short Run

Richard Johnston, André Blais, Henry E. Brady, and Jean Crête

In 1988, Canada's Conservative government fought and won an election on free trade with the United States. Almost everything about the event was extraordinary. Twice before, a party had made some form of Canada-U.S. free trade the issue. Each time that party lost decisively. History almost repeated itself: in the middle of the 1988 campaign, the government appeared to have lost its gamble. But this time the government fought back and ultimately won. No less extraordinary than the event was the identity of the protagonists. In advocating free trade, the Conservative government proposed to jettison whatever remained of its traditional role as the party of Canadian nationalism. The opposition was led by the Liberal party, historically the party of free trade.

Why would *any* party propose so risky a shift in the electoral agenda? Why was *this* particular party, given its legacy, the one to make the proposal? In part, the answers lie in the parties' search for political advantage. Parties eager to get or keep power that reckon that the existing agenda leaves them at a strategic disadvantage may be well advised to make the risky choice. But, for ideological or coalitional reasons, not all moves are available. For much the same reasons, not all moves will be credible. Intervening moves may be required before the ones of greatest value can be ventured. In the Canadian case, the 1988 election was the culminating installment of a process of issue evolution that began in the mid-1950s. First came a shift in the Conservatives' social base, a shift that exemplified Riker's (1982) notions of the issue foun-

The authors acknowledge the generosity of the Social Sciences and Humanities Research Council of Canada, under grants 411-88-0030 and 421-89-0002, and of the computing centers at the University of British Columbia and l'Université de Montréal. Fieldwork for the Canadian Election Study was carried out by the Institute for Social Research, York University, under the direction of David Northrup. Brenda O'Neill provided invaluable assistance in preparing this paper. Comments from Ted Carmines and William Riker have been valuable. None of the foregoing individuals or institutions is responsible for any errors of analysis or interpretation.

dations of party realignment. Although the realignment made it possible for the Conservative party to champion free trade, the earlier event was not founded in the particular issue reorientation that the Free Trade Agreement (FTA) represented. The issue evolution took a tortuous path altogether like that of the reorientation of the U.S. party system's racial basis (Carmines and Stimson 1989). Each Conservative move occurred against a background of political weakness.

In this essay, we supply an interpretation of the 1988 Canadian general election. In doing so, we also contribute to our general understanding of how the electoral agenda evolves. As an interpretive exercise, we address both the long term and the short term. As a general contribution, we argue (*a*) that policy reversals in a party system require several moves; and (*b*) that campaigns must be taken seriously as stages for rhetorical and heresthetical moves and countermoves. We also present methodological innovations: a "rolling cross-section" survey of a campaign and experiments designed to interact with the real-time campaign.

If the strategic circumstances on the eve of the election seem so propitious, why did the agenda gamble almost fail once again? And why did it ultimately succeed? Once free trade was proposed, the struggle over the agenda shifted to a lower level of issue aggregation. In the campaign itself, the battle was over what considerations Canadians should invoke in making up their minds about the FTA. In the early going, the opposition succeeded in implanting considerations unfavorable to the agreement. Later, the government succeeded in shifting the argument onto more favorable ground.

In this essay, we stake a claim that campaigns are, in their own way, a site for the heresthetics that Riker has identified as underpinning the long run of party alignments and as a staple of legislative life. They commonly turn on competing arguments about what the dimension that dominates evaluation should be. In staking this claim, we also wed to the social choice perspective a notion from the psychological literature on elections, the idea of priming (Iyengar and Kinder 1987). Indeed, we treat priming as the mass public result of heresthetic moves by elites. But if campaigns are a site for heresthetics and priming, so also can they be a place for outright persuasion, for rhetoric.

The Long Run: Realignment and Policy Reversal

The Status Quo Ante

Canadian commercial policy has traditionally been embodied in the National Policy of 1878–79. The National Policy was the Conservative party's legacy to the nation. The policy traditionally had three elements: railway subsidies, virtually free access to Dominion-controlled western lands, and protective

tariffs (Mackintosh 1964). Lands have ceased to be an issue, at least for our purposes. Railways continue to excite controversy but, again, not in a way that matters here. This leaves tariffs.

The National Policy created its own coalition. An import-substitution manufacturing sector emerged as a political interest in its own right. Allied with it was the new Canadian Pacific Railway, for which manufactures from Ontario and Quebec provided the westbound freight. The policy was not merely national; it was also imperial. The policy's first decade coincided with a renewed interest by Britain in its empire and with a growing desire in many English Canadians for a larger place in the imperial sun. The railway and the protective tariffs that helped sustain it were part of the All Red Route to India.

The first free-trade misfire came in 1891. In that year, a Liberal party invigorated by a new leader and facing a Conservative party grown old in office snatched defeat from the jaws of victory by committing itself to "Unrestricted Reciprocity" with the United States. No agreement would be required; the tariff wall would simply be knocked down. The Conservative party responded with the slogan, "the Old Flag, the Old Policy, the Old Leader." The leader in question, Sir John Macdonald, affirmed that he would die as he was born, a British subject.[1]

The Liberal government that finally formed in 1896 appeared to have learned its lesson. The principal commercial policy initiative of its first 14 years in office was a brilliant tactical coup: Imperial Preference. By reducing tariffs on British manufactures,[2] the party genuflected in the direction of its free-trade roots. By confining preference to imperial production, it neutralized arguments that the Liberal party was disloyal to the British connection. The timing was brilliant: the policy came into force in 1897, the Diamond Jubilee year.

These lessons seemed to be forgotten in 1910. In that year, the Laurier government won an agreement for reciprocal free trade in natural products from the Taft administration.[3] Canada enjoyed comparative advantage in most natural products. In wheat, the most important product of all, the agreement was essentially irrelevant; the United States and Canada were both exporters,

---

1. The best capsule account of the 1891 election is Waite 1971, 221–27.

2. The tariff reductions were not, strictly speaking, exclusive to the empire. The legislation offered reciprocal reductions to any country willing to match them. The United States was not among these, as it had just enacted the Dingley tariff. Britain was granted the preference by virtue of its standing policy of free trade. For some Liberals, the legislation was appealing as an inducement to U.S reciprocation. For others, the unlikelihood of the latter was a considerable relief. For all, the imperial gloss was a happy accident. See Colvin 1955.

3. On the U.S. side, the incentive for the agreement seems to have been to give a sop to Progressives, who were still smarting from the enactment of the Payne-Aldrich tariff. The classic source on the agreement is Ellis 1939.

principally to the European market. The agreement seemed politically unassailable in that it left protection for manufacturing essentially untouched.

These considerations did not carry the day. The principal argument against the agreement spoke of the "thin edge of the wedge": the agreement was cast as the harbinger of more comprehensive trade liberalization. The latter, of course, threatened the British connection. This time the slogan was "No Truck or Trade with the Yankees." The new Conservative government was formed with a two-to-one majority.

But the result may not have been quite the product of miscalculation that the barebones narrative suggests. The government was old and unpopular. Particularly bruising had been controversy over the government's Naval Bill of 1910, which created a Canadian naval service. In Quebec, the Naval Bill was opposed because it did too much for the empire. The Liberals may have gambled that Quebec voters would not desert them for the archimperialist Conservatives, whatever the trade issue.[4] Outside Quebec, imperialists opposed the Naval Bill as doing too little for imperial defense. In much of English Canada, this sentiment only reinforced the reaction to the Reciprocity Agreement. But Canada was still overwhelmingly agrarian. The new electoral weight of the Prairie region had reinforced the Liberal's traditional agrarian base in Ontario. The free-trade commitment may still have offset losses that the government would otherwise have incurred, especially in agrarian English Canada (Johnston and Percy 1980).

But the simplest lesson of 1911 was that free trade was electorally too risky. With this lesson in mind, no government dared submit free trade with the United States to the electorate for another 77 years. Canadian tariffs *increased* in the early 1930s and the differential between U.S. and empire products was only sharpened by the Empire Trade Agreement of 1932 (Drummond 1974). Tariffs on American products were reduced in 1936 and 1938, but not to levels below those set by the original National Policy (Easterbrook and Aitken 1956; Marr and Paterson 1980). In 1948, the government contemplated accepting a U.S. offer of complete reciprocity but recoiled before the electoral implications (Pickersgill and Forster 1970). For the most part, Canadian governments were prepared to shoulder the political risks of tariff reduction only in a multilateral context, through GATT.

Agricultural implement tariffs were the occasional exception that proved this rule. Farm implements violated the usual logic of tariffs: just as benefits were concentrated, so were costs, and costs became even more concentrated as the number of farmers decreased. The level of implement tariffs thus varied

---

4. As it happens, the Conservative party did not campaign in its own right in the francophone parts of Quebec, but was happy to count the Nationalists returned on the naval issue in its parliamentary ranks, at least for a while.

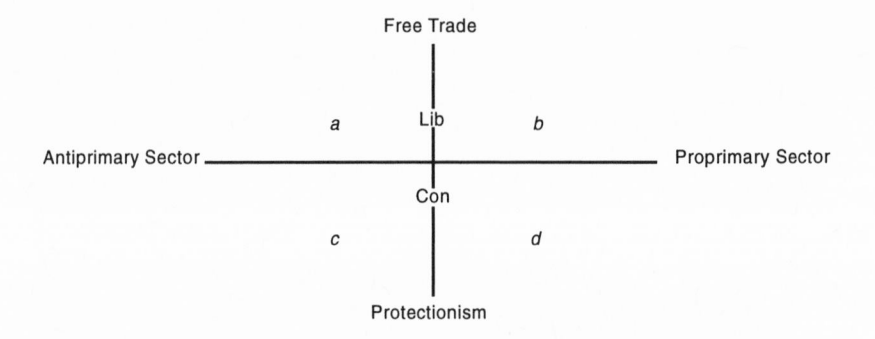

Fig. 1. Party positions on free trade and primary sector support before 1957

with the relative political strength of farming and manufacturing interests: tariffs were greatly reduced in 1919, 1922, and 1925, only to be increased again with the general raising of tariff walls in the 1930s. Reductions came in response to agrarian insurgency in the Progressive movement. The disappearance of Progressives in the late 1920s facilitated the tariff increases of the next decade. In 1944, implement tariffs were finally abolished.[5] Again, however, farmers had a strategic advantage: the CCF, with ties to the cooperative movement, reached its peak of popularity in that year and, indeed, defeated a Liberal government in Saskatchewan. The government was preoccupied, because of war, with the security of the grain supply.

The other exception to the rule was the creation of the Permanent Joint Board on Defense by the Ogdensburg Agreement in 1940. Although it liberalized Canadian-U.S. economic relations in defense production, the sector in question is, to say the least, intensely managed.[6]

By the 1950s, then, the parties' economic policy positions could be stylized as shown in figure 1. The vertical axis could be defined as willingness to truck or trade with the United States to paraphrase an earlier Conservative slogan. On this the parties had different locations partly because of their legacies but mainly because of their abiding nontariff differences: Conservatives expressed unease about U.S. direct investment while Liberal governments acted to facilitate it. The horizontal axis concerned willingness to aid the primary sector, especially agriculture. This axis existed only in potential; it was effectively suppressed by the parties' identical positions on it.

---

5. Fowke 1957, 292.

6. The one other exception, the Automotive Agreement of 1965, came after the realignment under discussion. Like the Ogdensburg Agreement, it was an example of managed trade.

The Realignment: Causes and Consequences

If protection for secondary industry was an issue that would not die, protection for primary industry was struggling to be born. Wheat was being marketed by the Canadian Wheat Board by this time and the federal government did pump money into agricultural research and field rehabilitation. But farmers did not receive cash transfers, nor did they have a price guarantee. Only limited forms of capital market assistance were available. The one attempt to create a comprehensive national products marketing scheme, in 1935, had been struck down by the Judicial Committee of the Privy Council.

Both parties resisted calls for support for farmers and other resource producers. Each had made concessions to agrarian pressure, but not out of any apparent conviction. A Conservative government established the National Wheat Board in 1935, but only as the last desperate act of a dying government. Otherwise, they resisted calls for assistance to the sector. Jimmy Gardiner, the Liberal Minister of Agriculture from 1935 to 1957, was in many ways an effective steward of the sector's interests. He successfully resisted attempts to bring farmers under the jurisdiction of the Wartime Prices and Trade Board and he negotiated an Anglo-Canadian wheat agreement that guaranteed Canada's continued access to its most important overseas market.[7] At no point, however, did he succeed in establishing price or supply management as operating principles.[8]

But new forces emerged in the 1950s. The United States began to dump its wheat surplus onto the international market, and the resultant glut sent the price plummeting. The political significance of this is best indicated by the path of per capita income in Saskatchewan, the province most completely dominated by wheat. In 1952, per capita income in Saskatchewan was over 110 percent of the national average; two years later, it stood at roughly 75 percent. The next two years brought a modest recovery, but, by 1957, Saskatchewan incomes were again below 80 percent of the national average.[9]

If these events seemed to pass the Liberal government by, the same was true for the Conservatives, until December, 1956. Farm support was an inadmissible issue for the leadership of the major parties. Both groups understood its political appeal, but both also seemed to regard it as verging on immoral. In effect, they tacitly adopted a gag rule. Only political desperation combined with a leader with no ties to the financial and manufacturing communities

---

7. Bothwell, Drummond, and English 1981, 71, 83ff.

8. See Ward and Smith 1990, 307ff. for a poignant account of Gardiner's waning influence in the Liberal cabinet.

9. The data in this paragraph are a synthesis from Bothwell, Drummond, and English, figs. 5, 6, 9.

would induce either party to break this rule. The Liberals had no incentive to break it; they were too successful. The Conservatives *were* desperate, but their natural supporters could not stomach the means of salvation.

What changed? First, the agricultural crisis of the 1950s suggests that the resource industry axis lengthened, at least for Westerners. The second key ingredient was a change in the Conservative leadership. The Conservative party had, in a sense, run out of its traditional alternatives. It had tried several business-oriented imperialists. It had genuflected toward Quebec with R. J. Manion. It had had several Westerners as leader but none who seemed to embody the sensibility of the region. Finally, despite front bench and ex officio resistance, the party's rank and file chose John Diefenbaker from Saskatchewan.

Diefenbaker more than symbolized the Prairie West. He delivered the goods. Beginning in 1957–58, the government supported nine commodity prices at 80 percent of their preceding ten-year average, credit facilities were greatly expanded, the Wheat Board began advance payments on the crop, and it sold the crop aggressively.[10] Altogether, direct transfers to Western wheat producers increased more than sevenfold in constant dollars between 1957–58 and 1961–62 and accounted for *all* of the Agriculture Department's budget growth. Payments had fallen back to nil by 1965–66,[11] by which date, significantly, the government was once again Liberal. To return to the Saskatchewan income-series mentioned above: its trend was positive through the Diefenbaker years and 1963 brought the highest income to the province of any year from 1954 to 1975.[12]

The Conservatives also went after oil producers. To protect the industry from imports of cheaper oil from Venezuela and the Middle East, the government reserved the bulk of the Ontario market for high-cost Alberta product. For the first time, central Canadian consumers were forced to subsidize a western industry that seemed to have no realistic prospect of comparative advantage in the world market.

These policies did not deliver power to the Conservatives in 1957 and 1958. The party's surge over those years is most easily explained as a reaction to 22 years of Liberal rule. What the policy reorientation did do was reshape that Conservative base that remained after the party was swept from office in 1963. It is not clear how much of this policy reorientation Conservative leadership convention delegates willed when they chose Mr. Diefenbaker in 1956. Mr. Diefenbaker himself, anecdotal evidence suggests, understood that

---

10. The 1963–64 export volume was 550 million bushels. Never before had Canadian exports exceeded 400 million bushels.
11. Berthelet 1985, 11; see also Skogstad 1987; Bothwell, Drummond, and English 1981.
12. Bothwell, Drummond, and English 1981, fig. 9.

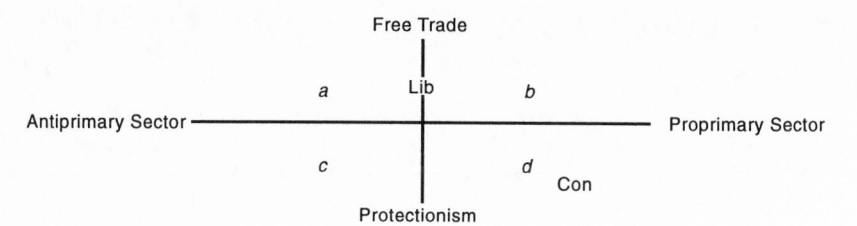

Fig. 2. Party positions on free trade and primary sector support, 1957–63

the wheat economy was in crisis early on.[13] The fruit of that understanding was an expanded electoral base. The party was still the subordinate one in the system, but its subordination was much less abject than it had been from 1935 to 1957.[14]

As a party now committed to defending the primary sector, the Conservatives had moved dramatically to the right on the proprimary-antiprimary axis (see fig. 2). The transformation did *not* occur because the Conservative party abandoned its commitment to the National Policy and to the ethos that supported it. John Diefenbaker was no more inclined toward closer ties with the United States than was the man with whose shade he seemed to be in constant contact, Sir John Macdonald. Instead, Mr. Diefenbaker committed his party to protection all around, squarely into quadrant d of figure 2. Thanks to this commitment to protection of the primary industry, the Conservatives became the dominant party in the West, the traditional home of free trade (for manufactured products) opinion. The Liberals were now hemmed into the heartland of the older, National Policy protectionism. But the sectional and sectoral reorientation that Mr. Diefenbaker had effected, for exquisitely protectionist reasons, prepared his party to abandon the National Policy.

The Canada-U.S. Free Trade Agreement

More moves had to be made, however. The regional and sectoral reorientation of the parties' electorates, and thus of their recruitment of activists, ensured that more moves would be made.

As the party of government, the Liberals made the first move. They preempted the Conservatives' traditional control of the nationalistic pole.

---

13. See Camp 1970, 187. Camp also supplies a skeptic's account of the 1956 convention (232ff.). On Mr. Diefenbaker's economic ideas more generally, see Bothwell, Drummond, and English 1981, chap. 22.

14. The Conservative party regularly won fewer than 20 percent of the House seats from 1935 to 1957. In contrast, the party's 1963–84 share was typically 30 to 35 percent.

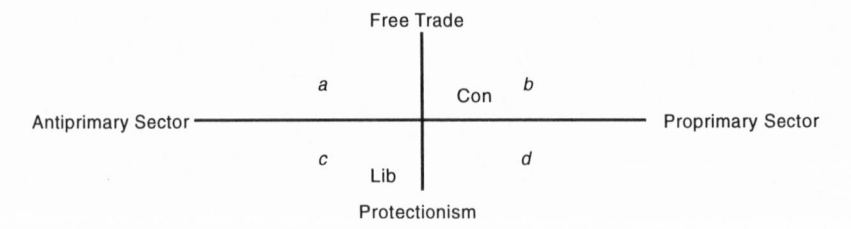

Fig. 3. Party positions on free trade and primary sector support, 1970–84

Liberal nationalism advanced on two fronts: they increased their commitment to protection for secondary industry and they attacked interests in the primary sector. In terms of figure 2, they moved significantly south and west.

One front, investment policy, looked to the enemy without. Now it was the Liberals who worried publicly about the weight of (mainly) U.S. investment. As the government, they were in a position to act on the concern, with the establishment, in 1974, of the Foreign Investment Review Agency (FIRA), with a mandate to review foreign takeovers of Canadian firms.

The other front looked to the enemy within, the energy sector. In the 1960s, energy producers were grateful for the protection that Mr. Diefenbaker had given them. In the 1970s, the protection no longer seemed necessary. Indeed, the policy instruments created to provide it were turned against the sector in a bitter struggle over rent created by the oil price increases.[15] This culminated in the National Energy Program (NEP) of 1980, which sought to reduce foreign ownership in the oil and gas sector and to increase the federal government's share of energy rents (Safarian 1985; James 1990).

Conservatives opposed all of this and so moved toward, and perhaps into, quadrant *b* (see fig. 3). They promised to loosen FIRA regulations and did so once in power.[16] They fought the NEP in Parliament and through their control of the key energy province, Alberta. At one point in 1982, they brought Parliament to a halt. In power, they abrogated the NEP's most objectionable features.

But they remained silent on free trade. Protection of manufactures had, after all, been *their* policy, one of the party's constitutive values. It had

---

15. Canada maintained domestic oil prices below world levels. Eastern Canadian consumption of offshore oil was subsidized by a tax equivalent to the difference between the domestic and world prices levied on exports to the United States from the West, mainly Alberta. This scheme was roughly self-financing as long as Canadian exports and imports were in balance. As the 1970s progressed, the trade in oil went out of balance and the fiscal foundations of the policy were undermined.

16. FIRA was renamed Investment Canada. At the renaming, the government announced that "Canada [was] open for business."

derived warrant not just on economic grounds but also as an expression of mutually reinforcing national and imperial interests. An attack on the National Policy had been vulnerable to being styled as an attack on the British definition of the nationality and on the connection that sustained it. But there lay the rub: the empire had disappeared. Conservatives' evaluation of commercial policy now had to be detached from imperial considerations. The remaining considerations that the party found congenial argued against protection. The party was poised to shift. Only tactical considerations held it in check: the party remembered 1911.

Even as Brian Mulroney was forming his Conservative government (formed in 1984), circumstances favoring a free-trade agreement were emerging.[17] The previous Liberal government, notwithstanding its nationalist orientation, had initiated discussion about sectoral free trade. These came to nought, however. It was increasingly clear that if an agreement was to be pursued, it would have to be comprehensive, with tradeoffs between sectors.

If, in the past, such an agreement was shunned, increasing protectionism in the United States proper forced the issue for Canadians. Typically, the U.S. target was not Canada, but Canada often seemed to get caught in the backwash. The momentum that the Omnibus Trade Bill seemed to be gathering was especially ominous. And one important dispute, over softwood lumber, had Canada as its specific target. An earlier attempt to have the International Trade Commission (ITC) impose a countervailing tariff on Canadian softwood imports had failed; the ITC had found the claim, which had originated in the U.S. Pacific Northwest, without merit. To Canadians, little in the specifically economic realm seemed to have changed since that earlier dispute; yet this time the bid for a countervailing tariff succeeded. That a U.S. tariff was ultimately replaced by a Canadian export tax (and thus that the imputed rent remained in Canada) did not mollify Canadian opinion. The dispute suggested that trade politics in the United States were shifting to a new level of toughness. Many Canadians concluded that Canada had better try to insure itself against the worst.

At the same time, a case for a U.S.-Canada agreement emerged from an independent source. On September 5, 1985, the Royal Commission on the Economic Union and Development Prospects for Canada, also known as the Macdonald Commission, delivered its report. The commission was a creature of the previous Liberal government and originally seemed tainted by that paternity. Despite early difficulties, the commission was able to establish its seriousness and legitimacy. Although Mr. Mulroney had apparently intended to shut down the commission upon forming his government, he was dissuaded

---

17. In the subsequent discussion, we draw heavily upon the narrative in Campbell and Pal 1991, chap. 3.

from this. Indeed, the commission's suspect origins worked to his political advantage. The commission, whose head had been an architect of Liberal government nationalist policies in the 1970s, staked a strong claim for the merits of free trade. The commission proposal was quite concrete and supplied a basis for the government to proceed. Official notice of intention to negotiate was given on September 26, 1985.

This brings us to the central question: were these external events so compelling that *any* government, not just a Conservative one, would have yielded to them? The fact that even the Liberals had begun sectoral discussions is awkward. We are skeptical, though, that a Liberal government, with the electoral coalition it had assembled, could have stomached the comprehensive agreement that seemed to be the only alternative to no agreement at all. For Conservatives, pressures to reach an agreement were not uncongenial, even if acceding to them was risky.

The risks, meanwhile, arguably diminished in salience in the months after the government declared its intent. For other reasons, September, 1985, the month of the declaration, came to be called "Black September." Scandals and a bank failure forced two resignations and embarrassed the whole cabinet. Other scandals and some unpopular policy initiatives also littered this period. The government's popularity, as indicated by published polls, plummeted over the autumn of 1985. By the beginning of 1987, the government had fallen as low as it seemed it possibly could. Free trade could pose no further risks. Pursuit of an agreement at least gave the government the appearance of purpose and political courage; these were electoral assets in their own right. If an agreement could be reached, Conservatives might hope, given the basic coalitional structure of Canadian elections, that its supporters would have to vote for them.

The negotiations, which began in 1986, had several rocky patches, but a draft agreement was struck in late 1987. Under it, most tariff barriers between the two countries would come down within ten years. A continental energy market will be created, as Canada has foresworn export taxes on Canadian production and has agreed that any rationing will fall proportionally across all North American contracts.[18] Canada has dropped barriers to U.S. provision of services, including financial services, and has greatly increased the asset threshold above which foreign investment becomes subject to review.[19]

Concessions on the U.S. side are much less dramatic. U.S. tariffs on Canadian goods will also disappear within ten years, but U.S. barriers were

---

18. The industry had long pressed for an end to the priority for Canadian consumers in the event of rationing. That priority had made Canada an uncertain supplier, a fact reflected in prices fetched by Canadian contracts.

19. Although Canada retains the right to pursue a 50 percent Canadian ownership objective in the energy sector.

smaller than Canadian ones to begin with.[20] The United States placed virtually no restrictions on Canadian capital movements before, and so had few to remove; indeed, from the mercantilist perspective historically dominant in Canada, the openness of the United States to Canadian capital was itself a problem. Ironically, in the area in which U.S. restrictions were greatest, banking, the provisions of the Glass-Stiegel Act remain in force. The United States has agreed to establish a joint review process for trade disputes. But the trade law to be jointly adjudicated remains that of the country in which the dispute originates. So far, no harmonizing of the two countries' trade subsidy legislation has occurred, although there now exists a commitment to effect it.

The political risks embodied in the agreement were enormous. Canadian opponents characterized it as a sellout: the United States gave up little while Canada bartered away its sovereignty, an argument that earlier trade initiatives had evoked. Passage through the Parliament proved impossible. The opposition raised procedural difficulties in the House, and the Senate declined to consider the trade bill before it had been referred to the people. This set the stage for dissolution of Parliament on October 1, 1988.

The Short Run: Free Trade in the 1988 Campaign

The Balance of Opinion

Figure 4 shows a daily tracking of each side of FTA opinion.[21] The daily data point is the five-day moving average $(t - 2, \ldots, t + 2)$. The campaign revealed the agreement's strategic vulnerability. Support for the FTA was sliding, and opposition was gaining from the beginning. By some time before the debates, the two sides appeared to be at a standoff: about 40 percent on

---

20. There was some debate about the effective rates of protection on both sides of the border in the status quo ante. With GATT reductions, both countries' tariffs on the existing mix of trade with each other had gone down. But Canadian advocates of the agreement claimed that many progressive tariffs remained on the U.S. books, such that Canadian attempts to add value were discouraged. These tariffs will now disappear.

21. The 1988 Canadian National Election Study's preelection component was a rolling cross-section administered by a form of computer-assisted telephone interviewing (CATI) that, among other things, accommodated experiments to mimic arguments in the campaign. An average of 77 interviews were completed per day from October 4 to November 20 inclusive. The day on which a respondent happened to be interviewed was, to all intents and purposes, a random event. A fresh sample was released each day, enough to yield the target number of completions. The bulk of the completions were recorded within three days of release, but numbers were kept open for two weeks and for as many as 15 callbacks (a few completions took even more callbacks than this). The first few fieldwork days saw fewer than 80 completions, as the system warmed up. By about day 4 (October 7) the daily pattern was set: 40 to 50 completions from that day's release, 10 to 20 from the previous day's sample, 5 to 10 from two days before, and scattered completions from a range of earlier releases.

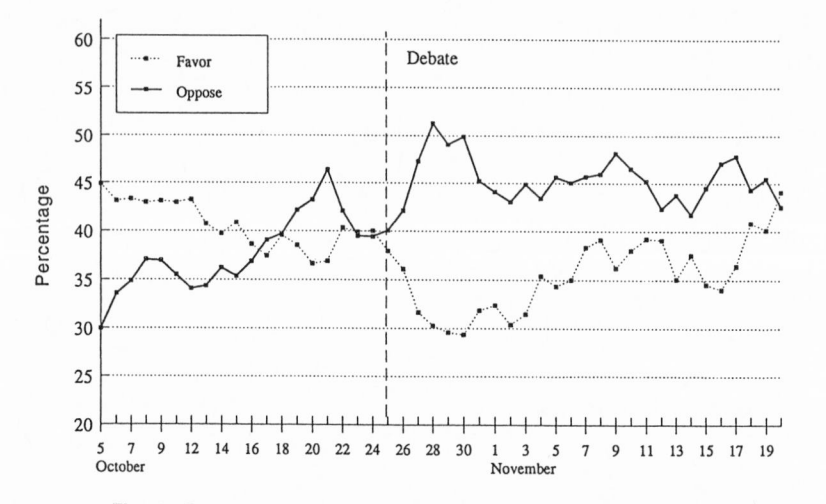

Fig. 4. Support and opposition to the Free Trade Agreement

each side. For supporters, the worst was yet to come. The decisive events were the leaders' debates, on October 24 (French) and 25 (English). In the three days that followed the English debate, support for the FTA plummeted.[22]

The recovery began immediately. By the end of the campaign, the government had undone most of the debates' damage. But the slowness of the recovery suggests that it could not be taken for granted; it had to be won. Certainly, the government seemed to think so, in light of the resources it and its allies poured into the fight. At the end, the standoff was restored. Given the split in the anti-FTA vote, the standoff translated into a Conservative seat majority.

What produced the shift against the FTA? The campaign tapped uncertainty about the negotiator and about the agreement itself, uncertainties that, before the campaign, were latent. Our design picked up each of these uncertainties. How was the recovery brought about? We are not as comfortable with our answers to this question as with our answers to the first one. But our design did pick up an important facet of the late campaign: the breaking of the link between the FTA and some of the arguments against it; one way in which

22. Party support shifted commensurately, indeed more than commensurately. The pre-debates drift against the FTA had no effect on party support. In the aggregate, the two were actually pulling apart. The debates brought them together, to the disadvantage of the Conservatives. The debates also rehabilitated the Liberals at the expense of the other anti-FTA party. See Johnston et al. 1991.

the Conservatives broke the link was by increasing the sense of uncertainty about life *without* the agreement.

Uncertainty Over the Agent

The critical moment in the English debate seems to have been an exchange over the FTA. Liberal leader John Turner's most memorable phrase was: "I happen to believe that you have sold us out." The sellout metaphor personalized concerns for sovereignty by joining them to fears about the agent. By confronting Brian Mulroney directly with his responsibility for the Free Trade Agreement, John Turner echoed weeks of preparatory rhetoric by both opposition parties and by nonparty advocates.

The rhetoric sought to take advantage of voters' natural tendency, in the face of uncertainties and complexities, to look to proxies, in this case to ask who was responsible for the negotiations. Liberal and NDP strategies believed that such a process could only work to the agreement's *disadvantage:* they repeatedly styled the FTA as "the Mulroney trade deal." The Mulroney government had regularly been attacked by the opposition as mendacious and unreliable. The government was plagued by conflicts of interest and petty corruption. Harmful in themselves, these problems sat poorly with the 1984 campaign's emphasis on honesty. The prime minister had become typed as habitually telling his immediate audience whatever it wanted to hear, heedless of contradictions with promises made to other audiences. And the prime minister seemed to have gained a reputation as someone who would do anything to close a deal, even at the expense of his own bottom line, if indeed he had one. The Free Trade Agreement thus seemed vulnerable to the reputed untrustworthiness of the agent principally responsible for it.

The government itself seemed to concede the point. In the early campaign, it adopted what might be called a third-party approach to the FTA: rather than emphasize its own responsibility for the agreement, it recited endorsements that the FTA had received from independent groups. And in contrast to the opposition's focus on the FTA-Mulroney nexus, the government downplayed the agreement.

To assess the agreement's vulnerability, we administered two FTA support-oppose items to our respondents. The assignment of respondents to one or the other version was random. The basic item was:

As you know, _____ has reached a Free Trade Agreement with the United States. All things considered, do you support the agreement or do you oppose it?

The experiment lay in who was named as reaching the agreement.

Half the sample was given the word *Canada*. This places a mild burden of proof on rejecting the agreement. To the extent that it does, this version mirrors Conservative rhetoric later in the campaign that asked: what would be the effect of rejecting the FTA on Canada's image abroad as a good faith negotiator? The other half of the sample was supplied the words, *the Mulroney government*. This treatment goes straight to the prime minister's reputation.

The experiment's greatest impact should have come early in the campaign. Indeed, much of the impact may have been absorbed by the time our fieldwork began, so intense over the summer had been the opposition's attempts to link the FTA to the prime minister. To the extent that opinion remained unmobilized in October, however, the "Mulroney" treatment should have had an adverse impact on support for the FTA. As the campaign wore on, this impact should have weakened. A consideration that might not be ordinarily accessible to the respondent's consciousness early in the campaign, and thus introduced into that consciousness might move survey response, may already be factored into the latent response disposition late in the campaign. At this point, invoking it serves only to reinforce opinion on one side and is likely to be discounted by the other side.[23] That is, by late in the campaign, the consideration's impact should be not so much *internal* to the experiment as *external* to it, in the ebb and flow of FTA support itself.

The data shown in figure 5 suggest that the opposition's pre- and early campaign strategy was well conceived. Here, FTA position is represented by a summary variable, scored $+1$ if the respondent favored the agreement, -1 if he or she opposed it, and 0 if the respondent was ambivalent or indifferent.[24] In the weeks before the debates, respondents in the "Canada" treatment were palpably closer to the supportive end of the FTA scale than respondents in the "Mulroney" treatment. In percentage terms, the typical predebate difference shown in figure 5 translates into about a 10-percentage point larger share of FTA support in the "Canada" group. The difference cannot be accounted for by chance.

The experiment's impact evaporated within a week of the English debate. FTA support fell in both treatment groups, but fell further in the "Canada" than in the "Mulroney" group. Thereafter, treatment-group differences were largely the result of sampling error.

23. See Schuman and Presser 1981; Zaller 1984. As Zaller puts it: "question wording changes which introduce new ideas, stimulate memory, or otherwise alter the context in which an issue is viewed often influence survey responses. Question wording changes which cannot plausibly be argued to have done any of these things less often affect survey responses" (23).

24. All apparent differences between the support-side and opposition-side dynamics can be reconciled with a model that posits that underlying dispositions on the FTA are roughly normally distributed.

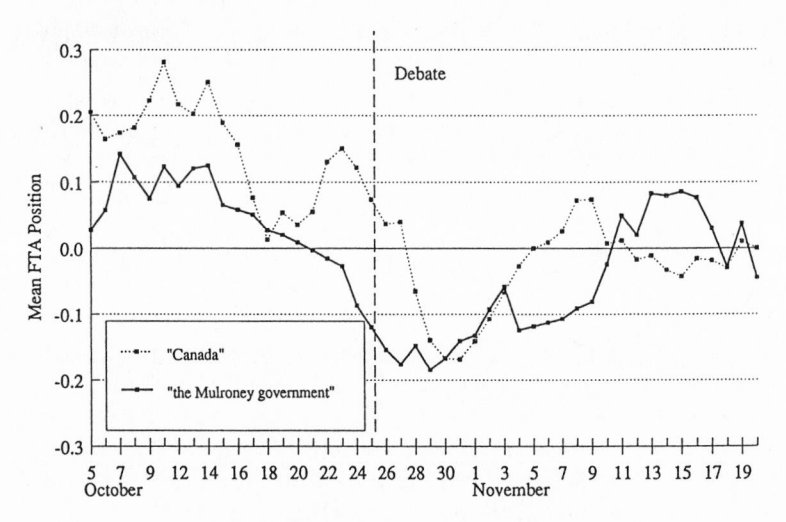

**Fig. 5. Identity of the negotiator and FTA opinion
(seven-day moving averages)**

The existence of an experimental impact before the debates indicated the potential for discrediting the FTA by linking it to Brian Mulroney. The disappearance of the experiment's effect after the debates indicated that the potential was realized in the campaign—the consideration we were experimenting on was now having an effect in the electorate at large. The debates must have implanted uncertainty about the agent in the electorate.[25] We had implanted such uncertainty in the "Mulroney" treatment group. After the debates, this treatment had little further impact: all respondents—even those assigned to the "Canada" treatment—now came to us with Mulroney-related doubts about the FTA already in place. We no longer needed to remind them of the linkage between the prime minister and the FTA; John Turner's accusation that Brian Mulroney had "sold us out" did the job for us. Consequently, both treatments yielded about the same level of support for the FTA, and the experimental impact faded. It faded as FTA support in the "Canada" treatment fell precipitously after the debates; "Canada" respondents got the message from the debates that "Mulroney" respondents had been getting all along.

Even though the average level of FTA support differed between treatment

---

25. Some of the impact that we attribute to debates may be from another factor roughly coincident with those events: the start of party advertising. Parties are not allowed to begin advertising until four weeks before the last day of the writ period. In 1988, this was Sunday, October 23. Early advertisements by the Liberals embodied the theme that Mr. Turner raised in debate, and so the exact assignment of responsibility need not detain us here. Work in progress suggests that the debates were, in fact, the critical events.

groups before the debates, both groups drifted against the FTA at roughly the same rate, with all convergence occurring after the debates. Clearly, something was working against FTA support even before the debates. But whatever it was, it must have been unrelated to uncertainty about the negotiator. Had the negotiator been the issue before October 25, the experimental differences would have narrowed. What else was at issue?

Uncertainty Over the Agreement's Impact

One plausible interpretation of the earlier decline in FTA support is in terms of debate over its substance. Three lines of attack seemed especially promising as the campaign began: the apparent abrogation of *sovereignty* over key elements of the economy; threats to Canada's *social programs;* and fear of *job displacement.* Arguments available to supporters of the FTA seemed politically weaker. Two such arguments, nonetheless, had emerged by the eve of the campaign: a standard comparative advantage claim in terms of *lower prices* and a historically specific argument in terms of insurance against U.S. *protectionism.*[26]

Each of these arguments was mirrored in a challenge contingent on initial FTA opinion. Supporters were given, at random, one of the three opposition arguments and asked if this made them less supportive. Opponents were given one of the two supportive arguments and asked if this made them less opposed. Respondents were not asked if they changed their minds, just if they felt less of whatever it was they initially claimed to be.[27] Again, we should expect the impact of challenges to follow the logic in Zaller 1984 and diminish as the campaign wore on.

---

26. Later in the campaign, a theme emerged that we had not anticipated correctly: a concern over access to a large market. We framed a market size item for the postelection wave and refer to it subsequently.

27. The supporters were challenged by the following statements.

1. Some people say that under this agreement Canada will lose its ability to control key sectors of the economy, such as energy;

2. Some people say that this agreement will make it very hard for us to maintain our social programs, such as medicare;

3. Some people say that under this agreement many Canadians will lose their jobs, in industries such as textiles, automobiles, and services.

The opponents were challenged by the following statements.

1. Some people say that this agreement will defend us against *American* protectionism, such as happened in the softwood lumber dispute.

2. Some people say that this agreement will lower the cost of many of the goods that Canadian families need.

After the challenge, the respondent was asked the following question.

Does this make you *less supportive* of [*opposed* to] the agreement, or does it make *no difference* to how you feel?

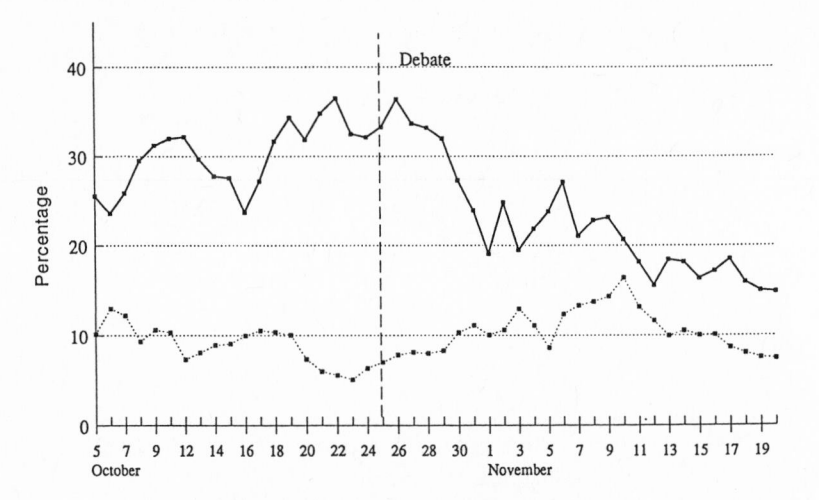

Fig. 6. The dynamics of the challenges

The data shown in figure 6 suggest that opponents did indeed have the tactical advantage. The figure combines response to each side's set of challenges and gives a daily tracking (seven-day moving average) of the percentage less supportive or opposed, as the case may be. Before October 28, arguments against the FTA moved two to three times as many FTA supporters as arguments for the FTA moved FTA opponents. In the last week of the campaign, however, the corresponding ratio was only about 1.5 to 1.0. All decay in impact was on the opposing argument side. The campaign had done its work, evidently, by helping FTA supporters cope with opposition arguments and by moving erstwhile supporters (who were truly vulnerable to opposition considerations) to the place where they belonged: the opposition camp.[28]

This interpretation still requires substantiation. It sits rather awkwardly with the exact time path of decay in challenges' effectiveness: anti-FTA challenges' impact *increased* before the debates and did not begin to drop until three days *after* the debates. A full estimation of the process must take account of a powerful selection bias that reflects the very force of the campaign's arguments: it is not unreasonable to expect that just as arguments reach their peak of intensity or effectiveness, the group to which they are directed is being depleted of its most marginal members. The interaction of

---

28. Reassuringly in this respect, respondents who claimed that the challenge's consideration might make them reconsider were more likely to report a pre-post election change on the FTA than were respondents who said that the challenge would make no difference.

Table 1. Impact of Substantive Arguments by Campaign Stage

Argument	Before October 29		October 29 and After		Postelection[a]
	Percentage	N	Percentage	N	
	Supporters[b]				
Control key sectors	26.2	227	21.1	234	−0.08
Social programs	39.5	190	21.5	180	−0.24
Loss of jobs	31.9	245	17.1	205	0.14
	Opponents[c]				
U.S. protectionism	6.4	335	12.0	384	−0.04
Price of goods[d]	12.4	337	3.2	378	0.45

[a]The entries for the postelection are mean ratings on an agree-disagree scale of −2 to +2; N = 2,922.
[b]Entries for supporters are those less supportive.
[c]Entries for opponents are those less opposed.
[d]This argument was recast as market size in the postelection survey.

endogenous resistance and exogenous force requires much more unpacking than we can give here.

Table 1 gives a crude periodization of the impact from specific challenges. Following the summary evidence shown in figure 6, the campaign wave was split between October 28 and 29. All along, the social programs challenge proved the most powerful. In the early going it was nearly four times as powerful as either challenge on the other side; indeed, it moved nearly two FTA supporters in five to reconsider.[29] On the pro-FTA side there is a hint that the "U.S. protectionism" challenge gained some bite. But, challenges to FTA opponents underlined just how hard pro-FTA arguments were to make. Typically, they failed to move all but one in ten of the agreement's opponents. In rhetoric, at least, supporters of the FTA occupied a strategically vulnerable position.

Hold the position they evidently did. Indeed, they regained ground. Can we get any purchase on the place of substantive arguments in the recovery? To this end we must resort to the postelection wave. There, four of the five challenges were recast as items asked of all respondents.[30] The challenge

29. A weekly breakdown indicates that the "key sectors" and "jobs" challenges eroded by the end; in the last week, their ability to provoke reconsideration was no higher than that for the "U.S. protectionism" challenge.

30. The items retained the campaign wave wording except for the "some people say that . . ." introduction. Agreement or disagreement was on a five-point scale.

about the price of goods was replaced by one about access to a large market, an argument that gained increasing prominence as the campaign progressed.[31]

The preelection-postelection contrast is startling. Table 1 also shows the mean postelection ratings for the five items. The results are a surprise in light of the record of campaign wave challenges. On the anti-FTA side, the rank order of ratings was the inverse of the rank order of challenges' impact. Respondents were *less* likely to agree with the "social programs" item than with any other. The balance of opinion was also slightly in disagreement with the "key sectors" and the "U.S. protectionism" claims. The two considerations to gain a favorable balance were the "job loss" and the (new) "market size" ones.

It seems unlikely that balance of agreement with the social programs consideration was so negative for the entire campaign. The power of the campaign wave challenge corresponded to the repeated invocation of the argument in the campaign and with the FTA's midcampaign free fall. The Conservatives themselves paid attention to the issue, once they awakened to the danger. In addition to stepping up advertising concentration on the consideration, they marshaled seemingly independent witnesses. Perhaps the key event was the press conference at which Mr. Justice Emmett Hall, whose Royal Commission years before was widely credited with bringing the health insurance system into being, claimed that that system was *not* at risk under the FTA. This received voluminous coverage and put the Liberal and NDP leaders on the defensive; were they prepared to call the father of medicare a liar? Whatever the exact ingredients, the data shown in table 1 suggest that one key part of the counterattack was not so much heresthetical as rhetorical: the Conservatives seem to have *persuaded* the electorate that its greatest fear was unfounded.

But did it also *distract* the electorate from the social programs question, that is, did it succeed in a heresthetic move? With the data shown in table 2 we try to see if the FTA agenda shifted over the campaign. Unfortunately, we cannot do this with items from the campaign wave itself. For good or ill, we put the key campaign wave questions to respondents on the wrong side of the issue, so to speak. But even if the distributions on the five FTA items shifted from before the election to after, the *rank order placement* of individuals ought not to have shifted, apart from random error. We should thus be

---

31. The usual form of the argument went: but for the FTA, Canada would be the only industrialized country without guaranteed access to a market of 100 million or more. In substance, this argument overlaps the "U.S. protectionism" item. But the emphasis in the large-market argument seems structural, on an abiding characteristic of the market for Canadian products. Rhetorical emphasis on U.S. protectionism seemed more in terms of active harassment, under countervailing proceedings, that could go on irrespective of tariff level. The Conservatives seemed to sense that mention of action protectionism might only arouse anti-U.S. sentiment. The protectionism challenge was the only one that provoked more than a trivial number of (unprompted) "more opposed" responses. The specific wording of the market-size item was: "The agreement is necessary to make sure we have a large market for our products."

TABLE 2.   The Impact of Considerations on FTA Support, Measured Weekly

Week	N	Intercept	Anti-FTA	Pro-FTA
1	258	0.328	−0.300	0.323
		(0.027)	(0.067)	(0.073)
2	436	0.354	−0.336	0.251
		(0.022)	(0.040)	(0.044)
3	438	0.349	−0.376	0.356
		(0.020)	(0.036)	(0.039)
4	434	0.315	−0.334	0.381
		(0.019)	(0.047)	(0.049)
5	475	0.296	−0.326	0.270
		(0.020)	(0.047)	(0.053)
6	415	0.296	−0.388	0.370
		(0.020)	(0.047)	(0.050)
7	466	0.339	−0.443	0.300
		(0.019)	(0.043)	(0.048)

Notes: Scales are standardized to a −1,+1 interval. Standard errors are in parentheses.

able to enter postelection self-placements into estimations with the campaign wave FTA opinion on the left-hand side. This we do in table 2, with weekly regressions of FTA support on summary pro- and anti-FTA scales.[32]

The pattern is *not* consistent with a shift in the agenda. Over the campaign, we might have expected to see coefficients on the anti-FTA scale shrink (at least late in the campaign) and coefficients on the pro-FTA scale grow. Neither occurred. The pro-FTA coefficients remained roughly stable and the anti-FTA coefficient may even have grown. In the week-by-week comparison, the real action was in the intercepts, which fell and rose roughly as the pro-FTA share did. This suggests that Canadians first became progressively more persuaded of the anti-FTA arguments and then progressively less so, and the same, mutatis mutandis, for arguments on the other side. This reinforces the emphasis that comes out of the postelection distributions on rhetoric.

The particular fate of the social programs consideration may be an object lesson in political vulnerability. Its vulnerability was the other side of its power. It touched Canadians' deepest fear, that U.S. pressure would somehow undermine one of Canada's distinctive features, its highly developed social services. But arguments about the impact of the FTA on the welfare state were highly speculative. As such, they could expand to make the agreement appear

---

32. The results were essentially the same for FTA opposition. We also did estimations with the five items entered separately and, again, no difference from the pattern described in the text emerged.

one step short of the apocalypse. For the same reason, they were vulnerable to rapid compression. By late in the campaign, the social programs arguments still available to FTA opponents were highly convoluted, strained in the telling. In contrast, arguments that the FTA entailed labor market displacement and a de facto loss of sovereignty were less controvertible.

This brings us to a parting question: where do heresthetics end and where does rhetoric begin? The distinction may become blurred when the axes of evaluation concern what an agreement will *do*. If a protagonist persuades a voter that social programs are not at risk, is that a rhetorical move or a heresthetical one? The axes of FTA evaluation were not quite like the dimensions that underlay, for instance, the game of U.S. federal aid to education. In that game, the Powell amendment was perfectly explicit in what it would do to the shape of education policy. What mattered is what members of Congress thought about the substance of the amendment. In 1988, there seemed little disagreement about the objectives that the FTA was alleged to promote or hinder; each side picked what it assumed to be strategically favorable arguments, and nothing in our data controverts their strategic sense. The debate was over whether the considerations were relevant, over the facts.

Discussion

Commercial policy has been notable mainly for its absence from the Canadian electoral agenda. Before 1988, the only successful moves in the domain were explicitly protectionist: the National Policy in the 1878 election and the Diefenbaker government's support for agriculture and gas and oil. Between 1878 and 1988, comprehensive liberalization was proposed only twice. The 1891 proposal does not seem to have been born out of desperation. It might best be regarded as a learning experience. The Liberal party's apparent failure to learn the lesson in 1911 may truly have been an act of desperation. A case could be made that the Reciprocity Agreement gave the Liberal government its best chance to reinforce its base, to stop its agrarian supporters from defecting, in retrospective disapproval of the rest of the record, to the Conservatives. It just was not enough. The 1988 move also had some appearance of desperation. When the intent to pursue negotiations was announced, the government's position did not seem that weak. But the weakness that later beset the government probably reinforced its determination to see negotiations through to the finish. In 1988, as in 1911, the government had an issue that, even if it alienated a significant proportion of the electorate, raised the defection stakes for its natural supporters.

But for the Conservatives in 1988 to occupy the same position as the Liberals in 1911, the Canadian party system had to undergo a complete reversal on commercial policy. The electoral realignment that started the

reversal, in the 1950s, was reminiscent of the U.S. alignment in the 1850s. A party long out of power reached for a hitherto inadmissible policy alternative and split the ruling coalition. But it also resembled a reorientation of the U.S system closer in time to the Canadian realignment: just as the critical U.S. realignment in 1958 that engendered a later racial policy shift did not come about solely for reasons of race policy (Carmines and Stimson 1989), so the 1957–63 Canadian change had nothing to do with tariff reductions. In each case, however, the original shift entailed further policy reorientations. There is a special poignancy in the Canadian example, as the architect of the Canadian shift, John Diefenbaker, was an archnationalist and would almost certainly have repudiated the entailment of his handiwork.

Once a strategic shift in the agenda is ventured, many tactical moves remain. The 1988 election exemplified a rich variety of both heresthetical and rhetorical initiatives. The most striking heresthetical ploy was the opposition's emphasis on the FTA's negotiator, to damn the agreement by association with an untrustworthy agent. On the substance of the agreement, heresthetics yielded to rhetoric, or so it might be argued: Canadians had to be dissuaded from certain views rather than merely distracted from them. The decline and recovery of support for the FTA seemed to reflect not shifts in which substantive consideration was important as in whether that consideration was factually true. At this point, though, rhetoric and heresthetics seem to merge.

REFERENCES

Berthelet, D. 1985. "Agriculture Canada Policy and Expenditure Patterns 1868–1983." *Canadian Farm Economics* 19:5–15.
Bothwell, R., I. Drummond, and J. English. 1981. *Canada since 1945: Power, Politics, and Provincialism.* Toronto: University of Toronto Press.
Camp, D. 1970. *Gentlemen, Players and Politicians.* Toronto: McClelland and Stewart.
Campbell, R. M., and L. A. Pal. 1991. *The Real Worlds of Canadian Politics: Cases in Process and Policy.* Peterborough: Broadview.
Carmines, E. G., and J. A. Stimson. 1989. *Issue Evolution: Race and the Transformation of American Politics.* Princeton: Princeton University Press.
Colvin, J. A. 1955. "Sir Wilfrid Laurier and the British Preferential Tariff System." In *Imperial Relations in the Age of Laurier,* ed. Carl Berger, 33–44. Toronto: University of Toronto Press.
Drummond, I. M. 1974. *Imperial Economic Policy 1917–1939: Studies in Expansion and Protection.* Toronto: University of Toronto Press.
Easterbrook, W. T., and H. G. J. Aitken. 1956. *Canadian Economic History.* Toronto: Macmillan.
Ellis, L. E. 1939. *Reciprocity 1911.* New Haven: Yale University Press.

Fowke, V. C. 1957. *The National Policy and the Wheat Economy.* Toronto: University of Toronto Press.

Iyengar, S., and D. R. Kinder. 1987. *News that Matters.* Chicago: University of Chicago Press.

James, P. 1990. "The Canadian National Energy Program and its Aftermath: A Game-Theoretic Analysis." *Canadian Public Policy* 16:174–90.

Johnston, R., A. Blais, H. E. Brady, and J. Crête. 1991. "Free Trade and the Dynamics of the 1988 Canadian Election." In *The Ballot and its Message,* ed. J. Wearing, 315–39. Toronto: Copp Clark Pitman.

Johnston, R., and M. B. Percy. 1980. "Reciprocity, Imperial Sentiment, and Party Politics in the 1911 Election." *Canadian Journal of Political Science* 13:711–29.

Mackintosh, W. A. 1964. *The Economic Background of Dominion-Provincial Relations.* Carleton Library Edition. Toronto: McClelland and Stewart.

Marr, W. L., and D. G. Paterson. 1980. *Canada: An Economic History.* Toronto: Macmillan.

Pickersgill, J. W., and D. F. Forster. 1970. *The Mackenzie King Record,* volume 4, *1947/1948.* Toronto: University of Toronto Press.

Riker, W. H. 1982. *Liberalism against Populism: A Confrontation between the Theory of Democracy and the Theory of Social Choice.* San Francisco: Freeman.

Safarian, A. E. 1985. "Government Control of Foreign Business Investment. In *Domestic Policies and the International Economic Environment,* ed. J. Whalley, 7–57. Toronto: University of Toronto Press.

Schuman, H., and S. Presser. 1981. *Questions and Answers in Attitude Surveys: Experiments in Question Form, Wording and Content.* New York: Academic Press.

Skogstad, G. 1987. *The Politics of Agricultural Policy-Making in Canada.* Toronto: University of Toronto Press.

Waite, P. B. 1971. *Canada 1874–1896: Arduous Destiny.* Toronto: McClelland and Stewart.

Ward, N., and D. Smith. 1990. *Jimmy Gardiner: Relentless Liberal.* Toronto: University of Toronto Press.

Zaller, J. 1984. "Toward a Theory of the Survey Response." Paper presented to the annual meeting of the American Political Science Association, Washington, D.C.

Contextualizing Regime Change: Transformation Windows and Systematic Reforms in Eastern Europe

George J. Graham, Jr.

The rapid transformation of regime structures in Eastern Europe provides a unique laboratory for considering how the fundamental agenda-setting processes of regimes are themselves changed, that is, how the constitutional foundation for a regime is itself placed into question and restructured. The fact that we were surprised to discover so many regimes transformed in a short time indicates that our theory has failed to provide adequate guidance in considering which contextual conditions must be present for system transformation. In this essay, I posit that we can clarify the theory by identifying regime transformation windows that parallel policy windows within a particular regime's processes. The primary issue is to decide whether we can identify conditions under which the *possibility* for regime transformation opens— conditions necessary but not necessarily sufficient for change.

The "regime transformation window"—like a "policy window" defined as an "opportunity for pushing one's proposals" (Kingdon 1984)—means only one simple thing: if action is taken, a change could occur. It does not mean a change must occur. It only means that, if the window is open and if an effort to transform a system occurs, it may be that "a transformation" will actually occur. Grasping the conditions for these windows of opportunity will allow better comprehension of the Eastern European transformations and better capacity to predict future transformations in different contexts.

The sovereignty of a regime depends upon the number of individuals who are willing to accept the political outcomes of the policy process. Each individual affected by a regime either does or does not grant sovereignty to it.[1]

---

1. Sovereign authority here refers to the capacity to make binding decisions in a given political space. This use might lead to some confusion because authority is often defined as legitimate power (Dahl 1963). The notion of legitimacy, as set forth by, for example, Max Weber, is the willing acceptance of an authority's power as distinct from coerced acceptance of an authority's power (see Weber 1958, 78–82 and 1964, 124–32, 324–92.) My concept of sover-

The "granting" may be of a positive sort, based on any of the grounds of legitimacy (see, for example, the Weberian types) or it may be a conceded sort given on such a simple ground as fear of coercive response. A regime, which defines the policy process, thus depends upon maintaining sufficient control over the preferences of individuals within its political space to maintain hegemony over policy. Since coercive power and legitimate power, in some mix, provide or deny sovereign control, by considering individuals' preferences one can outline the options for possible regime control.[2]

Our context is the sudden transformation of regimes in Eastern Europe and the former Soviet Union. How could so many experts on Eastern European politics have failed to see that regime transformations would quickly follow each other there? To be sure, some scholars have predicted the collapse of the Soviet system and its satellites, but in none of the predications of the failure have the contextual and temporal conditions been prearticulated. It is this failure that leads me to seek a way of at least identifying the window of opportunity for transformation and of grounding it in a theoretical framework. I will turn to the Eastern European setting in the final section, after I introduce the basic assumptions of my model.

Regime Transformation Assumptions

The model is based on assumptions about how citizens perceive a regime from below. I begin with three critical features that affect the "energy" entailed in possible regime transformation. The first feature is the individual's perception of relative well-being as compared with either earlier periods within the political space or alternative political spaces. This is an important and difficult feature because it is relative to both the information and the preferences of the

---

eignty, however, permits one to deal with the fact that all authorities blend a mix of coercive threat and legitimation techniques in maintaining their sovereign authority. This expansion is especially important for dealing with nondemocratic regime forms (Lasswell and Kaplan 1950, 177–85). The basic concept of sovereignty permits one to approach the assessment of policy systems as a whole, relying on the "public acceptability" of the regime (Graham and Graham 1976).

2. The set of individuals' preferences includes all actors within the political space. For our purposes, the interesting preferences are those held in common by individuals. These common preferences can be separated into three types, corresponding to different levels of consensus: (a) preferences for abstract ends or goals, (b) preferences for decision rules and procedures, and (c) preferences for shared particular political or social goals. The latter form of shared preferences is what is sought within a consensual deliberative process. The former sets (a and b) are ends that are shared or shareable by the totality of the members or smaller groups (families, groups, parties, etc.). In this analysis, one must not assume that an individual's set of preferences or a consensus among individuals will include agreement on logically or empirically consistent preferences (Graham 1984).

actors. If the perception is positive, the regime within the space should remain relatively stable. The second feature of special concern is risk aversion. The individuals most risk averse are assumed to be those with the least relative gains from the regime.[3] Thus, in terms of maintenance of a regime's hegemony within a political space, the individuals least well off are the least likely to be willing to risk change per se. One expects, therefore, that the individuals willing to test the regime (by, for example, demonstrations) would come from the better off and better educated groups, especially if there is a threat of retribution, which is, perhaps, disastrous to the least well off. If, however, communication, especially radio and television across national boundaries, reduces the perceived risk of retribution, then one expects increasing diversity in the mix of rebellious participants. The third feature is, of course, a regime's capacity to coerce as perceived by those within the political space. In Eastern Europe, this is made more difficult to define because of a history of real and threatened Soviet coercive intervention.

Since these three features all consist of individuals' perceptions, they thus depend on the rhetorical source of perceptions, mainly media coverage. This component of the model is a metacontextual variable: media provide resources for popular control and propaganda as well as sources for undercutting the same. It is metacontextual in the sense that it is beyond the complete control of any particular regime.[4] Television provides a window through which one can better see into political responses and threats, and also better see what other regimes return to those living within their given political spaces. Highly visible outcomes of material rewards are incorporated in ways that place counterevidence before the viewer and provide an in-home comparison of relative well-being.

The effort to project the range of moments within which a political

---

3. Although the growing research on heuristics may lead to a psychological explanation of this assumption, it is here posited from the tradition of political philosophy. This assumption is consistent with Scott's (1976) view of risk-averse peasants, and I make it even while acknowledging the aggregation problems pointed out by Popkin (1979). I use it with respect only to individual's risk aversion. The assumption interestingly relates to Rawls's maximin assumption (1971).

4. Communications advances, like other products of technological innovation, have an independent capacity to affect all sociopolitical settings. Like other metacontextual variables, such as multinational corporations, these variables are metacontextual because they insinuate themselves into contexts, are independent of current political space domination, yet are major forces in the unfolding of national and international political events. Indeed, both communications' and multinationals' expansions make estimates of national capacity problematic because the metacontext skews our indicators. For example, the resources of British Petroleum can move back and forth between London and Cleveland electronically: which nation-state is more powerful by the accident of place? These phenomena are metacontextual in that they transcend the definitions of political space as nation-states in which we are now frozen. Ironically, economic forces and communications are now worldwide, while "nationality" persists within all political states in all contexts.

movement or response could unseat a regime is not essentially different from the effort to project the range of policies that can potentially be placed upon a political agenda within a regime. Focusing only on the question of possible change, based on a window of opportunity opening for the policy (or regime) change, the window may be seen as open, but unused. If, in fact, the regime has insufficient resources to respond successfully to challenges, the challenges nonetheless require a challenger of sufficient force to unseat a regime. If the leaders of a contestation attempt to transform a regime, but the public remains too fearful to join the effort based on its current level of risk aversion, nothing at all could happen, except the arrest of the rebels. On the other hand, if the mass public is mobilized by reducing its fear and turning the shared disaffection against the regime, then *some* change can take place. The window provides a focus on the possibility of "some regime transformation" rather than upon a particular regime transformation. Indeed, the leaders who ultimately form the new regime may not be the same as those who provide the force behind the change.[5] In any case, the social context itself sets the limits on available belief systems (Bates 1991).[6] Put otherwise, consensual norms provide the ultimate limits of possible political regimes at any one time.[7]

The connections between actual leadership speeches and the beliefs of the public are direct. A leader, especially within the context of carefully calculated public presentations, seldom presents uncrafted statements. The speeches contain the contentions framed by the leader's beliefs concerning the shared symbols of the audience—the consensus. While the point is patently obvious, its implications for political analysis are not always apparent. If we are willing to assume that a leader will pursue his or her purposes rationally, then we must also be willing to assume that this pursuit is crafted within

5. The role of Thomas Paine's forceful rhetoric in the U.S. and French contexts provides a clear exemplar of how the individuals most significant in pushing a regime transformation window open may fail to contribute much to the particular changes wrought by their efforts. After the regime transformation, Paine's own visions of democracy and society were seen as dangerous and a threat to U.S. and French institutions.

6. Whatever package is advanced as a regime must have sufficient support among the individuals so that, with the legitimation *and* reserve of coercive capacity, the regime can maintain its claim to sovereignty. Reasons for support will differ in different settings, but, as stated above, "perceived relative well-being" under a regime provides grounds for granting sovereignty or denying it. Of course, the particular preferences condensed in an individual's judgment vary. It is here that the rhetoric and heresthetic of legitimation (and, obviously, transformation) become important. The "good reasons" of political discourse are often dedicated to providing grounds for "seeing the granting of sovereignty" as a wise, selfish choice.

7. The possible future regime forms derive from the same foundation as ongoing forms. The public's entire range of possible symbolic and linguistic structures are contained in the set of all individual's preferences. This set provides the political ontology of discourse and, thus, all the possible grounds for persuasion both in the deontological and teleological senses (Toulmin 1986, 137–43).

public statements made to develop or maintain support from his or her audience.[8] It seems clear that if one can assume that political economy links both institutional change and the purposes of actors, then one can fairly assume that statements by leaders are constructed to achieve the intentions of leaders in light of the receptivity of the political audiences (Alt and Shepsle 1990, 2).

If this is true, then the rational leader will select persuasive discourse that indicates (at least according to the leader's assumptions about audience beliefs) what beliefs are part of the preferences of the audience. A leader speaks to the audience and persuades to the degree that he or she is correct about the audience's beliefs. In principle, then, one should be fully able to map the consensual system within the set of all individual preference sets by careful assessment of the political discourse within the space.[9]

Of course, there are difficulties. The speakers within the system may well make serious mistakes. They may believe that a particular persuasive argument will work and discover that it backfires, rhetorically speaking. Or, as challengers, they may attempt to build a group in much the way Dewey (1927) discusses the creation of publics within a regime's space, thus focusing on groups poorly attended to by the regime and thereby risking failure. Moreover, despite the speaker's best efforts, he or she may not be aware that values, consensus, and meanings have changed over time. Implicit within the meaning of a mistake is the counter: mistakes are made by not following rules, a meaning based on the implicit assumption of rules.[10]

---

8. Those who study political discourse make the assumption that one must treat seriously what people say. The fact that a leader may decide to be silent, or even to lie, does not counter the assumption that successful leaders attend to what they say with great care. Indeed, one often discovers how changing contexts force leaders to speak differently. Widespread reporting on the content of speeches leads to a limit on the prospect of structuring a political speech to a single audience; war messages covered by an international media source available to both sides place limits on possible statements. Most important, however, is a simple point: it would be irrational, in the maximizing sense, for a leader not to craft speeches to the preferences of the audience in any regime form.

9. Different techniques for uncovering hidden assumptions are available, such as those developed by Polayni (1988) that demonstrate how common value commitments are "behind" the persuasive powers of such diverse discourses as law and self-help arguments for families with drug problems.

10. My interpretation of mistakes follows Wittgenstein 1953. The rule-following aspects of language-in-use permits one to uncover the cultural meanings of rhetorical appeals. A persistent problem in comparative political studies is the difficulty of generalization because of the uniqueness of cultures and the inability to replicate for interpretation. In the current language, this is the issue of "thick description" versus "thin description" (Geertz 1973, chap. 1). The mistake of generalizing without accounting for the culture meanings, however, can be avoided if we generalize about language-in-use. It returns one to the Weberian technique of studying ideal types in contexts that allow for systematic generalization (Weber 1949, chaps. 1–2). Perhaps the best general statement of the conceptual research problem is captured with the phrase "configuration analysis" (Lasswell 1965, chap. 1).

Riker's notion of heresthetic (1986) may be understood in terms of changing, often by rhetorical means, the *active* and *interested* participants. One shifts the collective saliencies. One uses *other* values to challenge the established rules or, put otherwise, to legitimate the new ground for choice. This is to say that the major shift in conditions opens up the set of relevant preferences within the political space: nonparticipants can be mobilized around *either* procedural ends (e.g., democratic decision making)[11] *or* particular ends, such as freedom of speech.

Of course, ultimately, no one changes the embedded preferences of the audience, but simply draws upon different unstated dimensions, evaluative or procedural, in restructuring a debate. When only policies are at issue, what occurs is clarification of the fact that *these* values are relevant to this question; *those* are important if you see it that way. Discussion remains in the deontological world of reasoning. Transformation of regimes, however, is *teleological:* it requires changing the shared rules and setting, changing the consensus, that is the constitution of the regime. When, furthermore, the preferences of the public are already *not* satisfied under the constitution, then the regime's perceived coercive capacity is the sole barrier to change.

The context of regime transformation is, at bare bones, the material resources available to individuals within a political space and the set of all preferences within the same space. The important preferences are those that permit justifications of a regime form responsive to the public. Because perceived relative well-being should summarize the material context as it affects regime transformation questions, it serves as a critical summary condition for all projections concerning legitimation of the sovereign. Because perceived coercive potential is, in the real world, the contextual variable of importance in dealing with coerced acquiescence, it summarizes the second basic variable critical to our appraisals. Thus, in order to identify the regime transformation window, we are interested in finding empirical indicators of when regime change thresholds open for possible mobilization for action.

The relationships can be portrayed as shown in figure 1. Sovereignty is granted by i if (i's perceived relative well-being under regime k) + (i's perception of the potential for coercion by regime k) is positive and at least as great as that of any other options available. Risk aversion is complex in this setting because it is greatly affected by each of the perceptions. Each actor's assessments are independent. The individuals can be seen as residing within the political space with their positions presented as in figure 1. The represen-

---

11. For example, in the rebellion preceding the massacre at Tiananmen Square, Chinese youth appeared more interested in changing participants rather than changing the regime. Note that the articulation of reasons for involvement differed greatly between students and the Western media interpreters. (See the interviews on the news reports on the demonstration at the Vanderbilt University News Archive.)

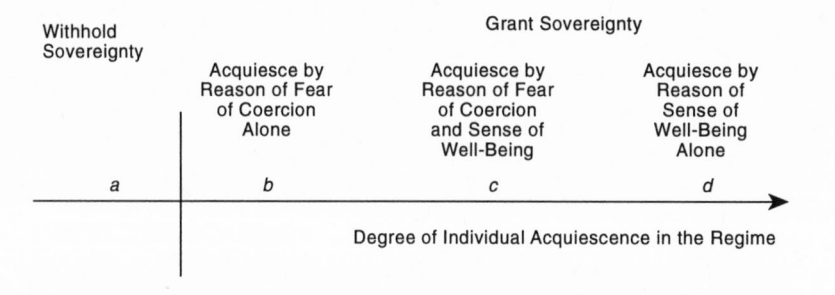

Fig. 1. Contextual setting for regime maintenance or transformation

tation includes type *a,* who have withheld sovereignty, and type *b,* who grant it only through the perception of coercive response. Transformation leaders must appeal to the mixed group, type *c,* on the basis of both considerations in order to maintain control. The flow of information concerning risk aversion is especially significant because removal of the external threat (in our case, the coercion potential from the Soviets) has an enormous effect on the individuals. In the contexts of Eastern European polities, the transformations became possible because the windows opened that had been well sealed by serious levels of perceived coercive reserves behind regimes, levels that were augmented with additional coercive potential from the Soviets.

Even in the setting of enormous coercive power—or perceived power—it is instructive to attend to the political discourse surrounding the conditions. The legitimating rhetorics that had been provided at various stages in justification of power were not without meaning within the evolving cultures of Eastern Europe (Stucky 1991). If viewed as persuasion within specific contexts, arguments concerning the necessity of short-term costs for achieving ultimate long-term gains as socialism strengthens its place in the world are not so different from arguments concerning investments in the future heard as the legitimating rhetoric within capitalist societies. We are mistaken if we discount such high rhetoric, once it falls, if we fail to trace through whether such reasons are treated as good by a populace at particular times. Lane's study of U.S. beliefs (1962) indicated that the less well off did, at that time, accept the systemic norms in the context of their hopes for their children, though this may well have changed by now. In any event, the rhetoric of legitimation depends upon linking the institutions and practices being legitimated with other values, beliefs, and aspirations, and upon the perceived relative well-being of those being persuaded. Control of coercive force, to be sure, assures domination of the discourse within the political space. The authority, if fully

sovereign, is the sole storyteller. The official narrative of conditions defines the context as understood by the listeners (Taylor 1989).

Beneath their superficial preferences, each individual holds some very strong ones that provide a check on all legitimation efforts. The power of coercion rests upon fear of a basic sort: concern over the capacity to continue to survive at a rudimentary level. This means that, when threatened, gross material concerns become very special preferences, especially if they expand with commitments to family. So fear of loss of resources for survival and fear of direct coercive responses are not unrelated. Thus, one is not surprised that those living marginal existences may choose to avoid risk. The grant of sovereignty because of fear may be the most rational response: fear of direct violence and fear of losing essential survival goods. Hence, other goods, including many freedoms, are bound to rank lower for the individual. Clearly, mobilization of support for regime transformation depends on the level of anticipated coercion as well as the level of belief that the transformation could better preserve the basic material needs of the actor.

In simple terms, i is a candidate for supporting a regime transformation if i's perception of i's own relative well-being and perception of the regime's coercive resources, together, are less than i's expected well-being under a different regime minus the cost of commitment to regime transformation. As the regime's coercive resources seem to decline and thus also lower the reason for granting sovereignty, so also the perceived cost of commitment to transformation declines. Although a decline in coercive power is common, there are two other perceptions that may not change in a correlated way: the perception of power in the relationship between the sovereign and the individual and the perception of the costs entailed in rebellion. These perceptions may not be directly correlated with objective changes in power because other dimensions of cost and personality may change at different rates. More important, there is a temporal difference between a conviction that it is possible to transform a regime and a desire to do so; and, of course, there is some uncertainty about whether any particular option could overcome the low estimate of relative well-being. (Activists often overestimate their chances of success while the risk averse often underestimate it.) In any event, a threshold must be crossed. Of interest is the realistic possibility that one can push across a threshold by drastically overstating the prospects or understating the cost. At the same time, the old regime has the opportunity of shifting the agenda, for example, in an effort to recapture sovereignty or to discredit the leaders of the revolutionary group.[12] The threshold is essentially the point at which sovereignty is

---

12. A strong case can be made that some of the responses of restructuring the Communist parties in Eastern European countries were efforts to prepare for change or alter the agendas within the failing regimes.

in balance. For the individual, it is a point of choice. The aggregate of the individual choices will identify whether the threshold has been crossed when sufficient actors decide to withdraw sovereignty. The window opens.

Once the window has opened, the old regime itself also becomes an actor on the larger stage, attempting to put together a coalition of individuals sufficient to redefine the regime and again win hegemony over the political space. In one sense it takes place in a single plane: all parties must appeal to the preferences of the component population. But such a simple view is probably unfounded in revolutionary times. Consider the choice between a regime based on Islamic fundamentalism or on economic development; the issue would first be a battle over which plane within which to construct a regime-supporting coalition. Indeed, one might expect to discover that different individuals, depending upon their contexts, are guided by potentially independent and perhaps mutually exclusive sets of interests (perhaps shared with subsystemic groups) but not shared by all within the political space.

Regime transformation, it seems to me, is currently occurring in many European settings—not just in the eastern portions—as shared economic sovereignty is being constructed. Similar shifts in the Pacific rim and even North America indicate that, on economic matters, political space itself may be undergoing transformation. Ironically, it also seems that, in many cultural settings, groups are confirming nationality in subnational settings that may affect the final definitions of political space at a different level. Quebec and Belgium seem to foreshadow further divisions, such as those that have already arisen in Yugoslavia and other Eastern European settings where there is no single nationality in the current political space. This is especially characteristic of nearly every segment of the old Soviet Union. When coupled with economic and/or religious distinctions, such differences greatly affect the molding of regime rules adequate to the maintenance of sovereignty. It is ironic because we see the nation-state under critical tensions from the pull of international economic organizations and international corporations at the same time that nationality distinctions erode important aspects of shared self-identity internally (Toulmin 1990). It seems that contrifugal and centripetal forces each tug at the nation-state. And the availability of information about life outside one's own space limits the possibility of convincing the less well off that they are better off than they would have been without the regime's authorities in power.

Whereas deontological arguments are set forth within the structure of current norms and practices—exploring how one ought to do the thing to be done—in resolving issues, the transformational arguments question the very rule and ends combined in the regime itself. They provide reasons for *not* resolving conflicts within the current regime form. Very often these arguments are best made by means of examples: we have condition x; the regime as-

sumes condition y; so our problem is insoluble in the old regime. The arguments can deal with economic or other preferences (they have more goods; they have less control over freedoms). Often, contestation employs a strategy of advancing evidence that a regime fails to make good on its own promised goods—promised goods that are shared as common ends in the supporting consensus (Graham 1971).

Opportunity for change within the political space will be most dependent upon the shifting context. The preferences of individuals, assuming some biological and human base, are not likely to be removed or added easily; indeed, one might posit that most wants change only in regard to their ordering or expansion within contexts—greatly affected by satisfaction and saturation. The context provides our basic variable for dealing with serious alterations within a regime or in the regime form itself. The basic task for transformational leadership is to employ changes in the context in order to undercut consensual and/or coerced acquiescence in the sovereign's authority.

A threshold exists for every regime beyond which its capacities cannot be extended. It is interesting, in tracing public statements, that leaders who are confronting challenge in international conflict shift, when conflict is about to break out, from analytic discussions of the conflict and potential enemy to nationalistic discourse.[13] The same sort of awareness of threshold seems to be involved when challengers of a sovereign turn from negative characterizations of the old regime and begin to propose what the consequences of acting might be. Of special interest as regime transformation windows approach is the change in framing news from systemic to particularized problems.

Regime Transformations in Eastern Europe

The series of regime transformation windows that appeared in Eastern European countries provides a valuable laboratory for exploring the prospects for our theory. Not since the transformations following colonization have so many test cases become available in close temporal proximity. And the problems faced in these countries should prove useful in identifying appropriate postdictive contexts in earlier historical settings. At this stage of testing our ideas, however, we are plagued with having only indirect information and evidence available to us. Nonetheless, these indirect measures—as they are more fully developed—should provide grounds for accepting (or rejecting) the promising notion of regime transformation windows.

The primary difficulty in specifying the particulars of context is attempt-

---

13. The phenomenon is traced by Hunt (1991), who follows leaders' positions via newspaper editorials and finds that the shift from analytic to nationalistic discourse predicts outbreaks of war quite well.

ing to set forth, in a systematic way, indicators of our basic dimensions: perceived relative well-being and perceived coercive resources. Nevertheless, the significant features of trade, troops, and resources should be reflected in the information sources and modes of presentation in both internally and externally received media.

State-by-state snapshots of conditions in each country could be presented from basic data. For example, Hungary's context includes many relevant particulars.[14] Agricultural employment in Hungary dropped from a high of 2,190,000 in 1949 (almost the same as 1941) to 986,200 in 1986. During the same period, industrial, trade, and transport work forces nearly doubled, and construction work forces expanded nearly fivefold. Of interest, too, is the growth of cultural activities in Hungary. Between 1950 and 1986, the number of books published per year grew from 1,880 to 8,206. The copies published grew from 20.1 million to 95.6 million. The number of periodicals grew from 334 (475 million copies) to 1,683 (1.44 billion copies). While theater visits remained relatively constant at 5 to 6 million per year after 1952, cinema attendance grew from 47 million in 1950 to a high of 140 million in 1960, dropping back to 67 million in 1986. Television licenses commenced in 1958 (at 16,000) and grew to 2.93 million licenses by 1986. The rural-urban divisions shifted systematically from 63.2 percent rural and 36.9 percent urban (17.3 percent in Budapest) in 1949 to 41.7 percent rural and 58.9 percent urban (19.7 percent in Budapest) in 1987. The picture of change herein reflected is of special significance because it occurs in the context of the effects of urbanization and media saturation that, in all settings, seems to atomize populations and to wear upon old norms. New freedoms are indicated alongside basic changes in the economy. But until one can work with full documents and diaries, the snapshots would not have led to a prediction of when Hungary could or would transform regimes.

Another way of focusing attention on the "historical" dimensions opens some view on the perceived coercive potential by means of interpreting amounts expended on the military. To be sure, the Soviet data are affected by other political commitments, but the relative number of armed forces populations per thousand inhabitants and military expenditures as a percentage of GNP (see table 1) provide at least a *feel* for the contexts of perception of citizens. Although the data in table 1 may be incorrect and greatly understated for all governments except the United States, the data indicate several things.[15] The proportion of the population in nonproductive roles is exceptionally high. Moreover, the cost of military expenditures in a period of

---

14. For the details cited, see Hungary 1988, 6, 25, 26.
15. The data brought together in table 1 and tables 3 and 4 are from Central Intelligence Agency 1990.

declining international threats dramatically contrasts the resources available for consumption as against other uses. The consequences of these expenditures are reflected, of course, in the public announcements and reasons given for the shifting commitments to maintain the military presence in the separate countries as well as in public discussions on the relationships between the superpowers. The limits of military expenditures on any efforts to redevelop the crumbling economic base in the various countries, which must have been obvious to all regime leaders, forced a decision about whether to invest in coercive force or attempt to find better mechanisms for maintaining sovereignty. We can only presume, at this point, to assert that the international economic and political contexts of the regimes placed enormous strains on the capacities of the regimes to maintain sovereignty. The cost of maintaining the military had to place enormous strains on other modes of development.

The intrusion of media into the political context of Eastern Europe is fairly complete. The data indicate a very broad distribution of media, which can be compared with the population data to show that households are likely to have access to the airwaves in multiple forms (see table 2). Although the specific implications of television coverage are difficult to characterize without tracing the content of the actual reception capacities and an analysis of the patterns of coverage in each nation, it is clear that news coverage has been available in many noncontrolled editions for quite some time. Moreover, the confluence of information about local economic conditions and reports from abroad provide a serious foundation for erosion of perceived well-being

TABLE 1. National Armed Forces and Military Expenditures

	Armed Forces[a]			Military Expenditures as a Percentage of GNP		
	1967	1976	1985	1967	1976	1985
Albania	26.40	23.74	14.1	8.6	10.2	5.3
Bulgaria	21.20	20.14	21.2	8.8	8.8	10.5
Czechoslovakia	18.10	14.10	13.5	6.9	5.6	6.6
German Democratic Republic	11.80	13.00	14.5	5.0	6.3	7.1
Hungary	15.30	11.10	11.0	5.2	5.4	5.3
Poland	9.62	12.70	11.8	6.5	5.9	7.0
Romania	9.84	10.20	10.4	5.5	4.4	5.5
Yugoslavia	15.00	12.79	11.2	4.7	5.0[b]	3.7
Soviet Union	16.50	17.90	15.4	12.1	12.6	12.6
United States	17.00	9.22	9.4	9.4	5.4	6.6

Source: Data from U.S. Arms Control and Disarmament Agency Reports.
[a]Figures are per 1,000 population.
[b]Data from 1975.

TABLE 2.   Literacy and Media Data for Eastern Europe, the Soviet Union, and the United States

	USSR	U.S.	GDR	Poland	Czech.	Hungary	Romania	Bulgaria	Albania	Yugoslavia
Literacy	99.0	99.0	99.0	98.0	99.0	99.0	98.0	95.0	75.00	90.5
Television sets	85.0	150.0	6.2	9.7	4.4	3.5	3.9	2.1	0.05	4.1
Radios	162.0	495.0	6.7	9.3	4.2	5.5	3.2	2.1	0.21	4.7
Population	290.9	250.4	16.3	37.8	15.7	10.6	23.3	8.9	3.27	23.8

Note: Literacy rates are expressed as percentages; all other figures are millions.

throughout Eastern Europe and the Soviet Union. One sometimes forgets that the Eastern street scenes carried by the Western media are experienced first-hand by those on the streets. The primary image of economic difficulties in a time when ideological justifications were not adequate responses by regimes indicate that one should have been aware of changed conditions setting the regimes' contexts. The enormous impact of seeing oneself in the light of other settings, of comparing one's well-being with what one knows is available to others (or to oneself in better times), removes the force of ideological suasion. A regime structure that permits no real choice opens itself to regime transfor-mation because there is no means for leaders to employ heresthetic techniques except to translate the political option into coercive force. And in the back-ground, on television, was the emerging story of glasnost.

As long as force is an available option, it can be very persuasive. But one's potential for force is related to other activities and options, such as economic productivity. To maintain sufficient force to control large popula-tions, one must assign resources that are not productive, and the double role of internal and external coercive capacity is an expenditure tl.at no economic system easily bears. Just as the impact of Vietnam affected the relative role of the United States in international competition, so the strain on the Soviet economy, which included financial subsidies for weak regimes as well as the maintenance of coercive force and the Afghanistan involvement, made it extremely difficult to maintain a power base for assuring sovereignty in East-ern European countries. In the early stage of internal control, Soviet ideologi-cal suasion may well have been augmented by increasing senses of well-being in contexts that provided solely historical comparisons of conditions for many within the political space.[16] As material conditions strangle hopes of eco-nomic growth, the regime's failure in the economic sphere may require other foundations for maintaining the regime. Clearly, some who see as negative their overall relative well-being have decided to withdraw support for sover-eignty.

---

16. It would be a very serious mistake to presume that the collapse of Eastern European regimes was evidence that, all along, only force maintained the systems. It is certainly reasonable to suppose that, in earlier contexts, many groups of individuals found their rewards and promise of future rewards under the system *positive*. Ignoring the contexts of earlier periods is just as much an error as our failure to observe the changed context in the 1980s. One might see how and why the political discourse went as it did in each of the earlier periods to attempt to grasp the meanings to those within the political spaces and times we select to analyze. The "good reasons" for accepting a regime may escape an outsider who fails to consider the discourse: a Yugoslav legislator in the 1960s reported that few of his colleagues took Marxism seriously, but that they all realized the consequences for the guilt of his nation if the ideology was treated as they saw it. The failure of the system (indeed, of the maintenance of the political space) and nationality bloodshed were seen as the likely result of undercutting the agreed upon regime. That would speak of power in the ideology that was not merely due to the coercive force of the military.

TABLE 3. Contextual Data on East European Countries, 1990

	Employment[a]			Telecommunication Stations			
	Industry	Agriculture	Other	AM	FM	Television	Relays
Bulgaria	33.0	20.0	47.0	15	16	13	1
Czechoslovakia	36.9	12.3	50.8	58	16	45	14
East Germany	37.5	10.8	51.7	23	17	21	15
Hungary	30.9	18.8	50.3	13	11	21	8
Poland	36.5	28.5	35.0	30	28	41	4
Romania	34.0	28.0	38.0	39	30	38	—
Yugoslavia	27.0	22.0	51.0	199	87	50	—

[a]Data are in percentages.

The differences among the regime contexts are interesting because they indicate how the particular production focuses (table 3) did not seem to provide barriers to collapse (and will provide interesting information for exploring later developments). The ease of access to media is indicated in the number of stations and relays in each country.

Internal cultural differentiations have significance for the perceived well-being of individuals under *any* regime claiming hegemony over power. Arguments for maintaining the consolidation of current regimes carry both positive and negative consequences. For example, the erosion of central power in Romania quickly opened serious controversy with Hungarian Transylvanians, who had long been unhappy over the domination of local schools by Rumanian nationals. The nationality differences (see table 4) have made the borders of Eastern European political spaces "flexible" over the centuries, but, more

TABLE 4. Internal Population Characteristics in Eastern Europe, 1990

Country	Religious Group[a]					Dominant Group	
	Orthodox	Other	Protestant	Roman Catholic	Muslim	Nationality	Percentage
Bulgaria	85[b]	—	—	—	13	Bulgarian	85.3
Czechoslovakia	2	28.0	20	50.0	—	Czech	64.3
East Germany	—	46.0	47	7.0	—	German	99.7
Hungary	—	7.5	25	67.5	—	Hungarian	96.6
Poland	—	5.0	—	95.0	—	Polish	98.7
Romania	80[c]	4.0	—	6.0	—	Rumanian	89.1
Yugoslavia	50	10.0	1	30.0	9	Serbian	36.3

[a]Figures are percentages of national population.
[b]Bulgarian Orthodox.
[c]Rumanian Orthodox.

to our concerns, it has made for serious differences within the political spaces—thus leading to the prospect of clusters of individuals who are low in their sense of relative well-being. From an external view, divisions may well seem irrational. However, the reasons can very well be viewed as essential, especially if individual actors sense a linkage of economic and social position associated with differences in religion or nationality. A "legislator," in Rousseau's tradition, might provide guidance toward forms of federalism, but such guidance depends upon a sense of trust and shared preferences that is difficult to achieve if old cultural divisions continue to play within the setting. What divisions may aid in opening the regime transformation window may well cause any future regime difficulties in finding ways to close them once again, especially when economic adjustment costs are inevitably going to be high and have differential effects upon segments of the populations at the very time that basic norms and rules are changing. Essentially, one may find common aspirations among those who reject the ancient regimes, but inevitably some will surely benefit as the movement is made to new modes of distribution.

My major effort is to demonstrate that one can provide an adequate set of indicators of perceptions of relative well-being and of coercive potential of regimes for a model of sovereignty maintenance, disruption, and displacement. My primary purpose is to show that a threshold is crossed that leads to a condition within which, in the specific context, a regime's hegemony over the policy and programs within the political space could be overthrown if challenged. Immediately before the threshold is reached, the regime could attempt to retain support through advancing policies and programs that appeal to relative well-being or it could increase its capacity—or belief in its capacity—to put down any challenge. In the Eastern European setting, this last condition was augmented, in earlier periods, by linkage with Soviet coercive potential—and sometimes justification (as in Poland in 1980–81) of one's own force as preferable to the Soviet force. Although hard data correlations might later be found to support such a general model, and permit one to predict without having information concerning individuals' perceptions and understandings of the conditions, I believe one can better grasp the conditions by focusing attention on the reports of public discourse within the political arena. One must expect that before the regime shifts in Eastern Europe, the problems with perceived well-being were high, that there was perception that elsewhere within the Warsaw bloc there were not exemplars of well-being to serve as grounds for aspiration (information from within the Soviet Union was well distributed), and that the justification for regimes had failed to yield promised returns.[17]

---

17. In attempting to conceptualize the relationships here, it is useful to consider efforts to deal with the persistence of regimes over time under conditions of stress and to see how internal feedback in the political regime is critical for the reinforcement of legitimacy (Easton 1965; Deutsch 1963).

In order to provide a rough map of the political discourse and actions leading to the Eastern European transformations, the indirect route of assessing the reports of conditions and actions by the three major television networks in the United States has been selected to provide evidence of general patterns. The media coverage is important because the stories carried on the evening news are selected by highly trained staffs whose job it is to isolate important events as they occur, independent of any judgments about why things occur as they do. One expects the news team to cover the significant events, and though their coverage can have the impact of creating a self-fulfilling significance for an event, an effort to test a theoretical explanation by postdictive assessment of the past can be achieved if the recorded news identifies the shifts in context that indicate how the policy windows were opened.

The questions to answer are simple. First, is there evidence that perceived well-being was drastically and consistently deteriorating within the various political spaces of concern? Second, is the perceived coercive capacity drastically and consistently declining? Third, is there evidence that willingness to employ external force (that is, Soviet intervention) was recognized as declining? Fourth, is the reverse of internal force sufficient to maintain perceptions of a significant level of coercive capacity to maintain sovereignty? And fifth, is sufficient information available to the participants to overcome risk aversion sufficiently to open a regime transformation window? If the response is positive, then, we would expect more diverse participants in mobilized activities as risk aversion diminished because of increased assurance that the answers were positive to the preceding questions. The metacontextual impact of information over the airways virtually reduces information costs; indeed, watching and/or listening to the news has entertainment value.

In providing answers to these questions, the television news broadcasts from 1988 through early 1990 are traced, demonstrating the sequence of reported events concerning (*a*) Soviet coercive capacities and commitments and (*b*) stories providing a reflection of internal unrest and reform both within the Soviet Union and Eastern European countries. The survey of all stories over this period includes all evening news broadcasts of the three primary U.S. television networks. Coding for this description of the news was entirely from the written indexes of the Vanderbilt Television News Archive. Stories that were presented as "background" or "commentary" pieces for the U.S. audience were not included in the counts. Specific references to ongoing events or conditions were all counted, with current interviews with non-Americans becoming a major means of sorting out background stories from reports. In some cases, the stories fit predominantly in one category, but are also appropriate for a second category. Presentations of findings have been condensed to monthly figures because the current purpose is solely to outline the general patterns over time. These breaks mean that the base is nonstandar-

TABLE 5. Monthly summaries of Time and the Number of Stories on Transformation Dimensions, January, 1988, through February, 1990

	East-West Positive	East-West Negative	Afghan Withdrawal	Eastern European Withdrawal	USSR Conflict	Eastern European Conflict	USSR Change	Eastern European Change
January, 1988	10:10 (3)	0:00 (0)	11:35 (10)	0:00 (0)	0:00 (0)	0:00 (0)	8:20 (6)	0:00 (0)
February	27:20 (17)	5:10 (3)	8:20 (3)	0:40 (1)	5:40 (5)	0:00 (0)	0:20 (1)	0:00 (0)
March	0:00 (0)	0:00 (0)	9:40 (6)	0:00 (1)	14:40 (13)	1:00 (2)	2:50 (1)	0:00 (0)
April	28:20 (13)	3:20 (3)	22:30 (18)	0:00 (0)	8:30 (5)	3:50 (3)	8:40 (5)	2:20 (1)
May	121:40 (49)	12:20 (3)	29:00 (16)	0:00 (0)	30:10 (20)	14:10 (6)	42:10 (5)	1:40 (1)
June	46:50 (18)	0:50 (2)	0:20 (1)	0:00 (0)	41:30 (29)	1:00 (3)	48:10 (17)	0:10 (1)
July	8:20 (10)	0:00 (0)	5:20 (3)	8:10 (9)	5:40 (12)	5:10 (3)	22:30 (8)	9:30 (3)
August	9:50 (15)	0:40 (2)	11:20 (9)	0:00 (0)	0:30 (1)	60:20 (39)	0:00 (0)	0:00 (0)
September	15:10 (11)	2:40 (1)	1:10 (3)	0:00 (0)	14:00 (11)	12:50 (12)	24:00 (13)	1:10 (3)
October	1:40 (1)	0:00 (0)	0:20 (1)	0:00 (0)	3:10 (2)	16:30 (19)	15:10 (11)	3:20 (1)
November	7:20 (8)	4:00 (3)	7:20 (3)	0:00 (0)	27:20 (21)	6:30 (8)	10:40 (8)	0:00 (0)
December	53:20 (15)	0:20 (1)	10:30 (6)	7:20 (4)	5:10 (4)	2:20 (2)	8:00 (10)	0:00 (0)

Month								
January, 1989	1:20 (4)	0:00 (0)	11:50 (9)	8:00 (5)	4:10 (4)	7:20 (10)	1:50 (5)	5:10 (5)
February	0:00 (0)	0:00 (0)	33:00 (11)	0:00 (5)	3:10 (4)	0:20 (5)	13:00 (5)	5:30 (5)
March	2:30 (2)	1:20 (4)	0:00 (0)	0:00 (0)	9:50 (2)	17:20 (13)	31:40 (5)	0:30 (6)
April	7:30 (5)	0:40 (2)	17:50 (7)	6:50 (6)	22:00 (6)	0:00 (0)	12:40 (9)	7:30 (1)
May	26:30 (17)	1:00 (3)	0:00 (0)	4:50 (5)	12:30 (21)	10:40 (11)	16:10 (11)	11:50 (8)
June	31:00 (18)	0:00 (0)	0:00 (0)	0:00 (6)	9:40 (6)	0:40 (2)	5:50 (7)	51:30 (11)
July	73:20 (26)	0:00 (0)	4:30 (3)	0:00 (0)	33:30 (13)	1:30 (1)	24:10 (27)	33:50 (27)
August	0:20 (1)	0:00 (0)	11:30 (3)	0:00 (0)	12:30 (31)	27:30 (19)	11:00 (6)	74:50 (37)
September	25:40 (16)	3:00 (2)	2:20 (1)	0:00 (0)	20:40 (12)	55:00 (27)	7:10 (6)	16:16 (12)
October	18:30 (8)	0:00 (0)	11:10 (7)	0:00 (0)	14:50 (11)	100:30 (47)	4:40 (8)	44:40 (32)
November	2:50 (2)	0:00 (0)	15:00 (7)	0:00 (0)	10:50 (13)	138:20 (48)	1:20 (8)	202:50 (32)
December	29:10 (10)	0:50 (2)	6:30 (6)	0:00 (0)	29:00 (12)	109:40 (46)	21:10 (2)	118:30 (80)
January, 1990	2:00 (2)	0:00 (0)	10:20 (11)	0:00 (0)	132:20 (17)	31:20 (26)	30:40 (12)	46:30 (70)
February	28:20 (15)	0:00 (0)	10:10 (9)	0:00 (0)	45:20 (54)	10:20 (11)	79:10 (30)	10:40 (12)

Note: The monthly times are given in minutes and seconds; figures in parentheses are the number of stories.

dized because of the length of the periods, but the sequences and comparative figures illustrate the major points in historical sequence. The coarse filters used make it clear that the figures are presented in a very general frame—one that always is affected by the relative length and numbers by other events—whether earthquakes or U.S. elections (see table 5).

Our interest in the coercive capacity of the Soviet Union is the central focus because the military strength and commitment of separate Eastern European countries slightly declined or remained stable through the crisis in most countries (see table 1), and the obvious shifting context involved rapidly changing conditions in the increased negotiations between the United States and the Soviet Union (bringing about a renewed potential for limiting military obligations of the Soviets) and the highly significant withdrawal of Soviet troops from Afghanistan. The discussions of reduction of Soviet troops within Eastern Europe, and the reduction of military commitments there, are of special interest largely because the efforts indicate that reassignment of troops from other regions would not increase the expectation of coercive potential within Eastern European countries. The number of stories and time devoted to East-West treaty negotiations and to summit arrangements and to the withdrawal of troops from Afghanistan provide good reason to assume that perceptions of the coercive capacity of the Soviet Union and its willingness to employ that capacity had drastically shifted (see fig. 2 and 3). Indeed, a configuration of forces in transition implicitly indicated a decline of the Soviet presence.

At no time during the period of my study did any of the indicators provide a hint that Soviet coercive capacities would be employed in salvaging the old regimes from even the most drastic innovations in Eastern Europe. A temporary hesitancy of the Soviets concerning German reunification quickly dissipated. Even internal Eastern European coercive efforts, with perhaps the exception of Albania, had, at best, only the power to delay transformation efforts (Romania), and more often had the simple impact of focusing protest. The consistent overall pattern of stories on the reduction of coercive capacities, seen in combined form in figure 7 that adds the four types of stories together, provides support for the belief that "perceived coercive capacity" had drastically changed during 1988 and 1989. Indeed, it is important to note that a visual review of the relevant stories on the military provide strong narrative support for these gross figures. One often senses a Geertz-type "wink" toward reform by Gorbachev when he is on camera that supports his policy directions (Geertz 1973).

The stories dealing with internal conditions in the Soviet Union and in Eastern European countries have been summarized into two major types (see figs. 4 and 5). The first are reports of all forms of unrest, conflict, and disturbances, providing a very rough picture of dissatisfaction and willingness

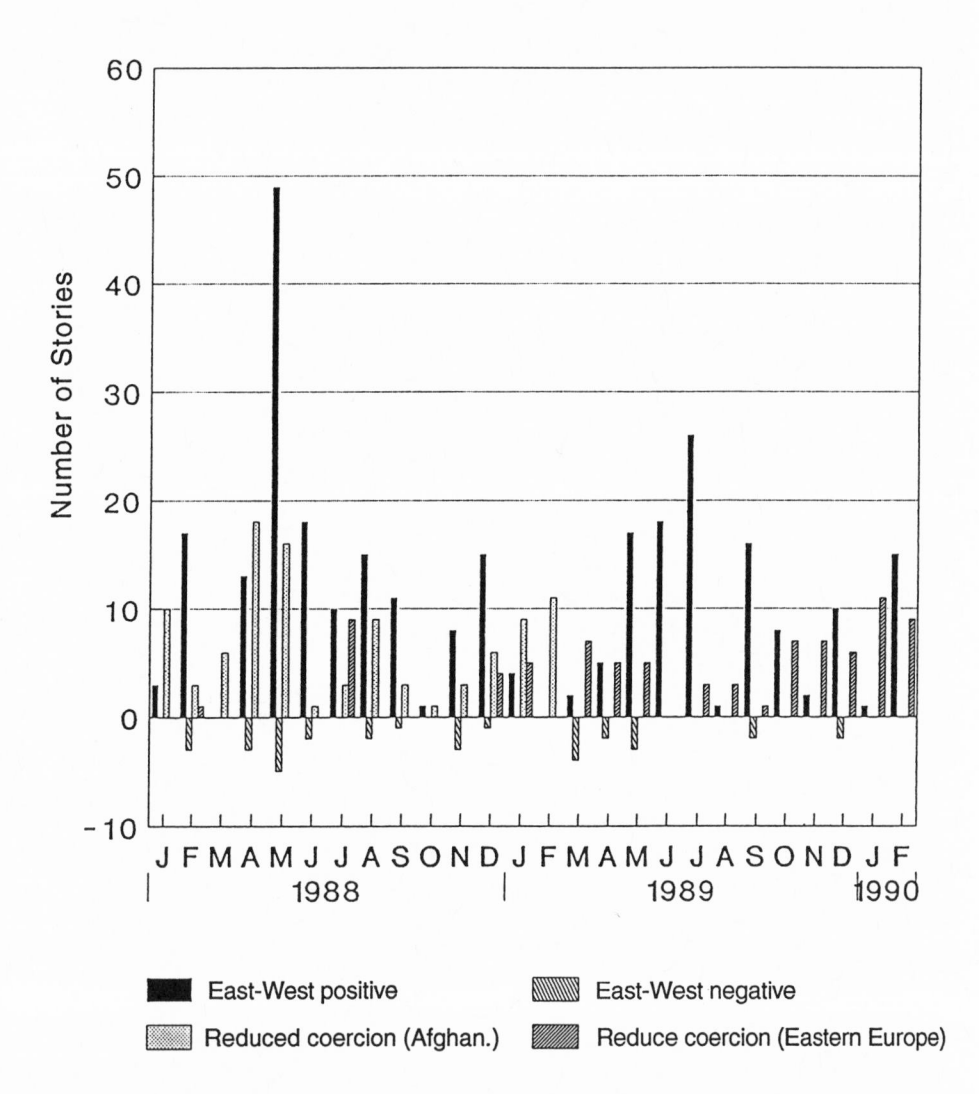

Fig. 2. The number of news stories indicating weakening commitments

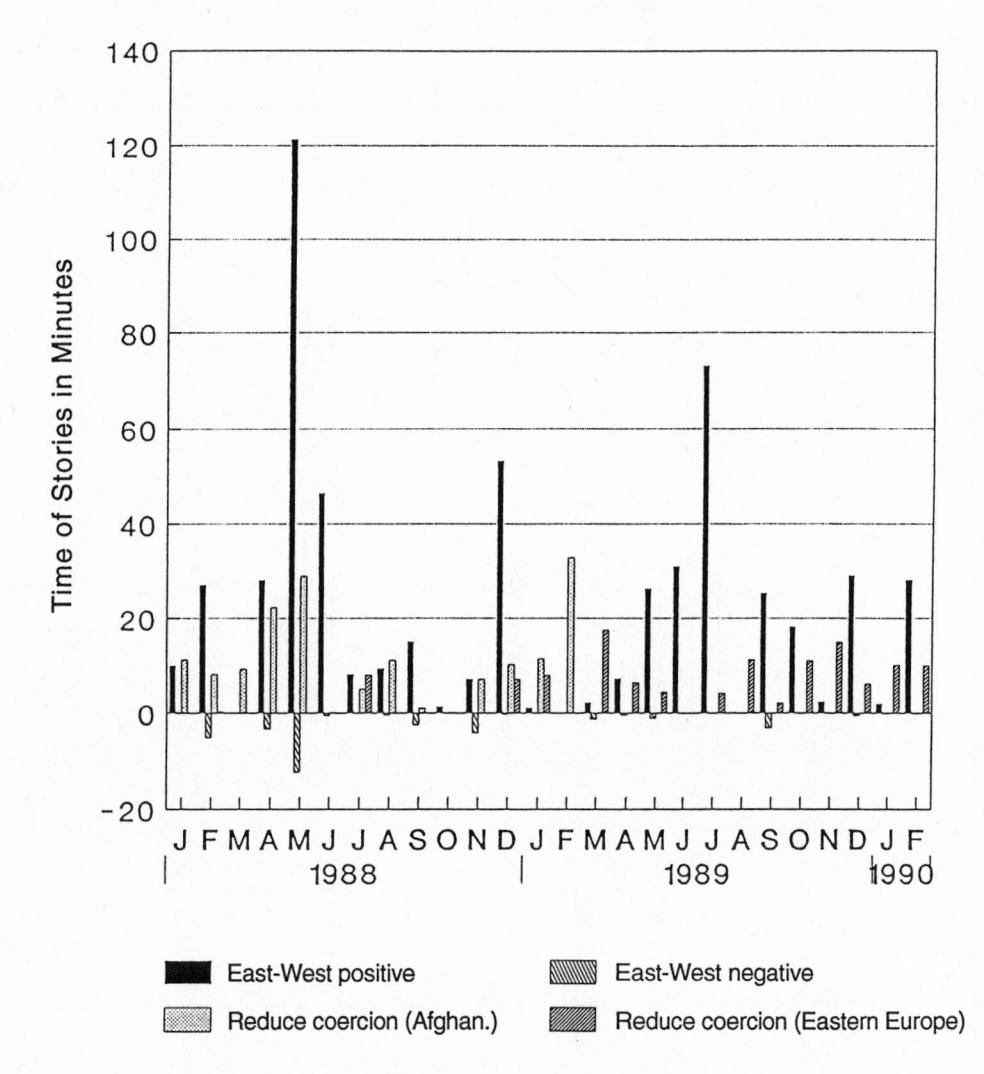

Fig. 3. The total time devoted to news stories indicating weakening commitments

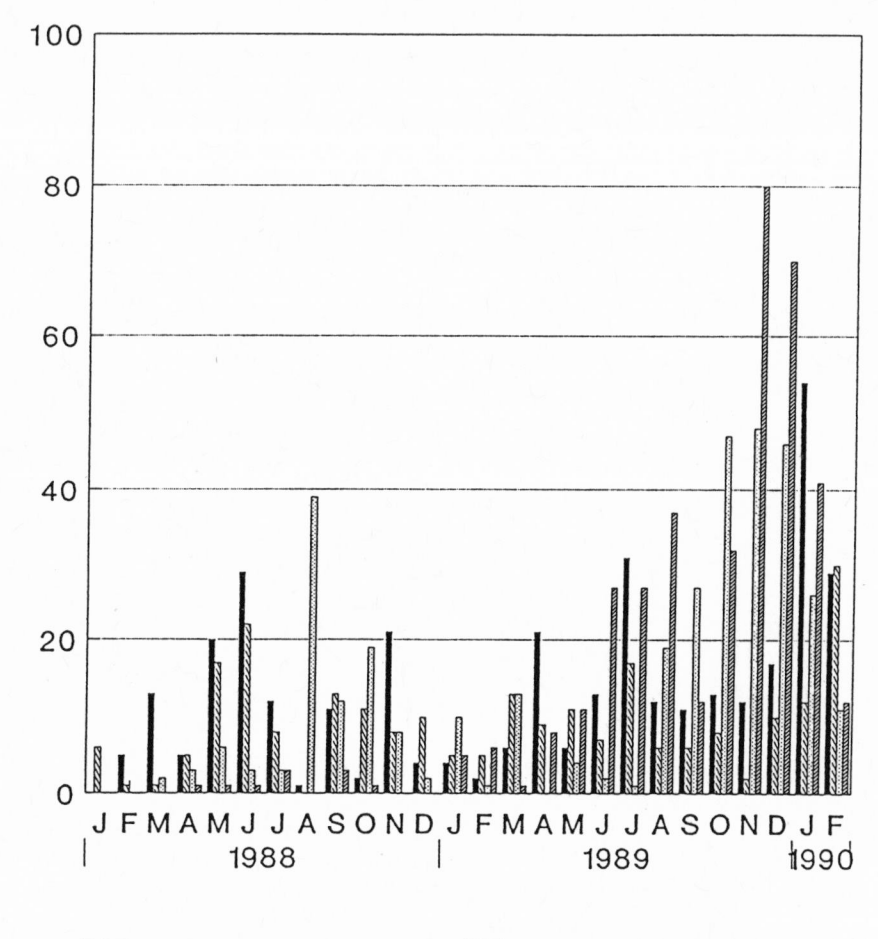

Number of Stories

J F M A M J J A S O N D J F M A M J J A S O N D J F
1988   1989   1990

USSR political conflict ▮   USSR political reform ▨

Eastern Europe ▨
political conflict

Eastern Europe ▨
political reform

Fig. 4. The number of news stories about politics and disorder

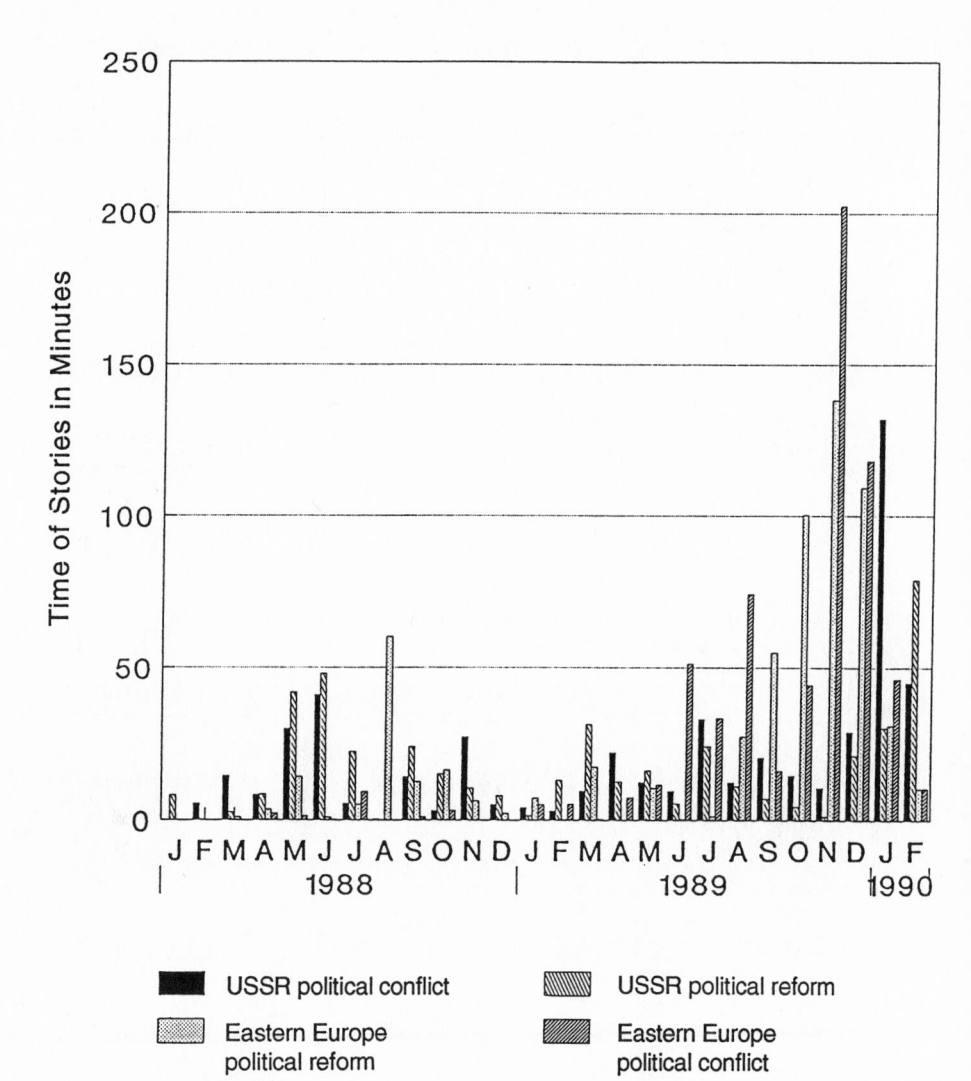

Fig. 5. The total time devoted to news stories about politics and disorder

to exhibit disagreements. The data shown in figures 4 and 5 provide an indirect way of assessing perceived relative well-being within the state. When the reported disagreements indicate that more-or-less ordinary politics is permitted, we find stories in the category for the second type, namely about social, economic, and political reforms. Further refinement of the sequence of these stories indicates responses increase as coercion threat diminishes, and continues under changes of regime form (see figs. 6 and 7).

The movement from conflict to reform measures by regime shifts *opens* new areas wherein the expression of desires for reform are released. The interesting patterns go beyond this study, but many postregime transformation conflicts arise connected with questions concerning the very definition of political space (Germany, Yugoslavia, and the former USSR itself are examples).

The sequence of national conflict to reform is followed by stories covering particular states. It appears that protests reported originally are more general expressions of dissatisfaction with relative well-being, but success in opening the transformation window introduces a more particular, focused context for selecting which regime form to adopt. This latter context is essentially an effort to set appropriate limits for political space and to determine which spatial model will apply for the new politics. "Usual politics" has been lost, but new rules are not established yet. A perhaps disappointing reflection on this is that it reinforces awareness of the centrality of coercive power and satisfaction of material well-being preferences, with little support for a sense that democratization is very important to the transformation.

The figures I have presented demonstrate the plausibility of my projections concerning regime transformation windows, though obviously they, at best, provide a representative case of how the images of coercive capacity and of relative conditions correspond with our assumptions. The news broadcasts provide a representation of the shifts in expressed preferences that would be required for a window to open. Longer historical periods in Eastern Europe or comparisons in other national contexts with more refined techniques might clarify this "picture," but such refinement will provide only a more certain representation of the events. This is to say that tests of the model will inevitably be case studies that assess the relevance of the model in different contexts. The merit of such results are that they provide a way of systematically collecting comparative case studies that might convince us that the regime transformation events do *not* take place when perceive coercive capacities or perceived well-being do not function as projected. Postdictive and predictive studies can be pursued using the events as reported in the media as a way of providing descriptions adequate for a search for disproof of the theory. The comparative study, moreover, will provide a way of assessing at which points, and in which contexts, the relative weight of each variable has remained at a level sufficient to offset the other.

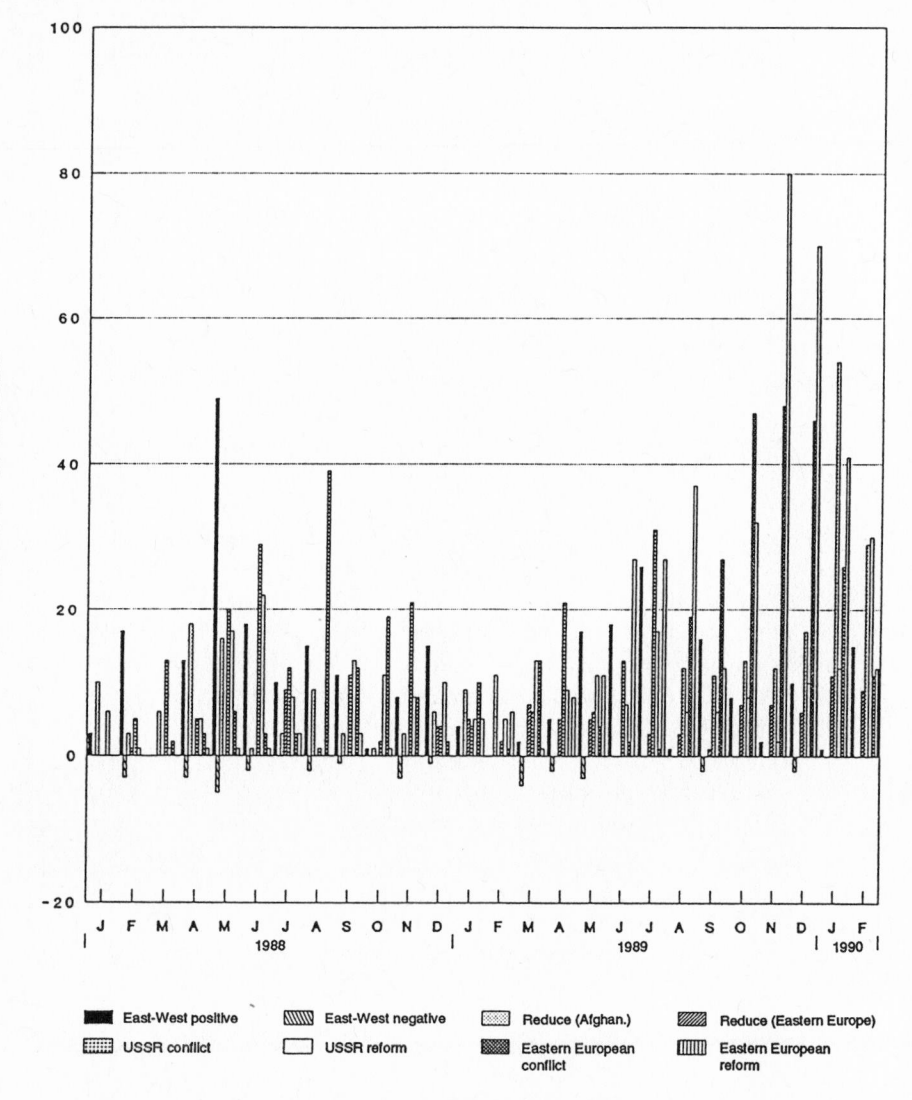

Fig. 6. The number of news stories about all transformation variables

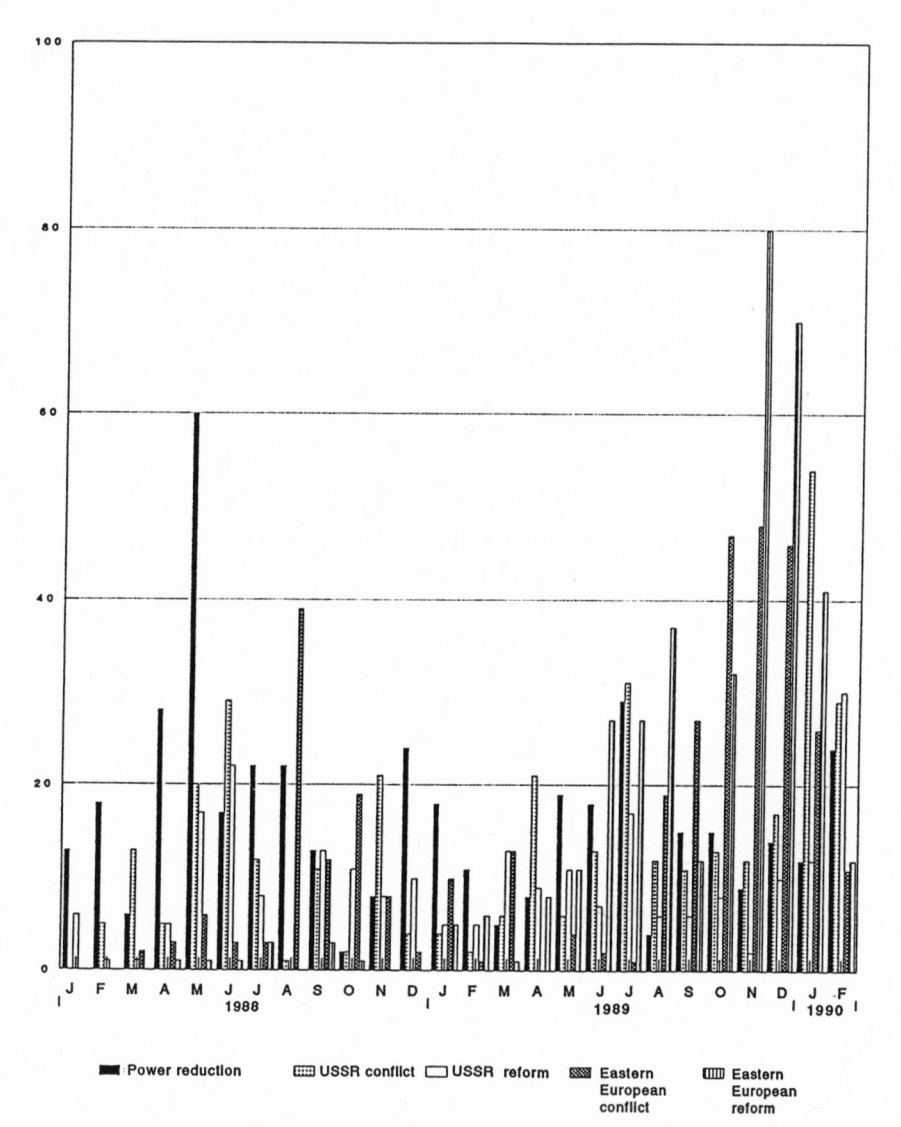

Fig. 7. The number of news stories about power reductions, politics, and disorder

Conclusions

The news stories about Eastern Europe, as reported by the three major networks in the United States, provide conclusions concerning the five particular questions I have raised. First, the number of protests consistently increased (and continues) throughout Eastern European countries and the old Soviet Union. The content of the stories makes clear that the protests vividly indicate perceived failure of the old regimes to satisfy the preferences of the public. Second, the decline in perceived coercive capacity is obvious. Third, and of great importance, was the evidence, often embedded in Gorbachev's rhetoric, that Soviet troops would not be maintained in Eastern Europe. The assignment of forces formerly in Afghanistan to the western Soviet borders could have been attempted to "close" the regime transformation window. Fourth, although tested in Romania, the use of internal coercive capacity was virtually absent, and quickly reported as counterproductive in systems that might have wished to challenge regime change. Fifth, the information flow from abroad was probably sufficient, but dependence on external radio and television was further reduced by internal reformation of television throughout the area. Success in one country was immediately known to others and generated similar events. One important implication is that removing information costs on the probability of coercive responses quickly changes one's willingness to risk challenging a regime.

The implications of my study are important because they focus on political events and the surrounding context as experienced by actors. The reports of a Soviet leader withdrawing support for specific actions, or suggesting following Soviet-style reforms in sister nations, have happened in many periods, not always leading toward "freedoms" as viewed in the West. The seriousness of the discourse of leaders is reflected in the media representation of their views, and the public responses seem clearly linked to such reports. At this stage, research into these relationships, especially given the limitations in accurately assessing and collecting relevant reports, show only that the research is worth doing, and that it can be guided by theoretical propositions that relate to major questions in political science. With the "news" reports on serious communications events, we can, if we develop the resources for systematically studying them, develop systematic tests of political theory in important, albeit difficult, areas.

REFERENCES

Alt, James E., and Kenneth A. Shepsle, eds. 1990. *Perspectives on Positive Political Economy.* Cambridge: Cambridge University Press.

Bates, Robert H. 1991. "The Economics of Transitions to Democracy." *P.S.: Political Science and Politics* 24:24–27.

Central Intelligence Agency. 1990. *The World Factbook 1990*. Washington, D.C.: Central Intelligence Agency.

Dahl, Robert A. 1963. *Modern Political Analysis*. Englewood Cliffs, N.J.: Prentice-Hall.

Deutsch, Karl. 1963. *Nerves of Government: Models of Political Communication and Control*. New York: Free Press.

Dewey, John. 1927. *The Public and Its Problems*. Chicago: Swallow Press.

Easton, David. 1965. *A Systems Analysis of Political Life*. New York: Wiley.

Geertz, Clifford. 1973. *The Interpretation of Culture: Selected Essays*. New York: Basic Books.

Graham, George J., Jr. 1971. "Consenso & Opposizione: Una Tipologia." *Revista Italiana di Scienza Politica* 1:19–36.

Graham, George J., Jr. 1981. "The Role of the Humanities in Public Policy Evaluation." *Soundings* 64, no. 2:150–69.

Graham, George J., Jr. 1984. "Consensus." In *Social Science Concepts: A Systematic Analysis,* ed. Giovanni Sartori, 89–124. Beverly Hills: Sage Publications.

Graham, George J., Jr., and Scarlett G. Graham. 1976. "Evaluating Drift in Policy Systems." In *Problems of Theory in Policy Analysis,* ed. Philip M. Gregg. Lexington, Mass.: Lexington Books.

Hungary. 1988. *Hungarian Statistical Yearbook 1986*. Budapest: Hungarian Central Statistical Office.

Hunt, W. Ben. 1991. "Getting to War: Mass Media, Preferences, and Decision Theory." Ph.D. diss., Harvard University.

Kingdon, John W. 1984. *Agendas, Alternatives, and Public Policies*. Boston: Little, Brown.

Lane, Robert. 1962. *Political Ideology: Why the American Common Man Believes What He Does*. New York: Free Press.

Lasswell, Harold D. 1965. *World Politics and Personal Insecurity*. New York: Free Press.

Lasswell, Harold D., and Abraham Kaplan. 1950. *Power and Society: A Framework for Political Inquiry*. New Haven: Yale University Press.

Polayni, Livia. 1988. *Telling the American Story*. Cambridge, Mass.: MIT Press.

Popkin, Samuel P. 1979. *The Rational Peasant*. Berkeley: University of California Press.

Rawls, John. 1971. *A Theory of Justice*. Cambridge, Mass.: Belknap Press.

Riker, William H. 1986. *The Art of Political Manipulation*. New Haven: Yale University Press.

Scott, James C. 1976. *The Moral Economy of the Peasant*. New Haven: Yale University Press.

Stucky, Mary. 1991. *Narrator-in-Chief*. Chatham, N.J.: Chatham House.

Taylor, Michael. 1989. "Structure, Culture, and Action in the Explanation of Social Change." *Politics and Society* 17:115–62.

Toulmin, Stephen. 1986. *The Place of Reason in Ethics*. Chicago: University of Chicago Press.

Toulmin, Stephen. 1990. *Cosmopolis: The Hidden Agenda of Modernity.* New York: Free Press.

Weber, Max. 1949. *The Methodology of the Social Sciences.* Trans. Edward A. Shils and Henry A. Finch. New York: Free Press.

Weber, Max. 1958. *From Max Weber: Essays in Sociology.* Trans. H. M. Gerth and C. Wright Mills. New York: Oxford University Press.

Weber, Max. 1964. *The Theory of Social and Economic Organizations.* Trans. A. M. Henderson and Talcott Parsons. New York: Free Press.

Wittgenstein, Ludwig. 1953. *Philosophical Investigations.* Trans. G. E. M. Anscombe. Oxford: Blackwell.

Contributors

Keith T. Poole, Carnegie-Mellon University

Howard Rosenthal, Carnegie-Mellon University

Ian Budge, University of Essex

William H. Riker, University of Rochester

Bruce Bueno de Mesquita, Hoover Institution

David Lalman, University of Maryland

Edward G. Carmines, Indiana University

James A. Stimson, University of Minnesota

Michael Laver, University College, Galway

Kenneth A. Shepsle, Harvard University

Richard A. Smith, Carnegie-Mellon University

Shanto Iyengar, University of California, Los Angeles

Richard Johnston, University of British Columbia

André Blais, Université de Montréal

Henry E. Brady, University of California

Jean Crête, Université Laval

George J. Graham, Jr., Vanderbilt University